Teaching Young Children to Read

FOURTH EDITION

Dolores Durkin
University of Illinois
at Champaign-Urbana

Allyn and Bacon, Inc.
Boston London Sydney Toronto

To the memory of my father

Copyright © 1987, 1980, 1976, 1972 by Allyn and Bacon, Inc.
7 Wells Avenue, Newton, Massachusetts 02159.

Library of Congress Cataloging-in-Publication Data

Durkin, Dolores.
  Teaching young children to read.

  Bibliography: p
  Includes index.
  1. Reading (Primary) 2. Reading readiness.
I. Title.
LB1525.D84 1986   372.4'1   86-17434
ISBN 0-205-10265-4

Series editor: Susanne F. Canavan
Production coordinator: Helyn Pultz
Editorial-production services: Grace Sheldrick, Wordsworth Associates
Text designer: Denise Hoffman
Cover coordinator: Linda K. Dickinson

Printed in the United States of America

10 9 8 7 6 5 4 3 2   90 89 88

Contents

Part II: Reading at the Beginning

4 Readiness for Beginning Reading   53

5 A Beginning Literacy Program   90

13 Comprehension   376

Part IV: Instructional Materials

14 Basal Reader Materials   414

15 Other Materials   448

Part V: Making Decisions

16 Decisions: Materials, Classroom
Organization, and Instruction   474

Preface

Like the earlier versions of *Teaching Young Children to Read*, this fourth edition provides specific, practical help for nursery school, kindergarten, and primary-grade teachers. The inclusion of nursery school and kindergarten teachers in the intended audience is not prompted by the belief that all four- and five-year-olds are ready to learn to read but rather by the assumption that some are ready and, in fact, may be reading when they come to school. Keeping in mind the other students, *Teaching Young Children to Read*, fourth edition, does not neglect what constitutes readiness for reading nor what teachers can do to foster it.

Fostering readiness as well as teaching reading itself should always include attention to oral language development. The direct dependence of reading on oral language is reflected in *Teaching Young Children to Read*, fourth edition, with the chapter that deals with that topic and even more with its intermittent references to the specific ways reading ability is either advanced, or curtailed, by a child's oral language.

Instructors who used previous editions of *Teaching Young Children to Read* will find in this newest version a much more extensive treatment of reading comprehension. The expansion reflects the fact that a considerable amount of information about comprehension and comprehension instruction accumulated since the publication of the third edition.

How to connect reading with writing activities is another topic that receives increased attention. Given the growing evidence that workbooks are invading kindergartens and even nursery schools, early childhood educators should also welcome the expanded treatment of appropriate ways to introduce pre-first graders to reading.

It should be noted that instructors of methods courses who used earlier versions of *Teaching Young Children to Read* will continue to find features that have characterized every edition: (1) specifically described instruction for all the topics covered, plus a generous number of suggestions for practice; (2) many references to observed classrooms, teachers, and children that add a note of reality to the content; (3) discussions of a great variety of materials, some of which are in the child's everyday world; and (4) constant recognition of the fact that children's interests as well as their abilities need to be kept in mind whenever decisions about instruction are made.

Since approximately 98 percent of the people who make decisions for teaching young students are women, feminine pronouns are used when references are made to teachers, except in cases in which a specific teacher was a man. To avoid ambiguity, masculine pronouns are used to refer to children, again with the exception of times when a specific girl is the referent.

D. D.

PART I

Introduction

A book concerned with teaching young children to read needs to consider what reading is, what successful teachers do and do not do, and what young children are like in the setting of a classroom. Even though all of these topics enter into the content of many chapters in this book, they are singled out for special attention in the first three.

Chapter 1, "Reading and Reading Instruction," begins by stressing the fact that reading and comprehending are synonymous terms. It goes on, therefore, to highlight the most important variables that enter into the successful processing of print. The chapter then considers what these variables indicate is necessary subject matter for an instructional program. In turn, the reference to important content allows for an overview of Teaching Young Children to Read.

Chapter 2, "Teachers in Classrooms," looks at individuals who provide instruction. It describes what classroom observation research has identified as being important characteristics of effective teachers. As is true of practically all the chapters in this textbook, Chapter 2 adds specificity to the descriptions with reference to actual teachers who represent a wide spectrum of effectiveness.

Chapter 3, which looks at the children being instructed, concentrates on behavioral patterns identified during many visits to classrooms located in a variety of geographical areas. Because later chapters in the book often refer to primary-grade students, the children that figure in Chapter 3 were seen in nursery schools, kindergartens, and first grades. With such a focus, Chapter 3 provides a framework for what is said about readiness in Chapter 4 and for what is done with beginning literacy in Chapter 5.

CHAPTER 1

Reading and Reading Instruction

PREVIEW

Not long ago, a reading specialist being interviewed on television was asked to define *reading*. Obviously embarrassed, the specialist explained that at one time, rattling off a one-sentence definition presented no special challenge; but with all that had been learned about the reading process starting in the 1970s, he now found that requests for a definition left him stuttering and stammering.

Like the specialist, Chapter 1 makes no attempt to begin with a one-sentence definition of *reading*. Instead, it explains what reading is by getting you consciously involved with comprehending a brief piece of text. By then analyzing the requirements for understanding the stated and implied content of the two-sentence text, the chapter makes apparent the important components of an instructional program.

How those components do, in fact, contribute to comprehension abilities is reinforced in all the chapters that offer information and advice for teaching. Attention to comprehension is thus frequent, and one chapter (Chapter 13) deals with only that topic. The generous coverage is a recognition that reading and comprehending are synonymous.

In addition to fostering conscious attention to variables that enter into comprehension, this first chapter also refers to the materials that continue to have a widespread influence on instruction: basal reader programs. The readers and workbooks that are a part of all such programs remain similar in many ways to what you yourself used in elementary school when you were acquiring reading ability. Basal reader series also include teaching manuals for each reader plus numerous ditto masters to supplement the workbooks. Since basal materials are referred to often and discussed in detail in Chapter 14, anyone who does not remember them should now take the time to browse through one or more programs. Because the beginning parts of basal programs (one or more reading readiness workbooks) are commonly used in kindergarten, they are dealt with in Chapter 4, "Readiness for Beginning Reading."

For now, let's see whether you learn something new about reading in Chapter 1.

Even though everyone would agree that comprehending is the very essence of reading, it wasn't until the early 1970s that widespread interest and considerable research focused on the inner processes that constitute the act of comprehending. Earlier, the major concern was for what is observable and can be tested. This meant that much more attention went to finding out what was comprehended (e.g., main idea, related details, mental images) than to the processes required to attain those ends. One consequence of the earlier interest for both classrooms and instructional materials was very little comprehension instruction but much comprehension assessment (4, 6).

This approach is now beginning to change as researchers continue to probe what underlies the successful processing of print. The work is not finished, but enough is known about the requirements of comprehending that teachers and authors of instructional materials should feel obligated to give as much attention to teaching students how to comprehend as they once gave to finding out if and what they comprehended.

SOME COMPONENTS OF
READING COMPREHENSION

One way to identify both the obvious and not so obvious components of comprehension is to examine what successful readers know and do. To prepare for such an examination, read the following:

> Facing each other, the girls were playing Checkers
> at the square table. The older one was winning.

Now that you have used certain knowledge and processes to comprehend the two sentences, let's consider the product or outcome of their use. To begin, list on paper everything that would go into a fully embellished picture (done in color) of what this brief, seemingly simple text says. When you have a list, compare it with the one that follows. We will then analyze what was necessary to enable you to draw in your mind the detailed picture of the girls.

POSSIBLE CONTENT OF DETAILED PICTURE

1. Two girls are sitting across from each other at a table.
2. One girl is bigger than the other.
3. The top of the table is square.
4. A smaller square piece of cardboard, divided into red and black squares, is on the middle of the table.
5. Round pieces of wood, some black and some red, are on the black

(continued)

squares. In some instances, one red piece is on top of another red piece.

6. Some black pieces are also off the board, placed in front of the bigger girl. A smaller number of red pieces are in front of the second girl.

To make explicit what proficient readers hardly think about but of what teachers need to be consciously aware, let me discuss what a person must know and be able to do in order to move from the two sentences about the girls playing Checkers to a picture that includes at least the details enumerated above. (Knowing that winners are usually happy and that a smile is associated with happiness, some of you, to cite a detail not listed, may have put a smile on the face of the older girl.)

Directionality of Written English

Comprehending the two sentences requires knowing that English words are written and read in a left-to-right direction. Even more basic is the knowledge that blank space shows where one word ends and the next begins. Also required is the knowledge that lines of text are read in a top-to-bottom order.

Typographic Signals

Comprehending the two sentences also requires an understanding of the functions of certain typographic signals. Knowing that a comma, for example, signals the need to pause briefly allows for segmenting the first sentence into two meaningful parts: (a) *Facing each other*, and (b) *the girls were playing Checkers at the square table*. In this instance, the second part can be further divided, or chunked, into the units *the girls were playing Checkers* and *at the square table*.

Knowing about one function of periods suggests the need for a pause following *table*. Acquaintance with another of its functions indicates that the brief passage is composed of two statements.

The capital letters in *Facing* and *The* reinforce the existence of two statements. The capital letter in *Checkers*, on the other hand, signals it is the name of something, in this case, the name of whatever it is the girls are playing.

Word Identification

Even though nothing can be gleaned from the two sentences if a reader is unable to name the words that compose them, a fully elaborated picture of the content makes it clear that word identification ability is only the beginning when comprehension is the goal. The fact that word identification ability is necessary but not enough to assure comprehension explains why children may experience problems with comprehending even when they can name every word in whatever they are trying to read. On the other hand, it is equally true that comprehension breaks down if too many words cannot be read both correctly *and* quickly (1, 7, 9).

Word Meanings

Just as the need for readers to identify words in their written form is obvious, so, too, is the need to know their meanings in a given context. With the two sentences being considered, using a context to decide on meanings is necessary for *Facing* (*Facing each other* vs. *facing on a sweater*), for *square* (*a square table* vs. *a square person*), and for *table* (*square table* vs. *table of numbers*).

Referents

To process the second sentence in the text under consideration (*The older one was winning*), a reader must know that *one* refers to one of the two girls mentioned in the first sentence. (That there are *two* girls is implied both by the comparative form of *old* and by the knowledge of how many persons play Checkers.) This suggests the need for a reader to be aware of the likelihood of interrelationships between sentences. In the case of the text being considered, the relationship is suggested by *one*, which refers to something or someone in the preceding sentence.

Inferences

As already mentioned, another requirement for comprehending is the ability to make explicit what an author only implies. This is effectively illustrated in the two sentences about the girls playing Checkers because drawing the picture suggested by the content of the sentences requires the reader to add (that is, to infer) the following:

1. There are *two* girls. (text-based and knowledge-based inference)
2. The two are *sitting*. (knowledge-based inference)
3. One girl is *bigger* than the other. (knowledge-based inference)

As these examples show, readers are able to make inferences not only because of the text but also because of what they know. In the case of the sentences about playing Checkers, familiarity with table games suggests that the players are likely to be sitting. Knowledge of Checkers (and of the comparative form of adjectives) indicates the players are two in number. That one of the two girls is likely to be bigger than the other comes from the knowledge that older children are commonly bigger than younger children. As mentioned, it is also possible that the older girl shows some sign of being pleased with her progress in the game.

World Knowledge

Obviously, what a reader knows about the world allows for more than just the ability to make inferences. In fact, many details in the requested mental picture derive not from the two-sentence text but from the reader's head — more specifically, from his or her knowledge of the game called Checkers. Lacking that knowledge, the best a reader can do is conclude that the girls referred to in the sentences are playing some kind of a table game.

How other kinds of knowledge (and experiences) allow for a highly embellished picture was demonstrated when a group of teachers were asked to draw a picture of the content of the same two sentences. For one teacher, the brief text brought many memories to mind because she and her older sister often played Checkers as children whenever it was too hot to go outdoors. (She was a native of the South.) As a result, her picture was rich with details that included two glasses of lemonade placed on the table.

Unexpectedly, the picture drawn by another teacher in the group had a beige and brown checkerboard along with beige and brown checkers. Asked about the colors, she explained that one of her most treasured possessions was a beige and brown Checkers game given to her by her father.

The fact that two sentences prompt noticeable differences in how their content is pictured makes it clear that reading is as dependent on what is in a reader's head as it is on what authors write. That is why reading is referred to as an *interactive* process in which readers use what is printed on the page in conjunction with what is in their heads in order to *construct* meaning (10). These facts point up not only that reading is anything but a passive activity but also that what ends up being comprehended may be different for different people. This suggests that reading is not as objective as many once believed it to be, a fact that teachers who think every question has only one correct answer should keep in mind whenever they use questions to assess comprehension.

SOME COMPONENTS OF
AN INSTRUCTIONAL PROGRAM

Although the previous section only scratches the surface as it considers what comprehending connected text requires, it is hoped that enough is said to allow you to identify as early as this first chapter the necessary components of an instructional program. Some of the most important parts will be referred to now. More detailed discussions of all the parts appear in subsequent chapters.

All such components should be viewed as a means for bringing into existence not only the ability to read but also the desire to read.

Providing Experiences

Since what is known about the world originates in direct and vicarious experiences, school attendance from the beginning to the end should be synonymous with experiencing and, as a result, with constantly expanding concepts and oral vocabularies. As you move through the chapters in this textbook, you will find frequent reminders and illustrations of the dependence of reading ability on both world knowledge and oral language.

Because evidence of the dependent relationship is not always found in how time is spent in classrooms, what can be done to add to both the size and the depth of children's oral vocabularies is not considered until Chapter 12. The delay reflects the conviction that by Chapter 12, enough illustrations of how oral language enters into the reading process will have been encountered that its importance will be apparent.

Developing Reading Vocabularies

A person's reading vocabulary is composed of all the words that can be identified automatically in their written form—typically as a result of repeated contacts with them—and whose meanings are understood. Such words are also referred to as a *sight vocabulary* because they are known on sight.

Some words in a student's sight vocabulary would have originally been taught as wholes. (A teacher says, "This word is 'do.' ") The initial recognition of other words (e.g., *me* and *time*) may have been rooted in their spelling, that is, in letter-sound relationships. Such relationships are the core of phonics instruction. Still other words (e.g., *unwanted, playfully*) might have come to be known with the help of both letter-sound relationships and a knowledge of word structure. Students may be able to read even more words—for instance, *down*—because they were initially encountered in contexts that were sufficiently helpful (e.g., *The swing went up and down*) that the known words suggested what the unknown one says.

How reading vocabularies come into existence points up some of the responsibilities of teachers who are working to change nonreaders into readers. Chapters covering what needs to be done insofar as the development of these vocabularies is concerned are noted in Figure 1.1.

As Figure 1.1 shows, regardless of the origin of help, practice is a requirement for *automatic* identifications—the only kind that facilitates comprehending connected text. Suggestions for interesting word practice are at the end of Chapter 7. More suggestions are scattered throughout other chapters.

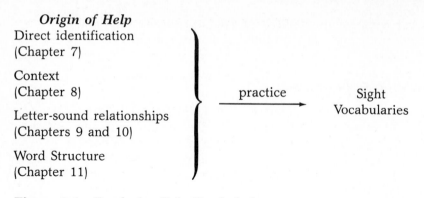

Figure 1.1. *Developing Sight Vocabularies*

Teaching Comprehension

Because the meaning of even a sentence requires knowing more than the words that compose it, developing oral and reading vocabularies is important but not sufficient to allow every student to realize his or her full potential for reading. What must be added to this responsibility is early *and* frequent comprehension instruction, which is made up of various combinations of descriptions, information, explanations, examples and nonexamples, questions, modeling, and so forth.

Some of what is done at the beginning to help with comprehension might deal with the fact that pronouns such as *that* refer to, and substitute for, other words that may be in a different sentence:

> Give me the pencil. *That* is mine.

Later, comprehension instruction may have as its objective the understanding that *that* can refer to, and replace, more than a single word:

> John didn't do his homework. He didn't do the assignments either.
> And when he got in line, he hit another boy. Because of *that*, he
> couldn't go out to recess.

Because reading *is* comprehending, many references are made to comprehension instruction throughout this book. In addition, Chapter 13 deals exclusively with that topic, and Chapter 14 ("Basal Reader Materials") shows how comprehension instruction should function in the context of a basal lesson. Chapter 15 illustrates how attention to writing may help not only with writing itself but also with understanding the words of another author.

INSTRUCTIONAL MATERIALS

Even though it is an indisputable fact that basal reader programs (which have now made their way into many kindergartens) exert unique influence on what is done with reading in school, much is said in this book about materials other than the readers, workbooks, and ditto-sheet exercises that make up such programs. Texts composed by children, by teachers, and by both are discussed, as are the rich but, for the most part, unused instructional materials found in the child's everyday world. A few examples of these "free" materials – which may be of much greater interest to children than examples taken from a textbook – are listed in Table 1.1 to show their potential for achieving important objectives.

Table 1.1. *Examples of "Free" Materials*

Source	*Text*	*Possible Topics for Instruction*
Sign in lot where bank is being constructed	"New Quarters for Your Quarters"	Multiple meanings of *quarters.* One function of underlining.
Sign on restaurant door	"No shirt. No shoes. No service."	Implicit cause-effect relationship.
Bumper sticker on truck	"Love thy neighbor. Tune they piano."	Importance of world knowledge for comprehension. Implied relationship between content of two sentences.

What will not be forgotten when materials are discussed is the use of literature, viewed as a means not only for advancing reading ability but, even more so, for fostering an interest in doing some. As has been said, "If you don't read, how will you *know?*"

OVERVIEW OF THIS TEXTBOOK

One of the many important points made in the more recent comprehension research is that having an overview of how a piece of text is constructed, or put together, enhances comprehension and also helps a reader retain what was comprehended (8). This is the case because the overall picture serves as a framework into which the various parts of the content can be placed to form both a meaningful and a memorable whole. With that finding in mind, let me end this introductory chapter by briefly describing the topics covered in *Teaching Young Children to Read*, 4th edition.

The content of Part I has already been outlined. Part II, entitled "Reading at the Beginning," deals with topics that merit generous coverage in a book entitled *Teaching Young Children to Read*. The first of the three chapters in Part II is "Readiness for Beginning Reading." Long the subject of both controversy and confusion, readiness as treated in Chapter 4 has to do with what is necessary for success when reading instruction commences. Considerations of readiness are mandatory since success at the beginning of any endeavor – be it roller skating or reading – is *uniquely* important. Therefore, those people responsible for getting reading started should read Chapter 4 with special care.

The second chapter in Part II, "A Beginning Literacy Program," shows one way the points emphasized in the chapter on readiness can be put into practice. Even though no assumption is made that what is recommended in Chapter 5 on beginning literacy describes *the* way to get reading started, what *is* described was at the core of a two-year program for four-year-olds that succeeded in fostering both achievement in, and positive attitudes toward, reading (3). For that reason, the content of the chapter merits consideration by anyone who believes that reading should get started before first grade, *if* what is done to teach it is appropriate for young children.

The final chapter in Part II looks at reading done orally and silently. The two kinds of reading are dealt with early in the book in order to identify their respective functions. Awareness of those functions should allow for an appreciation of the amount of time each kind of reading merits in an instructional program.

The seven chapters grouped together as Part III deal in very specific ways with how to teach the strategies, abilities, and understandings necessary for acquiring proficiency in reading. Because reading is comprehending, each of the seven chapters shows how the topic under consideration contributes to, and is even required for, comprehension.

Even though the material covered in Chapters 7 through 13 sometimes goes beyond beginning reading, those people teaching young children who are just starting to be readers will find the content useful for such reasons as the following. What needs to be done to get a word like *aisle* into a more advanced reader's sight vocabulary is not too different from teaching the word *one* to a beginner. To cite another example of the encompassing relevance of Part III, knowing about ways to develop oral vocabularies is just as important for the nursery school teacher as it is for the teacher working with gifted third graders.

Because it is next to impossible to deal with instruction without references to instructional materials, the latter are mentioned throughout *Teaching Young*

Children to Read. However, because instructional materials are so important, they also receive special attention in the two chapters in Part IV. Chapter 14 focuses on the most influential materials insofar as reading is concerned: basal reader programs. The purpose of this chapter is not to promote more frequent use; rather, the aim is to describe a *professional* use. Since a professional use of basal series inevitably requires supplementing them with other kinds of materials, the second chapter in Part IV deals with some of the other kinds, including material that children themselves write.

Like all competent professionals, competent teachers are knowledgeable and astute decision makers. Since many of the most important decisions for teachers have to do with individualized instruction, the chapter that constitutes Part V, Chapter 16, describes means for maximizing it. (*Individualized instruction* matches what one or more children need and are ready to learn and proceeds at a pace suitable for the individual or group being taught.) The first part of Chapter 16 looks at ways for organizing and managing classrooms; it also explains how to choose appropriate materials. The second part covers diagnosis, which has to do with attempts to learn what students do and do not know so that appropriate instruction, review, or practice can be planned.

CONCLUDING COMMENTS

So much for the plan of this book.

Throughout all of *Teaching Young Children to Read*, an attempt is made to be as specific as possible because only recommendations and procedures described with specificity are helpful to teachers. Other efforts are made to ensure that the book is realistic and authentic. This is often accomplished with references to classrooms that have been observed and to instructional materials. In some instances, samples of the latter are reproduced and are often accompanied by comments. At such times, you are urged to study both before proceeding with your reading.

To help with your reading, each chapter starts with a Preview; facing each Preview is an outline of the chapter's contents. Together, they are meant to give you an overview of what is to come, which should promote both comprehension and retention. Another overview, in the form of a Summary, appears at the end of every chapter.

You will also find a Review section at the conclusion of each chapter. The Review is intended to help you consider what you have read and to encourage you to see its implications for teaching. Since successful readers come to a text with a purpose, it is recommended that you examine the Review section before beginning a chapter. Reading the Summary ahead of time will help, too.

All this is to say that you should read *Teaching Young Children to Read* in much the same way that you would encourage your students to read whenever they need to acquire information from text.

SUMMARY

Chapter 1 began by demonstrating that successful reading—even of a brief piece of text—involves much more than the ability to name words. It was especially emphasized that success also requires active participation by readers in the form of (a) using what they know that is relevant, and (b) adding to the text what an author implies but does not state. This discussion of the requirements of comprehending allowed for an identification of essential subject matter for instructional programs. What *was* identified constitutes the topics covered in Chapters 7 through 13.

Chapter 1 next made a brief reference to the most widely used instructional materials—basal reader programs—which are discussed later in a separate chapter and also intermittently in a number of chapters. Serving as an illustration of material that can—and should—supplement basal series, samples of environmental text were quoted and their instructional potential named.

Finally, Chapter 1 provided a brief overview of the entirety of *Teaching Young Children to Read*. This was done on the assumption that having in mind a general picture of the content of a large body of text facilitates both comprehension and retention. Additional comments were made about the study aids available for each chapter.

REVIEW

1. Was anything said in Chapter 1 about the nature of reading that you did not know, or at least did not consciously think about, until you read the chapter?

2. It was said in the chapter that reading is an *interactive* process. What interacts with what?

3. Chapter 1 showed that what readers are able to comprehend is affected by their knowledge of the world. The chapter also implied that reading commonly requires both literal and inferential comprehension. Using the following sentence, explain (a) the meaning of *literal* and *inferential comprehension*, and (b) the role played by world knowledge in comprehension.

   The men were digging a hole for the new tree.

4. Another point made in Chapter 1 is that environmental text is not only of interest to children but also has much potential for realizing goals that will advance their ability to read. What could the following text, found on a pencil advertising a new furniture store, help to teach?

Don't gamble on quality.
See us first.

5. Let's say that a Head Start teacher decides that none of her children are ready to start reading, yet she wants to do whatever is possible to help them become ready. Based on Chapter 1 (much more will be said about this in Chapters 4 and 5) what can she do to maximize the likelihood that children will be successful when reading instruction begins?

6. A suggestion was made in Chapter 1 to read the Review section at the end of each chapter before reading the chapter itself. How is this recommendation related to a conception of reading that views it as *intentional thinking*?

REFERENCES

1. Adams, M. J.; Huggins, A. W. F.; Starr, B. J.; Rollins, A. M.; Zuckerman, L. E.; Stevens, K. N.; and Nickerson, R. S. *A Prototype Test of Decoding Skills.* Cambridge, Mass.: Bolt Beranek and Newman, Inc., 1980.
2. Durkin, Dolores. "Is There a Match between What Elementary Teachers Do and What Basal Reader Manuals Recommend?" *Reading Teacher* 37 (April, 1984), 734–744.
3. Durkin, Dolores. "A Language Arts Program for Pre-First Grade Children: Two-Year Achievement Report." *Reading Reserach Quarterly* 5 (Summer, 1970), 534–565.
4. Durkin, Dolores. "Reading Comprehension Instruction in Five Basal Reader Series." *Reading Research Quarterly* 16 (1981, No. 4), 515–544.
5. Durkin, Dolores. "A Six Year Study of Children Who Learned to Read in School at the Age of Four." *Reading Research Quarterly* 10 (1974–75, No. 1), 9–61.
6. Durkin, Dolores. "What Classroom Observations Reveal about Reading Comprehension Instruction." *Reading Research Quarterly* 14 (1978–79, No. 4), 481–533.
7. Hogaboam, Thomas W., and Perfetti, Charles A. "Reading Skill and the Role of Verbal Experience in Decoding." *Journal of Educational Psychology* 70 (October, 1978), 717–729.
8. Meyer, Bonnie J. F. "The Structure of Prose: Effects on Learning and Memory and Implications for Educational Practice." In R. C. Anderson, R. Spiro, and W. E. Montague (Eds.), *Schooling and the Acquisition of Knowledge.* Hillsdale, N.J.: Lawrence Erlbaum Associates, 1977, 179–200.
9. Perfetti, Charles A., and Hogaboam, Thomas W. "The Relationship between Single Word Decoding and Reading Comprehension Skill." *Journal of Educational Psychology* 67 (August, 1975), 461–469.
10. Rumelhart, David. *Toward an Interactive Model of Reading.* Technical Report No. 56. San Diego: Center for Human Information Processing, University of California, 1976.

CHAPTER 2

Teachers in Classrooms

PREVIEW

A welcome change among researchers is an interest in studying classrooms. At times, their curiosity about the teacher's instructional environment takes the form of ethnographic research in which one small element from the total, complex picture receives close scrutiny. In other instances, larger pieces of life in the classroom are the concern. Whatever the focus, the new interest is all to the good, because knowing as much as possible about the context of instruction is mandatory if major and lasting improvements in the educational process are to be made.

As the chapters in this textbook attest to, I have been observing in classrooms over a long period of time in order to ensure that as I made recommendations to teachers, I would understand where they work. Visits to schools have allowed me to know, for instance, that teachers are often kept from putting together superior instructional programs because of such constraints as administrators' expectations, poor instructional materials, uncooperative parents, excessively large classes, students' disruptive behavior, and last, but hardly least, deficiencies in their own knowledge, industry, and motivation.

Teachers in classrooms are referred to regularly in *Teaching Young Children to Read*. They are the major focus of Chapter 2; here, they are discussed within a framework in which reading is the central concern. The chapter identifies characteristics of teachers that seem especially necessary if children are to be given every opportunity to become the best readers possible.

Frequent references are made to what has been seen in classrooms not only to add a note of authenticity to the content but also because the observations, plus the classroom research of others, are the sources of recommendations made in the chapter.

Before starting Chapter 2, you may want at least to skim the Summary at the end to get a quick overview of its content. Since reading at its best is intentional thinking, looking at the questions in the Review section should help make your study of Chapter 2 more purposeful.

Although many people may think that good teachers are born rather than made, available studies of effective teachers inevitably point to such acquired characteristics as "industriousness" as setting these teachers apart from others who are less effective. One observer of classrooms has noted, for example, that "Contrary to popular myths, teachers in 'schools that work' are not charismatic figures generating unforgettable experiences. They are simply hard-working, organized teachers moving crisply through a well-planned day" (14, p. 3). Nothing I know about teachers gives me reason to question this observer's characterization, but it needs to be made explicit that superior teachers work hard on the right things. Making the same point, Madeline Hunter warns, "To teach exquisitely that which is not worth the effort or to set worthwhile goals that are never achieved are both manifestations of poor educational practice" (12, p. 170).

DECISION MAKERS

Just as some people may believe that good teachers are born, so others may assume that teachers are the sole source of decisions about instruction. Researchers specializing in classroom studies (2, 4, 5, 8) have put that myth to rest, too. Jere Brophy, for example, correctly states:

> Teacher education programs are often designed as if teachers were responsible for establishing appropriate educational objectives . . . , preparing appropriate curriculum materials, conducting and evaluating the outcomes of instruction, and making whatever adjustments prove necessary. . . . Teachers may have done all these things in the distant past, but at present, most of these functions are performed by school boards, school administrators, and commercial materials. (2, p. 11)

Researchers have increasingly given attention to commercial materials not only because of the major flaws in these products (6, 7, 9, 13) but also because of their unique influence on how both teachers and children spend their time (5, 8). Not to be forgotten is that as more and more children enter school at younger and younger ages, commercially produced materials are enlarging their influence to include pre-first-grade programs. That is why *all* teachers need to keep in mind that one of their primary responsibilities as members of a profession is to make and execute knowledgeable decisions about instruction that take into account the nature of the reading process as well as the age, interests, and abilities of the children in their classrooms.

To underscore this important decision-making responsibility, let's divide teachers into two groups, as shown in Figure 2.1.

Teacher A works from a goal-oriented perspective. Well acquainted with available materials, she selects topics for instruction that they recommend or

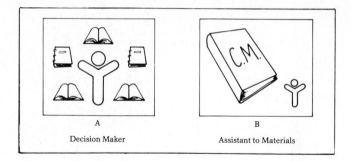

A
Decision Maker

B
Assistant to Materials

Figure 2.1. *Contrasting Teachers.*

that she herself believes to be important. Either way, what is chosen for attention reflects children's needs. Either way, too, specifically defined objectives shape what is done and also determine what will be evaluated. Samples of five objectives follow.

Students will understand that:

1. empty space shows where one word ends and another begins; or
2. a period, not the end of a line, marks the end of a sentence; or
3. the letter *s* at the end of a word may indicate it is plural; or
4. *there* may refer to one or more words in a previous sentence; or
5. an appositive, enclosed in commas, provides additional information.

Once Teacher A decides on an objective, her thoughts turn to materials (commercial and homemade) that might help achieve the objective. Commercially prepared materials are viewed, then, as a means to an end, not as an end in themselves—and, certainly, never as something that must be covered regardless of their value.

In contrast, Teacher B not only allows commercial materials to define instructional objectives but also relies on them for procedures to attain the objectives. Within this framework, a teacher is not a professional person but only an assistant to materials prepared by individuals who may know less about reading than she does and who know nothing at all about the students in her classroom. Teacher B is the reason researchers have concluded that days in school are sometimes planned around activities, not around necessary, clearly defined objectives that take into account both the nature of reading and the needs of students (2, 4).

Decisions for Instruction

Probably the best way to explain the goal-oriented instruction of Teacher A is with an example. The following lesson, which deals with the suffix *-er*, shows how what is known can be used to foster an understanding of what is unknown.

Objective: Children will demonstrate an understanding of *-er* as part of a root and as a suffix, and, further, an understanding of how *-er* functioning as a suffix affects meaning.

Materials: Chalkboard; pictures of someone climbing a mountain, building a house, painting a fence, buying meat in a grocery store, kicking a football, and of two men boxing.

Procedure: The teacher begins by writing the familiar word *her* on the board, which is promptly identified by an instructional group composed of 11 first graders. The teacher removes the *h* and asks, "How would you say this (pointing to *er*)?"

her

er

After *er* is pronounced correctly, the teacher continues, "In *her,* the *e* and *r* are part of the word. In fact, if I take *e* and *r* away from *her,* what's left? [*h*] Yes, nothing is left that is a word. Another word you know that is like that is *under.* (Writes *under.*) When I take *e* and *r* away from *under,* what's left is not a word. At least I don't know of a word like "und," do you? [No!] In some words, though, *e* and *r* at the end are different. In these words, they are added to a real word. Let me show you some words like this. [Writes the familiar word *help.*] What does this say? . . . Let's see if you can tell me what *help* says when I add *e* and *r* to it:

help

helper

What does this second word say? . . . What is a helper? . . . A helper, then, is a person who helps."

Using the same procedure with two more familiar roots, the teacher ends up with a board that looks like Figure 2.2.

Next, the teacher displays six pictures. After their content is discussed, each is labeled (*climber, builder, painter, buyer, kicker, boxers*). With the help of the labels, the teacher summarizes: "When *e* and *r* are added to a word, they

Figure 2.2

~~her~~	_____	caller	_____
helper	*help* _____	sleeper	_____
player	_____	seller	_____
over	_____	answer	_____
water	_____	teacher	_____
walker	_____	reader	_____
under	_____	ever	_____

Figure 2.3

mean 'one who.' A climber is one who climbs; a builder is one who builds; and so on. By the way, what is a learner? . . . Yes, it's somebody who is learning just the way you are doing right now. There's more than one of you, so we'd call you 'learners,' " just the way we called the two men fighting "boxers."

Copies of the sheet in Figure 2.3 are distributed next. Directions for using it are explained and illustrated in the first two words. Remaining at the reading table, the children quickly complete the sheet and then take turns answering an item aloud to allow for feedback. All are correct. (If any response was wrong, the teacher would explain why it was incorrect and what the right response is. Any child with an incorrect answer would correct the error.) To conclude the day's work with the suffix *-er*, papers similar to the one in Figure 2.4 are distributed. Each sheet shows a different base word. The

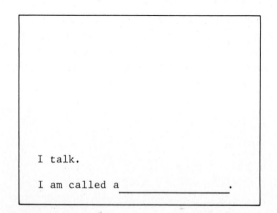

Figure 2.4

tasks for the children are to complete the second sentence with the appropriate derivative and to draw a picture that illustrates its meaning. Eventually, illustrated pictures will constitute a book for the classroom collection of free-choice materials that can be used whenever time permits.

Decisions for Practice

As is true of effective instruction, the details of fruitful practice are determined by its purpose. To specify the priority of objectives for practice as well as for instruction (and to show that practice need not be drudgery), some practice seen in classrooms in which young children were fortunate enough to have a Teacher A are described below.

Samples of Practice

Objective: Children will practice hearing /m/ and /t/ in initial position and associating those sounds with *m* and *t*, respectively.

Materials: Two plastic clothes baskets, one showing a card on which *m* has been printed and the other displaying a card with *t*; two large balls.

Procedure: When inclement weather requires indoor recess, playing "Phonics Basketball" is one way to spend the time. Two teams are selected, and a member of each gets a ball. Members take turns listening to the teacher say a word that begins with /m/ or /t/. If a child throws his ball into the correct basket, he moves to the end of the line, eventually getting another turn. Otherwise, he sits down. At some stipulated time, the team with the larger number of members is declared the winner. Other children form two more teams, and the game continues for as long as the children are interested.

Objective: Children will practice reading numerals from 1 to 5 and counting from 1 to 5.

Materials: Collections of paper squares, pebbles, buttons, straws, toothpicks, popsicle sticks, etc.; five numeral cards displaying *1, 2, 3, 4,* and *5.*

Procedure: Distribute one of the above collections among a small group of children. Show a numeral and have them count out that number of items. Afterward, have all the children name the numeral.

Objective: Children will practice reading the new word *family* and copying the words *My Family.*

Materials: Store catalogues; scissors and paste; pencils.

Procedure: Following a discussion of families and of the words *family* and *Family*, have children cut out people figures to match the makeup of their own families. After the figures are pasted on paper, have the children label their collections *My Family.*

Objective: Children will practice naming letters from *a* to *g.*

Materials: Piano; cardboard keyboard made the same size as an actual one with each white key labeled *a* to *g;* dittoed copies of: c c g g a a g f f e e d d c.

Procedure: Have the children read aloud the names of the letters on the dittoed sheet. Place the cardboard keyboard, standing up, behind the corresponding keys of the piano. Ask the children to rename the letters so you will know which keys to play. Play as they read. The results will be parts of two familiar songs ("Twinkle, Twinkle, Little Star" and "Alphabet Song") and a group of delighted children.

CLASSROOM MANAGERS

Even though entertainment is not the educator's concern, doing what interests children *is,* because when they are interested (and learning something, too), behavior problems are kept to a minimum. This fact is of obvious importance not only to teachers' mental health but also because reducing behavior problems is likely to add to the amount of time given to instruction. Such a conclusion is suggested by the fact that researchers studying classrooms are learning repeatedly that the generous use of workbook and ditto-sheet exercises found everywhere is related to teachers' worries over "losing control." Charlotte Taylor, for example, claims in her book *Transforming Schools* (15) that "Teachers keep their classes so perpetually occupied with busy work that neither chaos nor learning takes place" (p. 169). In an extensive study by Fisher et al. (10), the same point is made in the finding that students may spend as much as 70 percent of the time allotted to reading doing seatwork.

Not too many years ago, teachers of pre-first-grade children would not have to be cautioned about using assignments as a way of managing class-rooms. Now, however, with the introduction of workbook and ditto-sheet exercises into preschool classes, the need exists for all teachers to question themselves regularly about their motivation in using written assignments.

INTROSPECTIVE

"One of the most powerful techniques for producing professional growth," writes Hunter, "is introspection into one's own teaching" (12, p. 181). To promote introspection, I have teachers enrolled in my reading methodology course keep journals. One entry, written by a man in his first year of teaching, tells of the problems he was having with a difficult-to-manage class of second and third graders. The entry was prompted by my reminder in class that no matter how good the teaching, inattentive children cannot be expected to learn. His journal entry deals with this theme:

Your saying that attention and achievement go hand in hand put two thoughts into my head that are highly relevant for my own class. The first is that children cannot be expected to succeed if they don't know what they are to do; and they won't know what to do if their attention is not directed to a specific task and instructions for completing it. Yet yesterday, I gave the morning assignments when I had the attention of no more than half the group. The result was frustration for me—a seemingly endless stream of children came to me for help with their work—and more frustration for the kids because they didn't know what they were supposed to do.

Another thought prompted by your comment about attention and achievement is that children will be more attentive if what they are asked to do is interesting. Today's lesson on listening supported that. Since the beginning of the year, I have been concerned that my students rarely pay sufficient attention in class, so this afternoon I began the first of what will be a series of listening activities taken from some materials that were in the room when it was assigned to me in August. I think part of the reason for the success of today's work is that I had sense enough to wait at the start until I had everybody's attention. And I even stopped when anyone talked. But another reason for the success is that the lesson was interesting and included a story about "Lazy Ear Ranch" that everyone seemed to like. Something must have been retained because at the end of the day when I was trying to make some announcements, Joseph called a few children lazy ears because they weren't paying attention. And *I* must have retained something, too, because I have made the firm resolution not to start anything until I have everyone's ear.

Even though teachers of much experience and expertise might view this new teacher's efforts as hardly exciting or even worth mentioning, they do reveal one person's attempt to look at himself objectively and, based on what was seen, to try to improve what he was doing. This, after all, is how ordinary teachers eventually become extraordinary.

Another journal entry, written by a woman in her second year of teaching first grade, shows someone who is trying to become Teacher A:

When I arrived at school this morning, a police officer was walking around the building. I noticed, too, that water was running down the bricks from the second floor. When I got to the principal's office, I soon learned that my school had been vandalized during the night. Later, when the children arrived, they were naturally curious and excited. Once they calmed down, we walked to one of the damaged rooms to see what had been done. Needless to say, I laid aside my planned work and, with the help of the children, wrote an account on the board of what had happened to our school.

When the written description was done, I asked the children, first, to draw a picture of a vandal and to copy from the board the title "A Vandal."

(I quickly learned that several of the children thought someone by the name of Mr. Vandal had done the damage, so that confusion had to be taken care of.) Next the children were to draw a picture of something that had been damaged. While the children were busy with their drawings, I quickly made a ditto of our written account and ran off copies for the children to take home. Another copy was put in each one's reading folder.

We then discussed people in the community who might be at school this morning. The only ones named were reporters and T.V. cameramen; consequently, I asked the children to watch the six o'clock local news on T.V. to see what might be said about our school, and to have someone at home look in the newspaper for stories about the vandalism. The children were asked to bring the articles tomorrow so that I can read them aloud to see whether the reporters were correct in what they said.

I feel the children really learned about vandalism today. Everything had so much meaning for them. They were totally involved. In fact, one mother phoned this evening to find out what had been going on in school. She thought her son was making up a story.

Admittedly, I was a little nervous about laying aside the basal reader and all my lesson plans. However, I proved to myself today that I *can* do worthwhile things without textbooks. I look forward to moving to some combination of basal readers and other materials that deal more directly with the children's lives and experiences. While I don't want any more vandalism to occur—our building is a mess—its consequences demonstrated how discipline problems vanish when everybody is interested.

The third journal entry, written by an observer of another first-grade class, describes a teacher who exemplifies a professional decision-maker with definite objectives that determine what she does. What she does suggests she is also introspective. The observer writes:

Last week, we discussed characteristics of effective teachers. My observation this morning in a first grade provided a timely look at the same topic.

As I arrived, so too did the last of the children. The teacher, who had been greeting everyone at the door, went to the front of the room and quickly got everyone's attention with the statement, "I have something exciting to tell you." She then waited a couple of minutes to allow the children to finish a conversation or to put their lunch bags away.

Once she had everybody's attention, she explained that an important worker would be on the playground shortly to repair the wooden climbing apparatus. Together, the teacher and children went on to talk about the needed repairs. In the midst of the discussion, one child said, "I know who's coming. It's a carpenter!" "Right you are," responded the teacher. She walked to the board, quickly printed *carpenter*, and told the group that what she wrote was the word "carpenter."

She then got a picture book from her desk that told about carpenters. Everyone listened attentively while the teacher read the text and showed the pictures. With the help of the pictures, the children decided what tools to look for and what questions to ask when they went outdoors to see what the carpenter was doing. The teacher reminded the children that soon they themselves would be able to read books like the one that told about the work of carpenters.

When the teacher had a few minutes to talk with me, I asked why she had decided to discuss the carpenter. She said she thought it was very important for all children, but especially for beginning readers, to learn that information is available in books. Her objectives, she said, were two in number: to show the children that useful information comes from reading and, second, to encourage them to want to learn to read.

Other teachers who have been observed might have done things differently had they been more introspective and asked, "*Why* am I doing what I'm doing?" For instance:

A hard-working teacher took the time to print words in need of practice on dark red construction paper cut in the shape of apples. Since the words had been printed with a black crayon, it was extremely difficult to see the letters on the dark red.

To display colors and the words that name them, a teacher made a paper train, each car a different color. Attached to a car was a word card telling its color. In this case, all the printing was so small that the words were hard to read when the train was attached to a bulletin board.

To make numeral-identification practice appealing, a teacher drew the face of a clock on a paper plate. Numbers from 1 to 12 had been carefully printed around the edge. Unfortunately, the movable hand, made of stiff paper and attached to the center of the plate, was so long that it covered a numeral whenever it pointed to one.

More teachers who would have profited from monitoring their behavior also come to mind. One was unusually successful in assembling interesting bulletin-board displays that had much instructional potential. Enthusiastic responses from the children may explain an unfortunate development. As the school year passed, one attractive bulletin board was replaced by two. Gradually, the two were replaced by three until, by mid-year, every wall in the room was covered including the chalkboard. The lack of a chalkboard meant that it was impossible to show what the children needed to see, and the displays themselves became a distraction rather than what they were intended to be: instructional materials. "How easily means can become ends in themselves," was the thought that ran through my mind each time I visited this classroom.

Why the availability of chalkboards is important was demonstrated in a third grade in which the teacher was reviewing that titles are signaled by capital letters and quotation marks. Adhering to a basal manual's suggestion, the teacher asked an instructional group, "Does it make sense to say, 'A boy was listening to the ancient tree'?" Although the manual indicated that the children would respond negatively, one girl said "Yes" immediately, then went on to explain her response with the comment, "Something might be inside the tree that's making noise." For whatever reason (perhaps because a visitor was in the room), the teacher ignored the girl's explanation and proceeded to print on 8"-by-11" paper, *A boy was listening to "The Ancient Tree."* She then held up the sheet. (The manual had suggested writing the sentence on the board; however, the table at which the teacher sat was in the middle of the classroom, thus some distance away from two chalkboards.) The children who could see the words clearly enough to read them commented immediately, "Oh, it's a story" and "Oh, he's reading a poem or something." "That's exactly right," responded the teacher, who then proceeded to discuss referents for pronouns.*

What this teacher did prompted many questions, including one raised early in the chapter; namely, had she—as researchers claim—planned the day around activities rather than instructional objectives selected because they were both important and as yet not achieved? The same question came to mind in a classroom in which the teacher was listening to a group taking turns reading a basal story aloud. (It had not been read silently ahead of time.) When the end of a certain page was reached, the following interchange took place:

> *Teacher:* "All right. That's all we'll read today. It's too long to finish today."
>
> *Children:* "No, it isn't. There's just four more pages."

Adhering to the suggestion in the basal reader manual she was using, the teacher had the children close their readers and open their workbooks. Written assignments were made, which, according to the manual, would "allow for skill teaching and practice." Nothing that was assigned had any connection with the story the children had been reading.

Even though it may be tempting to put all the blame on commercial materials for some teachers' failure to be sufficiently introspective about what they have students do, classrooms in which a manual is nowhere to be found also have activity-oriented days. In one nursery school, for instance, the teacher and her assistant spent an entire morning having fourteen children take turns lying on large pieces of white paper so they could trace the outlines of their bodies. In turn, the children cut out the outlines and, with crayons, made eyes, a nose and a mouth, plus the clothes they were wearing. Time was

---

*Flitting from one topic to another is characteristic of basal reader manuals (6); consequently, flitting also describes the behavior of Teacher B (5, 8).

even taken to paste yarn on the heads to serve as hair. When all this ended, so had the morning.

Later, the teacher explained what had gone on with the comment, "The children love doing things like this." A more introspective teacher might have used the time-consuming activity—if she chose to use it at all—to talk about the meanings of words like *trace* and *outline*, to discuss possible uses of yarn, to show what words like *face* and *hair* look like when they are written, and, if needed, to review the names of colors. Instead, what turned out to be a very noisy—at times, even chaotic—morning was spent on a project that some children never did finish. Again, "Why am I doing what I'm doing?" was the question that needed to be asked.

PREPARED BUT FLEXIBLE

As emphasized, effective teachers are industrious and thus are well prepared for each day's work. In addition, however, they are flexible, which, for some, may be a more difficult behavior to achieve. Yet it is flexibility that allows for taking advantage of those unexpected events that have so much instructional potential—and so much interest for children.

The teacher at the school that was vandalized displayed flexibility, as did another who was observed during social studies. At the time of the observation, her class was working on a page in a new social studies workbook and discovered an error. According to the directions for doing the page, adding certain lines to a map would result in the outline of "a well-known animal." Because of what must have been one or more errors in the directions, nothing recognizable resulted, which immediately led the children to suggest, "Let's write to whoever wrote this page to tell them about the mistake!" At first the teacher said nothing, then responded, "I think that's a great idea. We've been learning how to write letters, so there's no time like the present to find out if you can write one." The workbooks were put away, and the writing began. Once the letter was finished, the teacher said she'd copy what the children had told her to write on the board, type the letter at home that evening, then bring it back in the morning so everyone could sign it.

Afterward, when I complimented the teacher for having practice that was really meaningful, she admitted her first thought had been, "But we haven't had music or health yet." Fortunately, "What a wonderful time to practice writing a letter," was her next one.

What might be called either structured flexibility or flexible structure has been seen in other classrooms, too. All the teachers described below were well organized, yet open to unforeseen possibilities:

While teaching the song "B–I–N–G–O," one teacher remembered to print the five letters on the board for all the children to see. This was in keeping with one of the current instructional goals: letter-naming ability.

A group of children were talking about a recent P.T.A. Carnival during a conversation period, after which the teacher wrote P.T.A. on the board and explained that it was an example of what had recently been discussed: abbreviations.

In another room, a child observed, "So many begin with *J!*" when attendance was being taken with the help of first-name cards. Since the children were learning about letter-sound associations, the teacher correctly took time to show and read the four names that started with *J*.

SENSITIVE

Any chapter designed to identify characteristics of the kind of teachers all of us would want our own children (or grandchildren) to have should include sensitivity. A teacher can be knowledgeable, industrious, goal-oriented, and both prepared and flexible, yet ineffective if she is not sensitive to children's problems.

I became consciously aware of the need for sensitivity when I began to visit classrooms on a regular basis. Its importance was initially made clear in a kindergarten in which there was an exceedingly bright girl—in fact, she was one of the brightest young children I have known. Yet, for reasons I would not pretend to understand, she became tense and anxious whenever she was asked to do something alone. It could be as simple as reading a word or pointing to a particular picture. The nature of the task did not matter, nor did her outstanding ability. Fortunately, she had a teacher who sensed the problem and went out of her way to avoid placing the child in any situation that called attention to her. Eventually, but very slowly, the girl was able to overcome the problem, although at the end of the year she still did not go out of her way to perform.

What on the surface also looked like excessive shyness characterized a boy in another kindergarten. For him, having to do anything physical seemed like an unbearable burden. During music, for instance, when the other children were merrily skipping or dramatizing the words of a song, he acted as if his greatest desire was to find a hole in which to hide. Sensitive to the problem, his teacher said nothing when he chose to remain apart from an activity. Occasionally she offered encouragement, but nothing more. Again, little by little, this boy was able to join the others—although with great hesitation at first.

Other combinations of sensitive teachers and children with problems were found elsewhere. In one first-grade class, a girl seemed unusually intimidated by children who knew more than she did. The teacher took cognizance of this when she organized instructional groups, always placing her in one in which she was likely to know either as much as, or more than, the others. The careful placement seemed to bolster the child's self-confidence; at least, by the end of the year she was not so readily squelched by children who knew more than she did.

Whole groups of children also benefitted from sensitive teachers. This became especially noticeable on days when restlessness pervaded an entire class. When it did, these teachers allotted more time to recess or, for example, planned a music period in which the children sang and also marched, skipped, jumped, and hopped. As one teacher commented, "On a day like this, I always make sure there's plenty of wiggle music."

SUMMARY

Thanks to an increase in classroom research, information is accumulating that not only describes what goes on in classrooms but, at times, also offers possible explanations for what occurs. Since no teacher—at any level—is so perfect as to make improvement unnecessary, this new body of data is very important. After all, what is not understood cannot be changed and presumably made better.

Why doing better with reading instruction is so important becomes clear whenever the consequences of limited reading ability are considered. Based on existing research, doing better will require some teachers to become more goal-oriented, thus to start their planning with such questions as, "What contributes to reading ability? Which among these contributions are my students now ready to learn?" Such an orientation contrasts with what Chapter 2 refers to as teachers who plan around activities, this time wondering, "What can I assign that will keep the children occupied?" Some research has suggested that planning a day around activities may be a way that is chosen, consciously or unconsciously, to control a class.

Clearly, controlling a class or finding ways to fill up a day with activities are not the primary concerns of the individual Chapter 2 calls "Teacher A." Teacher A is the professional person who makes her own decisions about instructional objectives, is knowledgeable about materials, and uses them in the way they ought to function: one means for accomplishing preselected objectives.

It could be said, then, that Teacher A, like this textbook, aims toward maximizing individualized instruction. As Chapter 1 explained, such instruction is any that deals with what is relevant for reading; that concentrates on what can be, but has not yet been, learned by an individual or a group; and that proceeds at a suitable pace.

REVIEW

1. Over time, the teaching ability of some persons matures; with others, it merely ages. Needless to say, teachers who get better work consciously on doing better. Based on Chapter 2, what are some guidelines or principles a teacher needs to keep in mind if "doing better than I'm doing now" is her aim?

2. Chapter 2 divided teachers into two groups, "Teacher A" and "Teacher B."
   a. How would you describe each group to somebody who had not read Chapter 2?
   b. Do you think the division is accurate, based on what you know about classroom teachers? Might a division into three groups, for instance, be more realistic? If so, what would characterize each group?

3. Chapter 2 talked about teachers who plan a school day around activities.
   a. Specifically, what does this mean?
   b. What are the drawbacks when teachers make decisions based on a concern for activities?

4. Chapter 2 illustrated some consequences when teachers fail to ask themselves, "Why am I doing this?" Skim the chapter so you can describe both the examples and the consequences of insufficient introspection on the teachers' part. What would be different if these teachers not only had objectives but also kept them in mind?

5. Individualized instruction was defined in Chapters 1 and 2.
   a. What *is* individualized instruction?
   b. Give an example of such instruction offered to 100 students.
   c. Give an example of instruction offered to one student that is not individualized.

REFERENCES

1. Anderson, Linda. "The Environment of Instruction: The Function of Seatwork in a Commercially Developed Curriculum." In G. G. Duffy, L. R. Roehler, and J. Mason (Eds.), *Comprehension Instruction: Perspectives and Suggestions.* New York: Longman, 1984, 93–103.
2. Brophy, Jere. "How Teachers Influence What Is Taught and Learned in Classrooms." *Elementary School Journal* 83 (January, 1982), 1–13.
3. Brophy, Jere. "The Teacher as Thinker." In G. G. Duffy, L. R. Roehler, and J. Mason (Eds.), *Comprehension Instruction: Perspectives and Suggestions.* New York: Longman, 1984, 71–92.

4. Duffy, Gerald G. "Context Variables in Reading Teachers' Effectiveness." Paper presented at National Reading Conference, Clearwater Beach, Florida, December 2, 1982.

5. Durkin, Dolores. "Is There a Match between What Elementary Teachers Do and What Basal Reader Manuals Recommend?" *Reading Teacher* 37 (April, 1984), 734–744.

6. Durkin, Dolores. "Reading Comprehension Instruction in Five Basal Reader Series." *Reading Research Quarterly* 16 (1981, No. 4), 515–544.

7. Durkin, Dolores. "Some Questions about Questionable Instructional Materials." *Reading Teacher* 28 (October, 1974), 13–17.

8. Durkin, Dolores. "What Classroom Observations Reveal about Reading Comprehension Instruction." *Reading Research Quarterly* 14 (1978–79, No. 4), 481–533.

9. EPIE Institute. *Annual State of the Art Report on Instructional Materials: Reading Textbook Programs*. New York: EPIE Institute, 1983.

10. Fisher, C.; Berliner, D.; Filby, N.; Marliave, R.; Cohen, L.; Dishaw, M.; and Moore, J. *Teaching and Learning in Elementary Schools: A Summary of the Beginning Teacher Evaluation Study*. San Francisco: Far West Laboratory for Educational Research and Development, 1978.

11. Guzzetti, Barbara J., and Marzano, Robert J. "Correlates of Effective Reading Instruction." *Reading Teacher* 37 (April, 1984), 754–757.

12. Hunter, Madeline. "Knowing, Teaching, and Supervising." In Philip L. Hosford (Ed.), *Using What We Know About Teaching*. Alexandria, Va.: Association for Supervision and Curriculum Development, 1984, 169–192.

13. Osborn, Jean. "The Purposes, Uses, and Contents of Workbooks and Some Guidelines for Publishers." In Richard C. Anderson, Jean Osborn, and Robert J. Tierney (Eds.), *Learning to Read in American Schools: Basal Readers and Content Texts*. Hillsdale, N.J.: Lawrence Erlbaum Associates, 1984, 45–112.

14. Salganik, M. William. "Researchers Team with Reporters to Identify Schools That Work." *Educational R and D Report 3*, No. 1 (Winter, 1980), 2–7.

15. Taylor, Charlotte. *Transforming Schools*. New York: St. Martin's Press, 1976.

CHAPTER 3

Children in Classrooms

PREVIEW

Even though the previous chapter focused on teachers and this chapter deals with children, what content belonged where is not always apparent. Such a dilemma is natural because how children behave and respond in school is closely tied to their teachers, just as teacher behavior is noticeably influenced by students.

The dependence of children's behavior on who happens to be their teacher was made clear in a longitudinal study (5) in which I followed a group of subjects from age four until they finished fourth grade. Even though the pre-established goal of the research was to learn about the effects of pre-first-grade starts in reading, the inclusion of classroom observations for all six years allowed for a large amount of data that went beyond the formal concern of the study. Clearly evident in the extra data was evidence of a teacher's influence not only on what individual children learned but also on how they behaved. In some cases, the effect on behavior was slight; in others, it was nothing less than dramatic.

Because this and other studies (3, 4) included parent interviews as well as classroom observations, the fact that a child's behavior in school and at home may be very different was also verified. Even though it is likely that multiple factors account for the discrepancy, different treatment by parents and teachers must surely be an important variable. The possible extent of these differences was brought to my attention at the time of a classroom observation. I was visiting a nursery school and was especially impressed with one girl's mature behavior and advanced learnings. Even though she was the smallest in the group physically, she certainly was the "biggest" both in her behavior and in how easily she learned everything. That was why I was surprised by what happened when her mother arrived at dismissal time. The mother met the girl at the door, picked her up as if she were about one year old, and carried her to a nearby car. I couldn't help but think, "I wonder how that child behaves at home."

In another case, I came to know a four-year-old boy quite well. At school, his behavior was so docile that I once commented to his teacher, "I think if you told that child to jump out the window, he would." According to his mother, however, he was willful at home, had frequent temper tantrums, and spent most nights sleeping on the living room sofa because of his refusal to stop watching television.

The comment of another mother is worth quoting. Speaking about her son, a first grader, she noted, "Why, when his teacher talks about him, it's as if she's describing a child I don't even know!"

What the various sources of information reinforce is the complexity of human behavior. Chapter 3 thus considers some topics related to children's behavior that are especially pertinent for teachers. As you read about the children, do not overlook the many suggestions for instruction and practice scattered throughout the chapter.

Classroom studies have grown steadily in number; those that focus on reading, however, appear to assume that its beginnings occur in first grade. This is suggested by the fact that the research rarely includes pre-first-grade classrooms. In contrast, this chapter considers young children—in particular, their characteristics that need to be taken into account by anyone trying to teach in the setting of a classroom. Because paying attention is both a requirement for learning and a concern of teachers, it is discussed first.

ATTENTION SPANS

For many decades, the idea that young children inevitably have short attention spans was cited as one reason reading instruction should not be initiated until at least first grade. Observing young children in classrooms, however, suggests that general statements about attention spans do not reflect reality (3, 4, 5).

To be specific, when the attention spans of children of the same age and in the same class are compared, they always vary—sometimes dramatically. Complicating the comparisons is the fact that even for one child, a single description or judgment is usually inaccurate. Here, I recall a boy in a kindergarten I visited regularly. In general, he had been classified as a hop-skip-and-jumper for, when allowed to do so, he switched quickly from one activity to another. Yet, put paper in front of him and crayons in his hands, and he was a different child—or so it seemed. Always the last to finish an art project, this boy consistently produced meticulously executed pictures.

Curious about the ever-present details in his art work, I once talked with him about a picture he had drawn of his parents and learned that he had taken the time to curl his mother's hair, to make her dress a floral print, and to put bows on her shoes. Naturally, she was carrying a nicely detailed purse. And with his father he had been just as careful: best hat with band and a tiny feather, handkerchief in suitcoat pocket, wide stripes in tie, and laces in shoes.

Had other visitors gone into the classroom at any time other than the art period, they would have assigned descriptions like "giddy" and "restless" to this boy's behavior. If observing only during art, however, the same persons could not help but be impressed by the steady, patient attention this boy gave to his work. Even though the behavior of other children in the classroom was not characterized by such extremes, it was still difficult—and also inaccurate—to label the attention span of each with a single description (13). More correct and realistic is the contention that each child had a collection of attention spans.

Classroom observations indicate that each child has a collection of attention spans for some of the same reasons that adults have a collection. Factors such as fatigue, illness, and mood, for instance, play important roles. In fact, in classrooms that were visited often over a period of a year or more, the relevance of children's moods became especially pronounced. Some children, of course, were less moody than others, but all had their good days and bad days. I often thought that wet weather brought out everyone's bad mood; whenever a series of rainy days occurred, a greater than usual amount of restlessness and behavior problems occurred, too.

Other factors had a positive effect on the amount of time children attended to something. If an activity related to themselves, or at least had a connection with what was familiar, it was likely to get and keep their attention. In addition, if previous involvement with something had led to achievement or praise, that activity was likely to succeed in involving them again. Also successful in holding the attention of children was whatever they themselves selected. When teachers kept such factors as these in mind when they planned a day's schedule, an observer would be impressed with how the children became and stayed involved. In these classrooms, traditional claims about the short attention span of a young child seemed highly questionable.

Many times, I was pleasantly surprised at the sustained attention of four-, five-, and six-year-old children; nonetheless, I was equally surprised at how easily young children could be distracted—and this was true even of those who seemed the most mature. The greatest distraction, I learned, is another child. Left alone, an individual might stay with something for what seemed like an endless amount of time. But then along would come a friend, and the picture changed. The more I observed, the more I also noticed that in just about every classroom, at least one boy or girl routinely interrupted others who were busy.

New acquisitions could also be distractions. For example, I once observed a boy with new cowboy boots and a girl with a new watch turn into intermittent sources of distraction for a whole day. At other times, in other classrooms, irresistible attractions were bracelets (especially those that dangle), bandages, combs, rings, and jewelry pins. On one occasion, I learned that even a piece of string could get in the way of a peaceful morning in school.

To sum up, classroom observations uncover variety rather than uniformity in attention spans. The variety is characteristic not only between children but also within a single child. What seems like an accurate conclusion, therefore, is that children have a collection of attention spans, each determined by many factors that work together to affect its depth as well as its length.

To show—if this is necessary—that what has been said about young children's attention spans applies equally to older students, let me refer just briefly to a fifth-grade boy who was in a case study involving three children (6). Everything that the three did during the time scheduled for reading was described and timed.

Of the 1,957 minutes spent observing the fifth grader, 411 minutes ended up categorized as "Noninstruction," a description used when a subject walked aimlessly about the classroom, sharpened a pencil, looked out a window, made an effort to find something, talked to another student about a topic not related to schoolwork, and so on.

By the time the study ended, one conclusion reached about the fifth-grade boy was that much of the behavior categorized as "Noninstruction" was a means for avoiding written assignments. Contrasting sharply with these "delaying tactics" was the same boy's use of what turned out to be 235 minutes allowed for "free reading." For that category, every minute of the allotted time was spent by this subject reading a book. Once more, then, a variety in attention spans was characteristic.

SELF-CONTROL

Although the topics "Attention Span" and "Self-Control" are related, they are sufficiently different to warrant a separate discussion of each. Like attention spans, self-control is considered in a way meant to be pertinent for teachers. In fact, the discussion begins with teachers, because one principle they need to keep in mind goes something like: Do not tempt children, for they *will* succumb. The importance of this dictum has been verified in many studies, which show without question that classroom discipline is "the most seriously perceived problem area of beginning teachers" and of many experienced ones as well (14, p. 153). The truth of the same dictum has been substantiated so many times during my own visits to classrooms that it is difficult to select from all the supportive examples a few that will both illustrate the exact meaning of the guideline and also suggest what can be done when children *do* succumb to temptation.

Let's start with what was seen in a first grade. At the time this observation began, the teacher was working with six children. While she was printing words on a chalkboard, the six were supposed to be looking at the words and identifying them. There was a problem, however. Next to the board was a small, low table on which had been placed clay figures of animals the children made the day before. As might be expected, two children were more interested in looking at the animals than at the words. Instead of taking this normal response into account and dealing with it immediately (by moving the table) the teacher scolded the children for not paying attention. The final results were wasted time and two children who persisted in giving more attention to the clay animals than to the words on the chalkboard.

A similar incident was seen in a third grade in which simple machines was the topic currently being studied in science. This is relevant to mention because, when the science period ended, the teacher placed some of the machines (pulleys, for example) in the front of the room next to the table where she met with reading groups. In this case, it took the teacher no more than about three minutes to realize the unwise placement because, for the first three minutes of her meeting with an instructional group, none of its members even looked at her. Without a word, she moved the equipment to a corner in the back of the room, returned to the table, and restated what she had said earlier when everyone had been gazing intently at the machines.

How a highly effective first-grade teacher handled distractions also merits a description. She had given three assignments to a group of children with whom she had just finished working. One made use of paper fans that had been made earlier in the week. This particular assignment required the children to select from a page of pictured objects those whose names began with /f/, to cut them out, and to paste them on the fans as a decoration. As soon as the fans were distributed, the group became excited and noisy, apparently forgetting the other work to be done. Aware of her mistake in passing out the fans too soon, the teacher wisely bypassed chastisement and said instead, "I don't think you'll have enough room on your desks for the fans. Maybe it would be a good idea to put them back on the table until you finish the two workbook pages. When I check them and find that all your answers are correct, you can put the workbooks away and then there will be plenty of room to do a good job with the fans." No child objected, and the practice period proceeded without further disruptions.

As illustrated, even the best of teachers need to be constantly on guard to avoid distributing materials too soon. I recall being in the classroom of an excellent teacher when she had planned some interesting listening comprehension activities requiring use of a workbook. After passing out copies, she asked the children to keep the books closed until she explained what they were to do. She then started to introduce the activity only to find herself looking at children who were so busy turning pages and looking at pictures that it is doubtful they even knew she was talking. She immediately looked at me and said, "I really do know better than to do what I just did."

EXCITABILITY

Parents as well as teachers know that children can become overly stimulated and that, at such times, behavior problems are common. Obviously, the problems are magnified when an entire group gets too excited. This means that classroom teachers have to be careful to avoid what may be excessively stimulating.

Admittedly, teachers accustomed to older students would be delighted if something they did or said was able to arouse interest in their otherwise blasé charges. What a treat to get the response that is common for those who teach younger children. What a joy, for instance, when children get excited because a teacher decides to use last names for attendance-taking rather than the customary first names. How rewarding when children get excited because they suddenly see in books words they can read: *go, the, house*. Equally refreshing is the enjoyment they find in acting out the meanings of words— *skip* and *sad*, for instance.

Even though this easily aroused excitement has obvious rewards for teachers, it has its problems, too. A teacher once pinpointed the major problems when she commented, "You sometimes get more than you bargained for." Earlier in the morning, in preparation for a story about frogs, she had introduced a group of children to a large stuffed frog who was to sit on a chair and listen to them read. The children were delighted. New words in the story included *hop* and *jump*. After they and other words had been written, identified, and discussed, the teacher asked eager volunteers to act out the meanings of *hop* and *jump*, which they promptly did with great gusto. Once the story was read, the children were allowed to jump and hop back to their desks, which they again did with obvious enjoyment. The problem? The whole class jumped and hopped for the rest of the morning.

In another classroom, the children had reached the point at which they could print their names quite well. They were also able to read a number of words, including *me*. To promote further interest in reading and printing, the teacher typed and dittoed a simple letter that began, "Dear Me." The children each received a copy in a stamped envelope addressed to themselves. What excitement!

A post office was close to the school, so off went the children and the teacher to mail the letters. It was a small office, and arrangements had been made for a tour and an explanation of the facilities. Upon their return to the classroom, excitement was everywhere. As the teacher observed, "They're really high now." And they were for the rest of the morning.

Since excitability *can* cause problems, let me have you read another journal entry written by a graduate student who was an aide in a nursery school. She worked with two teachers. Her entry is informative not only about causes of excessive excitement but also about constructive ways for dealing with it. The entry tells about Valentine's Day and begins in a very forthright way:

The day was a disaster. Excitement was high. The teachers should have been more prepared than ever, but weren't. The Valentine holder should have been ready and the hearts cut out. The children grew restless and noisy waiting for the lead teacher to finish the box. I tried to take advantage of the waiting by writing *Valentine* on the board for my group. We talked about the sound that *v* stands for, and I asked if they could think of any child's name that began with *V*. Several children thought of Vik immediately, and Steven said his name had a *v* in it, too. This led to a discussion (with examples) of the meaning of "beginning of a word." Later, the children said that *vest* and *vase* started the way *Valentine* began, so I wrote those words too.

Then the Valentine exchange! All the children took the cards they had brought and tried to put one card in each child's box. This resulted in chaos, and the confusion upset everyone.

If I had anything to say about the distribution of Valentines, I would have suggested that a teacher put the cards into the boxes, making sure that everyone had a card. Then we could have looked at the cards with the children, one group at each table with one teacher. We might have discussed the pictures, read the messages, and tried to find the word *Valentine*. If they were interested, we might have named letters, seen how many children's names could be read, and so on. As it was, the morning began and ended in confusion – and overly stimulated children.

Another journal entry, only part of which is reproduced below, was written by a kindergarten observer. This account deals with a more controlled and constructive kind of excitement.

In class, we talked about the effective teacher who recognizes and takes advantage of unexpected opportunities to encourage and introduce learning experiences. During this observation, I witnessed a teacher who did just that.

On the day of the observation, fresh snow was on the ground. Taking into account the excitability of young children – specifically, the excitement that the first snow of the year would generate – this kindergarten teacher took advantage of the situation to put the word *snow* into the children's reading vocabularies. The group was easily led into a discussion of snow, whereupon the teacher commented that it might be interesting to see what the word *snow* looked like when it was written. She printed *snow* on the board and identified it. While making sure that the children were looking at *snow*, she had them rename it, spell it, and say again what it said.

The teacher next brought out the book *Snowy Day* by Ezra Keats. Almost immediately, several of the children commented on the fact that *Snowy* had the word *snow* in it. (The teacher agreed, but failed to print *Snowy* directly under *snow* to highlight how the two words were the same and how they were different.) The children became absorbed in the story, for reading it on this particular day made it very special.

IMAGINATION

The excitability of young children results from many factors, one of which is their rich imagination. Observations have shown that imagination also brings reality and fantasy very close together, thus allowing young children to be an interesting combination of sophistication and naïveté.

The combination first became noticeable in a kindergarten occupied by children who were unusually sophisticated five-year-olds. They were highly verbal, learned easily, and were surprisingly aware of what was going on in the world. One day, after they had sung and enjoyed a song about a jack-in-the-box, their teacher suggested that each become one. Without hesitation, all these "sophisticates" did just that, hiding their heads in nonexistent boxes. Commenting that she could see nothing but boxes, the teacher inquired, "Where are the children?" Of course, the "lost" children were delighted and tried all the harder to curl up in their boxes. And the harder they tried, the more I thought, "Such an interesting combination of sophistication and simplicity."

That thought became increasingly common. With a first-grade group, for instance, a teacher was using a bulletin-board display to review some words. At the bottom, the board showed an airport. Over it were clouds, attached to which were small word cards. With this display, children took turns "flying." Using a small paper airplane as a pointer, they pretended to fly up and down in a variety of directions, touching cards and naming words.

To create interest in what was to be done, the teacher had first talked to the children about the trip they were going to take and the opportunity they would have to be pilots. Then the flying—and vocabulary review—began.

From the comments the children were making, it appeared that some thought a trip to a real airport was in their future. That this was true of at least two children was verified later. The teacher received phone calls from two mothers who wondered when the trip to the airport was to be, and how much it would cost. Before the teacher could explain, one volunteered to go along to help.

At another time, I had the chance to observe a teacher in a rural nursery school create interest in numeral identification with the help of a stuffed cloth hen and a group of imaginative four-year-olds. The hen had been placed on a pile of straw; under her were egg-shaped pieces of construction paper on which numerals from 1 to 10 had been printed. As the teacher took out the eggs, the children named the numerals. When one was correctly identified, the egg on which the numeral was printed was thumbtacked to a board. Eventually, all the eggs were counted. Then the children renamed the numerals as the teacher took down all but three from the board. The three remaining eggs displayed *3, 5,* and *8.*

Next came some printing. The numerals *3, 5,* and *8* had been selected for practice because most of the children had difficulty forming them correctly. As the children began to print, they made a considerable amount of noise because, of course, they still had much to say about the hen. Quickly but kindly the teacher reminded them that the hen was tired from laying so many eggs and needed to rest. No further disturbances occurred as the children proceeded with their work in what was an amazingly quiet room—considering it was filled with four-year-olds who had a hen in their midst.

Many other examples of young children who had imagination and enjoyed using it could be described. Once a group of children were restless when the teacher wanted them to listen to some directions. Their hands seemed especially busy. Instead of making the more usual request that they fold their hands, the teacher suggested that they be trains and that they hook their hands together the way they had seen train cars being attached. The willingness of the children to do this was immediate and lasted long enough for the teacher to finish the directions.

In another classroom, trains had also been discussed. Later, as the teacher collected pictures of trains drawn by the children, she told them she was a conductor and was collecting tickets. While this was going on, a little girl who always seemed to have trouble sitting for more than two minutes stood up. Instead of chastising her, the teacher suggested, "Oh, you had better not stand up. The train might start and then you'd fall and hurt yourself." Very agreeably, the child sat down.

In cases like these, it has to be asked, Who has the greater imagination — the teacher or the children? In other instances, the children do the imagining on their own. Here, I am recalling the number of times parents have told how their young children play school when they get home. (Their imagination freely allows them to use dolls as students.) Once the teaching begins, however, imitation rather than imagination takes over. According to the parents, both the words and the gestures of the teacher at school are imitated by the children with perfection.

IMITATION

The tendency of young children to imitate is well known, so I was hardly surprised to find them in classrooms copying the behavior of others. With some children, however, the tendency seemed almost like a compulsion. I recall a number of children (usually the less mature in a group) who, at least on certain days, copied everything they saw and heard. If the child next to them looked at a picture displayed on a board, they looked at it. If he accidentally fell off his chair, they fell off theirs. Fortunately, with the majority of children, imitative behavior was less frequent and seemed normal. For example, to see one child blowing bubbles while drinking milk with a straw and then to see all the others do the same thing seemed very natural.

Luckily, young children copy the good as well as the bad. I remember one incident in which a first-grade girl suddenly discovered that the color of each of her crayons was printed on its label. With great enthusiasm she began to copy each word with the appropriate color, a somewhat awkward task, as the crayon being used was the one from which the copying had to be done. But she persisted, printing *red* in red, *blue* in blue, and so on. Meanwhile, a classmate came along and asked what she was doing. It wasn't long before the second child was busy with the same task. She wasn't nearly so successful, however. Her first carefully printed word in purple was *crayola*.

In another classroom, I saw imitative behavior spread throughout the entire group. These first graders were busy drawing a picture of a dog like the one in a story just read to them. Before they started, the teacher had labeled each paper with the word *dog* at the bottom. When one of the boys finished his picture, he added what looked like a circle close to the dog's foot. He asked the teacher, "Will you write *food* here?" Soon, food and the second label were being added to everyone's picture.

SUGGESTIBILITY

Similar to imitative behavior is what might be called the suggestibility of young children. I mention this trait, as I have been reminded of the power of suggestion repeatedly while visiting classrooms.

At storytime, for instance, with all the children sitting on the floor in front of her, a teacher might comment, "Can everyone see?" Suddenly, once contented children say they cannot see and must move. Or, as was heard in a kindergarten class, the teacher says, "John, I don't think you can see the pictures from where you're sitting." Predictably, all the children decide they cannot see, so once again everybody must move. Or, to cite another example, because the teacher allows one child to examine a picture in detail, all demand to look at it.

The power of suggestion was also clearly evident in a nursery school where I watched as a teacher distributed numeral cards to each child in a group of four-year-olds. As she did so, she warned, "Now I don't want any of you to put these cards in your mouth." Very quickly, the cards were in their mouths.

On another day, I observed first graders finishing a writing paper. One child had completed his, so the teacher suggested, "Jeffrey, as long as you're finished you can stand by the door." (It was almost time for recess.) Suddenly, children who had seemed intent on being careful and correct changed into children who hastily scribbled the last few words on their papers and then eagerly asked, "Can I get in line, too?"

Fortunately, the power of suggestion also works for the good. A teacher participates in a word game with a group of children and says for all to hear, "I'm going to listen carefully so I'll be ready when it's my turn." As a result, at least some children in the group listen a little more attentively than they otherwise might have done. Or, a teacher says to a child, "I certainly like the way you put that *e* on the line," and then many *e*'s are very carefully placed on lines.

What also led to *e*'s on lines, of course, was the praise the children received. Like all human beings, young children respond positively and, in their case, very openly to praise, sometimes adding a little of their own. I recall one girl who, after being complimented by her teacher for offering a suitable suggestion, proudly said, "That was good head thinking, wasn't it?"

IMPATIENCE

What is not relished by young children — or by anyone — is the need to wait. Yet in classrooms occupied by large numbers of students and only one adult, waiting is the rule rather than the exception. Waiting to have a turn, for example, is very common. In this case, practice does not make perfect. Repeatedly, I have watched children become inattentive and get into trouble because they were unwilling, or perhaps unable, to be patient and wait their turn.

A behavior problem connected with waiting developed in a first-grade class while the teacher was working with ten children. Each child had been given word cards, and the teacher was building sentences by naming the words. For instance, she might say "the" and the child holding *the* would bring it to a card holder hanging in front of the group where he would tuck it into a slot. All went well, as long as a child was having a turn. When he was not, especially when all his cards were gone, restlessness and inattentiveness resulted. (Had the teacher been the one who placed the cards in the slot as they were brought to her, the routine would have moved along more quickly, and the children would have had more turns faster. In addition, more words and sentences could have been read.)

In another first grade, the teacher was also working with a group of about ten. She was combining printing and phonics. She named a word, then chose one child to write its initial letter on the chalkboard. For the child doing the writing, life was great. For all the others, however, it was dull. Why? For one thing, the selected child often took a long time to write a letter; for another, his "audience" was unable to watch as he wrote because he was standing in the way. Eventually, as might be expected, more and more children lost interest and soon there were discipline problems.

Although taking turns requires an amount of patience that young (and older) children do not always have, once the process is begun, no one is willing to have his turn skipped. One kindergarten teacher, taking advantage of concern about getting a turn, introduced and used alphabetical order. The practice in her classroom was to have a child hold the flag each morning while the others said the pledge of allegiance. Turns were assigned in alphabetical order. To help, a large alphabetical list of the children's first names was discussed and then displayed low enough for all to see.

Later on, when the children's eagerness to be first in line began to cause problems, the teacher assigned turns using another alphabetical list, this one composed of the children's last names. Predictably, the teacher never once had to ask, "Whose turn is it to be first in line today?"

Sporadically, when difficulties arose because several children wanted to do or use the same thing at the same time, it was common to hear one of them comment, "Let's take alphabet turns." Equally common were objections from children whose names might be Tommy or Vicky or, perhaps, Wilson or Zimmerman. Clearly, the concept of alphabetical order had been learned well.

NONPREDICTABILITY

It is possible that this discussion of characteristics of young children may have implied that their behavior is predictable. As any parent or experienced teacher will verify, it is not. What we know about children, for example, suggests that if four-year-olds are taken to a hatchery, they will be willing and even eager to discuss what they saw the next morning. Yet I was in a nursery school on the morning following just such a trip and heard one boy object to a discussion in which all the others could hardly wait to get a turn to talk. "How come we're still talking about chickens?" was his complaint.

Because academic accomplishments do make young children seem older than they are, unexpected behavior may seem to occur more often when pre-first-grade programs have academic goals. I recall one kindergarten girl, for example, who burst into tears when the teacher unintentionally passed her by when rhythm band instruments were distributed. Such a response was unexpected because the child in question was one who learned everything that was ever taught – or merely mentioned. Consequently, she did seem "too big" to cry about such a triviality, but cry she did.

A very able girl in another kindergarten also took everyone by surprise with her tears. In this case, the children were printing each letter in their last names on small square pieces of paper, which eventually would be pasted in correct sequence on a large sheet of paper. Expectedly, this bright girl had no trouble printing or arranging the letters in order; however, when she went to paste her unusually long name on the paper, it didn't fit. Then came the tears.

Other unexpected behavior has been observed as young children responded to lessons. I remember one teacher – always a careful planner – who used colorful pictures to introduce what she hoped would be an informative discussion of clouds. Once the children's curiosity was piqued, the teacher read a book that told some interesting facts about cloud formations. The children listened attentively and seemed interested. Then, just before they were to go outside to look at some clouds, the teacher held up another colorful picture that showed stars in addition to clouds. One child immediately responded, "Oh, it's the Fourth of July." Soon everyone was talking at once about fireworks. Gone was the carefully nourished interest in clouds.

Even with games, children may react in unexpected ways. I first learned this while watching a group of children play musical chairs. Inclement weather had made indoor recess necessary, so the teacher lined up chairs and the game began. But then problems developed when everyone wanted to be a loser. Why a loser? Because the loser got to carry away a chair, and that was special for a reason not at all obvious to the two adults who watched.

Probably the underlying lesson to be learned from all these accounts of young children can be summed up with a simple prediction directed to their teachers: Never will there be a dull moment.

CONCLUDING COMMENTS

At the start of the chapter it was said that, in earlier decades, many early childhood educators thought that preschoolers' attention spans were so innately short as to preclude success should reading instruction be offered earlier than first grade. The same educators further believed that the primary concern of pre-first-grade programs should be social and emotional development, which meant that goals like emotional stability, self-acceptance, independence, and ability to get along with others were emphasized (1, 8, 11). The question to consider now is, Do visits to pre-first-grade classrooms verify the need for such emphases?

Actually, classroom observations are not a prerequisite for appreciating both the importance and necessity of helping children of all ages with what might globally be called good mental health. One merely has to be alive to know that room for growth in this area always exists whether a person is a child or an adult. The need to justify concern for young children's social and emotional development, therefore, is nonexistent.

What still has to be questioned, however, was the tendency of the same educators to separate social and emotional goals from academic ones. A question about the separation is raised because the unfortunate result was either-or thinking and, consequently, either-or decisions. Should we emphasize getting along with others, or should we be teaching readiness for reading? Should we help a child grow in independence, or should we introduce simple mathematical concepts? These were the kinds of either-or questions asked, and traditional answers moved in the direction of social and emotional goals. What classroom observations suggest is that such goals should not be isolated because they are not achieved in a vacuum but, rather, as children participate in activities connected with other goals. Or, as Annemarie Roeper, a nursery school specialist, said as long ago as 1959, "Good adjustment is a basic necessity for learning, but learning also makes for good adjustment" (12, p. 8).

One assumption of this book parallels Roeper's observation: Social and emotional goals are achieved gradually in conjunction with academic goals. One further assumption is that the latter should include reading ability, if and when teachers are prepared to offer pre-first-graders opportunities to begin reading that are appropriate for their age and interests. More is said about such opportunities in the next two chapters.

SUMMARY

In some ways, students are students regardless of their age. In other respects, however, age makes a considerable difference. This latter fact explains why some teachers say they would never think of working with older students, whereas others feel they wouldn't even know what to do with young ones.

Chapter 3 singled out for attention a few characteristics of young children that have been both obvious and common during many visits to classrooms (3, 4, 5). Some of the traits make it a delight to teach young children; others make it difficult, especially when one unassisted adult has responsibility for a large class. Knowing about the characteristics—in particular, knowing how to put them to good use—is common among the best of teachers.

Chapter 3 concluded with a brief discussion of what has helped to keep academic goals out of pre-first-grade programs: concern for the social and emotional development of young children. It was especially emphasized that social and emotional goals are not attained apart from other kinds of goals, including the goal of providing ready children with suitable opportunities to begin reading.

REVIEW

1. Chapter 3 discussed a number of topics—imagination, self-control, impatience—as it described children seen in classrooms. The discussion was not exhaustive, however. What characteristics would *you* add to those discussed? Why do you feel the additions are sufficiently important to merit discussion?

2. Giving attention to what needs to be seen or heard is of obvious importance for learning. Because of the importance, let me describe what occurred in one kindergarten. The teacher was having the seventeen members of her class take turns spelling their first names as she showed cards on which they were printed. The procedure took a lot of time and thus resulted in a restless group. Later, when I inquired about the reason for the spelling, the teacher said, "Doing something

like that with an entire class encourages lengthy attention spans." Do you agree?

3. One inevitable concern of beginning teachers — and of some experienced ones, too — is disruptive behavior they may be unable to control. As Chapter 3 showed, it is possible for teachers to foster exactly what they dread: discipline problems. As you skim Chapter 3, list circumstances mentioned that created disruptive behavior that could have been avoided.

4. When children in classrooms were being described, references were made to a number of activities children would like and from which they would learn something important. Name four such activities, including the contribution of each activity to an instructional program.

5. In discussing elementary school supervisors, Madeline Hunter says, "The objective of supervision is not to clone oneself but to stimulate growth in another. Teaching behavior that fits the observer's style may not fit the teacher's" (10, p. 181). Reconsider the content of both this and the previous chapter. Do you think their content might stimulate growth or, on the other hand, do you think the two chapters portray one type of teacher whom the author of the chapters expects every other teacher to copy?

REFERENCES

1. Butler, Annie L. "Hurry! Hurry! Why?" *Childhood Education* 39 (September, 1962), 10–13.
2. Clay, Marie. *Reading: The Patterning of Complex Behavior*, Auckland, New Zealand: Heinemann Books, 1979.
3. Durkin, Dolores. "A Case-Study Approach toward an Identification of Factors Associated with Success and Failure in Learning to Read." *California Journal of Educational Research* 11 (January, 1960), 26–33.
4. Durkin, Dolores. *Children Who Read Early.* New York: Teachers College Press, Columbia University, 1966.
5. Durkin, Dolores. "A Six-Year Study of Children Who Learned to Read in School at the Age of Four." *Reading Research Quarterly* 10 (1974–75, No. 1), 9–61.
6. Durkin, Dolores. "What Classroom Observations Reveal about Reading Comprehension Instruction." *Reading Research Quarterly* 14 (1978–79, No. 4), 481–533.
7. Ferreiro, Emilia, and Teberosky, Ana. *Literacy before Schooling.* Exeter, N.H.: Heinemann Educational Books, 1982.
8. Heffernan, Helen. "Significance of Kindergarten Education." *Childhood Education* 36 (March, 1960), 313–319.

9. Holdaway, Don. *The Foundations of Literacy.* Sydney, Australia: Ashton Scholastic, 1979.
10. Hunter, Madeline. "Knowing, Teaching, and Supervising." In Philip L. Hosford (Ed.), *Using What We Know about Teaching.* Alexandria, Va.: Association for Supervision and Curriculum Development, 1984, 169–192.
11. Hymes, James L. "More Pressure for Early Reading." *Childhood Education* 15 (September, 1963), 34–35.
12. Roeper, Annemarie. "Nursery School: A Place to Adjust or a Place to Learn?" *Child Study* 36 (Spring, 1959), 3–9.
13. Stammer, John D. "Target: The Basics of Listening." *Language Arts* 54 (September, 1977), 661–664.
14. Veenman, Simon. "Perceived Problems of Beginning Teachers." *Review of Educational Research* 54 (Summer, 1984), 143–178.

PART II
Reading at
the Beginning

The first three chapters in this book, which comprise Part I, provide background information for dealing with the content of subsequent chapters. They do this by considering reading, teachers, and children.

The first chapter in Part II attends to the question, "When are children ready to begin to learn to read?" Since nobody wants to start teaching reading before children are able to be successful, Chapter 4 is especially important for anyone with responsibility for making decisions about the timing of beginning instruction. Although Chapter 4 was written with teachers and other professional educators in mind, what it says about readiness is pertinent whether the setting of instruction is a classroom or a child's home.

Chapter 5, "A Beginning Literacy Program," describes in some detail implications for instruction of the readiness concept proposed in Chapter 4. In doing so, Chapter 5 illustrates how pre-first-grade programs in reading can proceed in ways that recognize the inter-relationships of all the language arts: listening, speaking, reading, and writing. The illustrations further show how beginning instruction can use children's interests and everyday experiences to promote literacy. It thus steers away from commercially packaged programs.

Chapter 6 closes Part II by examining when reading should be oral and when it ought to be done silently—questions that teachers at all grade levels need to consider when they make plans for the time set aside to teach reading. As Chapter 6 looks at the two kinds of reading, it reinforces the importance of teachers' asking themselves, "Why am I doing what I'm doing?"

CHAPTER 4

Readiness for Beginning Reading

PREVIEW

Individualized instruction has been defined as any instruction that focuses on what an individual or a group needs and *is ready* to learn. "To be ready" is to have whatever is required (understandings, abilities, experiences, motivation, etc.) to achieve the intended outcome of the instruction.

Since readiness has to do with prerequisites for learning, it is as relevant for college instructors as for people teaching young children. Chapter 4, however, singles out only one aspect of the concept that can be identified with the question, "When are children ready to begin to learn to read?" The same question can be rephrased to ask, "When are children ready to be successful in learning what is taught at the start?"

As Chapter 4 concentrates on these questions, it reveals their complexity, thus the inadequacy of simple answers. Because of the complexity, many different subtopics are discussed. Minimally, reading the chapter should allow you to:

1. Define readiness for beginning reading.
2. Understand a way to assess a child's readiness.
3. See implications of the definition of readiness for instructional programs.

It is possible that your present conception of readiness for beginning reading and how it should be assessed is different from the one that underlies Chapter 4. If that is the case, persistent comparisons of your ideas with those in the chapter will add to your comprehension. The same comparisons may also add depth to your understanding of your own point of view. Thus, nothing will be lost and much may be gained by a careful reading of Chapter 4.

Even though requirements for excellence in teaching reading do not include knowing the history of reading instruction, a historical treatment of the topic "Readiness for Beginning Reading" allows for an identification of a number of problems that have persistently plagued the field of reading. Specifically, a historical analysis makes clear (a) the significance of the timing of a proposal for its acceptance or rejection and, related to that, the periodic emergence of popular ideas that are questionable because the popularity is not fostered by well-documented facts; (b) the major influence of publishers on both what is taught and how and when it will be taught; (c) the intermittent, regular appearance of old and once rejected wine in new bottles; and (d) the failure (or inability) of the profession to deal with issues in relation to individual children.

Because what the history of the readiness concept brings to the surface has widespread application, this chapter starts with an examination of the roots and dimensions of what will be called the traditional view of readiness. The description *traditional* is used because this initial interpretation was highly influential for an uncommonly long period of time.

TRADITIONAL VIEW OF READINESS

In American schools, a close association has always existed between starting school and starting to read. Because the age of six has been the common criterion for admission into first grade, a parallel development has been the expectation that "being six" and "starting to read" occur simultaneously. Not to be overlooked, however, is that some well-known scholars of years gone by objected to the assumption that entrance into first grade should automatically mean the start of reading instruction. Edmund Huey, still highly regarded for his 1908 text *The Psychology and Pedagogy of Reading* (33), quotes John Dewey as recommending the age of eight as an appropriate time to introduce reading. He was quick to emphasize, however, that Dewey was objecting as much to the mechanical and passive way in which the schools taught reading as he was to the timing of initial instruction.

Huey's own objections were also directed to the nature of available instruction. He especially complained about the "unnatural" ways in which the schools introduced children to reading. He added specificity to the complaint by describing the "natural, every-day activities" of preschool children that sometimes teach them to read. As seen in the following quotation, Huey's language is a little old fashioned, but the theme in his 1908 description of preschoolers is strictly up to date:

> The child makes endless questionings about the names of things, as every mother knows. He is concerned also about the printed notices, signs, titles, visiting cards, etc., that come his way, and should be told what these

"say" when he makes inquiry. It is surprising how large a stock of printed or written words a child will gradually come to recognize in this way. (33, p. 313)

It is true that a few educators spoke out against the routine practice of initiating instruction in reading at the start of first grade; however, it still must be concluded from a study of the literature that the years from 1900 to 1920 were relatively quiet about when to begin. Soon afterward, however, books and journals became laden with questions and answers about the best time to start teaching reading. Why the change?

One basic reason is what is often called the Testing Movement of the 1920s. During this time, psychologists put forth considerable effort to "elevate psychology to the status of a respected science" (45, p. 390). Among the results of the interest in making psychological data more objective, thus more scientific, was the appearance of many tests, including some for assessing reading. Once the reading tests became available, national surveys of achievement became popular. Of relevance to this chapter is a finding commonly reported: Large numbers of children are failing first grade, most often because of insufficient achievement in reading (12, 32, 43).

Within a short time, concern about this finding was widespread for at least two reasons. Success in teaching reading, then as now, was considered uniquely important among elementary school responsibilities. In addition, the failures resulted in first-grade classrooms that were occupied by a number of "over age" children. Behavior problems increased; so did concern about why first graders were having difficulty learning to read.

Logically, a study of reading problems—at any grade level and at any period of time—would look at such multiple, commonsense causes as inadequate teacher preparation, poor instructional materials, large classes, low IQs among the children, and, perhaps, a lack of motivation. However, in the study of beginning reading problems that went on in the 1920s and 1930s, the factor given singular attention can be summarized as follows: First graders are having difficulty learning to read because they were not ready when the instruction began.

Why beginning reading problems were attributed so exclusively to a lack of readiness and, in addition, why delaying instruction was soon proposed as the remedy can be understood only when the broader psychological and educational setting of the 1920s and 1930s is brought into focus. The following sections sketch that period, highlighting developments that had a distinct effect on how beginning reading problems were "explained."

Psychological Beliefs That Fostered the Traditional Interpretation of Readiness

To understand why readiness received so much attention in the 1920s and 1930s, it is necessary to go back to still earlier decades and discuss G. Stanley Hall. Hall was a psychologist who, because of his reputation and numerous publications, had a very apparent influence on psychological interpretations of human behavior during the beginning years of this century. Prominent in Hall's writings was his belief in the unique importance of heredity in human development. Equally prominent was his acceptance of the theory of recapitulation. This quotation from one of Hall's texts points up the tenets of the theory:

> The most general formulation of all the facts of development that we yet possess is contained in the law of recapitulation. This law declares that the individual, in his development, passes through stages similar to those through which the race has passed, and in the same order. (26, p. 8)

Hall's belief in recapitulation theory, combined with the importance he assigned to heredity, fostered a view of human beings that stressed a predetermined nature that unfolds in stages. This interpretation of growth and development had a pronounced effect on Hall's students, who included a number of prominent individuals including Arnold Gesell. Because Gesell's work is directly related to the concept of readiness, and because his writings were influential for several decades, he figures prominently in any attempt to explain why (a) lack of readiness and (b) postponed instruction were once viewed as the cause of, and solution for, beginning reading problems.

Arnold Gesell was a physician; thus, his special interest in the maturation process is natural. So, too, is his description of maturation in terms of distinct stages, since it clearly shows the influence of G. Stanley Hall (23, 24). Hall's influence seems even greater in Gesell's proposed explanation of the maturation process. Here, as Gesell and his students tried to account for developmental stages in children, they detoured away from such factors as learning and practice and instead gave the credit for development to what they called at various times "intrinsic growth," "neural ripening," and "automatic and unfolding behavior."

Traditional Interpretation of Reading Problems

Having read this sketch of the psychological climate of the 1920s, you should now understand why the first-grade reading problems uncovered in the surveys referred to earlier were explained with a reference to a lack of readiness rather than to such possible causes as poor instruction, excessively large classes, or inappropriate materials. The reasoning behind such an explanation is outlined below:

Early Interpretation of Beginning Reading Problems
1. Development takes place in stages that follow one another in an inevitable order.

2. Moving from one stage to another results from maturation (internal neural ripening), which occurs automatically with the passing of time.
3. The ability required to learn to read occurs at one of these stages.
4. Reading problems disclosed by the surveys suggest that some beginning first graders have not yet reached that stage of development and, therefore, are not yet ready to learn to read.
5. The solution is to postpone reading instruction so that, with the passing of time, the children will mature and thus reach the stage of development that allows for success.

Mental-Age Concept of Readiness

Given the circumstances of the 1920s, a concept of readiness for reading that related it to a vaguely defined stage in a child's development was not likely to win universal approval as it hardly reflected the interest in exact measurement that characterized the Testing Movement. Not surprising, therefore, were the efforts soon made to describe with more precision that stage of development thought to ensure a child's readiness.

The form these efforts took was influenced by the appearance of group intelligence tests, because with their availability came many reports about the relationship between intelligence and reading achievement. Commonly, the focus was first-grade achievement. As early as 1920, in fact, one writer was saying that children who had difficulty with reading and were failing first grade were children with mental ages of less than six years (12). Subsequently, other authors in the 1920s moved toward proposals that would establish a certain mental age as a requirement for starting instruction. Arthur, for example, writing in 1925, said that a mental age of 6.0 to 6.5 years was "necessary for standard first-grade achievement" (2).

The kind of thinking about readiness reflected in these reports was crystallized in an article that became widely known and uncommonly influential for a long period of time. The report by Mabel Morphett and Carleton Washburne in 1931 described the reading achievement of first-grade children attending school in Winnetka, Illinois (30). Based on their achievement as it related to mental age, the authors concluded:

> It seems safe to state that, by postponing the teaching of reading until children reach a mental age of six and a half years, teachers can greatly decrease the chances of failure and discouragement and can correspondingly increase their efficiency. (39, p. 503)

How seriously Washburne took his own proposal is reflected in an article he wrote in 1936 called "Ripeness." He observed:

> Nowadays each first grade teacher in Winnetka has a chart showing when each of her children will be mentally six-and-a-half, and is careful to avoid any effort to get a child to read before he has reached this stage of mental growth. (49, p. 127)

Evidence of how seriously educators took the Morphett-Washburne proposal is in reading methodology textbooks that appeared not long after their report and in others published as many as ten and twenty years later. In fact, some textbooks with publication dates of the 1960s were still taking it seriously.

Reasons for Acceptance of Mental-Age Concept

Knowing how influential and long-lasting the mental-age concept of readiness has been, you might wonder why findings from a study of one teaching method in one school system were accepted as being applicable to all children in all schools. You might also wonder why the acceptance persisted. A subsequent section in the chapter helps with the latter question; here, let me deal with why the Morphett-Washburne proposal enjoyed quick approval.

For one thing, the proposal fit in perfectly with the temper of the times in which it was made. It supported the "doctrine of postponement," because most children entering first grade do not have a mental age of 6.5 years. It also reflected the notion that development proceeds in stages that are achieved with the passing of time, and it honored the Testing Movement by being precise and objective.

Any attempt to explain the unique influence of the mental-age concept of readiness must also take into account the prominence of Carleton Washburne. He was superintendent of the Winnetka schools—widely admired and copied in the 1930s—and also one of the most prestigious leaders of the Progressive Education Movement. As a result, what Washburne said was listened to, and not only by reading educators. Even earlier than 1931, he had made specific proposals about what was to be taught in arithmetic and at which mental-age level (50). With these facts in mind, his mental-age description of readiness and the influence it wielded should not be surprising.

Early Objections to Mental-Age Concept

Although the mental-age concept of readiness was widely accepted, objections were not missing. The most important came from Arthur Gates, whose research raised serious questions about the concept. For example, in May 1936, in a report called "Reading Readiness: A Study of Factors Determining Success and Failure in Beginning Reading," Gates and Guy Bond described the reading achievement of children in four first-grades (22). Of relevance here is that, in March, he identified the ten lowest achievers and assigned them tutors. By June, all ten were enjoying success. Referring to that success, the authors wrote:

> The study emphasizes the importance of recognizing and adjusting to individual limitations and needs . . . rather than merely changing the time of beginning. It appears that readiness for reading is something to develop rather than merely to wait for. (22, p. 684)

In the same report, the researchers also pointed out:

> Correlations of mental age with reading achievement at the end of the year were about 0.25. When one studies the range of mental ages from the lowest to the highest in relation to reading achievement, there appears no suggestion of a crucial or critical point above which very few fail and below which a relatively large proportion fail. (22, p. 680)

The report concluded:

> The optimum time of beginning reading is not entirely dependent upon the nature of the child himself, but it is in a large measure determined by the nature of the reading program. (22, p. 684)

Similar conclusions were reached in research reported by Gates in 1937. This time, results of different methods of teaching reading in first grade were examined. Commenting on the findings, Gates observed:

> Reading is begun by very different materials, methods, and general procedures, some of which a pupil can master at the mental-age of five with reasonable ease, others of which would give him difficulty at the mental-age of seven. (21, p. 508)

As seen in these reports, the concept of reading readiness that emerged from Gates's studies was very much at odds with the Morphett-Washburne description. Within the Gates frame of reference, the burden of responsibility was moved to the instruction and away from the child. Questions were also raised about the wisdom of postponement and of equating readiness with a particular mental age. Essentially, then, Gates's message was: Improve your instruction and watch the children read! Apparently, the Morphett-Washburne proposal was more appealing, because just as the publications of the 1930s and subsequent decades provide ample evidence of the prolonged acceptance of the mental-age concept of readiness, they also reveal how little attention went to Gates's findings. His simply did not move with the stream of popular thought.

REVIEW QUESTIONS ABOUT TRADITIONAL
INTERPRETATION OF READINESS

Because many ideas have been covered in relatively few pages, here is a good place to stop and see what has been comprehended. The following questions allow for self-evaluation.

- Developmental stages
- Ripening Process

1. Describe the traditional interpretation of readiness for reading. *MENTAL AGE 6.0-6.5*
2. Using the time line in Figure 4.1, explain the relevance of each of the people named to the development of the traditional view.

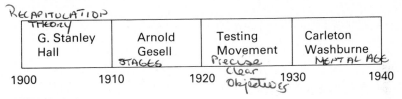

RECAPITULATION THEORY

G. Stanley Hall	Arnold Gesell *STAGES*	Testing Movement *Precise Clear Objectives*	Carleton Washburne *MENTAL AGE*
1900	1910	1920 1930	1940

Figure 4.1

3. Why can it be said that the discussion of readiness succeeds in showing that whether an idea is accepted depends as much on when it is proposed as on the quality of the idea itself?

VESTIGES OF TRADITIONAL VIEW
OF READINESS

Knowing about the traditional view of readiness will allow you to see vestiges of the earlier interpretation in current practices.

Physical Maturation and Readiness

Concern about the role played by maturation in readiness for reading is often found in readiness checklists. One such list (46) includes the following items under the heading "Motor Coordination":

1. Is the child able to perform the following tasks:
   a. hops on one foot?
   b. jumps?
   c. gallops?
   d. skips?
   e. kicks a ball?

The existence of highly proficient readers, young and old, who never could jump, gallop, skip, or kick a ball is enough to raise questions about the value of items like those just listed for decisions concerned with readiness; yet tests for motor coordination continue to be used in early screening programs (31) designed to identify children likely to have problems when they start school.

Other vestiges of the maturation emphasis are in materials that provide training in skills described at various times as visual-motor, perceptual-motor, and sensorimotor. Names like Frostig (20), Getman (25), and Kephart (36) are usually associated with these workbooks, worksheets, and tests that have children perform such tasks as matching geometrical forms, tracing lines arranged simply or in mazes, identifying figures embedded in more complex figures, and adding to certain shapes and forms to make them look like others. What motivates educators to use these packaged programs is not research data, because they have never supported the contention that exercises like those just mentioned help children become ready for reading (1, 9, 27, 28, 41, 49).

Reading Readiness Tests

Another vestige of traditional notions about readiness is the reading readiness test. Initial expectations for such tests are effectively portrayed in a 1927 issue of *Childhood Education*. Although they now seem naïve, the expectations clearly reflected both the Testing Movement and the maturational view of readiness:

> In the field of reading it is essential that a joyous attitude of success shall be cultivated from the first. This necessitates a stage of development in which the learner is capable of getting meaning from the crooked marks which symbolize ideas. When does this period come? . . . In which direction shall we look to discover the truth regarding this confused situation? Fortunately the scientific method points the way toward the solution of this and of other baffling problems. The first steps have been taken. First, the problem has been recognized. Second, a name has been coined for the characteristic which is sought, Reading Readiness, a term not only alliterative but meaningful. Third, tests are in process of developing [sic] which shall be applicable to any young child. . . . So we may look forward to the day when the measure of readiness will rest in objective tests and parent and teacher will both be governed thereby. (35, p. 209)

The tests referred to turned out to be group pencil-and-paper tests composed of subtests that typically covered vocabulary, visual discrimination, and auditory discrimination. For a vocabulary subtest, the usual task was to circle or underline a picture that went with a word named by the one administering the test, generally a teacher. Or the administrator might be directed by the test manual to read aloud a sentence; again, the children would be directed to select from a row of pictures the one that reflected its content.

Subtests for visual discrimination also relied on pictures. In this case, the *un*verified assumption was that if children noticed similarities and differences in pictures, they had the ability to see similarities and differences in letters and words. That the same questionable assumption held for geometrical figures also seems to have been accepted, because many of the subtests focused on circles, squares, triangles, and so on. With these figures, a child would be asked to look at the first figure in a row and to underline all the others that were the same as (or different from) the target shape.

Evidently, authors of readiness tests figured that sooner or later children would be taught phonics. This is suggested by the frequent inclusion of subtests for auditory discrimination. The kind most commonly tested focused on rhyme. In this case, the administrator might be directed to name each picture in a given row and to have the children underline or circle all the pictures whose names rhymed with the name of the first one.

In addition to explaining how tests were to be administered, manuals also offered suggestions for using the results diagnostically. That is, school administrators and teachers were urged to study subtest scores in order to identify each child's strengths and weaknesses. Low scores showed what needed to be taught; high scores indicated ways in which the child was ready for reading. What happened in practice, though, was quite different. Since what did occur involves readiness programs and readiness workbooks, they will be discussed next.

Reading Readiness Programs

When it was agreed in the 1930s that most children entering first grade were unready to read and that postponing instruction would ensure readiness later, a decision had to be made about what was to be done while the children were "growing into readiness." The term used to describe the product of the decision was *reading readiness program.*

Content of Readiness Programs.   Although called by the same name, what was done at the beginning of the first-grade year varied from school to school. Some of the variation, no doubt, reflected variation among teachers. But some also reflected differences in what the nature of readiness was thought to be. For example, educators who held staunchly to the notion that the passing of time automatically results in readiness naturally believed that the content of a readiness program did not have to be directly related to the reading process. In contrast, educators who thought that learning and practice made some contribution to readiness supported programs that had goals similar to those evaluated in readiness tests.

What also promoted attention to the tests—and this turned out to be uniquely influential over several decades – was the appearance of the reading readiness workbook. As it happened, the publisher of a readiness test often published the workbooks. Consequently, the contents of the tests and of the workbooks were very similar. In time, the contents of the workbooks and of the readiness programs were remarkably similar, too.

Duration of Readiness Programs.   In theory, a readiness program was for unready children and would last until they became ready. In practice, that was not the way it was. Instead, the typical procedure was to administer a readiness test (sometimes a group intelligence test was given, too) close to the start of the first-grade year. Evidently, the purpose was not to learn whether the children might be ready for reading but, rather, to see how much time was to be spent in a readiness program. The assumption seemed to be that it was good for everybody, ready or not.

If a school decided that the shortest amount of time to be spent on readiness was, let's say, two months, then first graders with the highest readiness scores were in the readiness program for two months. The remaining children participated for a longer amount of time, often determined arbitrarily and without consideration of individuals.

Other schools were more flexible. For instance, they might administer readiness tests more than once in order to make more frequent decisions about whether the readiness program needed to be continued. In these schools, nonetheless, total scores were still the concern. Probably very few educators ever used subtest scores diagnostically, carefully matching what was taught with what individual children needed to learn.

Reasons for Questionable Practices.   In retrospect, it is easy to be critical of practices like those described. However, one must keep in mind some of the reasons for them. Such reasons do not endow the flaws with quality, but they at least make them comprehensible.

Certainly one reason for many of the questionable practices was the large classes usually found in first-grade classrooms when the readiness concept was in the spotlight. Ideally, readiness programs should have been highly individualized and should have included only children who seemed unready. Being responsible for large numbers of children, teachers were not able to achieve the ideal.

Further, the whole idea of readiness and of readiness programs was new. In addition, the programs were viewed not humbly but as a means for solving all the reading problems. No wonder, then, that they were greeted with what now seems like naïve enthusiasm that appears to have resulted in the notion that readiness programs were good for everybody.

Why the content of the programs was often sterile and routine also has a very human explanation. When first-grade teachers were suddenly called on to do something other than teach reading at the start of the year, many, if not most, must have felt insecure, to say the least. After all, a good program—whether for readiness or something else—is not created overnight. It is no wonder, then, that readiness workbooks received a warm reception and just about took over when decisions were made about what to do with the time allotted to the readiness program.

Reasons for Maintenance of Questionable Practices.   Even though it is easy to see how questionable routines developed when readiness programs were a novelty, it is difficult to understand why they continued for so long. Yet, a number of reasons can be identified. One is the tendency of schools to be conservative. They often want to keep what they are doing and sometimes actively resist change. Another reason has to do with instructional materials—specifically, with readiness workbooks. Since most of the workbooks that continued to be published were a part of basal reader programs, it was easy to continue using them without asking, "Is all this necessary?" Not asking that question explains why so much time was spent on looking for differences in pictures and geometrical shapes even though these activities make little or no contribution to helping children see differences and similarities in letters and words (1, 9, 18, 49).

One other reason certain practices connected with readiness persisted relates to the tendency to place too much faith in test scores. This certainly has been true of readiness scores in spite of the fact that researchers have questioned their predictive value almost from the time the tests came into existence. Even though the critics did have a positive effect on the content of revised editions, they had little effect on their use. Readiness tests continued to be published over the years—and still are—apparently because they continue to be purchased.

Another reason for the longevity of certain practices connected with readiness assessment and readiness programs moves the focus away from the schools and toward psychology, because psychological conceptions of human growth and development changed very little from the early 1920s until the late 1950s. Supported by Gesell, his students, and his disciples, the popular view during the 1940s and 1950s mirrored that of the 1920s and 1930s: Readiness for various tasks—including reading—results from maturation. Therefore, the passing of time is the solution for problems connected with a lack of it.

In the 1940s and 1950s, support for such contentions came from psychologists other than Gesell. Willard Olson was especially popular among educators of young children, and his ideas about child development, expressed in terms of "organismic age," agreed with Gesell's (40). Robert Havighurst, also well known to educators, offered no reason to question traditional practices as he wrote about "developmental tasks" and referred to the notion of a "teachable moment" (29). In addition, early childhood educators themselves were making pronouncements like:

We have a mountain of evidence to prove that a perfectly "normal" child—
I.Q. 100—cannot learn to read until he is about six years six months old.
(30, p. 316)

Having little reason to do otherwise, schools continued the routine
practice of administering readiness tests in first grade and of having all the
children—ready or not—participate in readiness programs. But then came
Sputnik and what can accurately be called a revolution in education.

A NEW ERA

Although educational changes hardly occur on one certain day, it is customary
to designate the start of major, midcentury changes by citing the date when
Russia launched Sputnik I: October 4, 1957. Predictably, such an event
produced a variety of repercussions in the United States. One was considerable criticism of public school education, increasing the tempo of the already
existing debate about the quality of instruction in American schools (5). Now
the concern was for what seemed like the inferiority of our educational
endeavors compared to those of the Soviet Union (4, 11).

Resulting from the worry and criticism was an atmosphere characterized
by the plea, "Let's teach more in our schools, and let's teach it earlier!" Such an
atmosphere, as time has demonstrated, fostered rapt attention to new hypotheses proposed by psychologists. Relevant to this chapter's consideration of
readiness are hypotheses that highlighted not only the learning potential of
young children but also the unique importance of the early years for
intellectual development.

New Emphases in Psychology

One of the first publications to receive the blessing of the post-Sputnik era was
The Process of Education by Jerome Bruner (7). This book is an account of a ten-
day meeting "to discuss how education in science might be improved in our
primary and secondary schools" (7, p. vii). In the report, Bruner gave special
attention to the importance of the "structure of a discipline" in teaching that
discipline to others. More specifically emphasized was that the "fundamental
character" of a discipline enables one "to narrow the gap between 'advanced'
knowledge and 'elementary' knowledge" (7, p. 26). A chapter called "Readiness
for Learning" was introduced by a statement that was to be quoted with great
frequency: "We begin with the hypothesis that any subject can be taught
effectively in some intellectually honest form to any child at any stage of
development" (7, p. 33).

People who took the time to read all of Bruner's book found the statement
to have a meaning that was hardly startling. It simply urged in a somewhat

different way that the schools take another look at how they organized and presented instruction in fields like science and mathematics. Nonetheless, when the pronouncement was quoted out of context—and it often was—it fostered wishful thinking about the learning potential of young children.

That was the beginning. Later, in 1961, a book by another psychologist became unusually popular. This book, *Intelligence and Experience*, by J. McV. Hunt, was a review of earlier research (34). Among the many studies reviewed were those that had examined the effects of training and practice on certain aspects of development. According to the original interpretations, readiness to learn—whether a motor or an intellectual skill—was the product of maturation, not of training or practice. With Hunt's new interpretation, a great variety of practice and experience was thought to affect the emergence of a skill.* Especially highlighted in his hypothetical explanation was the critical importance of early experiences. With the broader concept of what constitutes practice, and with the new emphasis on the importance of early stimulation, it was natural that the young child's environment became a popular topic for discussion, even though much of the research reviewed and reinterpreted by Hunt included studies of animals.

Predictably, early experiences provided the theme for another book from which it became fashionable to quote. This book, *Stability and Change in Human Characteristics*, appeared in 1964 and was written by Benjamin Bloom (6). Like Hunt's work, Bloom's was a detailed reexamination of earlier research—in this instance, of long-term studies of the development of certain measurable characteristics. Concluding that the most rapid period for the development of many characteristics, including intelligence, is in the first five years of life, Bloom succeeded in reemphasizing the crucial importance of a child's early environment.

New Social Concerns

In the midst of the excitement about the importance of preschool environmental factors, another development occurred. It was a new interest in an old problem: children from the lowest socioeconomic levels start school with disadvantages that prohibit adequate achievement. This concern was unusually vocal and widespread in the 1960s because of the political, social, and economic climates of the times (47). Given the psychological climate, it was entirely natural for the concern to result in prekindergarten schooling (Head Start programs) for what were then called "culturally disadvantaged" children. Reflecting the same psychological climate was a 1966 statement by the Educational Policies Commission of the National Education Association (19) that referred to research that was never identified. In part, the statement said:

*To understand the new interpretation, one must read the whole of Hunt's book *Intelligence and Experience* (34).

A growing body of research and experience demonstrates that by the age of six most children have already developed a considerable part of the intellectual ability they will possess as adults. Six is now generally accepted as the normal age of entrance to school. We believe that this practice is obsolete. All children should have the opportunity to go to school at public expense beginning at the age of four. (19, p. 1)

Changes in the Timing of Reading Instruction

Given this collection of new interests and claims, it was natural that the traditional interpretation of reading readiness was questioned. After all, an era that supports "the earlier the better" is not likely to be sympathetic with school practices that postpone reading instruction on the assumption that the passing of time will automatically ensure readiness for it.

As the years have shown, the typical response to the questions and criticism was neither complicated nor imaginative. For the most part, schools simply altered the timing of traditional practices. Readiness tests were administered earlier, often in kindergarten, where readiness workbooks could be found, too. In first grade, reading instruction usually started sooner—although readiness programs continued in some first grades, especially in school districts that had no kindergartens. In a few places, the difference in timing was more radical: reading was introduced in kindergarten.

Results of Changes

What was learned from all this? Not much. The greatest difference, reading in kindergarten, was not usually accompanied by changes in materials or methodology. Instead, they tended to be like what existed in a typical first grade (16). Restrictions were thus placed on what could be learned both about earlier reading and about the basic nature of readiness. The result is that the 1960s, with all the excitement about young children and earlier learning, contributed little to what could have been a period of enlightenment. What about subsequent decades? Before they are described in the next chapter, this chapter concludes with a discussion of a conception of readiness for reading that, in my opinion, is difficult to dispute.

PROPOSED DEFINITION OF READINESS

The concept of readiness to which this book subscribes was articulated by Gates in the 1930s and at least implied by others since then. In 1959, David Ausubel stated it effectively in an article that dealt not with readiness for reading specifically but with readiness for any learning (3).

According to Ausubel, readiness is "the adequacy of existing capacity in relation to the demands of a given learning task" (3, p. 246). Let's examine the details of his definition to see what they say about requirements for success with beginning reading.

Existing Capacity

Nothing that we know about human beings indicates that heredity alone accounts for an individual's capacity to learn, nor does anything or anyone insist that only environmental factors are important. At various times, it is true, nature or nurture have been placed on a special pedestal of honor. Even amidst the adulation, however, the factor not getting attention was never cast aside completely. The assumption of this discussion, therefore, is that each child's capacity at any given time is the product of an interplay among genetic endowment, maturation, experiences, learning, and practice. Just how this interplay takes place awaits a definitive explanation. For now, it seems correct to say that a child's attained capacity at any given time is something he or she has inherited, grown into, and acquired.

Demands of the Learning Task

What learning to read demands, or requires, of children varies from situation to situation. One major reason for the variation is the selected teaching method. A beginning approach that expects children to remember the identity of whole words – to cite one illustration – has requirements different from another approach that stresses letter-sound relationships at the start.

But even when the method is the same, requirements for success are likely to vary. This is so because the quality of the instruction is critical, too. Applied to beginning reading, the point is that what teachers do with a method, how well they use it, and even how quickly or slowly they follow it determine what is necessary for success. This can be summarized by saying that what learning to read requires at the beginning depends on the type of instruction offered, its quality, and its pace.

Adequacy of Capacity in Relation to Demands

One of the most important features of Ausubel's definition is the explicit attention it gives to the relational aspect of readiness. It reminds us that the question of a child's readiness for reading has a twofold focus: (a) the child's abilities *in relation to* (b) available instruction. Practically speaking, the relationship means that "Is the child ready?" is an incorrect question because it is incomplete. Instead, the concern must be, "Is the child ready for this particular instructional program?" Implicit here is that we really need to think in terms of readiness*es* for reading, as some abilities will be prerequisites for one instructional program whereas a somewhat different collection is likely to be necessary for another.

The twofold focus was recognized by Walter MacGinitie when he said that because the large amount of readiness research that had been done ignored differences in reading methodology, "it tells us little about what abilities are important for success in any *particular* instructional program" (38, p. 879). The relational aspect of readiness also points up the folly of thinking that readiness is a uniform list of abilities that can be assessed in a readiness test.

HOW *SHOULD* READINESS BE ASSESSED?

Since readiness testing still takes place, it needs to be reconsidered in light of Ausubel's conception of readiness. What will get more attention here, however, is the kind of assessment implied in his conception.

Assessment with Readiness Tests

As explained, readiness tests are composed of subtests that typically deal with visual discrimination, auditory discrimination, and vocabulary. They thus yield subtest scores as well as total scores. Traditionally, total scores from readiness tests were used to decide whether children were ready or unready for reading. Based on Ausubel's conception of readiness, two major flaws characterize this use. First, it fails to recognize that different kinds of instruction require different abilities; and, second, it ignores the fact that the quality and pace of a given kind of instruction also affect what is required for success.

Another flaw in using total scores to decide who is, and who is not, ready for reading has to do with a questionable assumption; namely, that when reading instruction does get under way, children will have to learn everything immediately. This outlook, however, contrasts sharply with the reality of classroom instruction, which proceeds one small step at a time (a little today, a little tomorrow). Instead of being concerned only about what will be required *at the very beginning*, people who rely on total test scores to assess readiness appear to be looking at considerably more.

What they do not look at, on the other hand, is the possibility that coping with a readiness test may be more difficult than coping with beginning reading instruction. Such a possibility first came to my attention when I had the chance to compare readiness test scores achieved by first graders who had begun to read with those attained by classmates who had not (16). At first, it was surprising to find that some nonreaders did better than some of the readers. After a little reflection, however, the surprise vanished. The nonreaders had been in a kindergarten that offered readiness activities, usually in the form of workbook exercises. This made them very familiar with the format, the language, and the content of the readiness test. In contrast, the children who were able to read had been in a kindergarten that bypassed conventional readiness activities and, instead, involved the children in a reading program that progressed in a slow, carefully planned way. The result was readers, but not children who always did exceptionally well on a readiness test.

Thus far, only total scores from readiness tests have been considered. What about subtest scores? Authors of readiness tests commonly describe subtest scores as a source of help in diagnosing particular strengths and weaknesses. Instruction can then build on the strengths and work on the weaknesses. What about this?

In theory, the proposal sounds fine; in practice, problems exist. To begin, test authors do not agree on what constitutes essential subskills for beginning reading, which is natural given the fact that each author may have in mind a different type of beginning reading instruction. This means that a diagnostic use of low subscores could lead to time being wasted on nonessentials. The use of high scores, on the other hand, could foster unwarranted expectations, because what a child was able to do may not be necessary for success with the type of reading instruction that is provided. (For a further discussion of disagreement about essential requirements for beginning reading, see Figure 4.2 and the comments about it.)

More disagreement among test authors becomes apparent when different readiness tests are compared (44). Similar subtests are sometimes called by different names, and identical names are sometimes assigned to tests dealing with different abilities. Both types of discrepancies could foster inappropriate instructional remedies unless the people providing them take the time to go beyond subtest labels to see what was actually assessed.

Robert Calfee and Richard Venezky concluded that an even greater problem exists when a tested ability is lacking but the remedy is not apparent (8). They ask, What is the implication for instruction when children are unable to identify a short-haired dog from among poorly detailed pictures of a Doberman, a Saint Bernard, and a cocker spaniel? What is a teacher supposed to do when children fail to select a picture of a jet airplane when the given task is to find the vehicle that carries the most people? A more basic question is, What does this have to do with reading?

Even though these problems should be enough to raise questions about the diagnostic value of subtest scores, statistical considerations raise even more. From that perspective, the limited number of items typically found in a subtest do not allow for reliability, which means that retesting could result in a different score for the same child. In addition, intercorrelations between subtests are sufficiently high as to indicate that independent skills are not being measured.

The type of workbook exercise shown in Figure 4.2 continues to be a
frequently used task even though research has repeatedly demonstrated
that letters and words should figure in visual discrimination practice, not pictures. (Effective teachers attempt to salvage workbook pages like this one by
having children identify and discuss whatever is pictured. Such discussions can
clarify meanings or even add to children's oral vocabularies.)

Some readiness tests also use these kinds of items whereas others go far
beyond what is required for success with beginning reading no matter how it is
taught. For example, one test prepared by Richard Venezky and others (48)
includes a subtest in which children are asked to blend three given sounds into
words. Since blending sounds can be difficult even for children in the middle
grades (15), the inclusion of blending tasks in a readiness test has to be questioned. The inclusion illustrates how some tasks categorized as "reading readiness exercises" are more difficult than learning to read.

Other readiness tests continue to include subtests in which children are
required to make unfinished figures look exactly like other exceedingly complex
ones. For example, the *Clymer-Barrett Readiness Test* (10) includes a twenty-
item subtest called "Completing Shapes," which seems excessively difficult and
not related to anything that success with beginning reading requires.

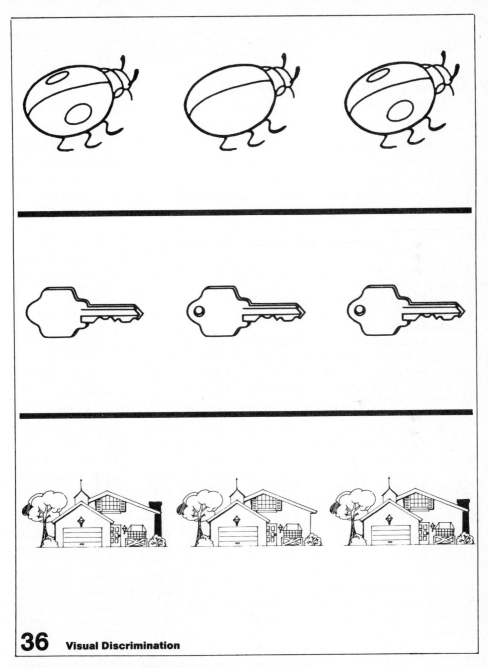

36 Visual Discrimination

Figure 4.2. *Current Readiness Workbooks and Tests*

From the *MCP Kindergarten Program*, Book K1: Auditory, Visual, and Motor Skills, 1980, p. 36. Reprinted with permission of Modern Curriculum Press.

To sum up, serious flaws continue to be found in readiness tests whether total scores are used to decide who is ready to begin to read or whether subtest scores enter into decisions about the details of instructional programs.

Assessment with Observations of Everyday Behavior

Having laid out problems associated with conventional readiness testing, let me move now to alternative methods of assessment. The first relies on observations of everyday behavior in the classroom from which inferences can be made about readiness. This method is illustrated with two partial reports of visits to classrooms, the first occupied by nursery school children. The observer of these children writes:

> There were two adults and 15 four-year-olds. The children were involved with free play when I arrived. The head teacher said she would be starting a lesson in five minutes and suggested that I look at samples of the children's work. While looking, I overheard the following conversation between two girls.
>
> Pointing to a book, one said, "See? This one's mine. It says Amanda. It's mine." Holding up another book, the second child responded, "This one is mine." "No, it's not," the first girl quickly answered. "That's David's. This one is yours. See? This says Katherine." Amanda pointed to several other books on the table and correctly read each child's name. Then Katherine pointed to a name on a book and asked, "David?" "No," Amanda replied. "That's Debbie."
>
> After the head teacher called the 15 children to the front of the room, she began discussing the letters *A*, *B*, and *C*. She first printed the capital and lower-case forms of each on the board, then said their names. She next asked if anyone's name started with "a big *A*." Amanda immediately responded, "Mine." The teacher repeated the question for *B*, whereupon one child said, "Anthony Barton." " 'Anthony' begins with *A*," the teacher explained, "but 'Barton' does start with *B*." The same question was asked for *C*; all the while nothing was written. All the while, too, an increasingly large number of children grew restless. As a result, the aide spent the time motioning to certain ones to sit up and reminding others to keep still and listen.
>
> I had to conclude that what I was seeing was a waste of everyone's time. It was clear that the children had different abilities, thus needed different kinds of help. Since an aide was available, the accommodation could have been made by dividing the class into groups so that members of each could do something that extended their abilities.

The second observation report, this one of a nursery school–kindergarten class, follows.

> Today I observed a group of 18 three- to five-year-olds, who had two teachers. The classroom was furnished with learning centers that lined

the walls, leaving a large unused area in the middle. There was no chalkboard, no signs displayed for children to look at or read, and no pencils.

I arrived before the children. After discussing readiness in class, I was interested to learn about the philosophy of the school regarding readiness; so I asked the head teacher whether any time was spent on reading. She said that the children were not of school age, thus were not ready for reading. (This reminded me of the discussion in the chapter about the traditional view that children aren't ready to read until they have a mental age of about 6.5 years.) I decided to look for some of the signs of readiness that we discussed in class.

As the children entered, I noticed an obvious affluency about them and even overheard one boy talking about the vacation his family was going to take in Hawaii. Another child came in carrying a well-worn, simply written paperback version of the *Gingerbread Man*, which he read to me after I asked if he knew any of the words. I naturally wondered why the teachers believed that the children weren't ready for reading when at least one had already begun. (It is possible, of course, that the reading was a memorized story. In any case, what the boy said was exactly what was printed.)

As the morning continued, I observed four children in the dramatic play center, reading labels on food containers. Although the library center was relatively small and not particularly attractive, five children went to it to look at one or more books during a one-hour period. Other children repeatedly asked the head teacher and assistant to write their names on their art work. (Both teachers did so in all capital letters even though lower-case are more common, thus ought to be used.) I observed another child who spotted a friend who had mistakenly gotten a piece of paper on which another child's name was written. He went to the child, showed her the name, and said, "That says *Carl*, not *Carol*!"

Repeatedly throughout the morning, I noticed behavioral signs of readiness in the interest displayed in books, in the recognition of names, and in the act of reading itself. The number of times that children displayed either readiness or reading ability during this one observation requires asking, "Why had the teacher said that none were ready?"

What the two reports of classroom observations make clear is that behavioral signs of readiness are neither obscure nor difficult to identify. Acquaintance with Ausubel's conception of readiness may have also suggested that the observation of everyday behavior could be combined with more systematic, preplanned efforts to assess readiness. Such efforts are described next.

Assessment with Preplanned Learning Opportunities

Since the preplanned efforts to assess readiness that are described reflect Ausubel's conception of readiness, his definition is displayed in Figure 4.3.

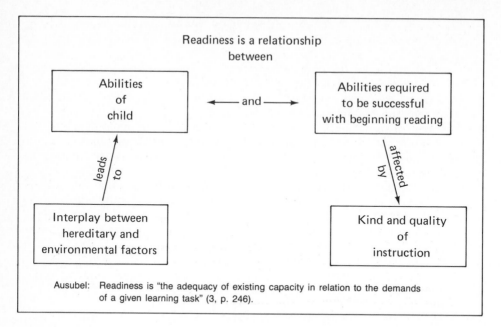

Readiness is a relationship
between

| Abilities of child | ←— and —→ | Abilities required to be successful with beginning reading |

leads to

affected by

| Interplay between hereditary and environmental factors | | Kind and quality of instruction |

Ausubel: Readiness is "the adequacy of existing capacity in relation to the demands of a given learning task" (3, p. 246).

Figure 4.3

If, as Ausubel suggests, readiness is the adequacy of existing capacity in relation to the demands of the learning task, it follows that the best way to test for adequacy is to give children opportunities to learn to read in order to see what their capacity actually is. Such opportunities should vary in methodology, because a child may be able to succeed with some methods but not with others. By observing what individual children do or do not learn from each method, much can be gleaned both about their readiness and about the kind of instruction that makes maximum use of their abilities and interests.

You might now be wondering how this recommendation could be put into practice in a classroom—say, in a kindergarten. Let me show you with illustrations featuring typical kindergarten activities. (The next chapter shows how these activities can be scheduled.)

Some time in every kindergarten goes to taking attendance. Mundane though it is, attendance taking can be an opportunity for five-year-olds (or four-year-olds) to learn to read, and for a teacher to learn something about existing capacities. Specifically, at the beginning of the year the teacher could take attendance by showing first names on cards. Later in the year, the children could indicate their presence by selecting their name card and putting it on an attendance board. This simple routine could teach the children to read their names and others' names as well. In addition, it allows a teacher looking for behavioral signs of readiness to learn which children remember (read) names easily, which have some difficulty, and which remember few if any names.

Art activities can be another means for assessing readiness because, in addition to being valuable forms of expression, finished art products are a reason for kindergartners to learn to print their names and, later, to write captions and to read those composed by other children. Pertinent to the theme of assessment is that these activities give a teacher the chance to identify individuals for whom writing and spelling might be an easy way into reading, to identify children who remember what particular words say with a minimum of exposure to them, and to become aware of other students for whom the motor skill of writing is a formidable task or for whom it is difficult to compose even the briefest of captions.

Reading to children, another kindergarten activity, should always be for enjoyment; occasionally, however, a story can be used as a vehicle for learning more about readiness. Let's say, for example, that a couple of stories have been about a parrot called Sam. Let's also say that children named Steven and Sandy are members of the class. In such a case, a kindergarten teacher might decide one day to print *Sam* on the chalkboard and then ask, "Does anybody [pointing to *S*] have a name that starts the way *Sam* starts? If you do, I'll write your name up here with Sam's." Soon the board shows:

> Sam
> Steven
> Sandy

Other questions (their number and kind will depend on the children's abilities and interests) follow: "Does anybody know the name of the letter [pointing to *S*] at the beginning of these three names? . . . Have you ever seen any other word that begins with *S*? . . . Now we have five words that start with *S*. I'll read them. As I do, listen to see if you can hear how they all start with the same sound. . . . Can someone tell us the sound that these words start with? . . . I'll say them again. Watch my mouth as I begin to say each one. Listen to the way each word starts. . . . Can someone tell us the sound that's at the beginning of all these words? . . . Can someone think of other words that start the way *Sam* and *Steven* and *Sandy* and *six* and *Sue* begin? If you can, I'll write them up here, too."

On another day, another word and letter might receive attention; or the teacher might decide to repeat the attention given *S*, using a different collection of words to illustrate a sound it commonly records. Whatever the decision, the opportunity exists for children to respond and for a teacher to identify individuals who know letter names and even have skill in auditory discrimination. At the same time, the teacher is also likely to become aware of other kindergartners who appear to have no knowledge of letter names or, more likely, no understanding of what is meant by "begin with the same sound."

Perhaps these few illustrations of ordinary activities are enough to give specific meaning to what has been proposed for assessing readiness: Give children varied opportunities to begin reading and note what they are able to learn.

Implied in the illustrations are other ideas that are important for teachers. These ideas can be communicated with descriptions of two children in the kindergarten just referred to who were present when the teacher wrote *Sam*, *Sandy*, and *Steven* and asked questions about them.

STEVEN.   Steven has all the signs of being mentally slow. Even his physical movements are sluggish and awkward. When the teacher wrote *Sam* on the board and asked whether anyone had a name that began with the same letter, he remained silent. A concentrated look from the teacher plus a nudge from the child sitting next to him (Sandy) led to Steven's volunteering his name. Once his name appeared on the board he seemed interested in the discussion, although he remained silent. The question now is, What meaning did the discussion and questioning have for both Steven and the teacher?

For his teacher, they gave further evidence of Steven's slowness. Even though *S* was in his name, and even though he had seen it many times before, he didn't seem to be aware that his name and Sam's began the same way. It was also unlikely that Steven had any understanding—at least his behavior showed none—of the concept *sound alike* when applied to parts of words.

For Steven himself, the situation was interesting because everybody was talking about his name. He didn't remember anyone telling him before—they had, actually—that the first letter in his name was *S*. And he didn't know until the day of the *Sam* lesson that other words started with the same letter.

Now, what about Sandy? What did the very same discussion and questioning mean for her? Something quite different, as the following account reveals.

SANDY.   Sandy is an alert child who doesn't believe in hiding her candle under a bushel basket. In the discussion of words beginning with *S*, she quickly informed the teacher that she knew its name because it was in her name and in her big sister's name (*Sue*). She said she could write her sister's name, and her mother's and daddy's names, too. As the discussion proceeded, she enjoyed making the sound that *S* stands for—this seemed to be new for her—and quickly recalled words beginning with *S*. *Six*, *seven*, and *Sue* were her contributions when the teacher asked, "Can anyone think of words that begin the way *Sam* begins?"

Obviously, what the discussion and questioning meant for Sandy was essentially different from what they meant for Steven. With both children, though, the teacher had an opportunity to assess readiness. In the case of Sandy, much was learned—including the fact that she had already begun to read. Sandy also knew the name of *S*, enjoyed making the sound it records, and was able to name words beginning with /s/. That she did some writing at home and was attentive to words in her environment also became clear.

While the teacher was looking for behavioral signs of readiness, what was Sandy getting out of the discussion and questions? Primarily, they helped her recall, and then use, what was known. New learnings seemed to be the understanding that words have a beginning sound and that a sound that *s* represents is /s/. The teacher's assessment, then, was an opportunity for Sandy to have reading instruction, specifically, instruction in phonics.

What the discussion and questioning turned out to be for both children is summarized in Table 4.1.

Table 4.1. *Results of Sam Lesson for Two Children*

	Assessment	Readiness Instruction	Reading Instruction
STEVEN	X	X	
SANDY	X		X

Table 4.1 and the description of the two kindergartners offer important reminders for anyone concerned about children's readiness for reading:

ASSESSING READINESS FOR READING

1. A meaningful way to assess readiness begins by providing children with varied opportunities to begin to read. What is or is not learned allows for inferences not only about their readiness but also about ways to teach reading that seem to be easiest and of greatest interest.
2. Assessment carried out this way provides more than just diagnostic information. It can be readiness instruction and even reading instruction itself.
3. The results of any opportunity to learn something depend on the children's abilities. For some children, an opportunity will only be preparation for reading. For other, more able individuals, it will be reading instruction.

One further point about readiness needs to be stressed and is made with a description of another child in the kindergarten just discussed.

JOEY.   Joey is an active participant in all activities. At the start of the year, he generally went to the blocks at free-choice time, but quiet table games and puzzles soon became attractive. He also is enthusiastic whenever the teacher makes other choices available: "Today, I'm going to be reading a story over in that part of the room" or "Today, I'm going to be playing a game" (e.g., bingo played with numerals, letters, or words). When words enter into a game, Joey is both interested and successful because of his ability to remember words with minimal help. He learned to read all the days of the week from the quick, early-morning discussions related to "What day is today?" And because of the attention given to *September*, *October*, and *November* in connection with the calendar in the room, he can read those words, too.

While using words in games, Joey's teacher has heard him make interesting comments. When *Sunday* was shown, he observed, "Sandy's name looks like a short Sunday." On another day, when the teacher wrote *silk* on the board while discussing fabrics and textures, Joey quickly observed, "That almost looks like *salt*." Asked, "Where did you see *salt*?" he explained, "It's on our salt shaker at home."

What is pertinent for this discussion is that Joey's keen observations and excellent visual memory are not matched by equal excellence in auditory discrimination. He rarely responds, for instance, when the teacher makes requests like: "I'm going to say two words. Can you tell me whether they start with the same sound or a different sound: *hand, fence?*"

What all these observations correctly indicate is that in certain ways Joey is more than ready for reading—he has already begun. In other ways, however, he is still learning to be ready. What the same observations mean more generally is that efforts to assess readiness should not have an either-or focus. That is, a teacher's thoughts ought not to be "Is he or is he not ready?" but rather "In what ways is he ready and in what ways is he not?"

This more correct perspective has implications for the way we think about instruction. It reminds us—or should—that readiness instruction and reading instruction go on simultaneously. With Joey, for instance, reading ability is developing from help with whole word identifications. At the same time, the attention going to sounds is readiness instruction for him. Graphically, this important point is shown in Figure 4.4.

How different the conception shown in Figure 4.4 is from the traditional, all-or-none practice of separating the readiness program from the reading program (see Figure 4.5).

Another important point can be made from the observations about Joey and the other children: Readiness assessment is a daily occurrence, not a special event. All the reasons this is so were summed up perfectly by MacGinitie when he said: ". . . when a child is taught a little, he is then ready for a little more" (37, p. 399).

The disarming simplicity of MacGinitie's comment should not overshadow a significant implication; namely, that beginners in reading are just

SIMULTANEOUS READINESS INSTRUCTION AND
READING INSTRUCTION

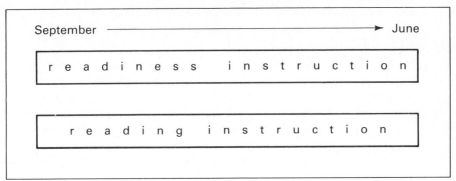

Figure 4.4

READINESS PROGRAM SEPARATED FROM READING PROGRAM

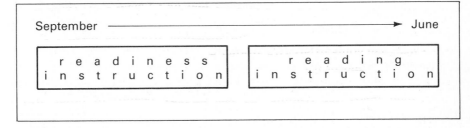

Figure 4.5

that—beginners. As such, they do not have to be able to master *immediately* all that constitutes "reading ability." Instead, they achieve that ability piece by piece over a long period of time. Practically speaking, this means that if reading instruction begins with the identification of a few carefully chosen words, the only requirements are the abilities to distinguish among the words and to remember what each says. If it happened—but this is unlikely—that each word began with the same letter and sound and, as a result, the teacher decided to introduce a little phonics, then new requirements come into existence: the ability to see that each word begins with the same letter and the ability to hear that each begins with the same sound. With such abilities, a child is ready to be taught one letter-sound relationship.

Even these few comments should identify a major flaw in traditional questions and tests dealing with readiness. They appear to be concerned with the whole of reading instruction rather than with the beginning steps that, when joined with many subsequent steps, *eventually* culminate in reading ability.

SUMMARY

The timing of beginning reading instruction is the concern of this chapter. It merits detailed attention because a child's initial experience with any activity is of unique importance.

In considering the best time to start teaching reading, psychologists and educators whose views dominated from the 1920s to the 1950s correctly gave attention to the concept of readiness. They asked, "When are children ready to be successful with reading?" Some answered, "When they have a mental age of about 6.5 years." Others turned to special testing to get an answer, and so was born the reading readiness test. Commonly, the interest of people who administered it was not in the possibility that some beginning first-graders might be ready for reading but, rather, in the question of how long each child should spend in a readiness program, conceived of as being separate and distinct from the reading program.

The chapter went on to identify flaws in the early interpretation and use of the readiness concept. One flaw was an exaggerated appreciation of the contributions made by heredity, maturation, and the passing of time. In contrast, the readiness concept supported in Chapter 4 assumes that readiness for reading is the product not only of genetic endowment and maturation but also of experiences, learning, and practice. Within this framework, much about readiness is teachable.

One of the most important points emphasized in the chapter is the need to look at both instruction and children's abilities when readiness is being considered. With the twofold focus, flaws can be seen in the question that the earlier psychologists and educators asked—Is the child ready? It seemed to assume that success with every type of reading instruction requires the same abilities and, therefore, that readiness can be assigned a single meaning.

This chapter tried to show that the correct question is more specific as it asks, Is the child ready to succeed with this particular kind and quality of instruction? Such a question recognizes the equal significance for success of the child's abilities and the instruction that will be available. Put differently, the question reflects the relational aspect of readiness—an aspect effectively underscored in Ausubel's conception of readiness as being "the adequacy of existing capacity in relation to the demands of a given learning task" (3, p. 246).

Ausubel's conception also has implications for how readiness can be assessed: Give children varied opportunities to learn to read; what they do or do not learn tells something about their readiness as well as the way of teaching reading that takes advantage of their particular abilities and interests. This type of assessment, the chapter showed, has the advantage of being two other things as well. It will be readiness instruction for some children and reading instruction for others who are more able. Because this way of assessing readiness makes use of different methodologies, teachers will also learn that <u>most children are neither totally ready nor totally unready for reading</u>. Such an awareness ought to encourage schools to give up the idea that "getting ready to read" and "beginning to read" occur at separate points on some time line, as well as the related practice of having a readiness program followed by a reading program. Instead, *readiness instruction* <u>will be viewed as reading instruction in its earliest stages</u>. What a reading program in the earliest stages might look like is the subject of the next chapter.

REVIEW

1. Even though readiness for beginning reading is not the concern of middle- and upper-grade teachers, they should know something about it. If a fifth-grade teacher, for example, was asked the following question in a parent-teacher conference, she ought to be able to answer. How would *you* respond to a parent who says:

   I have four children. My oldest is the brightest, yet she wasn't taught to read until some time after she started the first grade. Now my youngest, who is five and not nearly as bright, is in kindergarten and is being taught to read. Why the difference?

2. Chapter 4 says that a historical account of how the readiness concept has been interpreted identifies characteristics of the field of reading as a whole. Reference is made to such characteristics as:

   a. Proposals and recommendations are sometimes accepted and even become popular before the existence of well-documented facts that support them.

   b. Proposals for education rarely deal with issues in relation to individual children.

   c. Publishers of instructional materials commonly exert more influence on what is taught, and even on when and how it is taught, than do professional educators.

   With specific examples, show how the historical account in Chapter 4 illustrates these three characteristics.

3. Chapter 4 also pointed up the influence of psychological theories on the field of reading. Specify how the chapter illustrates the influence.

4. What might explain the fact that a child does poorly on a reading readiness test, yet—soon after the test was administered—he progresses well when beginning reading instruction starts?

5. That good teachers are astute observers was illustrated in Chapter 4.

Especially highlighted was their ability to detect behavioral evidence of readiness for reading. Such evidence, it should be noted, sometimes shows up in places other than classrooms. For example, while waiting in line in a grocery store, I watched a girl approach a gumball machine. I judged her to be about three or four years old. Noticing the hand-printed sign taped to the machine that said, "Out of order," the girl immediately asked a passerby, "What does that say?" Told what it said, she quickly inquired, "What does that mean?" Upon hearing the explanation, the child walked away, perhaps to look for whoever brought her to the store. What behavioral evidence of readiness was apparent in that brief episode?

6. Let's say that you are David Ausubel and have just finished giving a talk to a group of teachers. How would you respond to the first question posed after the talk?

> I teach first grade in a school in which we are required to use the _____ basal reader program.* All my children are doing well with the exception of two boys. Evidently they are not yet ready to read. What readiness material would you recommend for them?

7. When the readiness concept was considered in decades gone by, the notion of there being a teachable moment was often mentioned. Do you think there is a particular moment when it is best for a child to begin to get help with reading?

REFERENCES

1. Arter, Judith A., and Jenkins, Joseph R. "Differential Diagnosis – Prescriptive Teaching: A Critical Appraisal." *Review of Educational Research* 40 (Fall, 1979), 517–555.
2. Arthur, Grace. "A Quantitative Study of the Results of Grouping First Grade Children According to Mental Age." *Journal of Educational Research* 12 (October, 1925), 173–185.
3. Ausubel, David P. "Viewpoints from Related Disciplines: Human Growth and Development." *Teachers College Record* 60 (February, 1959), 245–254.
4. Benton, William. *This Is the Challenge.* New York: Associated College Presses, 1958.
5. Bestor, Arthur E. *Educational Wastelands, the Retreat from Learning in Our Public Schools.* Urbana: University of Illinois Press, 1953.
6. Bloom, Benjamin S. *Stability and Change in Human Characteristics.* New York: John Wiley and Sons, 1964.

---

*The program named starts instruction by concentrating on phonics. The pace of instruction is fairly fast.

7. Bruner, Jerome. *The Process of Education.* Cambridge: Harvard University Press, 1960.
8. Calfee, Robert C., and Venezky, Richard L. "Component Skills in Beginning Reading." In K. S. Goodman and J. T. Fleming (Eds.), *Psycholinguistics and the Teaching of Reading.* Newark, Del.: International Reading Association, 1969.
9. Chall, Jeanne S. "Decade of Research on Reading and Learning Disabilities." In S. Jay Samuels (Ed.), *What Research Has to Say about Reading Instruction.* Newark, Del.: International Reading Association, 1978.
10. Clymer, Theodore, and Barrett, Thomas C. *Readiness Test,* rev. ed. Santa Barbara, Calif.: Chapman, Brook and Kent, 1983.
11. "Crisis in Education." *Life* 49 (March 24, 1958), 26–35.
12. Dickson, Virgil E. "What First Grade Children Can Do in School as Related to What Is Shown by Mental Tests." *Journal of Educational Research* 2 (June, 1920), 475–480.
13. Dickson, Virgil E. *Mental Tests and the Classroom Teacher.* New York: World Book Co., 1923.
14. Durkin, Dolores. "A Case-Study Approach toward an Identification of Factors Associated with Success and Failure in Learning to Read." *California Journal of Educational Research* 11 (January, 1960), 26–33.
15. Durkin, Dolores. *The Decoding Ability of Elementary School Students.* Reading Education Report No. 49. Urbana: University of Illinois, Center for the Study of Reading, May, 1984.
16. Durkin, Dolores. "A Six-Year Study of Children Who Learned to Read in School at the Age of Four." *Reading Research Quarterly* 10 (1974–1975), 9–61.
17. Durkin, Dolores. "When Should Children Begin to Read?" *Innovation and Change in Reading Instruction,* chap. 2. Sixty-seventh Yearbook of the National Society for the Study of Education, Part II. Chicago: Distributed by the University of Chicago Press, 1968.
18. Dykstra, Robert. "The Use of Reading Readiness Tests for Prediction and Diagnosis: A Critique." In T. C. Barrett (Ed.), *The Evaluation of Children's Reading Achievement.* Newark, Del.: International Reading Association, 1967.
19. Educational Policies Commission. *Universal Opportunity for Early Childhood Education.* Washington, D.C.: National Education Association, 1966.
20. Frostig, M., and Home, D. *The Frostig Program for the Development of Visual Perception.* Chicago: Follet Co., 1964.
21. Gates, Arthur I. "The Necessary Mental Age for Beginning Reading." *Elementary School Journal* 37 (March, 1937), 497–508.
22. Gates, Arthur I., and Bond, Guy L. "Reading Readiness: A Study of Factors Determining Success and Failure in Beginning Reading." *Teachers College Record* 37 (May, 1936), 679–685.
23. Gesell, Arnold L. *The First Five Years of Life.* New York: Harper and Bros., 1940.
24. Gesell, Arnold L. *The Mental Growth of the Preschool Child.* New York: The Macmillan Co., 1925.
25. Getman, G. N., and Kane, E. R. *The Physiology of Readiness.* Minneapolis: Pass, Inc., 1964.
26. Hall, G. Stanley. *The Psychology of Adolescence.* New York: D. Appleton and Co., 1904.

27. Hammill, D.; Goodman, L.; and Wiederholt, J. L. "Visual-Motor Processes: Can We Train Them?" *Reading Teacher* 27 (February, 1974), 469–478.

28. Harris, Albert J. "Practical Applications of Reading Research." *Reading Teacher* 29 (March, 1976), 559–565.

29. Havighurst, Robert. *Human Development and Education.* New York: Longmans, Green, and Co., 1953.

30. Hefferman, Helen. "Significance of Kindergarten Education." *Childhood Education* 36 (March, 1960), 313–319.

31. Helfeldt, John P. "Test Review: The Brigance K & I Screen for Kindergarten and First Grade." *Reading Teacher* 37 (May, 1984), 820–824.

32. Holmes, Margaret C. "Investigation of Reading Readiness of First Grade Entrants." *Childhood Education* 3 (January, 1927), 215–221.

33. Huey, Edmund B. *The Psychology and Pedagogy of Reading.* New York: The Macmillan Co., 1908.

34. Hunt, J. McVicker. *Intelligence and Experience.* New York: The Ronald Press Co., 1961.

35. Jenkins, Frances. "Editorial." *Childhood Education* 3 (January, 1927), 209.

36. Kephart, N. C. *The Slow Learner in the Classroom.* Columbus, Oh.: Charles Merrill Co., 1960.

37. MacGinitie, Walter H. "Evaluating Readiness for Learning to Read: A Critical Review and Evaluation of Research." *Reading Research Quarterly* 4 (Spring, 1969), 396–410.

38. MacGinitie, Walter H. "When Should We Begin to Teach Reading?" *Language Arts* 53 (November/December, 1976), 878–882.

39. Morphett, Mabel V., and Washburne, Carleton. "When Should Children Begin to Read?" *Elementary School Journal* 31 (March, 1931), 496–503.

40. Olson, Willard. *Child Development.* Boston: D. C. Heath and Co., 1949.

41. Paradis, E. E. "The Appropriateness of Visual Discrimination Exercises in Reading Readiness Materials." *Journal of Educational Research* 67 (February, 1974), 276–278.

42. Pikulski, John. "Readiness for Reading: A Practical Approach." *Language Arts* 55 (February, 1978), 192–197.

43. Reed, Mary M. *An Investigation of Practices in First Grade Admission and Promotion.* New York: Bureau of Publications, Teachers College, Columbia University, 1927.

44. Rude, R. T. "Readiness Tests: Implications for Early Childhood Education." *Reading Teacher* 26 (March, 1973), 572–580.

45. Samuels, S. Jay. "Resolving Some Theoretical and Instructional Conflicts of the 1980s." *Reading Research Quarterly* 19 (Summer, 1984), 390–392.

46. Sanacare, Joseph. "A Checklist for the Evaluation of Reading Readiness." *Elementary English* 50 (September, 1973), 858–860.

47. Shaw, Frederick. "The Changing Curriculum." *Review of Educational Research* 36 (June, 1966), 343–352.

48. Venezky, Richard L.; Pittelman, Susan D.; Kamm, Marga R.; and Leslie, Ronald G. *Prereading Skills Tests.* Chicago: Encyclopaedia Britannica Educational Corporation, 1978.

49. Washburne, Carleton. "Ripeness." *Progressive Education* 13 (February, 1936), 125–130.

50. Washburne, Carleton. "The Work of the Committee of Seven on Grade-Placement in Arithmetic," *Child Development and the Curriculum*, chap. 16. Thirty-eighth Yearbook of the National Society for the Study of Education, Part 1. Bloomington, Ill.: Public School Publishing Co., 1939.

51. Williams, Joanna P. "Teaching Decoding with an Emphasis on Phoneme Analysis and Phoneme Blending." *Journal of Educational Psychology* 72 (February, 1980), 1–15.

CHAPTER 5

A Beginning
Literacy Program

PREVIEW

My initial experience with pre-first-grade reading occurred in 1958 in connection with longitudinal studies of children who began to read at home before they started school (9). The abilities of the children, as well as the easygoing way in which they acquired them, were sufficiently impressive that an experimental school program was developed based on information about what the early readers did, liked, and learned in the naturalistic setting of their homes (11, 12). Although the major purpose of the two-year program was to provide opportunities to begin to read, it had a language arts focus, first, because oral language had been encouraged in a variety of ways in all the early readers' homes and, second, because some of the subjects had been more interested in learning to print than to read. In fact, it was through printing and their questions about spelling that these particular children started to read. (What was uncovered in the two studies of preschool reading was what eventually came to be called "emergent literacy" [7, 21, 34].)

The half-day experimental program started with four-year-olds, because the previous research with preschool readers revealed that age four is a common time for children to show interest in print, both as something to read and as something to produce.

This chapter, based partially on the experimental program, shows how pre-first-grade children can be eased into reading with instruction that reflects a language arts focus as well as the eclectic approach implied in Ausubel's conception of readiness. The chapter also shows with a number of examples how the beginning stages of literacy can proceed in ways that are of interest to young children, that are nonthreatening, and that allow success to accumulate.

Although Chapter 5 does not cover the specifics of the various kinds of instruction that are referred to--subsequent chapters do that—its description of one possible program is sufficiently detailed that it should allow for a well-defined picture of what can be done and how it can be done at the beginning.

Before describing one possible program for developing beginning literacy in kindergarten (or nursery school), a few preliminary comments will be made. Initially, they are historical in nature.

CHANGES FOLLOWING THE 1960s

As the previous chapter points out, an unprecedented belief in the intellectual potential of young children and in the special importance for intelligence of learning opportunities during the first five years of life was often expressed in the 1960s. Requests for schools to teach more and to teach it earlier were a natural consequence in such a setting.

What the results would have been for school programs had the interest in the intellectual development of young children continued to receive generous financial support from government and private sources is an unanswerable question for such reasons as the following. In contrast to the 1960s, the 1970s witnessed a major recession in the national economy and, along with that, reduced spending for education by both federal and state agencies. Sizable cuts were also made repeatedly in local school budgets, leading to faculty layoffs and, very often, to the elimination of such "nonessentials" as teacher aides. Retrenchment became the new (and threatening) buzz word.

In spite of these problems, the public's desire for educational reform remained visible and even vocal, fostered now by such catalysts as widely circulated reports of reading problems and steadily dropping scores on college entrance examinations. By the time the 1980s arrived, the country as a whole had become increasingly more conservative; consequently, it was not unexpected that "return to the basics" was once again proposed as the cure for educational ills. Not in conflict with the recommendation was an increase in the use of both statewide and citywide competency tests, scores from which were sometimes used to make such major decisions as whether a student would receive a high school diploma.

In a sense, all these concerns and complaints were welded together in a federally sponsored report called *A Nation at Risk* (29) released in 1983. Although the document focused mainly on high schools, its claims about falling test scores, watered-down curricula, ineffective teaching, and growing numbers of discipline problems naturally raised questions about elementary schools. For the most part, the report fostered more rigid notions about schooling and hardly put a damper on the growing tendency to equate academic excellence with high test scores, even when they derived from instruments that did little more than assess what is easiest to put into a format that allows for computer scoring (3). It was no wonder, then, that knowledgeable, conscientious educators worried about a growing phenomenon: assessment was driving instruction.

IMPACT OF CHANGES ON
PRE-FIRST-GRADE READING

Before the post-Sputnik era, kindergarten programs were fairly similar, thanks mostly to some highly influential early childhood educators who persisted in their convictions that the most important purpose of kindergarten was to promote social and emotional growth and that the best vehicle for accomplishing that goal was play. When, in the 1960s, interest began to emerge in the possibility—even desirability—of initiating reading instruction in kindergarten, the same educators were quick to retaliate with articles that forcefully opposed such an innovation on the grounds that teaching reading earlier would inevitably put pressure on five-year-olds and take time away from more important concerns (4, 18, 23). Meanwhile, the schedules of some kindergartens were altered to include either reading readiness activities or reading instruction itself. But, as the previous chapter explains, such changes for the most part would have to be described as "doing the same old thing" but doing it earlier (10, 13).

Because, unlike first grade, kindergarten was not yet burdened with assumed expectations for reading, the 1970s was a perfect time for experimental programs designed both to arrive at a better understanding of readiness and to develop methods and materials for teaching reading that were suitable for, and of interest to, younger children. Unfortunately, as previous sections in the chapter point out, funding for this kind of innovation was not available on any generous or widespread scale.

Meanwhile, interest in getting reading started earlier persisted. As a result, more and more kindergarten teachers found themselves in a position where they were expected to teach reading—whether or not they were ready and whether or not the children were ready (10). It was probably sudden administrative "requests" that made workbooks like those published by Modern Curriculum Press in 1972 so attractive. Called the "MCP Kindergarten Program" (31), the five workbooks covered what was typical of others that soon became available: Auditory, Visual, and Motor Skills; The Alphabet; Consonant Sounds; More Consonant Sounds; Introduction to Vowel Sounds.

While publishers were exerting an ever-widening influence on the kindergarten curriculum, what were colleges and universities doing to help teachers of young children learn about appropriate ways to meet the expectation that they would teach reading? A letter received in the mid-1970s from a kindergarten teacher unknown to me provides one answer. In part, her letter said:

> I have taught kindergarten for ten years. During that time, more and more children arrived at school so ready to learn to read; yet, there I was, ill-prepared to know what to do, because at the time I was an undergraduate nothing was ever said about reading. Although I saw many of my friends

who are teachers turn to workbooks, that was not the route I wanted to follow. Instead, I decided to take a leave of absence to do full-time graduate work to get a master's degree in early childhood education. I took it for granted that one result of the year's work would be the ability to put together a kindergarten program that would do exciting things with reading while not neglecting other, equally important parts of the curriculum.

While I enjoyed the year—I've always liked being a student—the little I learned about reading that met my needs was a major disappointment. I took three courses in early childhood education, but only one even mentioned reading. Actually, what was most helpful in that particular course was a paper I wrote on "Kindergarten Reading." The only reading methodology course that was available covered kindergarten through grade six; consequently, very little time went to topics directly related to my interests and concerns.* I did get help from a course in children's literature and, of course, I picked up lots of ideas from other teachers whom I met in classes. The chance to observe in eight kindergartens was helpful, too, both in pointing out what I would never do and in identifying some things that I'll try when school begins next month.

In spite of all that I learned, I still am disappointed and feel much less ready to do a good job with reading than I had expected to be after a full year of courses.

This letter suggests the possibility that a lack of coordinated leadership from early childhood and reading specialists is one reason kindergarten reading instruction grew like Topsy in the 1970s. The lack of leadership may also explain why representatives of publishers found it so easy to sell workbooks and ditto sheets to anxious administrators and teachers. The same reason may account for the fact that anyone who now observes in kindergartens will find that the bulk of what is done to teach reading comes directly from basal reader programs, which have been expanded to include manuals for kindergarten teachers and workbooks for kindergarten children. Such a development cannot help but bring to mind what MacGinitie said in an article published in 1976:

> I only hope that as early reading programs become more institutionalized, they do not become more institution-like—more formal, more uniform, more demanding, less tolerant of deviation. (27, p. 882)

What can happen when kindergarten reading does become "institution-like" is effectively revealed in a journal entry written by a kindergarten teacher. The account could be called "The Reluctant Birth of a Teacher B":

---

*The scarcity of reading courses for teachers of young children at the pre- and in-service levels was verified in a survey sponsored by the International Reading Association that included both the United States and Canada (2).

Although prior to this course, I had had little training in the teaching of reading, I knew intuitively that each year for the past few years, some of the children in my class were very ready to learn to read. Certain ones, in fact, arrived already reading. Thanks to a workshop that I took that dealt with language experience materials and to a large number of articles that I had read, I gradually developed procedures and materials that succeeded in teaching a number of words and a few sounds to everyone. Once the ability to read began to develop with some children, it couldn't be stopped. With others, not too much was learned, but I always saw to it that they felt proud of whatever it was that they were able to accomplish.

All this changed a year ago last fall. For a long time, our school system used the same basal program, which did not have anything for kindergarten—or, if it did, those materials were never purchased. Just over a year ago, a different series was adopted and even though I had nothing to do with its selection, I was expected to use the kindergarten part of the program, which consists of an excessively thick manual for me and two workbooks (plus ditto sheets) for each child. Only a small part of the manual is helpful—some of its suggestions for readiness, in fact, are ridiculous. However, what caused me great concern is that the children's materials introduce 19 words and cover 15 consonant sounds. Because such expectations are beyond the reach of some children and devoid of challenge for others, I decided to use the basal materials sparingly and to proceed with my own way of teaching reading, which had always been viewed positively by my principal.

This year, however, things are different. The first-grade teachers who have children from my last year's class have complained that not all of them know the 19 words and 15 sounds, thus are not prepared to use the initial first-grade materials. As a result, I have been told by my principal to use the basal program's kindergarten workbooks regularly, including all the end-of-unit, end-of-level tests. He even hinted about the possibility of retaining in kindergarten any child who does not pass the final test, which, for the most part, deals with phonics.

Although I have tenure, I've decided that I had better do what I can to please everyone, if only for the sake of the slower children. I hardly want them to be labeled "slow" before they even have a chance to begin. To please myself, I intend doing what I have always tried to do in the past: Match my program to the children. To do anything else is not something I'd find easy to live with.

Even though the details of how this teacher works when she does what she wants to do are unknown, the program described in this chapter is one she would probably find acceptable. The program is also one that would allow her children every opportunity to learn the nineteen words and fifteen consonant sounds that one basal series has arbitrarily established as being the subject matter for a kindergarten reading program.

RECOMMENDATIONS FOR A PRE-FIRST-GRADE READING PROGRAM

Although the focus of this chapter is reading, the recommendation to persons working with pre-first-grade children is to view teaching reading within a framework that recognizes the interdependence of oral language (listening and speaking) and written language (reading and writing). The broader view, which we'll call a language arts perspective, is recommended for a number of reasons.

To begin, the broader context should encourage teachers of young children to spend time on whatever aspect of language needs attention. In practice, this means that teachers will not let reading take over (even though ability in reading might be a major instructional goal) when it is obvious that the oral language of some or all of the children suffers from serious limitations. This point needs to be stressed because it is too easy for teachers to allow themselves to be guided by a narrow view of what it means to teach reading, or to prepare children for it.

To illustrate, I recall observing in one kindergarten in which the teacher was fortunate to have the highly desirable combination of a full-time aide and eighteen children. Surrounded as this urban school was by extreme poverty and deprivation, my immediate thought as I entered the room was, "What a wonderful opportunity to help these children grow in their ability to use language!" Within a few minutes, surprise and disappointment replaced the feeling of hope because, in this classroom, the aide functioned (at least during the observation) only as a disciplinarian. Both she and the teacher walked about the room, constantly reminding children not to talk—not even to ask questions—as they completed two pages in a reading readiness workbook. Later, when I asked the teacher why the observed procedure was used, she responded without hesitation, "If these children are going to learn to read, they have to learn to be quiet." In this particular school, an explanation like, "If these children are going to learn to read, they have to learn to talk" would be easier to defend.

A more widespread disregard for viewing reading in relation to other aspects of language is now found in kindergartens and even nursery schools. I refer to the already-mentioned practice of drilling children on phonics before they have had the opportunity to learn what reading and learning to read are all about, or even before they understand what "word" means. As their teachers follow manuals, use charts, and distribute workbooks and ditto sheets, basically important matters such as the connection between oral and written language are slighted, resulting in children who have no understanding of why their teachers continue to refer to something called "beginning sounds" or why they are constantly talking about words that rhyme.

In addition to preserving the basic importance of oral language for reading, the broader language arts focus allows for the likelihood that the easiest way to become a reader is different for different children. Recall from Chapter 4 the description of Joey. With his wonderful visual memory, he readily recalled written words, yet had obvious difficulty with auditory discrimination. The program being recommended could accommodate him by providing many opportunities to learn to read words; at the same time, other opportunities are made available to prepare for phonics.

Another kindergartner could also be accommodated. Frank, unlike Joey, shows little interest when the chance to learn to read words is offered, and he does not get excited when questions are asked about the sounds of words he knows. Frank, however, is interested in learning to write and, in fact, has been printing at home since age four. Like other young "pencil-and-paper kids" (9), his interest in writing is accompanied by a curiosity about spelling. Often, his questions in school include, "How do you spell _____?" Although showing little interest as yet in reading per se, he is still doing some – thanks to help with printing and, when asked for, with spelling. Eventually, Frank's teacher hopes to use his interest in printing letters to teach him about the sounds some of them record. Meanwhile, his frequent decision at free-choice time is to print on one of the small chalkboards that are available from time to time. (Putting the chalkboards away for a while makes them more attractive when they become available.)

Steven must not be overlooked in this discussion of kindergartners. He is the child who is slow in everything. Yet he, too, can fit into a program that places reading in a language arts context. Within such a context, for example, his teacher feels no pressure to work on reading with every child. In addition, the same context helps put Steven's shortcomings into a correct perspective. He has a great need to experience many new things, to acquire concepts, and to learn the words that go with them. Even while all this is occurring, attention is being given to such personally captivating words as his own name. Steven can identify its written form, knows the name of *S*, and gets excited whenever he sees it in words displayed in the room. When opportunities to learn to print are available, he is eager to participate even though his progress does not match his interest.

When teachers keep all the language arts in mind, another important kind of accommodation is facilitated. This one has to do with the obvious fact that young children openly love nobody quite as much as they love themselves. Whether this reflects what Piaget calls the "egocentric stage" is less important for this discussion than whether teachers take advantage of the fact that young children love to listen to – and talk, read, and write about – themselves. Teachers who fail to take advantage of these love affairs are missing a great opportunity.

The language arts perspective offers the wise teacher unending opportunities to use the factor of self-interest. Consider the names of children, for instance. I watched one kindergarten teacher use a year-long interest in name cards (approximately 5-by-12 inches) not only for attendance-taking but also to give attention to instructional objectives related to:

the meaning of *word*
word boundaries
visual discrimination
letter names
capitalization
printing
auditory discrimination
letter-sound relationships
alphabetical order

In this classroom, one positive by-product of the children's direct involvement with names and attendance-taking was a heightened awareness of who was absent. As a result, an absentee's return to school was greeted with unusual enthusiasm, which must have contributed to that child's positive feelings both about school and about himself. (Another teacher's account of her use of children's names comprises Table 5.1.)

Table 5.1. *A Kindergarten Teacher's Account of How She Used Children's Names to Attain Certain Objectives*

Objectives	Procedures
1. To introduce school with a personal emphasis	1. Used name tags ("Hello" tags) for each child during the first week. Used sheriff's badges for second week and bracelets during third week.
	2. Took Polaroid picture of each child. Displayed on bulletin board with first names under pictures. (Later, taken home in envelopes marked with children's names.)
	3. Used place cards on tables at snack time during early weeks.
2. To teach identification of first names	1. Printed first names on all papers. Encouraged children to print all or part of their names themselves.
	2. Displayed name cards on two bulletin board displays: a. on balloons b. on large red school

(continued)

	3. Gave smaller name cards to children to compare with cards on bulletin board.
	4. Let children take own attendance by removing name cards from card holder.
	5. Each day had children read names of those who were absent (or present).
3. To encourage attention to individual letters	1. Using large name cards, discussed names beginning with same letters. Named those letters.
	2. Helped individual children look for words with letters that were in their names. Named the letters.
	3. Gave each child white squares on which a letter in his name was written. Distributed name cards. Had children arrange letter-squares in a sequence to make their names. Had them paste letter-squares on paper. Later, they drew pictures of themselves above their names.

One more advantage of a language arts perspective should be mentioned. It is the possibility that its broadly conceived base can discourage use of the label "early reading program." This by-product may seem less important than it really is unless it is kept in mind that such a label typically leads to the expectation that every child in the program *will* learn to read. Whenever that happens, pressure is put not only on children but also on teachers. One result is what is all too common now: routine, uniform instruction that comes directly from commercially prepared manuals.

EXPECTATIONS FOR RECOMMENDED PROGRAM

All one has to do is visit nursery schools and kindergartens located in a variety of communities to learn that no single list of instructional objectives will ever be appropriate for everyone in these age groups. I have observed in nursery schools in which some children were more linguistically sophisticated than others I had seen in first grades. Similar discrepancies are found in behavior. To cite one illustration, I used a day to observe in the kindergartens and first grades in one school. In the kindergartens, I saw children whose behavior suggested greater maturity and independence than would ordinarily be expected of five-year-olds; yet, when I visited the six-year-old groups, I saw others whose behavior patterns were those associated with considerably younger children.

This suggests that the academic expectations established for any pre-first-grade program should vary from community to community, from school to school, and even from one group to another in the same school. In practice, such variation will result in programs in which children are neither bored nor bewildered. The variability in expectations also means that all this book can do is suggest possible instructional objectives. In turn, teachers must select from them whatever seems appropriate for the children who are their responsibility.

REQUIREMENTS OF RECOMMENDED PROGRAM

In addition to showing a pervasive concern for both oral and written language, the recommended program also requires – like all effective instructional efforts – flexible scheduling and careful planning. Let me deal first with flexibility, as that is especially necessary in programs for young children.

Flexibility

Just as it is unrealistic to think in terms of one list of instructional objectives for all pre-first-grade programs, so is it unrealistic – and even narrow – to think that one schedule is best for every situation. Still, teachers of young children do need to make decisions about who will do what and when. Before one sample schedule is discussed, the importance of flexibility needs to be explained.

When young children are having their first experience with attending school, they need ample time to learn its routines as well as the expectations for behavior. This means that only minimal attention can go to academic goals – although, as Table 5.1 shows, even the start of a year allows for a relaxed type of work with children's names, the names of letters, and so on. Nonetheless, much consideration needs to be given at the beginning to what might globally be called the children's adjustment – in this instance, to new adults, to new children, and to new expectations.

Eventually – the exact amount of time will vary, sometimes considerably – increased attention can go to academic objectives dealing with one or more of the language arts. At first, it will take a long time for the children to do just a few things; but then, as time passes, more will be done more quickly. One consequence of this natural change and growth is the need for an alteration in schedules, because a static schedule inevitably leads to idle and mischievous children.

The need for another kind of flexibility is identified in the behavior of teachers (at all grade levels) who persist in executing a plan even when it is obvious that all is not well. The children are uninterested or, perhaps, totally frustrated or obviously bored; and yet the teacher continues.

Once, when I was working with a group of new teachers, one among them had this characteristic to such a degree that it caused discipline problems. When we discussed her tendency to persist, come what may, she said she was painfully aware of the problem but saw no solution. She explained that she panicked every time she had the feeling of losing the children but, not knowing what else to do, continued with her original plans. Since one plan plus three emergency plans for each instructional period was hardly a practical solution, a simpler alternative was offered: Keep books close by to serve as a security blanket. During a period set aside for letter identification, for instance, it would be appropriate to have an alphabet book close at hand. Should it happen that what was planned did not work out successfully or, perhaps, did not take as long as anticipated, the book would be available to allow the children to do such things as look at and discuss illustrations, name letters, and identify colors and shapes.

Later, it was interesting to see how an available book added tremendously to this new teacher's security. In a short time, a "blanket" was unnecessary. As she gained self-confidence and began to know the children better, her plans were almost always successful, probably because she put them together carefully and executed them with the right amount of flexibility.

Carefully Planned Schedule

How various activities might be scheduled in a half-day kindergarten program will now be discussed. Those of you who work (or plan to work) in nursery schools or with first graders should find in this illustrative schedule bits and pieces that are appropriate and possible for your program, too.*

The schedule shown below was followed (with flexibility) in a kindergarten in which there were twenty-three children, a teacher, and an aide. As scheduled activities are discussed, they point out possible goals for pre-first-grade programs.

8:30– 8:45 A.M.	Conversation groups
8:45– 9:00	Attendance-taking; attention to date, weather, and current interests

*Schedules different from the illustrative one used in this chapter are described else-where (30).

9:00– 9:20	Academic period for one group
	Free-choice for other group
9:20– 9:40	Groups reversed for above activities
9:40–10:00	Music
10:00–10:30	Playtime, bathroom, milk
10:30–11:00	Art
11:00–11:30	Storytime
11:30–11:40	Preparation for home

At conversation time, the children divided spontaneously into two groups of approximately equal size, although on some days the boys made up one group and the girls composed the second. The teacher sat at a table with one group while the aide conversed informally with the other in a different part of the room. Usually, conversations were spontaneous. At times, however, a particular theme was introduced with a picture or an interesting object.

The next period of approximately fifteen minutes began with taking attendance and ended with discussions of current interests. (Later, the children took attendance themselves by placing their name cards in a chart when they first arrived.) All the children were together for this period, sitting on the floor in front of the teacher. Meanwhile, the aide prepared materials for use later on in the morning.

At about nine o'clock, the academic goals of the program received explicit attention. (As explained later, more casual attention went to them at other times.) At the start of the year, the academic period on Monday was a time to provide help with color identification. Materials such as clothing, crayons, traffic signs, bulletin board displays, flowers, and construction paper were used. Books about colors were read, too. Soon afterward, teaching color words became the objective. Still later, Monday was the day when either extra help or extra challenge (with anything) was provided. On Tuesday, the names of letters and how to print them received special consideration, although attention went to both at other times, too. For the more advanced children, Tuesday soon allowed for help with phonics. (How letter names, printing, and beginning phonics can be taught is the subject of Chapter 9.)

On Wednesday, ready children were given carefully planned opportunities to learn to read some words, generally selected in relation to the interests of the children or to current activities. As words were learned, sentences were constructed, and homemade books began to accumulate. Thursday was a time for the teacher to get her bearings and do whatever needed to be done. Once more, the usual activity was work with small numbers of children who needed additional help or challenge. On Friday, the academic period singled out the names of numbers for attention. In this case, instruction progressed with the help of birthday cards, calendars, measuring tapes, television dials, clocks, store catalogues, and telephones. As the year moved along, simple mathematical concepts were introduced. Although not officially in the schedule, the teacher's special interest in word meanings affected everything that was done. In addition, she commonly used an academic period to do something special with meanings.

While the teacher worked with one group of children (selected on the basis of ability), the aide was with the others. Her responsibility was to supervise, or participate in, activities that the children selected from among prescribed possibilities that included, at the beginning of the year, playing with blocks, trucks, dolls, dishes, telephones, and so on. Possible choices were gradually altered to include such activities as working puzzles, and playing with sequence cards, concept cards, or bingo cards that, at different times, displayed colors, numerals, letters, or words.

Eventually, three learning centers were established (Listening, Reading, Writing), and the aide divided her time among them. At this point in the school year, the children could be found listening to taped stories using earphones, making signs for block constructions, dictating descriptions of their pictures to the aide (which gave them the chance to see spoken language turned into print), and playing with a variety of number and word games. Some children might also be found printing on small chalkboards and slates, copying words the aide had printed at their request, or making their own words with magnetic letters or lettered blocks.

At approximately 9:20, the children who were with the teacher changed to free-choice activities; those who had been with the aide started their work with the teacher. (Ability groups varied each day, depending on what was being taught.)

Music followed the academic periods and was a time for fun and relaxation. In ways that would not take away from either objective, songs were occasionally used to help with academic goals.

Next came playtime. For that, the children went outdoors whenever weather permitted. Bathroom and refreshment needs were taken care of afterward.

For art, which lasted approximately thirty minutes, both the teacher and aide worked with the children. Usually the teacher gave directions and then both she and her assistant distributed materials and, later, helped or talked with individuals. During art, the atmosphere was relaxed but never rowdy. Conversations among the children and between teacher and child were taken for granted. At times, art projects were also used to help with academic goals. Early in the year, for example, sponge paintings of autumn trees were used to discuss and name colors.

Next came a story, and then it was time to prepare for going home.

Teacher Aides

Even though the assistance of the aide contributed substantially to the success of the program just described, it could still be carried out without the extra help. Certain things would have to be done differently, however.

At the start of the year, the children would require some time to learn to work independently. For a while, therefore, the teacher would supervise while the entire class was engaged in free-choice activities. Once the children seemed to know what was expected, academic periods could begin. Whenever new free-choice possibilities were made available, more temporary supervision would be necessary, this time to make certain that everyone knew how to use the new materials or activities. Essentially, then, the program would be the same whether or not the teacher had an aide. Without the extra adult, however, it would progress more slowly and probably less smoothly.

Because the assistance of a competent adult can make major contributions to school programs for young children, it seems appropriate to describe what one school system did when money for teacher aides was cut from the budget. Since most mothers of the children worked, volunteer parents were not available to replace the sorely missed aides. Parents did take the time, however, to put together a successful recruitment program directed to older people in the community that stressed the theme, "Are You Looking for Ways to Spend Your Days?" Advertisements in stores and the local newspaper, followed by interviews with persons who inquired about assisting in classrooms, resulted in a volunteer aide for any teacher who wanted one, plus names of other senior citizens who expressed interest in helping with walks through the community, field trips, and whatever else required more than the usual amount of supervision. Because the interviews disclosed a number of hobbies and experiences that would interest children, the recruitment efforts also resulted in school visits by individuals who talked about their hobbies and travels, often with the help of slides and artifacts. "Where there's a will, there's a way" is the moral of this successful enterprise.

Successful recruitment of aides is just the beginning, of course; the mere presence of one more adult is no guarantee that an instructional program will be improved. This important point is reinforced with descriptions of some contrasting uses of aides.

In one nursery school attended by twenty children, the teacher had the help of an aide plus a parent volunteer. At the time the class was observed, it was divided into three groups, each sitting at a table with an adult. One group was tracing a variety of geometrical shapes on ditto sheets; another was coloring a dittoed picture of a clown; those at the third table were putting sticks into groups based on their color. Conversation was not encouraged; in fact, the children were unexpectedly quiet.

Approximately twenty minutes later, the same tasks were reassigned. The children who had been tracing shapes were switched to coloring; those who had been coloring worked with the sticks; and those who had been sorting sticks received a copy of the geometrical shapes. After another twenty minutes, each group again stood up and moved to the next table. By this time, one could not help but think that in spite of all the extra help, activities during the observation were matched to tables, not to children.

A kindergarten in which there were a teacher, an aide, and twenty-seven children provides a contrast. Thanks to the aide, the teacher was able to work with individuals and small groups. Meanwhile, the aide did many things: answered children's questions; offered reminders to some; re-explained and checked assignments; read to small groups; discussed pictures; listened to individuals read brief sentences on cards; wrote captions for art work; helped with spelling when it was requested; demonstrated how to make certain letters; helped with the printing required to name buildings that two boys had constructed from milk cartons and shoe boxes. Clearly apparent was team work that began with a teacher who knew what needed to be done to achieve individualized instruction and who was fortunate enough to have an assistant who allowed her to do just that without interruptions.

How another kindergarten teacher took advantage of the help of two volunteer parents is described by the teacher herself:

I like to take each class that I have to a local grocery store early in the school year because it's rich with opportunities to extend experiences and language. The manager and I talk briefly before each trip to let him know what I'm trying to accomplish. This year, I'm preparing a unit on fruits and vegetables for vocabulary building, so I asked the manager to spend extra time in the produce section.

Before going to the store, we made a shopping list on the chalkboard. (On the day following the trip, we'll have a fruit and vegetable tasting party, so we needed to purchase the food.) We also talked about the reasons why people make lists.

At the store, we spent a long time in the produce department. The children identified familiar fruits and vegetables, and the manager and I named those that the children didn't know. We also discussed where some of the items were grown. We compared the colors and sizes of the various products, too.

Other parts of the trip that were particularly useful included a tour of the preparation and storage rooms. A meat cutter demonstrated his work with sausage, hamburger, and porkchops. In the "deli," the children were shown how doughnuts are filled and how bread and meat are sliced. They also sampled cold meats and pumpernickel bread. (They had a lot of fun saying – or trying to say – "pumpernickel.") As we walked around the store, the children read a number of labels. (I plan to take advantage of their interest in this kind of reading by bringing packages and boxes to school.*) We finished the trip by purchasing some fruits and vegetables. Before leaving, each child got an apple from the manager.

---

*It is encouraging when children read labels, but praise for their responses may be misleading for the children if they are using background cues rather than words to do the "reading" (16). This possibility points to the need for teachers to isolate names of products by printing them on cards or a chalkboard. This practice will help children understand that it is the words that "say" something.

When we returned to school, we wrote a thank you note together, which one of the volunteer parents duplicated. Each child then signed his or her note and drew a picture of something that had been seen at the store. The parents and I labeled the pictures according to each child's suggestion. The notes and pictures will be sent to the manager.

Since some of the children have been working on the hard sound of *c*, I asked them if they remembered anything that had been seen that started with that sound. I wrote their responses in a column on the board. Answers were *Crang* (the manager's last name), *cabbage, corn, coconut, Coca Cola, cake, cookies, carrots*, and *casing*. The latter is a new word acquired when we watched sausage being made.

Perhaps you can see why I take these trips. Inevitably, they provide opportunities to learn about many things—in this case, words, sounds, sequencing, nutrition, classification, and even careers.

A Pervasive Language Arts Concern

The earlier discussion of one possible kindergarten schedule refers to instructional periods, which might have prompted the conclusion that language arts goals received attention only at stipulated times. Not so. The language arts focus that underlies the recommendations in this chapter pervades the whole of a program. It is a concern that permeates teachers' thoughts, reminding them to be constantly searching for interesting, natural opportunities to give attention to any and all aspects of language. Because of the special importance of this point, let me make it more graphic with illustrations that show that work with listening, speaking, reading, and writing are not confined to specified periods. As a start, the usefulness of art projects is illustrated.

On the day that one kindergarten teacher discussed the sound that *v* records with about half the class, she had all the children make paper vases when art was scheduled. On each vase, she carefully printed *vase* and called the children's attention to the fact that it started with *v*. One child enthusiastically called everyone's attention to his knowledge of its sound, which he promptly produced. Since the vases seemed empty without flowers, the teacher suggested that on the following day, paper flowers could be made to fill them.

When art began the next day, the vases were brought out. All the children were asked to look at *vase*, to name and spell it, and to make the sound that *v* stands for if they remembered it. The teacher then suggested that it would be a good idea to fill the vases with a flower whose name also started with *v*. Thanks to a grandmother who had a large collection of violets, her grandson immediately suggested violets. Not by accident, colored pictures of the flowers were in a drawer. They were taken out by the teacher, discussed by the children, then thumbtacked to a bulletin board along with a card on which *violets* had been printed. By this time, the children were more than ready to make violets for their vases.

In early April in another kindergarten, the teacher was especially pleased with the number of words most children had learned to read but uncomfortable about the possibility of their forgetting everything they knew over the long spring vacation. To encourage fruitful play at home, she had them make spring baskets, which, during the week before vacation, were gradually filled with small, egg-shaped pieces of construction paper of various colors. On the day set aside for color identification, the children — in small groups — reviewed colors. As each child successfully named a color, an egg of that color went into his basket. The same type of review and reward were used on subsequent days with numbers, letters, and words that also appeared on egg-shaped paper. The week thus ended with a thorough review as well as with well-filled spring baskets and delighted children.*

Like art, music can also help with oral and written language. In one nursery school, for example, the children began the year completely unfamiliar with the Alphabet Song; consequently, it was taught early (and learned quickly). Sometimes the children sang it while they were having a midmorning snack; when they did, the teacher took the opportunity to discuss, and hang up, one more alphabet card. (This was how all the cards eventually got on the wall.) Later, either the teacher or a child pointed to the letters as the song was sung or listened to on a record.

When most children could name most letters, each received an alphabet book. It was a three-page dittoed copy of the Alphabet Song arranged as shown in Figure 5.1. At first, the teacher and the children talked about the page numbers. The children were next asked to point to the letters as the teacher sang part of the song very slowly. When they got to page 3, some of the children quickly identified *I* and *me*, which were part of several earlier bulletin-board displays. At this point, the teacher printed *I* and *me* on the board and asked everyone to tell her what they said. Afterwards, she slowly sang the words of the song, again encouraging the children to point to each letter and word. Before the books were finally taken home, the children made covers, most of which incorporated letters of the alphabet in one form or another.

In addition to helping with letters, music can highlight words. Singing songs with numerous verses, for example, might be facilitated with labeled pictures. Take "Old MacDonald" as an illustration. With all its verses, how natural to show a picture of an animal as a cue for the next verse to be sung.

---

*I learned about this art project not from the teacher but from a parent of a girl in her class. Her mother told me that the basket and eggs had become one of her daughter's most treasured possessions and that it was frequently used when she and her older sister played school. Because playing school is a common occurrence with young children and their older siblings (10), teachers should keep that activity in mind when they make plans for materials that will be taken home.

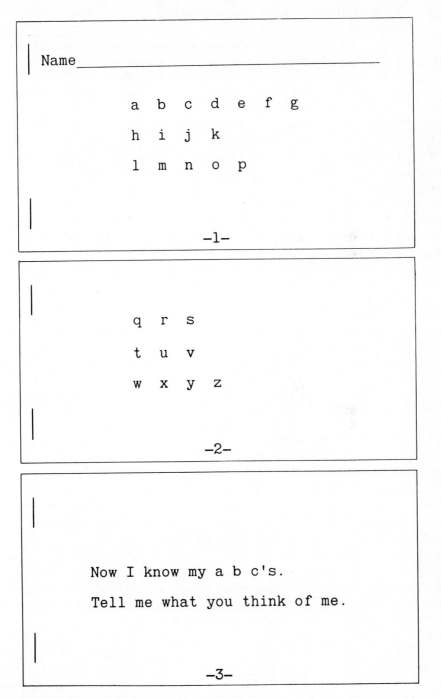

Figure 5.1. *Format of the Alphabet Book*

Later, the same pictures might be labeled with the animals' names. Eventually, only the labels are displayed. This would take place over several weeks, interspersed with opportunities for the children to examine and discuss the pictures and to look carefully at the written names.

Song lyrics themselves can be another source of help with words when a teacher prints the chorus so she can point to each word each time the refrain is sung. In addition to showing the word-for-word correspondence between what is sung and what is written, the repetition may be enough for some children to learn to read one or more words. Song picture books are also available for use later on (24). Other uses of songs can help with word meanings and, at times, highlight the fact that some words begin with the same sound.

Hopefully, these illustrations are sufficient to show how all the language arts can get attention at more than just the periods of time scheduled for them. The illustrations should have also indicated that opportunities to extend children's abilities in spoken and written language can be offered in ways that are personal, interesting, and free of pressure.

INSTRUCTIONAL GOALS

Like all effective instructional programs, those at pre-first-grade levels should be guided by carefully chosen goals. This is not the same as saying that a uniform list of goals should be established for all pre-first-grade programs, as that hardly takes into account the widely diverse backgrounds of children enrolled in these programs. (I'm reminded here of a recent conversation with a three-year-old who had much to say about a class he was taking called "Bugology.") The difference in backgrounds means that a uniform list of goals could be just right for some children but a source of bewilderment or boredom for many others.

GOALS FOR BEGINNERS

Because some pre-first graders are real beginners insofar as literacy is concerned, the persons responsible for selecting appropriate goals sometimes need to be reminded of the basic needs of such students. I refer to the fact that these children may require many opportunities:

To acquire an understanding of what reading and learning to read are all about.
To learn to want to be a reader.
To learn what is meant by "word."

To understand the function of empty space in establishing word boundaries.

To learn about the left-to-right, top-to-bottom orientation of written English.

What needs to be underscored immediately is that this list is not meant to suggest a sequence for attending to what is listed, nor should it be interpreted to signify that one goal must be realized before another is considered. Correctly interpreted, the list cites what some children might need to learn when they are at the very beginning of the long road to literacy. On any given day, therefore, a teacher of such individuals may be working on one or several of the listed goals.

Because language experience materials serve so well in accomplishing what needs to be learned at the very beginning, they are featured in the illustrative material that follows.*

Narrowly defined, *language experience materials* are children's accounts of their experiences told in their language. As realized in classrooms, the term expands considerably to encompass any written material, long or short, that deals with the in-school or out-of-school experiences of children in a given classroom. In many instances, the children's own words make up the account; in others, the words are similar but not identical. In other cases, the words are a teacher's. The critical element is that the content pertains to a particular group of children or to one individual. All other details (e.g., Should the teacher do the writing? Should a child's words ever be altered?) are determined by the reason for using the material.

Use of language experience materials is now discussed in the context of realizing what was listed earlier as beginning goals. The following illustrations are not meant to suggest that a single use of a particular text clinches things. Typically – certainly with slower children – repetition in some form is required for both understanding and retention. To be noted, too, is that each illustration starts with a statement of what the teacher is attempting to accomplish. The statement is intended to remind you that what is done and how it is done ought to be determined by why it is being done.

To Show the Connection between Spoken and Written Language

By the time children arrive in school, they have learned language but many have not learned about language. That is, they lack conscious knowledge of the properties of language even though they understand and produce it themselves. One of the things that many children do not understand is that

---

*How language experience materials function beyond the beginning stage is discussed in Chapter 15.

spoken words have written counterparts. No better material exists to promote that understanding than written accounts of what the children themselves say. That is why a teacher might ask, "Who wants to tell us something that happened yesterday when you weren't in school?" and why she would print on a chalkboard brief pieces of text like the following. (As words are printed, they are read to the children.)

> *Billy:*   I cut my leg yesterday.
>
> *Patricia:*   A fire engine woke me up last night.

At another time, children might be encouraged to tell about a picture they have drawn. Then, as they watch, a teacher or an aide prints and reads aloud exactly what they said in order to show that what is said can be written. If what children say is nonstandard English, that is what is printed. (See Figure 5.2 for examples of what two nursery school children had to say about their pictures.)

One-word traffic signs can also demonstrate that written language is not as strange as it might at first appear to be. Before the initial outdoor walk, a teacher might show signs attached to two long sticks. One sign displays *stop*, printed in large, lowercase letters; and the other displays *go*. After identifying the two words (and then giving the children a chance to "read" them), the teacher explains that she will hold up *stop* whenever there is the need to stop walking, and the *go* sign when everyone can begin again. (Although this procedure originated in the teacher's desire to show the connection between spoken and written words, *stop* and *go* will end up in the reading vocabulary of some children. This is another example, then, of offering opportunities to learn to read.)

To Teach What "Word" Means and to Show the Function of Space in Indicating Word Boundaries

Reading instruction, especially at the beginning, often highlights individual words in a way that is foreign to spoken language. With the latter, one word flows into the next so rapidly ("betcha" for *bet you*, "wanna" for *want to*, for example) that what we hear is a steady stream of sounds that yields a message. Only at certain times do individual words win our attention. This explains why children may arrive in school not knowing what *word* means and certainly not knowing that in written text, empty space shows where one word ends and the next begins. The use of language experience material that is as short as two words can be instructive for such children.

To illustrate, let's say it's a very foggy Tuesday, so a kindergarten teacher decides to use the children's interest in fog to begin to give meaning to *word*. (As you will see, what is done will also give the children the chance to learn to read *fog* although that is not the central concern.) Following the children's

Figure 5.2. *What Two Nursery School Children Said about Their Pictures*

many comments about the foggy morning, the teacher adds a few of her own: "You certainly know lots about fog, don't you? Let me show you what the word *fog* looks like when I write it. . . . This is what the word *fog* looks like when it's written."

On the next foggy morning, the same teacher might decide to repeat what was just described and also to add to it. Now, after printing *fog* on the board, she says, "Since you've been in kindergarten, you've certainly told me lots of interesting things about a foggy day. Let me show you what those two words, *foggy day*, look like when I write them. . . . This word (pointing to *foggy*) says 'foggy.' Did you see how I moved my hand over before I wrote the next word, the word *day*? I left an empty space so that you could see that I was writing two words, not just one. What do these two words say?" (Points to each as the children read, "foggy day.")

For another illustration of how text about children's experiences can help explain what a word is and also how empty space separates words, let's say it is the fall of the year and the children have been out gathering leaves. Back in the classroom, their teacher assembles the group to examine and discuss the collections. Leading questions about the leaves are posed periodically—for instance, "What colors are they?" "How do they feel?" "Are they all the same shape?" "Does this shape remind you of anything?" "How could we use these leaves?" "What can we now say about our collection?" Group contributions eventually lead to a written account, printed on the board by the teacher. (See Figure 5.3.)*

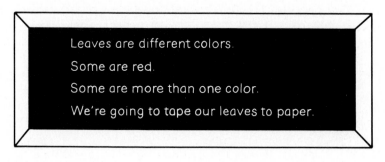

Leaves are different colors.

Some are red.

Some are more than one color.

We're going to tape our leaves to paper.

Figure 5.3

The following guidelines are pertinent for the teacher who chooses to use the text about leaves to teach children what *word* means.

*Sometimes, what is written on the board should be transferred to chart paper so that when children eventually become more skilled in reading, it can serve not only as practice material but also as evidence of their progress. Or, even if the sentences can't be read, a copy could be taken home to be shared with parents.

**GUIDELINES FOR USING LANGUAGE EXPERIENCE
MATERIALS TO TEACH THE MEANING OF "WORD"**

1. Say each word as you print it.
2. Read the entire account in a natural speaking fashion, pointing to each word as it is read.
3. Suggest to the children that they might like to read it, too. (As the children "read," read along with them, all the while moving your hand across each line of text from left to right.)
4. Point to and identify words that appear more than once. If the children seem interested, let them "read" these words.
5. Make a comment like, "There are so many words up here!" Then count them, pointing to each one. Show how a space separates one word from another. Next, let the children count the words. Point to each as it is counted.
6. Reread the entire account. Encourage the children to read with you.

In addition to specifying what a word is and indicating the function of space to show word boundaries, the language experience activity just described (a) demonstrated that words are read from left to right and that lines are read from top to bottom; (b) pointed out that identical words look alike when they are written; (c) gave the children a chance to pretend they could read; and (d) gave them the opportunity to learn to read some words. (In contrast, examine Figure 5.4 to see what commercially prepared workbooks provide, supposedly to teach about the left-to-right orientation of written English and, in the case of the reproduced page, to work on motor skills.)

If the group that collected and discussed the leaves was fairly small, or if the help of an aide was available, the teacher might also have asked each child for his favorite word in the account. Named words could be printed on small cards to be taken home so they could be read to parents and anyone else willing to listen. And so, reading vocabularies continue to grow.

To Motivate Children to Want
to Learn to Read

It would be difficult to dispute the assertion that the most successful (and enjoyable) way to interest children in acquiring the ability to read is by reading to them frequently from carefully chosen books. What is sometimes overlooked is that the *usefulness* of reading ability is another motivating factor. This point is made now because language experience materials can help to demonstrate how written text is helpful—to those who can read it—in

Figure 5.4

From the *MCP Kindergarten Program*, Book K1: Auditory, Visual, and Motor Skills, 1980, p. 11. Reprinted with permission of Modern Curriculum Press.

preserving information, thoughts, and feelings. To show the value of written records, thus the value of knowing how to read, a teacher might elect to use language experience material in the following way.

For purposes of illustration, let's say that each day in a certain classroom starts with a discussion of the weather, a topic of considerable interest to children since it affects their play life. One Monday morning, the teacher comments, "This certainly is a beautiful morning, isn't it? Was last Monday as nice as it is today? Can someone tell us what it was like last Monday?" Responses begin with guessing and end with the conclusion that nobody remembers. Thus, it is time for the teacher to propose, "If I were to write some words that tell us what this Monday is like, then next Monday we could look at what I write, and it would tell us. We wouldn't have to work so hard trying to remember." A discussion of the day's weather then begins and leads to the teacher's printing *sunny* and *clear* at the left side of a very wide sheet of paper. By the end of the week, the sheet displays:

Monday	*Tuesday*	*Wednesday*	*Thursday*	*Friday*
sunny	cloudy	cold	rainy	sunny
clear	warm	dark	windy	clear
		windy		

A few weeks later, the same teacher makes another proposal: "We seem to use the same words over and over, don't we? (Points to and reads *sunny, cold, windy*, and so on.) If I print these words on cards, we could use them again and again, depending on what the weather is like." Soon, a weather chart with slots for cards is attached to a bulletin board. In the meantime, all the children work hard at remembering what each card says so they will be able to select appropriate descriptions each morning. And so, reading vocabularies expand still more.

BEGINNERS AND THE LANGUAGE OF INSTRUCTION

Like all effective teachers, those working with beginners make certain that the words they use when instructing are understood. What results when the language of instruction confuses rather than helps can be pinpointed with illustrations.

In one kindergarten, the teacher wrote *you* and *me* on the board, then asked the children, "How many words did I just write?" With enthusiasm the group responded, "Five!" (I was impressed with both the quick counting and the confusion about the meaning of *word* and *letter*.)

At another time, I had been invited to observe in a classroom occupied by four- and five-year-olds who were being prepared for reading. It was early in the year, and the teacher was working on visual discrimination. On the day of the visit, she had placed word cards in the slots of a chart and was asking individuals in a small group to find any two words that were the same. (Earlier work had concentrated on smaller combinations of letters, beginning with comparisons of just two.) All went well until the teacher pointed to a card displaying *Monday* and asked if anyone could find the same word on the chalkboard. (At the start of the morning, *Monday* and *October* had been written and discussed.) Now, in contrast with the earlier work, nobody could. On reflection, the children's failure to respond was no longer unexpected — although at the time it was because of the earlier success. *Monday* had been printed on the board in large, white letters, whereas much smaller letters in black appeared on the card. What these children still needed to learn was the meaning of *same* and *different* applied to words. Eventually, they needed to learn that to all of the following, the same response must be given: flag, FLAG, flag , and *flag* .

Other observers have also heard misinterpretations of instructional terms. In a report entitled "Component Skills in Beginning Reading," Calfee and Venezky (5) describe an experience that is as pertinent for teachers as it is for researchers:

> Although many children use the words *same* and *different* . . . , their interpretation of these terms . . . may be different from the experimenter's. The writers ran headlong into this problem early in their testing program when one of the children replied "different" when shown two cards containing identical geometrical forms. When asked to justify his answer, the child pointed out that one of the cards had a smudge on it. With older or more test-sophisticated children, it is easier to communicate the dimensions with regard to which identity is to be judged. With younger children . . . the relevant dimension may be extremely difficult for the child to interpret. (p. 107)

Just how complex the language of instruction can be is also underscored in some observations made by Thomas Sticht:

> It seems likely that many children who are being taught to read may not know what they are to look for and focus upon, and may therefore have difficulty in learning to read. . . . For instance, suppose the teacher says, "Look at the word 'cat' on the blackboard." The child must aud the message, comprehend what a word is, understand that the utterance "cat" is a word in the spoken language, direct the gaze to the blackboard, visually examine the printed configuration and somehow understand that

all three letters—not just "c" and "t" or "c" and "a"—are important elements of the graphic display of the spoken word "cat."

The foregoing is quite different from the child's ordinary looking which is subservient to the child's self-imposed cognitive task. The teacher-imposed task may completely bewilder the child, making looking an almost pointless activity. This may be especially important if the teacher at one time expects the child to focus on whole words and at other times on elements of words. . . . A type of looking confusion could result, in that the child would not precisely know where to direct his focal attention. (33, p. 62)

Although of immediate importance, the meanings of words that figure in instruction are not something best taught in a given lesson on a given day. Instead, they come to be understood gradually with the help of many examples. Meanwhile, teachers of beginners need to bear in mind that when incorrect or unexpected answers occur, they may be rooted in confusion about auditory and visual language concepts that are an integral part of the language of reading instruction. It has been found that similar confusion may also have negative effects on test scores (8).

SUMMARY

The chapter began with some historical information to show why studies of the best ways to introduce pre-first graders to reading have been noticeably scarce. It continued by pointing up the influence of the publisher, which, in many school systems, has resulted in equating beginning instruction with the use of phonics workbooks and ditto sheets.

The chapter then proceeded to illustrate a pre-first-grade program that would allow for both individualized and personalized instruction. Adhering to the major implication of Ausubel's conception of readiness, the instruction referred to was eclectic in nature. Attention thus went to instruction that focuses on whole words, phonics, and writing. Recognizing the interdependence of all the language arts, the program that was described highlighted both oracy (listening and speaking) and literacy (reading and writing). It also reflected the contention that "the ideal educational system meets each child at his level of competence and leads him as far as possible in the direction of the desired instructional goals" (5, p. 93).

Since subsequent chapters deal with the various aspects of reading instruction in considerable detail, this chapter selected for attention goals especially important at the very beginning. Even though some pre-first graders are beyond the beginning, initial goals were identified in order to remind teachers of important prerequisites for success at the start.

How to teach some of the prerequisites was illustrated. Particularly emphasized was the value of language experience materials both to attain certain objectives and to make instruction personally interesting. Attending to whatever is of interest is vital, since involvement and achievement go hand in hand.

REVIEW

1. Based on Chapters 4 and 5, summarize developments occurring between the launching of Sputnik and the present that have affected both the timing of beginning instruction in reading and the kind of instruction often provided.

2. The need for carefully planned schedules as well as the importance of flexibility were stressed in Chapter 5. Are schedules and flexibility incompatible?

3. Working with a group of eight, a kindergarten teacher printed *red* on the board, told the eight what it said, then had them read it. Next she asked, "Can you think of anything that is red?" One child named fire trucks, which resulted in an animated discussion of fires and fire fighters. Calling the group's attention back to *red*, the teacher pointed to it and asked, "What is this word?" Immediately the children responded, "Red fire trucks!"

   a. Based on the children's response, what do they need to learn?

   b. With specificity, describe what the teacher can do to teach what is needed.

4. Facts presented in Chapter 5 include the following:
   a. Young children are very interested in their own names.

   b. Young children are sometimes confused by the language used in reading instruction.

   Describe how first names can function in teaching children the meaning of "beginning of a word."

5. Repetition is a natural part of songs. Repetition (practice) also is a requirement for word learning. Keeping those two facts in mind, select a song likely to be of interest to young children; then describe how it might help to get reading vocabularies started. OLD MAC DONALD

REFERENCES

1. Allan, Karen K. "The Development of Young Children's Metalinguistic Understanding of the Word." *Journal of Educational Research* 76 (November/December, 1982), 89–93.

2. Bailey, Mildred H.; Durkin, Dolores; Nurss, Joanne R.; and Stammer, John D. "Preparation of Kindergarten Teachers for Reading Instruction." *Reading Teacher* 36 (December, 1982), 307–311.

3. Buros, Oscar K. "Fifty Years in Testing: Some Reminiscenses, Criticisms, and Suggestions." *Educational Researcher* (July–August, 1977), 9–15.

4. Butler, Annie L. "Hurry! Hurry! Why?" *Childhood Education* 39 (September, 1962), 10–13.

5. Calfee, Robert C., and Venezky, Richard L. "Component Skills in Beginning Reading." In K. S. Goodman and J. T. Fleming (Eds.), *Psycholinguistics and the Teaching of Reading*. Newark, Del.: International Reading Association, 1969, 91–110.

6. Clay, Marie. *The Patterning of Complex Behavior*. Auckland, New Zealand: Heinemann Educational Books, 1979.

7. Clay, Marie. *What Did I Write? Beginning Writing Behavior.* Exeter, N.H.: Heinemann, 1982.

8. Cummings, Jack A., and Nelson, R. Brett. "Basic Concepts in the Oral Directions of Group Achievement Tests." *Journal of Educational Research* 73 (May/June, 1980), 259–261.

9. Durkin, Dolores. *Children Who Read Early*. New York: Teachers College Press, Columbia University, 1966.

10. Durkin, Dolores. "Facts about Pre-First Grade Reading." In Lloyd O. Ollila (Ed.), *The Kindergarten Child and Reading*. Newark, Del.: International Reading Association, 1977, 1–120.

11. Durkin, Dolores. "A Language Arts Program for Pre-First Grade Children: Two-Year Achievement Report," *Reading Research Quarterly* 5 (Summer, 1970), 534–565.

12. Durkin, Dolores. "A Six Year Study of Children Who Learned to Read in School at the Age of Four." *Reading Research Quarterly* 10 (1974–75, No. 1), 9–61.

13. Durkin, Dolores. "When Should Children Begin to Read?" In Helen M. Robinson (Ed.), *Innovation and Change in Reading Instruction*, The Sixty-Seventh Yearbook of the National Society of Education, Part II. Chicago: The University of Chicago Press, 1966, 30–71.

14. Gentile, Lance M., and Hoot, James L. "Kindergarten Play: The Foundation of Reading." *Reading Teacher* 36 (January, 1983), 436–439.

15. Goldstein, Bobbye S. "What's In a Name?" *Reading Teacher* 37 (May, 1984), 911.

16. Goodall, Marilyn. "Can Four Year Olds 'Read' Words in the Environment?" *Reading Teacher* 37 (February, 1984), 478–482.

17. Hare, Victoria C. "What's in a Word? A Review of Young Children's Difficulties with the Construct 'Word'." *Reading Teacher* 37 (January, 1984), 360–364.

18. Heffernan, Helen. "Significance of Kindergarten Education." *Childhood Education* 36 (March, 1960), 313–319.

19. Henderson, Edmund H. *Learning to Read and Spell*. DeKalb, Ill.: Northern Illinois University Press, 1981.

20. Hiebert, Elfrieda H. "Developmental Patterns and Interrelationships of Pre-school Children's Print Awareness." *Reading Research Quarterly* 16 (1981, No. 2), 236–259.

21. Holdaway, Don. *The Foundations of Literacy*. Sydney, Australia: Ashton Scholastic, 1979.

22. Holden, M. H., and MacGinitie, W. H. "Children's Conceptions of Word Boundaries in Speech and Print." *Journal of Educational Psychology* 43 (December, 1972), 551–557.

23. Hymes, James L. "More Pressure for Early Reading." *Childhood Education* 40 (September, 1963), 34–35.

24. Jalongo, Mary R., and Bromley, Karen D. "Developing Linguistic Competence through Song Picture Books." *Reading Teacher* 37 (May, 1984), 840–845.

25. Lesiak, Judi. "Reading in Kindergarten: What the Research Doesn't Tell Us." *Reading Teacher* 32 (November, 1978), 135–138.

26. Lloyd, Mavis J. "Teach Music to Aid Beginning Readers." *Reading Teacher* 32 (December, 1978), 323–327.

27. MacGinitie, Walter H. "When Should We Begin to Teach Reading?" *Language Arts* 53 (November/December, 1976), 878–882.

28. Morris, Darrell. "Concept of Word: A Developmental Phenomenon in the Beginning Reading and Writing Processes." *Language Arts* 58 (September, 1981), 659–668.

29. National Commission on Excellence in Education. *A Nation at Risk: The Imperative for Educational Reform.* Washington, D.C.: U.S. Department of Education, April, 1983.

30. Nurss, Joanne R. "The Schedule: Organizing for Individual Instruction." In Lloyd O. Ollila (Ed.), *The Kindergarten Child and Reading.* Newark, Del.: International Reading Association, 1977, 56–67.

31. Polish, Virginia. *Starting Off with Phonics.* Cleveland, Oh.: Modern Curriculum Press, 1980.

32. Schickedanz, Judith A., and Sullivan, Maureen. "Mom, What Does U-F-F Spell?" *Language Arts* 61 (January, 1984), 7–17.

33. Sticht, T. G.; Beck, L. J.; Hauke, R. N.; Kleiman, G. M.; and James, J. H. *Auding and Reading.* Alexandria, Va.: Human Resources Research Organization, 1974.

34. Temple, Charles A.; Nathan, Ruth G.; and Burris, Nancy A. *The Beginnings of Writing.* Boston: Allyn and Bacon, Inc., 1982.

CHAPTER 6

Oral and
Silent Reading

PREVIEW

Before Part III deals with the specifics of instruction, the final chapter in Part II focuses on when reading in classrooms ought to be oral and when it should be done silently.

References have been made to the two kinds of reading. In Chapter 1, when the requirements for comprehending two sentences about girls playing Checkers are discussed, a silent reading of the text is assumed. On the other hand, when Chapter 5 proposes the use of language experience material as a means for showing children the correspondence between spoken and written language, it is taken for granted that the material will be read aloud. No matter what kind of text is used to teach the referent for "word," that objective, too, calls for oral reading, as does phonics instruction, since its objective is to teach about relationships between spellings and pronunciations. What these illustrations reinforce, then, is the need for introspective teachers who habitually ask, "*Why* am I doing what I'm doing?" When such teachers have oral reading, silent reading, or some combination of the two provides the focus for Chapter 6.

As Chapter 6 discusses oral and silent reading, an activity in which all of us participated as elementary school children will be highlighted: round robin reading. This is the practice of having one member of an instructional group read aloud while, presumably, other members follow the same text silently. Why the routine use of round robin reading year after year is highly questionable receives generous coverage in Chapter 6. What is not slighted, however, are the times when oral reading is not only desirable but even necessary.

As Chapter 6 looks at both oral and silent reading, terms are used that may be unfamiliar. All are in italics and are defined. Even though most of these terms would not be discussed with children, they are terms about which teachers and people preparing to teach should be knowledgeable.

Whether an adult reads voraciously or rarely, it is safe to predict that the question, "Do you usually read orally or silently?" would result in an identical answer: silently. In spite of the numerous purposes that call for silent reading and, in contrast, the relatively few that require oral reading, large amounts of time in school are nonetheless allotted to the latter, especially in the primary grades. Is this as it ought to be?

Before an answer is offered, the contributions that oral reading can make both to instructional programs and to readers themselves need to be identified. For purposes of discussion, the contributions are divided into three categories that have to do with instruction, sharing, and diagnosis.

ORAL READING FOR INSTRUCTION

As mentioned, attaining certain instructional objectives requires oral reading. This is the case when the meaning of "word" is the concern, for example, or when the need exists to show that spoken language has a written counterpart.

Once children know that what is said can be recorded, they are ready to learn about the ways in which written text signals the pauses and unequal stress that characterize speech and that facilitate listening comprehension. Since oral reading allows for an overt demonstration of both pauses and stress, it should be used in comprehension instruction whose intent is to impart such information as:

Comma indicates pause.
Period signals longer pause.
Underlined word, word in italics, and word in all capital letters may suggest special stress.

To be noted immediately is that what is done with punctuation should always make explicit its significance for meaning. Often, this can be facilitated with the use of contrasts. For example, when children know about the function of commas in setting off both (a) the person addressed, and (b) an appositive, identical strings of words like the following are helpful:

Tom, my son is your age.
Tom, my son, is your age.

Teacher-questions about the meaning of the two sentences, coupled with an appropriate oral reading of each, serve well in highlighting the significance of commas (and pauses) for attaining meaning from print.

Other contrasts that help point up how typographic signals as well as stressed words affect meaning are listed below.

How Commas Affect Meaning
Joan, Sue Ann, and I walked to school.
Joan, Sue, Ann, and I walked to school.

However, clear understanding takes effort.
However clear, understanding takes effort.

How a Variety of Typographic Signals Affects Meaning
His mother said who would be invited.
His mother said, "Who would be invited?"

Karen said her sister is outside playing.
"Karen," said her sister, "is outside playing."

How Stress Affects Meaning
That's my *new* car.
That's *my* new car.

I *won't* go with you.
I won't go with *you*.

Other kinds of comprehension instruction also require oral reading. One example follows.

Earlier, the children in question learned with the help of illustrations in basal reader stories that authors reveal the traits of a character in various ways: with direct descriptions, by what the character says and does, and by what others say about him or her. Now the teacher wants the children to see how authors use the silent medium of print to state or imply how characters say what they say. Having already worked on direct statements (e.g., "Joel snapped back" and "Amy whispered"), the teacher shifts to less direct information.

To get started, the teacher has the children read an unfamiliar story silently for the purpose of seeing what the outstanding traits of the protagonist are and, second, what the author did to reveal them. (The protagonist, in this case, is a man named Mr. Graves, who becomes angry at the slightest provocation and, in the end, loses what he wants most because of his quick, uncontrolled temper.)

Once the story is read and discussed, the teacher selects passages containing dialogue spoken by the protagonist when he is experiencing a variety of emotions. (In none of the examples does the author directly state how the words were spoken.) The teacher's question for each passage is, "Who can read what Mr. Graves is saying in just the way he is likely to be saying it?" Oral reading that correctly reflects the protagonist's emotional states provides evidence that the reader used content from the story to infer how the words were likely to have been spoken. Depending on the children, the teacher might request evidence from the text to support the conclusions reflected in the oral reading. The evidence may be read either silently by the group – then discussed – or orally by an individual.

This example of instruction correctly has children use information from the text to arrive at an inference about how something is said; commercially prepared teaching manuals, however, commonly recommend procedures that turn expressive oral reading into an end in itself. Contrast, if you will, the procedures just referred to with typical recommendations in teaching manuals:

> Select children to read the sentences as if they were frightened.
> How would Betty say that if she was disappointed?

What these manual recommendations reflect is an *elocutionary* concept of reading that portrays it as a performance. At such times, saying words with suitable expression is what counts. If that is not only what counts but also what wins a teacher's praise, children are likely to become confused about the nature and purpose of reading. Right from the beginning, then, teachers must do whatever is possible to show that reading is a *cognitive* process that is concerned, not with giving a message, but with getting or constructing one.

ORAL READING AS A MEDIUM FOR SHARING

Once a reader does construct an author's message, he or she may want to share it with others. Obviously, this requires oral reading. Not to be forgotten, either, is that certain kinds of material were written as much for their sound as for their sense and are fully appreciated (much as if they were music) only when read aloud. Some might say, for example, that "silent poetry" is a contradiction in terms.

Since oral reading done for the purpose of sharing should not be overlooked when plans are made for the time in a day's schedule that is allotted to reading, additional comments about that function follow.

Requirements for Oral Reading as a Medium for Sharing

Whenever oral reading is done to communicate to other people, teachers should make sure that two requirements are met. To begin, the oral reader ought to have an audience (big or small) that has a desire, or at least a willingness, to listen. Whether a genuine audience is likely to exist depends on a combination of factors, one of which is the material being read. If it is dull or familiar, nobody should be surprised if the listeners fail to pay attention. On the other hand, if the material is something like a letter from a former classmate now residing in another city, attention is apt to be very apparent.

A second factor that affects whether an oral reader is likely to have a genuine audience is the quality of the reading. This suggests a second requirement for oral reading done to share: preparation. If what is to be read is short and simple, a quick skimming is usually sufficient. On the other hand, if the material is difficult or lengthy, adequate preparation might be a complete, careful (and silent) prereading.

Developing Effective Oral Readers

Preparation without knowing what constitutes effective oral reading is meaningless; consequently, this section focuses on what teachers can do to define and promote effective oral reading.

In any consideration of how to help students become adept communicators, it is important to keep in mind that some will never be more than minimally successful. This is so because how effectively anyone reads aloud is partially dependent on factors outside the domain of a teacher—for instance, on personality and quality of speech. This means that children who are shy or quiet or somewhat stumbling in their speech do not usually excel. Better performances come from individuals who are more aggressive or self-confident or who have a little of the "ham" in them. In this group there might even be a child who is able to read a telephone directory and make it sound interesting.

Fortunately, reading programs have no obligation to produce students who read directories with gusto. Instead, the more modest aim is to help them read orally with a moderate amount of skill. In some instances, individual children will go far beyond this goal. In other cases, they will not reach it; that is acceptable, too, because it is comprehension through the medium of silent reading that is of primary importance.

The fact that comprehension *is* what matters is not always reflected in classroom practices. Here I recall a conversation with a third-grade teacher who works with low achievers. Surprisingly, her overwhelming concern was for an effective oral delivery expressed with the complaint, "I just can't get these children to read fluently even when I have them practice reading the same material over and over again." Such a worry suggests that this teacher may hold to an elocutionary concept of reading in which success is equated with expressive oral reading. Yet with her students, who are still struggling with basic skills, such reading is like frosting on a cake—nice but not necessary.

To work on the frosting, when this seems appropriate, teachers can allow time for a number of activities, some of which are discussed here.

Reading to Children.   One assumption of this text is that good oral reading is as much caught as it is taught. This assigns importance to the occasions when a teacher reads to students because they provide a model. Ideally, the reading will demonstrate the importance of careful pronunciation and enunciation of words, appropriate volume, and an expression that succeeds in communicating feelings as well as facts. Since children always enjoy being read to – assuming appropriate material is selected and presented effectively – teachers at *all* grade levels should allow time for reading to their students on a regular basis.

To provide desirable models for oral reading, beginning teachers often find it helpful to rehearse. This practice develops confidence and also allows for sufficient acquaintance with the material that eye contact can be made with their audience from time to time. A rehearsal also frees teachers to show illustrations at appropriate times.

An interesting article by Sterl Artley (3) reminds all teachers of how students both enjoy and remember being read to. The article is based on responses from junior and senior education majors when they were asked to recall elementary school experiences in order to identify "what turned them on or off reading." After describing the bleak picture drawn by the college students' responses, Artley shifts to the positive and notes:

> The greatest number said that teachers reading to the class on any level was the thing they remembered and enjoyed most. In some cases the teacher read the opening chapter of a book or an interesting episode from it as a starter, the pupils then finishing it themselves, in some instances having to wait in turn because of the book's sudden popularity. Other teachers read a book to completion, chapter by chapter. . . . Some students reported that their teachers frequently talked about books they thought some of them might enjoy, and in other cases a teacher told about a book that she was reading for her own information or enjoyment. In this way the pupils saw that reading was important to the teacher. (3, p. 27)

Choral Reading.   In addition to reading regularly to children, another way to foster effective oral reading is with choral reading (also called *choral speaking* or *verse choirs*). For students whose potential for oral reading is diminished by shyness, choral reading can be especially effective because it allows them to forget their fears. At the same time, the repetition of words commonly found in material suitable for choral reading allows for word practice that is not tedious.

For teachers, the most important point to remember about choral reading is that it should not be treated as an end in itself. Perfect performances are fine for the theater but unnecessary in the classroom. In fact, demands for perfection may become petty, ignoring the reasons for having choral reading, which are the promotion of ability in oral reading *and* enjoyment. With the twin goals in the foreground, choral reading will be handled with an appropriate amount of seriousness.

Books are available to help teachers choose material, organize students, and plan the details of a reading (6, 17, 27). For any teacher who lacks experience with choral reading or who wants to use plays from time to time, the Benefic Press Oral Readers provide a suitable starting point. (See Figure 6.1.) They offer explicit directions and include material that ranges from a first- to a third-grade level of difficulty. The books also include other types of text that call for oral reading—riddles and tongue twisters, for instance.

Additional Ways to Provide for Practice. Three more examples of practice in reading aloud to an audience follow. All combine writing with reading.

> Prepare written descriptions of objects and scenes. Direct students in an instructional group to draw a picture that corresponds to a description. Later, each student will display his drawing and read the description. Others will be asked to listen in order to see whether all the details appear in the picture.

COMMENT: This activity illustrates how a single assignment can achieve more than one goal. First, students practice reading aloud to communicate to an audience; they also practice reading silently in order to get a mental picture, which, at times, is important for comprehension. Notice, too, that the oral reader has a chance to preread the material while the audience is given a definite purpose for listening.

> Collect wordless picture books covering a wide variety of topics.* Let individual children who are interested compose anything from brief captions to a well-developed text to go with the pictures. Later, a composer can read what he wrote while the teacher or another student displays the illustrations to the audience.

COMMENT. Reading one's own material is another type of oral reading practice. As just described, the material on some occasions might be written in connection with commercial picture books. Another possible stimulus is a student's own artwork. Either way, an audience should be available.

The third example of oral reading practice is described by an observer of a second-grade class:

> In the second grade that I visited this morning, I saw oral reading used appropriately and effectively near the end of the reading period. The teacher explained that the children had written ghost stories for Halloween and that she had discussed the need to read only a few at a time "so that they could really enjoy them." Three children were practicing in the library corner while the rest of the class and the teacher talked about the following:

*Reference 11 at the end of this chapter lists more than 100 wordless picture books.

Courtesy: The children related personal experiences at movies and concerts and described good listening.

Role of Announcer: After one child said that Johnny Carson was an announcer, the group discussed what an announcer should say (the person's name and the title of the story). An announcer was quickly chosen and went to the library area to get the necessary information from the three children.

Showing Appreciation: One child asked if they should clap at the end, which resulted in practicing "courteous" clapping. Why yelling was not the best way to show appreciation was the final topic considered.

The three readers were ready now, and their oral reading proceeded with the group's complete attention and interest. The planning session, which lasted about ten minutes, certainly succeeded in producing a genuine audience while the preparation time resulted in reading that was as effective as it could be, given the brevity of what had been written. One reader even added sound effects, which he said were meant to make his story "real spooky."

When I complimented the teacher, she said that a student teacher at some time in the past had used oral reading in this way. She added that she had learned a great deal from that student.

Some Final Comments.   To conclude the discussion of oral reading done to share, a few additional comments need to be made because of questions teachers frequently raise; for instance, "When a child is reading to others and is unable to identify a word, should I tell him what it says?" As with many other questions about teaching, the answer to this one is found in purpose and goals. Since, in this case, the reason for the oral reading is communication, the only response that makes sense is to supply the word so that the reader can move on.

A consideration of purpose also provides an answer for any teachers who wonder what to do when an oral reader misidentifies a word. If the misidentification distorts or confuses meaning, it should be corrected in a nonpunitive way. Otherwise, a correction is unnecessary.

Should it happen that one or more students frequently require help when they read aloud, it might indicate insufficient preparation. This should be discussed and remedied. It might also be that the material is too difficult, in which case a change to easier text should resolve the problem.

ORAL READING AS A MEDIUM
FOR DIAGNOSIS

Although the usual reason for reading aloud is to communicate to others, oral reading in school is sometimes used to identify a student's abilities and

Figure 6.1. *A Play for Oral Reading*

Only certain kinds of material are suitable for oral reading. This means ➤
that whenever a decision is made to have oral reading done for sharing,
thought must go to what will be read. The page shown here is from a series of
six successively more difficult books that contain material appropriate for sharing. Selections, therefore, include poems, riddles, choral readings, and plays.
Since all this oral reading is for communication, it should be preceded by silent
preparation in order to ensure an effective presentation.

You Can't Please Everybody
An Aesop Fable

Storyteller: This all happened in one walk when a man and his ten-year-old son were going to market. They took their donkey along to bring back what they might buy.

As they went on their way, they met a young woman who stopped and stood watching. She looked very cross.

Woman: Shame on you, sir! You are making that poor boy of yours walk in the hot sun. Why don't you let him ride?

Father: I guess you are right. Son, get up on the donkey. It is not right for you to be walking in this hot sun.

Son: Thank you, Father. I am hot and tired. It will feel good to ride a while.

Storyteller: So the boy got up on the donkey. Then they went on. Soon they met a lame old man. He looked crossly at the boy.

Old man: Boy, shame on you! You let your poor father walk while you ride. You are young and can walk. It is your father who should be on the donkey. It is not right for him to be walking in the hot sun.

From *Glad Sounds*, by Mildred A. Dawson and Georgianna Newman, p. 23. Benefic Press, Westchester, Illinois, 1969. Reprinted with permission of Benefic Press, Westchester, Illinois.

shortcomings. Serving that purpose, oral reading has different – in fact, opposite – requirements from what it does when the goal is communication. Now, a child should not have a chance to prepare, as the intent is to learn what he does in the act of reading. Since flaws are likely to show up, this oral reading should be done as privately as possible, preferably with only the teacher listening.

Let me now summarize requirements for two of the functions that oral reading serves:

Requirements for Oral Reading
To share: audience
              familiar material

To diagnose: privacy
              unfamiliar material

Since diagnosis is the concern of Chapter 16, it is not discussed now. Instead, the most common way in which oral reading is used in classrooms is analyzed. I refer, of course, to round robin reading. To lay the groundwork for taking a knowledgeable look at this combination of oral and silent reading, significant differences between oral reading and silent reading are discussed.

DIFFERENCES BETWEEN ORAL AND SILENT READING

Oral and silent reading are similar in some ways, dissimilar in others. Because it is the dissimilarities that are pertinent for the forthcoming discussion of round robin reading, three differences that set oral and silent reading apart need to be identified.

Vocalization

The most apparent difference between oral and silent reading is that the former is heard whereas the latter is not. The observable pronunciation of words that is the essence of oral reading is referred to as *vocalization*.

Vocalization contrasts with *subvocalization*, which is commonly present in silent reading. As the name suggests, subvocalization (also called *inner speech*) is a mental pronunciation of words that is neither heard nor seen.

Whether subvocalizing assists with comprehension is one of the many questions about reading that lacks a carefully documented answer. When Gibson and Levin (13) reviewed existing research on this topic, they noted the difficulties in studying subvocalization and the conflicting findings when it was examined. They suggested, nonetheless, that subvocalization may facilitate comprehending difficult material by focusing the reader's attention on meaning.

Frank Smith has a different hypothesis about why difficult material and an increase in subvocalization often go together (26). He says "the explanation is more likely to be that reading a difficult passage automatically reduces speed, and we have a habit of articulating individual words when we read at a speed slow enough for individual words to be enunciated" (p. 200).

Until facts about the relationships among subvocalization, difficult material, and comprehension are available, the position taken here is as follows:

1. Probably everyone subvocalizes too much, even with easy material.
2. Such subvocalization not only reduces the speed of silent reading but also is "annoying and difficult to turn off" (13).
3. Since the ability to comprehend at a reasonably fast rate is desirable, anything that may foster needless subvocalization should be avoided.
4. It is possible that the day-by-day, year-by-year practice of having children take turns reading orally while others are expected to follow the same material silently may increase subvocalization.

More is said about the final point later. For now, let's continue the discussion of differences between oral and silent reading.

Eye Movements

Before explaining how eye movements account for a second difference, let me discuss the movements themselves. To do that, some research is briefly reviewed.

Studies of Eye Movements.   When researchers first began to study reading, ideas about it were often generated from the method of introspection (18). That is, research subjects reported what was happening within themselves as they read. Based on the reports, hypotheses were formulated, some of which included hunches about eye movements. Among the latter was the notion that people's eyes sweep steadily across each line of print as they read.

Later, this conclusion was replaced by another because newly invented cameras allowed for eye movement monitoring that was both more objective and more precise.* Although cameras did not figure extensively in research until the 1920s and 1930s, initial studies using them showed that a reader's eyes stop intermittently as they move rapidly across a line (2, 5). Eye behavior is thus characterized not by a steady sweep but by stop-and-go movements. The active part is called *saccades* (sŭ cādé); the periods of inactivity are called

---

*Current research using computers verifies the ensuing description of eye movements (22, 23).

fixations. (To understand eye movements correctly, it is essential to keep in mind that each eye fixation is so brief that its duration has to be measured in milliseconds.) Research also showed that "the leaping eye" (which makes the fastest movement that occurs in a human's body) "is practically blind" (26). Consequently, "the reading of text occurs only during fixations" (23). What seems like visual continuity, then, is provided by the brain, not by the eyes.

Another characteristic identified with the more sophisticated research is that the eyes move backward on occasion. The right-to-left movement, referred to as a *regression*, has a variety of causes. In some instances, readers miss one or more words and have to return to pick them up. At other times, a person might be reading something like the following paragraph. To read it is to identify still another reason for regressions.

> The boys' arrows were nearly gone so they sat down on the grass and stopped hunting. Over at the edge of the woods they saw Henry making a bow to a little girl who was coming down the road. She had tears in her dress and also tears in her eyes. She gave Henry a note which he brought over to the group of young hunters. Read to the boys it caused great excitement. After a minute but rapid examination of their weapons they ran down the valley. Does were standing at the end of the lake making an excellent target. (4, p. 87)

The paragraph you just read was written by Guy Buswell for one of his eye movement studies. Reading it demonstrates that homographs (identically spelled words with different pronunciations and meanings) are another reason for regressions. A different but related reason is that reading involves certain expectations. When a text does not conform to them, regressive eye movements occur in order to correct what was erroneously anticipated.

Another reason for eye regressions is linked to a reader's need to move from the end of one line to the start of the next. (This essential right-to-left movement is called a *return sweep*.) If it happens that the eyes miss what is at the beginning, a return sweep is likely to be followed by one or more regressions.

One further reason for regressions relates only to oral reading — specifically, to what is called the *eye-voice span*. Before discussing that, let me synthesize this more general discussion with definitions that allow for a review of what has been said about eye movements.

> *Eye fixation:* Pause in eye movements at which time print is seen. Duration of fixations is so brief it is measured in milliseconds. (One msec. = 1/1000 of a second.)
> *Saccade:* Movement of eye from one fixation to the next. "The average length of saccades during reading is about 8–10 letter positions. . . . This is about the size of the region seen during a fixation" (23, p. 163).

Eye regression: Backward (right-to-left) movement caused by such factors as missed words, homographs, concern or confusion about meaning, and incorrect predictions.

Return sweep: The necessary right-to-left eye movement required by the start of each new line of text.

Table 6.1, which summarizes data from another study done by Buswell (5), shows that progress in silent reading is characterized by a reduced number of fixations, by shorter fixations, and by fewer regressions. (A postscript to these data is the fact that the pattern of an individual's eye movements is not the same at all times. Difficulty of material and the person's reason(s) for reading it are two factors that account for changes [22].)

Table 6.1. *Children's Eye Movements during Silent Reading at Different Grade Levels*

Grade	Average Number of Fixations per Line	Average Duration of Fixation Pauses (msec.)	Average Number of Regressive Movements per Line
1	18.6	660	5.1
5	6.9	252	1.3
11	5.5	224	0.7

Differences in Eye Movements during Oral and Silent Reading. The reference to Buswell's data noted that they were collected while subjects read silently. That was essential to mention because eye movement records for the same children reading the same material aloud (with the possible exception of the first graders) would yield noticeably different data. You should be able to predict the differences once *eye-voice span* is explained.

With oral reading, it is necessary to pronounce and carefully enunciate every word, which takes much more time than the eye requires to span the same material. The difference in rate accounts for the *eye-voice span,* which is "the number of words or letter spaces that visual processing is ahead of oral reading" (15, p. 640). The difference in the rates at which the eye and voice can deal with text naturally causes a conflict. Of necessity, the voice wins out as the eye yields (unconsciously) to the slower pace. While accommodating the voice, the eye is still active; as it waits, it wanders and regresses. Regressions "operate to reduce the separation between the eyes and the voice" (2, p. 125). The eye also fixates longer than would be the case were the reading being done silently.

All of these consequences of the eye's accommodation to the voice can be verified when eye movement records of a person reading the same material orally and then silently are compared. Predictably – at least when the reader is past the initial stage of learning to read – eye movements for oral reading show more and longer fixations and also more regressions. These findings thus indicate that eye movements for oral reading are inefficient for silent reading.

It is relevant to note in this context a conclusion reached by Roberta Golinkoff (15) after she reviewed research on comprehension: "Poor comprehenders' eye movements showed greater correspondence in oral and silent reading than did the good comprehenders' eye movements. Poor comprehenders seemed to continue laborious word-by-word reading even when reading silently" (p. 637).

Functions

The third difference between oral and silent reading to be mentioned lies in their respective functions. With silent reading, the purpose is to get or construct an author's message. Other purposes may also exist – for instance, to critique the message. Nonetheless, the first concern is to comprehend it.

In the case of oral reading, the customary function is similar to that of speaking: to communicate to one or more listeners. An effective oral presentation often indicates that the reader understands what the author says, but comprehension is not an essential requirement. What *is* necessary are correct pronunciations and phrasing, suitable volume, and appropriate expression. These aspects can be present when the oral reader does not understand everything the author has written.

IMPLICATIONS OF DIFFERENCES FOR INSTRUCTIONAL PRACTICES

The previous sections highlight differences between oral and silent reading that have to do with vocalization, eye movements, and functions. Implications of these differences for instructional programs are dealt with now in the context of round robin reading, since our own recollections of elementary school, plus data from classroom observation research (7, 8, 9, 25), support the following conclusions:

1. Round robin reading consumes a considerable amount of the time allotted to reading in primary-grade classrooms. At upper levels, it continues to be used but less frequently. When it is used with older children, they are usually the poorest readers in a class.
2. Round robin reading in which the entire class participates is common in middle- and upper-grade classrooms when social studies is taught. In this case, it is viewed as a way to cover the content of social studies textbooks.

The large amount of time spent on round robin reading, combined with the growing tendency for kindergarten programs to do what has been customarily done in first grade, suggests the need to scrutinize this particular combination of oral and silent reading. In the following sections, such scrutiny is carried on in a framework defined by the three differences between oral and silent reading identified earlier.

Round Robin Reading and Subvocalization

Regardless of the position taken on the function of subvocalization, most people would agree, based on introspection, that much of the subvocalizing that goes on in silent reading results in little more than needlessly slow rates — plus annoyance. If that is so, what must be taken seriously is the likelihood that the habitual practice of having children follow silently what another is reading aloud is encouraging the silent followers to pronounce mentally the words they are hearing. Or, said differently, a regular use of round robin reading is likely to foster what nobody wants in children's silent reading: purposeless subvocalization.

Round Robin Reading and Eye Movements

The possible connections between round-robin reading and excessive subvocalization have not yet been formally studied, but one researcher did look into the effect of round robin reading on eye movements. Luther Gilbert (14) reported a study, entitled "Effect on Silent Reading of Attempting to Follow Oral Reading," whose findings have been neither supported nor questioned as subsequent research was never done.

Gilbert studied children in grades 2 through 6 by photographing their eye movements while they read silently and, next, while they followed silently what another subject was reading aloud. (Gilbert deliberately chose oral readers with varying abilities.) When the two sets of eye movement records were compared, predictable differences were found. Eye movements for the silent reading that was accompanied by oral reading showed more fixations and regressions than did the silent reading done independently. As expected, the fixations were longer. It was also shown that the poorer the quality of the oral reading, the poorer (that is, the less efficient) were the eye movements of the subjects who were following the material silently. The latter finding prompted Gilbert to write, "The data are unmistakable in condemning the routine practice of requiring silent readers to follow the oral reading of poor and mediocre readers" (14, p. 621). Since observations in classrooms uncover a paucity of excellent oral reading when around-the-group oral reading takes place (7, 8, 9), Gilbert's data offer a second reason to question the day-by-day use of round robin reading.

Round Robin Reading in Relation to Function

The primary purpose of reading is to comprehend, which is usually accomplished more easily with silent reading. In contrast, the usual goal of oral reading is to communicate the content of a piece of text to other people. Keeping the two functions in mind, let's take yet another look at round robin reading, both when it is preceded by a silent reading of the text and when it is not.*

When silent reading does not come first, the logical reason for round robin reading is comprehension. However, why a silent-oral combination is more likely than silent reading to achieve that goal is unclear, especially when it is remembered that the oral reading is likely to be a halting, listlike rendition of a text that bears little relationship to the spoken language with which children are familiar. For that reason, the oral reading commonly heard during round robin reading may obscure rather than elucidate meaning.

Even though the oral reading is usually better when the selection *was* read silently beforehand, the reason to have oral reading under these circumstances is hardly obvious, except when certain parts of the selection are read aloud for such specific purposes as clarifying or verifying a point, identifying a sentence that explains a word's meaning, recalling a vivid mental image, finding examples of what was taught recently (for example, the function of commas in setting off appositives), pointing out the clue that suggested a particular outcome, and so on.

What we have, then, is another reason to question the routine use of round robin reading: It fails to make distinctions between the respective functions of silent and oral reading.

REASONS FOR CONTINUED USE OF ROUND ROBIN READING

The fact that round robin reading has received much criticism over a long period of time (1, 18, 21) should hardly come as a surprise, given the kinds of possible consequences just identified. In light of those consequences, what may be puzzling is the persistent presence of round robin reading in classroom after classroom. Undoubtedly, unexamined habits is one reason for its longevity. Another reason is teachers' unexamined dependence on basal reader manuals, which continue not only to encourage round robin reading but also to support an elocutionary concept of reading. One first-grade manual, for example, after suggesting that a selection with little content be

---

*Although teaching manuals typically recommend that silent reading come first, teachers do not always follow the suggestion (7).

read orally twice, states: "The major emphasis during the oral reading period should be placed on reading the text with the voice intonations—emphases, pauses, and inflections—called for by the situation in the story" (10, p. 24). This point of view may explain why it was not unexpected in one study to hear a fourth-grade subject say that the most important reason for reading her basal textbook was "to learn to say all the words right and with expression" (29, p. 351).

When questioned, teachers have their own explanations for scheduling round robin reading. The most common ones are examined now in a reason-response format.

Reason: If I do not have the children read a selection aloud, how will I know whether they are remembering the new vocabulary?

Response: Monitoring word identification ability is important, but what any child remembers can be uncovered during round robin reading only when he has a turn to read aloud. Since that usually is done with a brief passage that may include neither new nor troublesome words, reliable conclusions are ruled out. Because teachers do need to know which words are or are not being retained, alternative ways for learning about word identification abilities are considered in later chapters.

Reason: Expression tells me whether the oral reader is comprehending.

Response: This claim is common but unfounded, as an effective oral delivery may be little more than expressive word naming (12). A related problem is that early, persistent attention to expression can lead children to conclude erroneously that reading is a performing art, not a thought-getting process. When such a conclusion *is* reached, children might not comprehend even when they read silently because they do not know that is what they are supposed to do. Kenneth Goodman offers another thought about expression and comprehension. He observes:

> There are periods in the development of reading competence when oral reading becomes very awkward. Readers who have recently become rapid, relatively effective silent readers seem to be distracted and disrupted by the necessity of encoding oral output while they are decoding meaning. Ironically, then, poor oral reading performance *may* reflect a high degree of reading competence rather than a lack of such competence. (16, p. 489)

Reason: The children like round robin reading. They would object if I did not have it.

Response: Some children do seem to like round robin reading but only until they get their turn to read. After that, off-task behavior is common—which, actually, is a saving feature as the lack of attention to the text helps minimize problems related to subvocalization and inefficient eye movements. However, the lack of attention generally means that the children are attending to other matters and getting into trouble as a result. Anyone who observes round robin reading inevitably concludes that it is a potential source of discipline problems; nonetheless, it persists.

> *Reason:* Even though oral reading is not as important as silent reading, I still think children should have a chance to read aloud—especially the young ones. That is why I have round robin reading.

Response: As seen in this and other reasons cited, many teachers seem to think that the only way to allow for oral reading is to have round robin reading. Yet, as earlier sections in this chapter point out, many opportunities exist for oral reading that are free of the negative consequences likely to occur when round robin reading is used day by day and year after year.

ACCEPTABLE COMBINATIONS OF ORAL AND SILENT READING

With all the criticism directed to round robin reading, you may have concluded that the implication is to eliminate every combination of oral and silent reading. To correct that erroneous conclusion, descriptions of a few acceptable combinations bring this chapter to a close.

Read-Along Tapes

The use of read-along tapes merits initial attention; these tapes have children follow text that was recorded by a proficient oral reader. Comments—which are not more than conjecture—about this silent reading–oral reading combination follow.

1. For beginning readers who actually follow the text as it is read on the tape, this activity may help them read silently at a faster, smoother rate. (They will also get some word practice.) The oral reader will also be modeling correct phrasing, which is necessary for comprehension.
2. For more advanced readers, this watching-listening activity—if done often—might be detrimental by slowing down the rate at which they read silently.

3. With children who do not follow the text, hearing an effective reading of an interesting story may add to their desire to become better readers themselves.

Reading Plays

Reading plays is a second acceptable combination of oral and silent reading. In this case, let's assume that certain children need to improve their oral reading; their teacher thus decides to use a play to help. (See Figure 6.1.) Because the concern is oral reading and not a perfect play, the teacher bypasses memorization. Instead, she has members of an instructional group read from a script, which requires one child to read aloud while the others follow the text silently in order to be ready with their parts. For special occasions, the teacher might combine play reading with puppet making. In that case, speaking parts for the play are taped by the children, which frees them to give full attention to manipulating the puppets while the pretaped dialogue runs smoothly in the background. (Reference 28 at the end of the chapter provides directions for making various kinds of puppets: paper bag, stick, sock, finger, fist, and hand.) What is pertinent for this discussion is that dramatizations—whether simply or elaborately presented—occur infrequently and, thereby, differ from the habitual use of round robin reading that is being questioned.

Other Combinations

You might now be wondering, What about day-by-day practices? Should they ever combine oral and silent reading? Surely, but only in certain ways. To illustrate, let's say that a teacher is working with nine students. The group has just finished reading a selection silently, which might be material the teacher wrote, a story in a textbook, or, perhaps, a newspaper article. What was read does not matter; what does is how the teacher combines silent and oral reading. (It is possible, of course, that oral reading will not be used.) In this case, the teacher might decide to discuss the questions that were raised before the silent reading began. If some questions call for a subjective answer (Which paragraphs include descriptions that make you feel as if you were right at the scene?), the teacher might have individual students read aloud the passages that succeeded in transplanting them right into the scene of the story or article. But, please note, the other students just listen while the paragraphs are read.

It could turn out that even factual questions elicit different responses. Should this happen, oral reading again might be required, this time to allow for comparisons and verification. As individual children read aloud, the others listen—critically, it is hoped.

At other times, a teacher might choose to have parts of a selection read aloud in order to review what was taught earlier. For instance, if the use of italics appears in a selection to indicate the need to stress certain words, individuals might be asked to read aloud sentences that include the italicized words in order to see whether they remember the significance of the special print.

To sum up, certain circumstances do call for combinations of silent and oral reading. Such circumstances are not a daily occurrence, nor are they usually a time to require students to follow silently what another is reading aloud. To hold to such a requirement, which is the case when round robin reading occurs, is to encourage needless subvocalization and inefficient eye movements among the silent followers.

SUMMARY

Since what can be done to help children become proficient silent readers is the focus of subsequent chapters, this chapter singled out oral reading for attention.

At the start, samples of instructional objectives that require the use of oral reading were described. This was done, first, to point out one of the contributions of oral reading and, second, to reinforce the need for teachers habitually to ask themselves such questions as, "What am I trying to accomplish?" and "What is the best way to accomplish it?"

The importance of the same two questions should have remained apparent when the chapter proceeded to identify two additional contributions that oral reading makes to an instructional program. This is so because the two contributions (allows for sharing and for diagnosis) have opposite requirements. More specifically, when oral reading functions in allowing children to share a piece of text, preparation and an audience are required. On the other hand, when oral reading is the medium for diagnosis, it should be of unfamiliar material that is read under circumstances that permit maximum privacy. This indicates that indiscriminate uses of oral reading do not characterize the instructional programs of introspective teachers.

After acknowledging the three contributions of oral reading, Chapter 6 went on to make the point that the silent-oral reading combination known as round robin reading is one that needs to be considered more carefully than is usually done. To prepare for a critique of this exceedingly common activity, Chapter 6 discussed differences between oral and silent reading having to do with vocalization, eye movements, and functions. The discussion was intended to show how a frequent use of round robin reading is likely to foster what nobody wants when children read silently: needless subvocalization and inefficient eye movements.

Having criticized how round robin reading combines oral and silent reading, the chapter concluded with references to acceptable combinations of the two kinds of reading.

REVIEW

1. Questions about the habitual use of round robin reading are raised in Chapter 6. Because some of the misgivings are linked to subvocalization and eye movements, this review of the chapter starts with a request to define the following terms:

<table>
<tr><td>subvocalization</td><td>eye regression</td></tr>
<tr><td>eye fixation</td><td>eye-voice span</td></tr>
</table>

2. Using both the terms above and the information in Chapter 6 about subvocalization and eye movements, critique round robin reading from the viewpoint of children following silently what a classmate is reading aloud.

3. Neither subvocalization nor eye movements are topics to discuss with children. Why not?

4. Whenever teachers consider the possibility of scheduling oral reading, they need to ask whether its purpose will be sharing or diagnosis, as each purpose has different requirements for the oral reading. What are the requirements of each purpose?

5. Chapter 6 identifies three contributions that oral reading makes to an instructional program.
   a. Name the three. Diagnosis \ SHARING \ Instruction
   b. Keeping the three contributions of oral reading in mind, critique round robin reading from the viewpoint of the oral reader, first when the selection being read aloud was read silently beforehand and, second, when it was not.

REFERENCES

1. Adams, Marilyn J.; Anderson, Richard C.; and Durkin, Dolores. "Beginning Reading: Theory and Practice." *Language Arts* 55 (January, 1978), 19–25.
2. Anderson, Irving H., and Dearborn, Walter F. *The Psychology of Teaching Reading*. New York: Ronald Press, 1952.
3. Artley, A. Sterl. "Good Teachers of Reading—Who Are They?" *Reading Teacher* 29 (October, 1975), 26–31.
4. Buswell, Guy T. *An Experimental Study of the Eye-Voice Span in Reading.*

Supplementary Educational Monographs, No. 17. Chicago: University of Chicago Press, 1920.

5. Buswell, Guy T. *Fundamental Reading Habits: A Study of Their Development.* Supplementary Educational Monographs, No. 21. Chicago: University of Chicago Press, 1922.

6. Cullinan, Bernice E. *Literature and the Child.* New York: Harcourt Brace Jovanovich, Inc., 1981.

7. Durkin, Dolores. "Is There a Match between What Elementary Teachers Do and What Basal Reader Manuals Recommend?" *Reading Teacher* 37 (April, 1984), 734–744.

8. Durkin, Dolores. "A Six Year Study of Children Who Learned to Read in School at the Age of Four." *Reading Research Quarterly* 10 (1974–75, No. 1), 9–61.

9. Durkin, Dolores. "What Classroom Observations Reveal about Reading Comprehension Instruction." *Reading Research Quarterly* 14 (1978–79, No. 4), 481–533.

10. Durr, William K.; LePere, Jean M.; Pikulski, John J.; and Alsin, Mary Lou. *Teacher's Guide for Boats.* Boston: Houghton Mifflin Company, 1983.

11. Ellis, DiAnn W., and Preston, Fannie W. "Enhancing Beginning Reading Using Wordless Picture Books in a Cross-Age Tutoring Program." *Reading Teacher* 37 (April, 1984), 692–698.

12. Erickson, Sheryl E. *Conference on Studies in Reading.* Washington, D.C.: U.S. Department of Health, Education and Welfare, 1978.

13. Gibson, Eleanor J., and Levin, Harry. *The Psychology of Reading.* Cambridge, Mass.: MIT Press, 1975.

14. Gilbert, Luther C. "Effect on Silent Reading of Attempting to Follow Oral Reading." *Elementary School Journal* 40 (April, 1940), 614–621.

15. Golinkoff, Roberta M. "A Comparison of Reading Comprehension Processes in Good and Poor Comprehenders." *Reading Research Quarterly* 11 (1975–76, No. 4), 623–659.

16. Goodman, Kenneth S. "Behind the Eye: What Happens in Reading." In Harry Singer and Robert B. Ruddell (Eds.), *Theoretical Models and Processes of Reading.* Newark, Del.: International Reading Association, 1976.

17. Huck, Charlotte S. *Children's Literature in the Elementary School,* 3rd ed. New York: Holt, Rinehart and Winston, 1979.

18. Huey, Edmund B. *The Psychology and Pedagogy of Reading.* New York: Macmillan, 1908.

19. Johnson, Richard. "Reading Aloud—Tips for Teachers." *Reading Teacher* 36 (April, 1983), 829–831.

20. Karwoski, Arleeta O. "Practicing Oral Reading Skills." *Reading Teacher* 36 (March, 1983), 690.

21. Lewis, William D., and Rowland, Albert L. *The Silent Readers.* The John C. Winston Company, 1920.

22. McConkie, George W. "Studying the Reader's Perceptual Processes by Computer." Reading Education Report No. 34. Urbana: University of Illinois, Center for the Study of Reading, May, 1982.

23. McConkie, George W.; Hogaboam, Thomas W.; Lucas, Peter A.; Wolverton,

Gary S.; and Zola, David. "Toward the Use of Eye Movements in the Study of Language Processing." *Discourse Processes* 2 (July–September, 1979), 157–177.

24. Manna, Anthony L. "Making Language Come Alive through Reading Plays." *Reading Teacher* 37 (April, 1984), 712–717.

25. Shavelson, Richard J., and Borko, Hilda. "Research on Teachers' Decisions in Planning Instruction." *Educational Horizons* 57 (Summer, 1979), 183–189.

26. Smith, Frank. *Understanding Reading*. New York: Holt, Rinehart and Winston, 1971.

27. Sutherland, Zena; Monson, Dianne L.; and Arbuthnot, May Hill. *Children and Books*, 6th ed. Glenview, Ill.: Scott, Foresman and Company, 1981.

28. Weiger, Myra. "Puppetry." *Elementary English* 51 (January, 1974), 55–64.

29. Wixson, Karen K.; Bosky, Anita B.; Yochum, M. Nina; and Alvermann, Donna E. "An Interview for Assessing Students' Perceptions of Classroom Reading Tasks." *Reading Teacher* 37 (January, 1984), 346–352.

PART III

Instruction

Although many points have been made about instruction, the next seven chapters discuss it with considerably more specificity. To allow for specific descriptions and recommendations, the seven chapters divide instructional responsibilities into those concerned with developing reading vocabularies and others involved with connected text.

Regardless of the focus, two facts have a pervasive influence on the chapters. The first is deceptively simple: reading is comprehending. The second fact that is persistently influential is that it is senseless to teach reading in ways that discourage children from doing any. Two themes of this part, then, can be summed up by saying that the purpose of Part III is to assist teachers and persons preparing to teach to put together instructional programs that allow every child maximum opportunity not only to learn to read but also to learn to want to read.

Common sense suggests that children are more likely to attend to what is being taught or practiced if they understand the value for improving their reading. Thus, these chapters also stress the importance of teachers' taking the time to explain the relevance for reading of what they themselves do and of what they ask children to do. Admittedly, attempts to provide such explanations may sometimes make apparent the lack of relevance. Should this occur with some regularity, it may suggest that "Why am I doing what I'm doing?" is not asked often enough. A frequent lack of relevance may also be evidence of an excessive, nonselective use of commercially prepared materials.

Because nothing suggests that the use of these materials will become less common, these chapters have reproductions of some, plus commentary about them. This material is included to specify or illustrate a point and to reinforce how essential it is to be Teacher A.

Since knowledge of what needs to be taught to turn nonreaders into readers is a basic requirement for becoming Teacher A, the hope for all the chapters in Part III is that they cover the content and requirements of reading instruction in a way that is clear and helpful.

CHAPTER 7

Whole Word Methodology

PREVIEW

You will recall from an earlier chapter that David Ausubel's conception of readiness supports eclecticism for instructional programs. Applied to the development of reading vocabularies, his definition indicates the need to provide children with a variety of ways to learn words—assuming that they know what "word" means and that they understand that the oral language they know and use has a written counterpart.

When prerequisites like these exist, teachers who agree with the need for variety in methodology still must decide what method to use first, because all methods cannot be used immediately. Although beginning reading instruction is often equated with phonics—thanks to the widespread influence of commercial materials—the position in this book is that whole word methodology should be used initially for the following reasons.

As it focuses on words, whole word methodology deals with what is familiar. (This approach contrasts with phonics, which deals with such *un*familiar facts as [a] a word is composed of more than one sound; [b] a word has a beginning sound; and [c] letters stand for sounds.) A second reason is that starting with whole words allows for real reading quickly (e.g., *green grass, a cloudy day*). Not to be overlooked is that the words taught can be used later to illustrate letter-sound relationships for phonics instruction.

What about beginning methodology that concentrates on printing, thus also on writing and spelling? It is true that some young children are more interested in learning to print than in learning to read (7), but they do not constitute a majority. In addition, some children who are interested in printing do not yet have the motor coordination it requires.

For these reasons, then, the recommendation is to begin instruction by focusing on entire words and gradually to supplement that teaching with attention to phonics and printing in a way described in Chapter 5 and explained in greater detail in Chapter 9.

This chapter discusses whole word instruction, answering such questions as:

1. What words should be taught initially?
2. Exactly what is done to teach a word?
3. What impedes word learning?
4. What fosters permanently correct responses to words?

Since nonstandard dialects may affect how children respond to text, that topic is also covered.

Whole word methodology is the direct identification of entire words. To illustrate, a child is outdoors walking with his father, sees a sign, and asks, "What's that word?" In response the father says, "Stop." Or, to take another illustration, September is printed on a chalkboard in school and the children are told, "This is the name of the new month. This word is 'September.' " In both cases, whole words were identified; thus, whole word methodology was the teaching procedure, used first by a parent and then by a teacher.

The idea that telling a child what a word is constitutes a teaching procedure does not seem to be universally known. This is suggested by the fact that in interviews with parents of children who learned to read before starting school, they commonly expressed the belief that nobody had taught their children (7). It was not unusual, therefore, to hear such comments as, "He just learned by himself." Some parents had even concluded that reading is a natural, spontaneous ability for some children. Yet, when questioned further, these same parents recalled how often they had spent time conversing with their youngsters, how the children had asked so many questions, and how they themselves had tried to take the time to answer them. Not surprising was that "What's that word?" was one of the most common queries as the children got older. As would also be expected, other instances of whole word learning originated in sources like television commercials, in which words flashed on the screen were read by a narrator.

In addition to being called "whole word methodology," naming words is also referred to as a sight method. This description reflects the expectation for it: Children will be able to read words on sight without going through any conscious type of analysis. Another synonym is look-say methodology, reflecting the assumption that its use will allow children to say (or think of) a word as soon as they look at it.

Regardless of the label, it appears that anyone with a little reading ability could use this method. For that reason, some explanation about why an entire chapter deals with whole word methodology might be in order.

One reason is that telling a child once what a word is rarely leads to permanent learning. Because nothing less than permanent learning should result from school instruction, it is imperative that the professional teacher know how to foster permanent recall of words. This accounts for the discussion of such topics as cues and practice in the chapter.

Because children must learn many more words than those they ask about, the professional also needs to know how to select words and, further, what to do to interest children in learning them. These requirements are other reasons for a chapter on whole word methodology.

READING VOCABULARIES

Since the intent of whole word methodology is to bring reading vocabularies into existence, a brief discussion of these vocabularies is warranted.

A person's *reading vocabulary* is all the words she or he is able to identify in their written form. Within the context of an instructional program, *identification* is usually defined (explicitly or implicitly) as knowing what a written word says and means. Even though both pronunciation and meaning are stressed in school, it should nonetheless be remembered that reading (comprehending) only requires an understanding of meaning. More specifically, if a person does not know the pronunciation for *quay* but does know what it means, he or she can still read a sentence like *He will meet them at the quay*. On the other hand, if the same individual can pronounce *solo* (with the help of phonics) but does not know its meaning, that person's understanding of *She sang a solo for the first time* is restricted. The fact that meanings are more important for reading than are pronunciations is something teachers need to keep in mind as they allot time to the various dimensions of an instructional program.

SELECTING WORDS

When whole word methodology is used at the beginning, three factors need to be considered for word selections: interests, usefulness, and instructional materials.

Interesting Words

With all that has been said in earlier chapters about the importance of capitalizing on interests, it should go without saying that words chosen at the start should include some that relate to the children. Selections, then, might include *September, boys, girls*, and *school*. Apparently, many teachers of young children think that words like *door* and *table* should be taught early, since labeling objects in a classroom is a common practice. What about this?

If at the start of the year *and in the presence of the children*, a teacher prints some labels, reads them, and then attaches them to appropriate objects, the children might be learning – presuming this is not already known – that the unfamiliar looking marks we call words refer to what is familiar. In this context, labeling is a way of demonstrating that written language is not as foreign as it might first appear.

Another purpose labeling might serve relates to the topic of this chapter: word learning. Consequently, it is fitting to ask whether children will be able to read *door, table, pencils*, and so on when the labels appear elsewhere – in a book, for instance. In this case, the answer depends on what a teacher does with the labels in addition to displaying them on the objects they name. If the decision is to do nothing, it is likely that only a few children will be able to read *door, table,* and *pencils* for reasons that have to do with what is referred to in learning theory as the principle of least effort. Applied to labeling, the principle suggests that children are much more likely to attend to the objects than to the more demanding (and less interesting) details of the words that are their names. Not to be forgotten, either, is that labels displayed too long eventually blend in with the total classroom environment, becoming, if not invisible, not eye- or mind-catching either. This means that teachers who want labels to get into reading vocabularies must plan ways for the children to name them when they are not affixed to the objects. (When affixed, they should be printed in lower-case letters.)

Whether early vocabulary selections are *table* and *door*, or *school* and *September*, making choices with children's interests in mind indirectly reflects an important guideline: At the beginning, words ought to be selected from those in the children's oral vocabulary.

To show that there are exceptions to every rule, let me mention what occurred in a first grade when the teacher happened to use "huge" to describe a building. Immediately one child inquired, "What does 'huge' mean?" The teacher explained, then printed it on the board along with other words that the children could read: *tall, big, fat.* As a result of the attention to both the meaning and written form of *huge*, two consequences were possible for the children. First, "huge" was added to their oral vocabulary and, second, it ended up in their reading vocabulary, too. In spite of the potential value of occurrences like this one, the best practice to follow, at least most of the time, is to select for a reading vocabulary only words whose meanings are familiar. Because initial success is critically important to future success, one further recommendation is to concentrate on words that are of special interest. Later, when children have experienced the joy of success and have also developed some self-confidence, then it is time to start introducing words that may not be appealing but are basically important because they are so common.

Useful Words

Even if a teacher of beginners started out with the resolution to select only words that interested children, she would soon have to face the fact that words with little or no appeal are necessary because of their frequent appearance in text. Three categories of such words are described next.

Function Words.   Certain words must be taught almost immediately because even the briefest of phrases and sentences require their use. Since they function in forming the structure of a phrase or sentence, they are referred to as *function*, or *structure*, words. Function words, which have grammatical rather than lexical (dictionary) meaning, are prepositions (e.g., *off, over, at*);

articles (e.g., *the, a, an*); conjunctions (e.g., *but, and, or*); and parts of the verb *to be* (e.g., *were, been, am*). Although hardly interesting, some function words need to get attention early to allow children to read connected text. Other function words will be necessary later—for instance, *however* and *nonetheless*.

Service Words.   Anyone's list of useful words is bound to have function words; other words that are meaningful in and of themselves (e.g., names of colors) will also be included because they, too, show up regularly in written material. One of the earliest efforts to collect such words was made by Edward Dolch (6). Figure 7.1 displays his well-known list of 220 *service words*. (They are called "service" words because their frequent appearance in print makes knowing them highly serviceable or useful.)

Subsequent to the work of Dolch, other reading specialists continued the task of identifying high-frequency words (12, 17). Even though factors like cultural change and the availability of computers result in slightly different lists, the one compiled by Dolch has been reproduced because, first, it is the best known and, second, it is the standard against which more recent lists are compared. As one would expect, Dolch's list (and those of others) includes function words like *as, but, for, if, of, so, the, to*, and *upon*, as well as words such as *go, we, one, little, good*, and *ask*. Whatever the list, the point is that certain words appear frequently in print, which means they should be learned both early and well.

Words in Written Directions.   If a classroom is to function smoothly and efficiently, children must be able to cope with written directions so they can work alone while their teacher spends uninterrupted time with individuals or subgroups. This necessity suggests that other words ought to get into children's reading vocabularies as soon as possible. These words include *color, make, draw, read, line, under*, and *around*.

Words in Required Textbooks

Until something like a basal reader becomes a required textbook, it is only necessary for teachers to consider the two factors that have been discussed (interests and usefulness) when selections are made for reading vocabularies. When required materials do exist, their vocabularies naturally have to be taken into account. Since words in something like a basal reader are selected with children in general in mind, the meanings of some words may be unfamiliar to particular children. Whenever that is the case, meaning should be clarified before studied attention goes to the written form of a word.

Typically, basal manual suggestions for teaching new words are flawed in two ways. For one thing, the same procedures are recommended repeatedly.

a	could	had	may	said	under
about	cut	has	me	saw	up
after		have	much	say	upon
again	did	he	must	see	us
all	do	help	my	seven	use
always	does	her	myself	shall	
am	done	here		she	very
an	don't	him	never	show	
and	down	his	new	sing	walk
any	draw	hold	no	sit	want
are	drink	hot	not	six	warm
around		how	now	sleep	was
as	eat	hurt		small	wash
ask	eight		of	so	we
at	every	I	off	some	well
ate		if	old	soon	went
away	fall	in	on	start	were
	far	into	once	stop	what
be	fast	is	one		when
because	find	it	only	take	where
been	first	its	open	tell	which
before	five		or	ten	white
best	fly	jump	our	thank	who
better	for	just	out	that	why
big	found		over	the	will
black	four	keep	own	their	wish
blue	from	kind		them	with
both	full	know	pick	then	work
bring	funny		play	there	would
brown		laugh	please	these	write
but	gave	let	pretty	they	
buy	get	light	pull	think	yellow
by	give	like	put	this	yes
	go	little		those	you
call	goes	live	ran	three	your
came	going	long	read	to	
can	good	look	red	today	
carry	got		ride	together	
clean	green	made	right	too	
cold	grow	make	round	try	
come		many	run	two	

Figure 7.1. *The Dolch Basic Sight Vocabulary of 220 Service Words*

Used repeatedly, they lead to dull routine. The second flaw is the insufficient amount of attention manuals give to new words. However, since the typical manual offers too many recommendations both for oral reading and for post-reading interrogation, teachers can easily achieve a better balance by adding to what is done with new words and reducing (or deleting) proposals for oral reading and comprehension assessment questions. What is added can sometimes take the form of flashcard practice with words and short phrases printed on cards cut in the shape of something that relates to whatever the selection is about (16). Bone-shaped cards for a story about a dog and fish-shaped cards for one about fishing illustrate possibilities. As Judith Martin states, "Almost every story has a good symbol embedded in it. And you (the teacher) won't forget which flashcards belong with a particular story" (p. 118).

Exposure Words

As previous chapters indicate, the philosophy of this textbook includes the contention that providing children with opportunities to learn words in natural settings will lead to larger reading vocabularies than would be the case were such opportunities unavailable. Exposing children to *huge* at the time that it puzzled a child exemplified both an opportunity and an *exposure word*.

Unlike words that are preselected for special attention, exposure words take on significance because of what is being said or done. Sometimes they are featured alone, as was *huge*; sometimes, with other words. An example of the latter occurred in a kindergarten in which the teacher and eleven children were naming and discussing objects that included a spoon, cup, plate, and napkin. Eventually, all the objects were displayed, labeled, and grouped according to function. In this instance, children were exposed to, and thus had the opportunity to learn, such words as *cup, glass*, and *for drinking*.

Other examples of exposure words have been seen elsewhere. One first-grade teacher, for instance, had a Guess Center featuring weekly contests explained by signs like *Can you guess how many beads are in this jar?* or *Is there more water in Bottle A or Bottle B or Bottle C?* There also are the practical exposure words that tell children what is in various drawers or that warn *Don't feed the gerbil!* or that suggest *Look but don't touch*. In all these cases, children are exposed to text in meaningful ways, which is a desirable goal in and of itself. At the same time, opportunities exist for their reading vocabularies to grow.

A Summary

All the sources for words that have now been discussed are listed below.

**SELECTING WORDS
FOR A BEGINNING READING VOCABULARY**

Deliberately Selected Words
1. Interesting words
2. Useful words
   a. function words
   b. service words
   c. words in written directions
3. Words in required textbooks
Exposure Words

TEACHING WORDS

Exposure words may or may not be learned; the expectation for deliberately selected words, however, is that they do end up in children's reading vocabularies. How this can be accomplished, whether the child is a beginner or a more advanced reader, is explained in following sections of this chapter.

New Words and Contexts

Whether new words ought to be introduced alone (*road*) or in the company of other words (*on the road*) is a common concern. Even though the question has to do with verbal contexts, nonverbal ones should not be excluded from consideration as they often make verbal contexts unnecessary. This was illustrated most dramatically in a classroom that was observed on the morning after a tornado had struck the community. Correctly, the teacher was writing and discussing words like *tornado* and *demolish*—and without the help of additional words. In this case, recent experiences provided all the context required to make the words meaningful. But what about verbal contexts? When are they necessary?

Function Words and Contexts. A verbal context is always required for function words, since their meaning derives from their relationship to other words that have meaning in and of themselves. Words that are themselves meaningful are called *content words*. Content words are nouns, verbs (with the exception of the verb *to be*), adjectives, and adverbs.

With function words that are prepositions, phrases are natural contexts. Other function words, such as connectives, call for something else (e.g., *up and down, pie or cake*). How one teacher introduced the function word *and* in an unusual but highly effective context merits a description.

She started by praising members of an instructional group for all the color words they had succeeded in learning. While the children recalled the colors, she wrote (and read) their names in a way that allowed for extra space between each one and that stretched the words clear across the chalkboard— to the great delight of the onlookers. The teacher then started to reread the words, this time adding "and" between the first and second colors. Immediately she stopped to observe, "Oh, oh. I put in a word that isn't here. Did anyone hear the word I said that isn't on the board?" Immediately the children responded, "And!" The teacher continued "If I'm going to say 'and', I had better write it. Watch me write 'and.'" Each time it was written between two color words, the children named, spelled, and renamed it. Finally, the entire line of words was read with great enthusiasm.

Now it was time for more practice that made use of cards prepared ahead of time. They displayed contexts like the following.

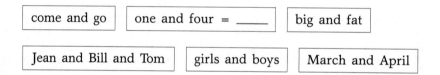

At the end, *and* was printed alone, then read, spelled, and read again. And so a very interesting presentation of an uninteresting function word came to a close.

It should be noted that the importance of meaning for reading is not the only reason for introducing function words in contexts. Another is that they receive so little stress in oral language (e.g., "black 'n blue") that when one is named apart from a context ("and") children might not even be aware it is a word they use repeatedly in their own speech. For two important reasons, then, function words ought to be introduced to children in a context that might be as brief as *black and blue* or as long as a sentence.

What can happen when contexts are absent was revealed during a classroom visit. The teacher wrote "am" on the board (this was a new word), then read it for the group she was instructing. It happened that her pronunciation of "am" was similar to the name of the letter *m*, which generated a puzzled expression on one girl's face as well as the comment, "Mrs. ____, that's not just *m*. That's *a* and *m*."

When teachers do use contexts, words other than the one being introduced ought to be in the children's reading vocabularies. If "or" is presented in the context *up or down*, for example, the words *up* and *down* should be familiar. This guideline indicates that some content words need to be taught before any attention goes to function words. This makes sense for another reason. Content words are more interesting, thus are easier to learn.

Content Words and Contexts.   As has been demonstrated, contexts are not always necessary when content words are taught. What can happen, however, when contexts are omitted was illustrated during another classroom visit. In this case, the new word was "find." After writing and naming it, the teacher requested examples of sentences that included *find*. The first sentence was very revealing, for with great pride a boy suggested, "It is a fine day."

That this kind of confusion is common at all grade levels is verified almost daily in classrooms. Witness the following examples:

- A series of stories in a basal reader dealt with the theme "South of the Border." This prompted the teacher to ask, "What does the word 'border' mean?" One child immediately volunteered, "It means somebody who lives with you." "No," the teacher said, "that's a different word." Another child then proposed, "It means when you get bored. Like when you're tired of playing the same game."
- When the meaning of "cone" was requested in another classroom, one child explained, "It's like when you comb your hair."
- In another room, the content word getting attention was "bold." Asked for its meaning, one child said, "It's like when you go bowling." Disagreeing, another child explained, "No, it's like when a man doesn't have any hair on the top of his head."
- When a fifth-grader was asked for the meaning of "prism," he explained, "It's where they keep the crooks."

These children's explanations were unexpected; so, too, was their teachers' failure to write anything on the board even though *visual* comparisons were clearly called for:

border	cone	bold	prism
boarder	comb	bowl	prison
bored		bald	

It should be emphasized that letting children see a word is important even when only one word is getting attention. The importance was reinforced in a recent third-grade observation, during which time the word "ancestor" was discussed but never shown. Later, when the children were writing, one girl spelled it *auntsister*.

Inherent in all these examples is an important message for teachers: Work close to a chalkboard so that words can be written, compared, discussed, and seen. Why seeing homonyms and homographs in a context is always necessary can be explained with definitions. *Homonyms* are words that have more than one meaning (e.g., *park, dress, run*). Introducing them in a context, therefore, is necessary to reveal the intended meaning. *Homographs*, which are words with identical spellings but different pronunciations and meanings (e.g., *tear*, *wind, does*), should be introduced in a context in order to indicate the pronunciation, which, in turn, will suggest the meaning.

Remembering Words: Distinctive Features

When children do not know about letter-sound relationships or word structure, all that is available to help them remember a word is the sequence of its letters. That is why it is helpful at the beginning to have children spell words, since this fixes attention on sequence. (The recommendation assumes that their letter-naming ability is automatic. Otherwise, attention will be divided between trying to remember the word and trying to recall the names of the letters that compose it.)

Using contrasts is another way to encourage attention to the distinctive features of words. This means that if *talk* is a new word, a teacher might print one of the following lists on a chalkboard, once *talk* had been identified and discussed.

take	take
talk	talk
	tall

Contrasts like the ones shown above help solve two problems that account for word-learning deficiencies: (a) ignoring letter order, and (b) attending only to the beginning of a word.

When *talk* is a new word, relevant questions about *talk* and *take* include: "Which of these words is 'talk', the first or the second one? . . . Yes, the second word is 'talk'. How did you know the second word says 'talk'? . . . To be sure that you'll remember this word when you see it again, would you say it and spell it? . . . What word did you just spell?"

All this can be summarized as follows:

ONE PROCEDURE FOR TEACHING NEW WORDS WITH WHOLE WORD METHODOLOGY

1. Show the new word either alone or in a context.
2. If a context is used, read it.
3. Call the children's attention to the new word. Name it. Have the children name, spell, and name it again.
4. Make certain its meaning is known, in particular, the meaning it has in the selection in which it occurs.
5. If the new word resembles other words, list one or more of them with the new word. Talk about similarities and differences.
6. Erase all the words except the new one. Have the children name, spell, and name it again.

This procedure is productive, but it should not be used with every word or with every child. To do so invites monotony. The procedure also overlooks children who remember a word forever after it has been named once or twice. No matter what procedure is followed, however, one detail is always essential: Be sure children are looking at the new word *at the time* it is being named. Neglect of this important detail is one reason so much instruction with words, whether offered to young or older students, is either inefficient or nonproductive. The importance of attention at the right time also suggests that new words should not be presented to as many as an entire class, because with a large number of students it is impossible to get everyone to attend when attention is critical.

LEARNING WORDS: CUES

As mentioned, one apparent distinctive feature of a word is the sequence of its letters. Sequence, for example, accounts for the fact that *tap, pat*, and *apt* are three different words. This essential feature is the reason different-looking symbols such as *young, Young*, and *YOUNG* require the same response. For word learning, then, letter sequence is a relevant cue. (Other relevant cues are letter-sound relationships and word structure, topics discussed in Chapters 9, 10, and 11.)

A *cue* is what is used to help establish a connection between a given word (stimulus) and its name (response). Or, to put it somewhat differently, some aspect (cue) of a written word is selected as a prompt for what should be said (or thought) in response to it. If what is selected fixes the correct response permanently, it is a *relevant* cue. If what is selected (consciously or unconsciously) gives only temporary assistance and eventually fosters confusion and erroneous responses, it is an *irrelevant* cue. Since time in classrooms is sometimes spent on irrelevant cues, they are discussed further with examples.

One observed teacher was trying to help children learn *red, blue*, and *green*. Thinking it would facilitate the learning, she printed *red* with red chalk, *blue* with blue, and *green* with green. Predictably, the children had no trouble "reading" the three words. Equally predictable, however, is that any student who had trouble remembering *red, blue*, and *green* before the colorful display would experience the same difficulty when the words were subsequently found in books, or written with white chalk or black ink. Why? The teacher used an irrelevant cue (color) to establish connections between stimuli (words) and correct responses to them.

More recently, a similar misuse of color was found in a basal reader workbook. One page, described as providing practice in reading two new words, required children to read sentences that contained the words. Unexpectedly, each time one of the words appeared in a sentence, it was printed in red. Whenever the other new word appeared, it was shown in blue. All the children had to do, therefore, was to attach a response to a color. (Not every use of color, it should be noted, exemplifies irrelevant cues. Having children underline color words with the color they name is one good way to learn whether the children can read these words. With a sentence like *The wagon is yellow and black*, correct [and informative] responses would be a yellow line under *yellow* and a black one under *black*.)

Other kinds of irrelevant cues have also been seen in classrooms. In one first grade, for example, a teacher said of *look*, "This word is easy to remember. It says 'look', and it has two eyes in the middle – just what you and I use when we look at something." What about this help? It would be relevant only if the one word in our language that had "two eyes in the middle" were *look*. As it is, the help offered was an irrelevant cue because of words like *took*, *tool*, and *boot*. (Interestingly, soon after the teacher made the comment about *look*, one child responded to it with "see.") What another teacher said when she was teaching *monkey* also highlighted an irrelevant cue. She explained that it was an easy word to remember because, like a monkey, it had a tail at the end. Unfortunately, so do *donkey* and *money*.

A student teacher used another type of irrelevant cue when she was teaching *up* and *down*. She began by printing *up* at the top of a chalkboard and *down* at the bottom. Then, as she named the two words, she assured the children that they would have no trouble remembering them because of where she had placed the words – and they didn't, as long as *up* was up and *down* was down.

It wasn't too many years ago that commercially prepared materials routinely encouraged teachers to call attention to another type of irrelevant cue: configuration. *Configuration* is the shape, or contour, of a word. For example:

Like other irrelevant cues, configuration might offer children temporary assistance; however, since so many words have the same shape (*over, came; game, pain; word, work*), making shape apparent and calling children's attention to it foster confusion. In spite of that, one colorful page in a workbook provides "help" for remembering *bed* by tucking it into one:

$$\sqcap bed \sqcap$$

The problem, of course, is that many words (e.g., *bet, bell, led, tub*) have the same configuration.

Children also use irrelevant cues. I recall one kindergartner who readily volunteered information about her strategy for remembering *Alexander*, the name of a book in the classroom library. She explained, "I always know that word because it has an *x*." In this instance, using *x* as a prompt for a correct response might serve this child well for some time because, for a long time, *Alexander* may be the only long word she will have to learn that has an *x* in it. Nonetheless, the use of one letter in a nine-letter word is depending on a shaky if not an irrelevant cue for its identification.

Word length is yet another type of irrelevant cue selected by children. Its use explains why a word like *something*, often taught early along with much shorter words, is so easily remembered—at least for a while.

Other irrelevant cues are pictures—for instance, illustrations in basal readers. Because basal manuals sometimes direct teachers to have children "look at the picture" when they cannot recall a word, this use of pictures requires further discussion, which can begin with a reference to what was heard in a classroom. A child who was reading aloud could not recall the word *toys*, so his teacher suggested, "Look at the picture." (On the page was a picture of a girl playing with some toys.) Immediately, the child said "toys" not even looking at the written symbol.* It seemed safe to predict that should *toys* be encountered again by this student, the same problem would occur because the cue offered (picture content) was not only irrelevant but also outside the word itself.

A negative response to an unfortunately common practice is not meant to deny the importance of pictures for instruction. As noted, pictures serve such valuable functions as specifying the meanings of words and encouraging children to talk and to write. Used as cues for word naming, however, they cause problems.

Two other kinds of irrelevant cues, which are also outside the word itself, can be identified with teachers' comments. I refer to one like, "Here [pointing to the word *chair*] is the new word we had yesterday." In this case, children do not even need to look at *chair*; all that is necessary is to recall the word introduced the day before. Another irrelevant cue is offered by the teacher who, after writing the troublesome word *what* on the board, asks, "Does this say 'that' or 'what'?" in a way giving such stress to "what" that even the slowest in the group is quick to respond correctly.

---

*The frequency of this behavior is great enough to warrant repetition of an earlier reminder: Be sure children look at a word *when* it is being named. Teachers who use round robin reading have special need to keep this in mind because, when they help an oral reader with a word, the child commonly looks at them rather than at the word.

WORD PRACTICE

When children are encouraged to use relevant cues and when sufficient practice in naming words is provided, most find themselves with constantly growing reading vocabularies. Before samples of word practice are described, questions related to practice will be considered.

How Well Should Words Be Learned?

Ideally, a word should be learned so well that the time lapse between a reader's seeing it and identifying it is virtually zero. Such instantaneous identifications are desirable because "When decoding can be accomplished with no attention (that is, automatically), attention is available for purposes of comprehension" (27, p. 85). *Automaticity* is the term often used in connection with instantaneous, "unthinking" identifications (26).

Since instantaneous identifications free readers to attend to the meaning of text, it is important for teachers to know the difference between word identification and word recognition. (For purposes of this discussion, we will assume that the meaning of all the words referred to is known but that their visual form is unknown.)

Word *identification* refers to a reader's ability to name a word without assistance except for the help that derives from the word's spelling. In contrast, word *recognition* is the ability to name a word with help.

To illustrate the two kinds of responses, let's consider the word *cold*. Children who can identify *cold* are able to read it whether it appears alone or in a context such as *It is cold in winter*. In contrast, children who are only able to recognize *cold*—probably because it has not been practiced enough—can name it when it appears in helpful contexts or, for instance, when somebody such as a teacher says, "This word means the opposite of 'hot'."

Since help in the form of various prompts is not always available, word recognition is not always sufficient for reading. In spite of that, recognition is what is typically evaluated in workbooks, competency tests, and standardized tests. A list of several words, for example, may be placed beside a picture; the task is to underline or circle the word that goes with its content. In another type of assessment, a number of words will be in a box, and the child is directed to underline or circle the word named by the teacher or test administrator. As it happens, however, readers do not start with named words from which they make a selection. Instead, they begin with written symbols they have to name, and doing the naming is word identification. (Please take the time to examine Figure 7.2 and the commentary about it.)

Because of the significance of word identification for comprehension, a sizable sight vocabulary (all the words that can be identified "on sight") is one of the most important instructional outcomes in the beginning years. In spite of that, the highly influential basal reader programs give surprisingly little attention to new vocabulary and practice. One possible consequence is incorrect conclusions about reading problems. More specifically, teachers end up thinking that certain children have comprehension deficiencies when, in fact, the basic problem lies with insufficient sight vocabularies. Another consequence is children who are turned off by reading because every time they attempt it, they have to struggle so hard with essential words that they are unable to comprehend even a brief piece of text. The unrewarded efforts of such children are highly visible by second and third grade because by then, many unknown and uncertain words have been allowed to accumulate.

Perhaps this is the time to re-emphasize what contributes to comprehension — and to a reader's self-confidence. (See Figure 7.3.) What moves a word from one level of "knowing" to the next is practice. At the early levels, practice should be supervised to allow for immediate feedback and to prevent children from learning incorrect responses. Once children can identify a word, unsupervised practice can be used for the purpose of speeding up responses.

How Much Practice Is Required?

Even if children were the same in word-learning ability, varying amounts of practice would be required to learn particular words for reasons such as the following. When children are just starting to learn to read, vocabularies often grow quickly with relatively little practice. This is especially true when the words being introduced are highly discriminable from each other. To illustrate, if the first words are *September, me, puppy*, and *white*, there might be few problems in recalling them because such observations by the child as "The long word is 'September'," "The little one says 'me'," "The one with all the *p*'s is 'puppy'," and "The word that starts with *wh* says 'white' " are helpful even though they focus on insufficient cues. As more words are introduced, however, such cues diminish in value. Now, *white* might be confused with *what, happy* seems to look like *puppy*, and *October* is almost as long as *September*. All this points up that the amount of practice required is affected both by the words to which the children have already been introduced and by the type of cues they used to help recall those words.

Since letter-sound relationships are a source of relevant cues, the amount of practice required for learning words is also affected by a child's knowledge of phonics. With the words mentioned in the previous paragraph, knowing about letter-sound relationships would reduce confusion and, at the same time, reduce the amount of necessary practice. The importance of such relationships for learning words explains why phonics should be introduced as soon as possible.

As mentioned, a word with a familiar meaning can be counted on to be easier to learn than one that is little more than a sound. Still easier are words whose referents are not only familiar but also of interest. The significance of

Figure 7.2. *Word Recognition*

The format of the workbook page shown in Figure 7.2 should be familiar, as ◀ publishers of reading materials have been assessing word recognition in this way for a long time. This means they have also been fostering inflated estimates of reading vocabularies for an equally long time.

Even though identification, not recognition, is what contributes to reading ability, identification is tested much less frequently. One obvious reason is that assessment like that shown in Figure 7.2 can be done with a group. A group procedure that begins to approach word identification might show in a box such words as *red, grow, brown*, and *yellow*, for which the directions are: "Read all the words in the box. Circle the word that is not a color." This procedure has the advantage of promoting attention to meaning as well as approximating word identification.

If it happens that close attention to spellings and sounds is what a teacher is interested in promoting, a box of words may show a list composed of *like, lake, look* and *luck*, or of *chop, shot, drop*, and *blot*. Even though directing children to draw a circle around "lake" or around "drop" is still only word recognition, it is nonetheless fostering what the teacher had intended: paying close attention to sounds and spellings. Once again, "Why am I doing what I'm doing?" is the question to ask when appropriate assessment procedures are the goal.

170

1. reads bed (books) is	2.(Linda) to pigs one	3. plays (has) cooks likes	4. cook in looks (Jim)
5.(big) Pat wolf for	6.(are) the Meg three	7. little sees two (fun)	8. bed (little) house Don
9. book likes (a) Meg	10. Jim (book) cook pig	11. are two plays (helps)	12.(Pedro) Don wolf in
13. one (look) fun has	14. bear for (play) house	15. Goldilocks (is) two are	16. Bob three has (good-by)
17. is house likes (bed)	18. and (for) in books	19. beds (see) come wolf	20. Jim (bears) helps to

Level 3: "Don Reads," pp. 54–63. (Vocabulary)
Objective: To acquire a basic reading vocabulary. **Directions:** Your teacher will read one word in each box.
Circle the word that he or she reads.

43

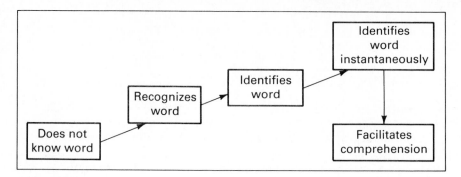

Figure 7.3. *Levels of Knowing a Word*

meaning and interest explains why content words require much less practice than function words. What this suggests (unfortunately) is that the easiest words to learn are often the least useful, whereas the more difficult ones are constantly needed.

Should Words Be Practiced in Isolation or in a Context?

It was pointed out that when function words and certain text-dependent words are introduced initially, they should be presented in a context. It was also mentioned that, at some point, all words should be isolated to allow children to scrutinize their details. Now, what about practice?

Since practice should be similar to reading itself, much of the work done to develop sight vocabularies should center on contexts—*the book* and *a big house*, for example, rather than on *the, book, a, big,* and *house*. Such a recommendation is not meant to discourage all uses of single-word practice, nor to minimize the importance of isolating words when confusions indicate the need for close scrutiny or comparisons. Instead, the recommendation is made to remind teachers who use nothing but isolated word practice (often in the form of lists) that it not only is inefficient but also can have an undesirable consequence for children, one effectively portrayed by Hayes (11) as follows:

> They,
> read,
> as,
> if,
> every,
> word,
> were,
> followed,

by,
a,
comma.

Which Words Should Be Practiced?

As pointed out in previous sections of this chapter, some words are important because they appear with such regularity in all kinds of text. Other words are less critical because, being closely linked to certain content, they show up in print much less frequently. In a story about a Thanksgiving celebration, for instance, *cornucopia* may appear on every page. In practically all other selections, however, it is not likely to show up even once. This suggests that high-frequency words should make their way into children's sight vocabularies as soon as possible. Other words should be practiced as often as time permits.

Should Games Be Used for Practice?

Although games are used for more than just word practice, they are probably used for that purpose most often. This is an appropriate time, therefore, to comment about them.

Chosen with care, games can both enliven practice and make it productive. Some games also allow for the use of what has been learned, thus demonstrating to children that it makes sense to learn to read. Both goals are obviously desirable; still, a few guidelines about using games are important to keep in mind:

USING GAMES: SOME GUIDELINES

1. A game and the details for playing it should be simple. Otherwise, more time will go to teaching children how to play it than to the educational reason for having the game.
2. Participants should be children who will learn from the game. "*Why* am I using this?" is a good question for any teacher who relies on games to enliven practice.
3. If teams are required, the teacher should select members. When children do the selecting, much time is wasted. Hurt feelings can be another undesirable consequence.
4. If a game is competitive, children who are frightened by competition should not participate, nor should children who do not have a chance to win.
5. Interest in a game erodes if it is available all the time or is played too often.

SAMPLES OF PRACTICE

Although, in theory, only interesting practice should be offered, that is not always possible to achieve. When it is not, it is especially important to tell the reason for the practice. A sufficient explanation may go something like, "I've noticed that some words are still causing problems. At times you know them, and at times you don't. Let's look at, and say, these words several times so that when they are in a story you're reading, you'll know them right away. A story isn't fun to read when it has a lot of words that you don't know." (Actually, "informed training" is best no matter what is being taught or practiced [20].)

Since an author's thoughts are customarily portrayed through connected text, the descriptions of possibilities for word practice will begin with samples that center on sentences whose difficulty can be matched to children's abilities.

Sentence Practice

If newly introduced vocabulary includes *bus, want*, and *buy*, they can be reviewed first, after which silently read sentences printed on cards will be the focus. Questions about sentences allow for attention both to word identification and comprehension. For instance:

> The children want me to see a toy bus.

Possible Questions:
What do the children want you to do?
Is the bus big or little?
Why do you think so?

> A man wants to buy a big red bus.

Possible Questions:
This tells something about a man. What does it say about him?
Is this also a toy bus?
How do you know?
What words tell about the bus?

When the suffix *-ing* has been taught and there is the need for practice in reading roots to which *-ing* has been affixed (e.g., *crying*), silently read sentences can be productive not only for the use of word structure but also for attending to various aspects of comprehending. For instance:

> The little boy is crying.

Possible Questions:

Does this tell about a child or a big person?
Is it about a girl or boy?
What does it say about the boy?
What else does it tell about the boy?
Does it tell why he is crying?
Why do *you* think he's crying?

In addition to providing for repeated responses to words (and for demonstrating that reading is comprehending), sentences with new vocabulary can personalize practice by incorporating children's names. In this case, an instructional group will again read a card silently, this time for the purpose of knowing what one of them should do or say. For example, see Figure 7.4.

> What color are your shoes, Marcia?

> Billy, please give something to Trish.

> Write a number on the board, John, and then come back to us.

Figure 7.4

Word cards, plus small card-holders, allow children to construct their own sentences with words that are almost in their sight vocabularies, as in Figure 7.5.

Once children have acquired a little printing ability, they can complete sentences that begin with recently introduced vocabulary. To illustrate:

In my family _____
When I'm in school _____
Every morning _____

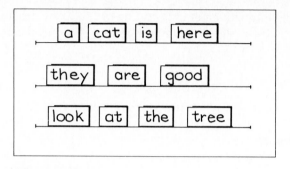

Figure 7.5

As illustrated in Chapter 5, songs are rich with opportunities for practice because of the repetition of words. In addition to having children sing from copies of simple refrains (or follow a Sing-Along filmstrip), teachers can use cards like the following, plus appropriate music, to allow for both physical activity and word practice:

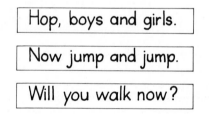

Easy addition allows for attention to important function words. Sentences like the following can be put on a ditto sheet for independent work:

> 2 caps are red.
> 1 cap is green.
> 2 and 1 are _____.

Activities selected to extend oral vocabularies also have potential for practice. Using her words, let me describe how one teacher maximized the contributions of a trip to a hatchery, which was taken for a social studies unit.

I began by reading a story called *The Wonderful Egg* to create interest in the trip and to prepare the children for what they were to see. What they did see gave specific meaning to words like *hatchery, incubator,* and *temperature.*
Thanks to my Polaroid camera, a bulletin-board display of photographs

was ready for the children to enjoy the next day. Once the pictures had been carefully examined ("Where am I?" was the most popular question), I mentioned that a visitor might wonder what the pictures were all about. This led to a group-composed description, which I printed on the chalkboard:

> Look at the baby chickens.
> Look at the boys and girls too.
> Can you find me?

The next day, I put the same three lines of text at the bottom of the bulletin board. At art time, I gave each child a sheet of white paper folded twice to allow for a four-page book, the first page being its cover. Printed at the bottom of the three following pages was one line from the text. Each became a caption for a page. Above each, appropriate drawings were made by the children. (As they did them, I circulated around the room to make sure that individuals were identifying the captions correctly.) The result was little books that the children enjoyed taking home to show their parents.

Another teacher combined art and word practice in the ways shown in Figures 7.6–7.8. The teacher-composed text in each example is not the best, but it does allow for repeated contact with recently introduced vocabulary.

Word and Phrase Practice

Even when single words are practiced, attention can still go to meaning. This is important because unless children are required to consider meaning, they are apt to think only about pronunciations. The ideas for practice that follow, therefore, deal with both "What does this say?" *and* "What does this mean?" Each sample can be adapted for varying abilities.

- Group words together. Then tell the children in writing what to do. For example:

  1. children   2. wall   3. walk
     father   lamp   run
     pony   tree   sleep

Directions:

1. Read the three words. Draw a line under all the words that name people.
2. Draw a line under the name of something that gives light.
3. Draw a line around all the words that tell what you can do.

Come With Me

1. I see something.
2. Look boys and girls.
3. I want to ride.
4. See me ride up and down.
5. See me jump.
6. See me jump fast.
7. "Come ride with me," said Diane.
8. See me ride the funny merry-go-round.
9. It is yellow, green, red and blue.

Figure 7.6. *Art and Reading*

Beginning readers sometimes have problems keeping the place when sentences in a continuous text figure in practice. To help, each sentence can be numbered so that if a child does lose his place, he can be directed back to it with a reference to a numeral.

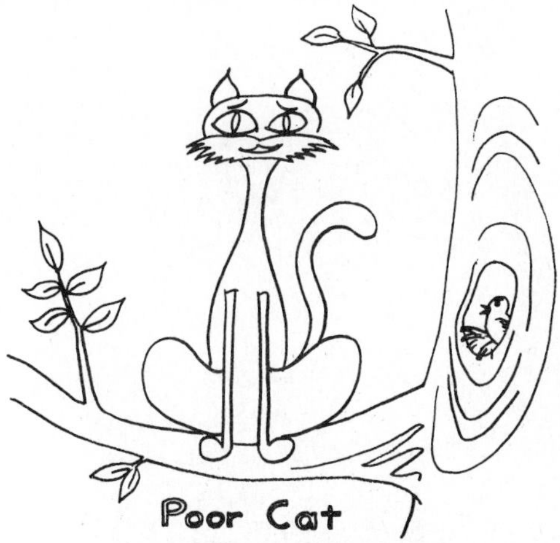

1. I like my cat.
2. My cat likes me.
3. My cat is yellow.
4. She likes to eat fish.
5. She likes to drink milk.
6. She likes to go up a tree.
7. She can not come down.
8. Poor cat!

Figure 7.7. *Homemade Material for Word Practice*

This teacher-composed text also has numbered sentences to help readers keep their place. Sometimes, paper markers (narrow, rectangular pieces of construction paper) are used to keep children from getting lost on a page. Should they be? Like all crutches, a marker ought to be used only when it is necessary and, secondly, only for as long as the need exists. If used, a marker should be placed above what is being read, since putting it underneath (as is the custom) fosters line rather than sentence reading.

I See Something

1. I see something.
2. "It can jump," said Tom.
3. It can jump up and down.
4. The something can go fast.
5. "It likes to play," said Kane.
6. My something is funny.
7. It is my dog.

Figure 7.8. *Comprehending*

Forming mental images based on written descriptions can get started early.
Above is one child's conception of what is communicated in a simple text.
Using the names of children in a class personalizes the practice.

- For better readers, word lists and other kinds of directions are possible: (1) Cross out the word in each list that does not belong with the others. (2) Above each list, write a heading for the three words that do belong together.

plate	bench	wide	grandfather	rocket
cup	stool	high	aunt	train
glass	table	tiny	grandmother	bird
mug	chair	heavy	sister	airplane

In place of headings, sentences can be requested that explain why one word did not go with the others.

- Attach the following to two boxes:

Have children put small cards into the boxes according to meanings (e.g., *red* [color]; *tiny* [size]). More than one word might be printed: *very big, dark green, extra large, quite small, deep blue.* The five senses provide other ways for calling attention to meanings by categorizing. (Ice cream cartons covered with gift wrapping paper make attractive containers.)
- Divide a bulletin board into four parts with the following titles: *Fall, Winter, Spring, Summer.* As children read words on cards (e.g., *cold, swimming, snow, football, school*), have them decide to which part of the board a card should be attached. Request reasons for the decisions.
- Have children sort small cards into pairs with opposite (or similar) meanings: *big, small; up, down; here, there;* and so on. Cards can also display phrases: *up the tree, down a tree; under the tree, above the tree; toward the street, away from the street.*
- After distributing a pebble or button to each child in an instructional group, show cards displaying such function words as *on, behind, over, above,* and *in;* or combinations like *in front of, in back of, to the left of.* The job for the children is to demonstrate meanings by performing an appropriate action with the pebble or button—for instance, placing it *on* the table.
- Have children pantomime the meanings of such words as *rub, bend, feed, rip,* and *tug.* (Like all the other examples of practice, this one can be adapted to varying abilities. With more advanced readers, pantomiming could be done with words like *crumple, gnaw, flee, quiver,* and *wince.*)
- Write phrases in a numbered list. Let the children take turns selecting numeral cards from a grab bag (ordinary grocery bag). The numeral chosen indicates which phrase is to be read. Correct responses allow a child to keep a card; otherwise, it is returned to the bag.

■ A bank game can give children a reason to work on hard-to-remember words. Word cards, turned upside down, are arranged in three piles, the most difficult called the $10 words, the least difficult the $1 words. Participants may choose a word from any of the piles. Correct identifications mean the bank gives them $10, $5, or $1, depending on the pile from which a card was selected. When all the cards have been drawn, the richest participant is the winner. (Before starting the game, participants are likely to be more than willing to have a warm-up practice period with the words.)

To attend to words that were new or causing problems, teachers have been observed doing the following:

■ One cut out a snowman's face from white construction paper. With black crayon, she made its eyes and mouth. She also cut out a hole for the nose. She then pasted a long narrow sheet of heavy paper to the back of the snowman in such a way that words printed on the paper could be pulled through the nose and shown one at a time. Used with children, it elicited the comment, "This is just like TV!" Next time it *was* a television set with a cardboard screen replacing the snowman's face. (Less work is required if an envelope is used. In this case, a "window" can be cut in the middle of one side. By making slits at both ends of the envelope, a long, narrow sheet of construction paper (with phrases printed on it) can be pulled through in a way that allows a phrase to show through the window.)

■ Another teacher cut out ghosts and printed a word on each. She put them in a trick-or-treat bag, then took the cards out one at a time for the children to read. Later, the ghosts were part of a bulletin-board display.

■ Another teacher prepared bingolike cards on which words were printed. She used the cards to play word bingo.

■ From newspaper headlines, a teacher cut out high-frequency words. She pasted them on a large sheet of cardboard, making a design. The sheet was used both for word practice and to encourage children to make designs themselves from words they found at home in old newspapers, magazines, and greeting cards. Subsequently, some brought their designs to school. These were displayed on a bulletin board for additional practice that gave children the opportunity to see a word written in different sizes, colors, and type faces.

More ideas for word practice are illustrated in Figures 7.9 and 7.10.

Book Practice

Reading a book allows not only for word practice but also for the consolidation of skills and abilities. It is important, therefore, that teachers do whatever

Figure 7.9. *Practice with Words, Phrases, and Sentences*

Once children are acquainted with Humpty Dumpty, a display can be prepared for word practice. (Some of the bricks in the wall have flaps that can be picked up to show words, phrases, and brief sentences.) The display is used by having children take turns being Humpty, which they do by holding a miniature figure resembling him. With Humpty in hand, a child tries to climb the wall by reading the words and sentences. An incorrect response means that, like Humpty, the child takes "a great fall." Another child is then given the chance to climb. If successful, his name is printed on a miniature figure.

Figure 7.10. *Word Practice*

This pond was made by covering the lower part of a bulletin board with cellophane paper that was attached on three sides. It can be used in a variety of ways. For example, as the teacher catches fish, the children name them. All such fish can be attached to the side of the board, eventually allowing for a review of all the fish caught. At other times, two children can take turns fishing for, and naming, words. (When this is done, one child should be an able reader in order to make certain that words are named correctly.) A box painted blue inside is another "pond" that can be used.

184

they can to encourage this more extensive reading. At the start, when reading vocabularies are limited, so are opportunities to have children read longer pieces of text. The types of "stories" found in the easiest books in basal reader programs do not provide a solution, for many are as mindless as:

> I will go.
> Will you go?
> I will go.

At the very beginning, it seems more advisable to concentrate on sentences in ways described earlier in the section "Sentence Practice."

I wish I could say that once children acquire larger vocabularies, all are eager to read books. I cannot, however, for I have been in too many classrooms in which the response to books was not much better than indifference, even when they were attractively displayed. It needs to be asked, therefore, what else can be done to foster better attitudes and more reading?

It should go without saying that one of the most effective solutions is effective instruction. After all, who wants to do what can only be done with great effort? Other motivation for reading comes from the availability of books that match interests and abilities. This means that variety (easy, hard; fiction, nonfiction; long, short) must be the mark of classroom libraries. (Reference 5 at the end of this chapter discusses and lists easy-to-read books.) If classroom libraries are to be used, not just looked at, free-choice reading is necessary. Some teachers also report a noteworthy increase in interest when both they and the children participate in *sustained silent reading* (15, 30). This is a scheduled period when everyone reads what they want to read without interruption.

Other ways in which teachers promoted book reading are described below.

- Whenever certain children display interest in a topic, our school librarian and I look for books that pertain to it. Initially, I meet with the group of interested children to discuss the topic, to distribute books, and to set a date for a subsequent meeting. Often, the post-reading discussions are as interesting as any that might be conducted by adults. Too, special-interest groups give less able readers a chance to make significant contributions, for what was in their books may be just as informative as what the more able readers learned from more difficult sources.
- If children enjoyed a book, they may, if they wish, tell in writing in any form they choose why they enjoyed it. Recommendations are displayed on a board to help anyone who is looking for a book. If I am able to get multiple copies of a really good book, I feel no compunction about asking certain children to read it. Before the reading begins, we meet as a group so that I can introduce the book and set a date for getting

reactions to it. The next time we meet, I am ready with questions, but I ask them only if something is needed to get a discussion started. If the children appear to have enjoyed the book, I am ready to show others by the same author or similar books by other authors. I also encourage games like Twenty Questions, in which one child pretends to be a character from a book and the others ask questions to try to identify the character.

- Many informational books – even those written at fairly simple levels – are more interesting than textbook sources. Children like them better, too. That's why I encourage groups to do extra reading on topics that often originate in social studies and science. With the supplementary reading, we sometimes get contradictory information, which usually results in good discussions and still more reading.

- Sometime during each year, I suggest the possibility of looking for interesting new words in self-selected books. To fan some interest, I couple the suggestion with a few examples that I've come across in my own reading. At a designated date, interested children and I get together to talk about our findings.

- By the time they get to third grade, some children are effective oral readers. With guidance from me or the school librarian, they select books that kindergartners and first graders would enjoy. After reading the books silently, they read them aloud to small groups of the younger children.

- Whenever adults in the community have interesting hobbies, I invite them to tell the children about them. I then try to find books that relate to the hobbies. Parents who have traveled and have taken slides also speak to the children. Again, I try to find books about the places each person has been.

- I have a series of filmstrips and tapes pertaining to books that tell about American folk heroes. When I show a filmstrip, I make certain that copies of the book itself are in our classroom library.

- Although I avoid the usual book report, I still encourage children to do something with a book once it's been read. Popular activities include making ads, posters, book jackets, mobiles, and scroll-like illustrations showing the sequence of events in a story.

What all these teachers demonstrate is an attitude toward books that is essentially different from the one depicted in the following dialogue:

Teacher: Do your workbook.

Child: I did it.

Teacher: Have you done all the worksheets?

Child: Yes.

Teacher: Did you check your spelling?

Child: I did that yesterday.

Teacher: Are you sure you've done everything?

Child: Yes.

Teacher: Well, then, go get a book!

NONSTANDARD DIALECTS AND WORD IDENTIFICATION

Because of the dependent relationship between oral language and reading, nonstandard speech sometimes affects responses to written text. Consequently, nonstandard dialects need to be considered before this chapter comes to a close.

Confusion about the Nature of Reading

The great amount of time spent on oral reading in primary-grade classrooms both reflects and encourages confusion about the purpose of reading. What should be clear (but doesn't seem to be) is that reading is a *receptive* process. It is an effort to get (or construct) an author's message, be it simple or profound, direct or obscure. Done aloud, however, reading also takes on a *productive* function: to communicate the author's message to others. With the added function, oral reading is as much like speaking as it is like reading. In this lies some potential problems, especially when the speech of the reader/speaker is nonstandard English.

Oral Reading and Nonstandard Speakers

What children say when they read aloud is affected by both what is printed and their own speech patterns. When the patterns are standard English, a child's oral reading should mirror what is on the page, as that, too, is standard English. In such cases, clear differences exist between right and wrong responses to written words.

With children who speak nonstandard English, the difference between right and wrong is less obvious. However, keeping in mind that the intent of reading is comprehension allows for distinctions. With a written sentence like *She is happy,* for example, a correct response for the nonstandard speaker would be "She is happy," but "She happy" would also be acceptable, since that is a translation of the written sentence into the reader's dialect. To illustrate further, an accurate response to *They are coming* is "They are coming," but a translation like "They is come" would be acceptable, since the latter is evidence of successful comprehension.

None of these comments are meant to suggest, by the way, that all deviations from an author's words are acceptable. Rather, the point here is that what *is* acceptable is determined not only by what is printed but also by the reader's dialect. Wolfram, a sociolinguist, specifies this point when he says that if a child reads a passage "in such a way that it systematically differs from standard English where his indigenous dialect differs, he has successfully read the passage" (29, p. 16). In speaking of poor black inner-city children, Hayes, the linguist, adds, "A child who says he 'bruvver' when he sees *his brother* has absolutely no reading difficulty at that point. He has understood so well that he has translated the written English into the natural speech he understands" (11, p. 6).

Goodman, an educator, refers to such deviations from text as *dialect-based miscues*, and maintains:

> . . . rejection or correction by the teacher of any dialect-based miscue moves the reader away from using his own linguistic competence to the teacher's expected response to the text. Word-for-word accuracy, in a narrow sense, becomes the goal rather than the meaning. . . . In encouraging divergent speakers to use their language competence . . . and accepting their dialect-based miscues, we minimize the effect of dialect differences. In rejecting them, we maximize the effect. (10, pp. 11–12)

Goals for Speaking and Reading

Proposals to accept dialect-based miscues often raise questions about the school's responsibilities. When reading the previous discussion, for example, some of you may have thought, "Are we giving up all our standards?" To respond, a distinction must be made between a school's responsibilities for speaking and for reading.

Without question, one serious responsibility of every school is to give students the opportunity to become speakers of standard English. This is important if only because of the relationship between speech and career opportunities. Even while acknowledging this responsibility, however, one fact must not be overlooked: compared to other variables in a child's life, schooling is relatively ineffectual in altering speech. More influential is the family; still more so is the peer group as a child gets older. In time, vocational interests may take on paramount importance. Or as Hayes puts it so well, "It has been said that the reason *I ain't got no money* is bad is that if you keep on saying it, you 'ain't gonna have no money' " (11, p. 5).

When it comes to teaching reading, the school has a much greater chance of succeeding, especially when teachers remember that reading is comprehending standard English, not mimicking it. When that is kept in mind, so, too, will it be remembered that, for some children, reading is translating what is printed into their own more meaningful dialect.

Are such translations difficult to make? As of now, too little is known to answer. Two points can still be made, however. The first is the possibility that the need for a translation makes learning to read more difficult for the nonstandard speaker than for the child who speaks standard English. The second point is that nonstandard speakers have been translating spoken standard English long before instruction in reading ever begins. As Goodman observes:

> They build an ability to understand the dialects of others. . . . This acquisition of receptive control over other people's dialects is a simple matter of survival. If you don't understand what teachers, policemen, store clerks, TV announcers, and other high-status people are saying, you are in big trouble. This does not mean that divergent speakers learn to talk like the teacher; that involves productive control. But it does mean that what they find in print is not as hard to deal with as we once thought. (10, p. 8)

What can happen in a classroom when teachers either forget or reject the guidelines that have been proposed for working with nonstandard speakers was revealed during an observation of a second grade in an inner-city school. The teacher was with a group of ten children who were seated on the floor in front of him taking turns reading aloud from a basal reader. Whenever an oral reader deviated even slightly from what was printed, he was corrected. Whenever a child responded to a question without using a sentence, he was required to "Say that again, but this time use a complete sentence." Combined, the responses to what the children were reading and saying created a negative, almost punitive atmosphere. That was why it was surprising to hear the teacher say during the post-observation discussion, "These children seem to have no interest in discussing what they read."

SUMMARY

Comprehending language, whether spoken or written, requires attention not to individual words but to what they mean when they are assembled into phrases, sentences, and more. To free a reader to attend to meaning, words must be identified "without thinking." Automaticity, therefore, is one requirement for successful reading. Since it is, getting sight vocabularies started is an important responsibility of anyone teaching beginning reading. Keeping their development going is a responsibility for all subsequent teachers.

To bring reading vocabularies into existence, Chapter 7 recommended the use of whole word methodology. It further recommended that other methods be introduced as soon as possible. Whole word methodology was singled out as the way to begin for several reasons. One is that words (unlike individual sounds) are familiar, thus of interest to children. In addition, even a small reading vocabulary allows for immediate attention to comprehension.

Factors to consider in selecting words for reading vocabularies were discussed next. They included both usefulness and interests. These two factors are all that is necessary in nursery schools and kindergartens, but the common and extensive use of commercial materials in all subsequent years means that their vocabularies must also be dealt with when plans are made for instruction and practice.

The discussion of instruction explained why function words need to be introduced in contexts. It also stressed the importance of relevant cues as well as the need to avoid irrelevant ones. The distinctive features of words and of how they can be highlighted was another topic discussed.

Since practice (repeated responses) is essential for automaticity, it merits a place in all instructional programs. The importance of getting and keeping children's attention is the reason many samples of interesting practice were provided. They demonstrated that meaning can be stressed along with identifications even when single words are the focus.

The equation of "reading" with "getting meaning" explains why speakers of nonstandard English were discussed. How the receptive-expressive nature of oral reading can lead to incorrect priorities (word-for-word accuracy over comprehension) was explained. The need to know about dialect differences in order to distinguish between errors and dialect-based miscues was also considered.

How other methods for developing reading vocabularies can gradually be added to an instructional program provides the theme for upcoming chapters.

REVIEW

1. A fairly large number of terms are introduced in Chapter 7. Some are listed below:

   content words   service words
   function words   structure words

   a. See whether you can define these terms and cite examples of each.
   b. Why is it important for teachers to know about these classifications?

2. What distinction does the chapter make between word identification and word recognition? Does reading require identification or recognition? Why?

3. Chapter 7 also distinguishes between verbal and nonverbal contexts. What is the difference? When is a verbal context required for whole word instruction?

4. During a visit in a third grade, the teacher was working with twelve children, who started reading a basal selection even though no attention had gone to new vocabulary. Later, when I asked the teacher about the omission, he said, "Sometimes I write the new words on the board, but today I wanted to work on getting the main idea." What do you think about this teacher's explanation for omitting attention to new words?

5. In another third grade, the teacher followed the recommendations of a basal reader manual for introducing new vocabulary. She thus wrote the new words on the board and, after naming each one once, said to the children, "Who can come to the board and draw a line under the word that means the opposite of 'go'?" Other questions that came directly from the manual included, "Which word means the same as 'big'?" Was this Teacher B providing practice in recognizing or identifying the new words? Explain your response.

6. Whole word methodology has been recommended as the way to get reading started. What would be the consequences were a teacher to use nothing but this method for an extended period of time?

REFERENCES

1. Adams, Marilyn J.; Anderson, Richard C.; and Durkin, Dolores. "Beginning Reading: Theory and Practice." *Language Arts.* 60 (January, 1978), 19–25.
2. Barnard, Douglas P., and DeGracie, James. "Vocabulary Analysis of New Primary Reading Series." *Reading Teacher* 30 (November, 1976), 177–180.
3. Barnitz, John G. "Black English and Other Dialects: Sociolinguistic Implications for Reading Instruction." *Reading Teacher* 33 (April, 1980), 779–786.
4. Ceprano, Maria A. "A Review of Selected Research on Methods of Teaching Sight Words." *Reading Teacher* 35 (December, 1981), 314–322.
5. Cunningham, Pat. "Books for Beginners." *Reading Teacher* 34 (May, 1981), 952–954.
6. Dolch, Edward W. *Problems in Reading.* Champaign, Ill.: Garrard Press, 1948.
7. Durkin, Dolores. *Children Who Read Early.* New York: Teachers College Press, Columbia University, 1966.

8. Fasold, R. W., and Wolfram, W. A. "Some Linguistic Features of Negro Dialect." In Ralph W. Fasold and Roger W. Shuy (Eds.), *Standard English in the Inner City.* Washington, D.C.: Center for Applied Linguistics, 1970, 41–86.

9. Fry, Edward. "The New Instant Word List." *Reading Teacher* 34 (December, 1980), 284–289.

10. Goodman, Kenneth J., and Buck, Catherine. "Dialect Barriers to Reading Comprehension Revisited." *Reading Teacher* 27 (October, 1973), 6–12.

11. Hayes, Alfred S. "Language and Reading: A Linguist's View." New York: Harcourt, Brace and World, 1969.

12. Johnson, Dale D.; Moe, Alden J.; and Baumann, James F. *The Ginn Word Book for Teachers.* Lexington, Mass.: Ginn and Company, 1983.

13. Karlsen, Bjorn, and Blocker, Margaret. "Black Children and Final Consonant Sounds." *Reading Teacher* 27 (February, 1974), 462–463.

14. Lesgold, Alan M., and Curtis, Mary E. *Learning to Read Words Efficiently.* Pittsburgh: University of Pittsburgh, Learning Research and Development Center, 1980.

15. McCracken, Robert A., and McCracken, Marlene J. "Modeling Is the Key to Sustained Silent Reading." *Reading Teacher* 31 (January, 1978), 406–408.

16. Martin, Judith L. "Spicing up Vocabulary Study and Review." *Reading Teacher* 38 (October, 1984), 118.

17. Monteith, Mary K. "A Whole Word List Catalog." *Reading Teacher* 29 (May, 1976), 844–847.

18. Moss, Joy F. "Using the 'Focus Unit' to Enhance Children's Response to Literature." *Language Arts* 55 (April, 1978), 482–488.

19. Nemko, Barbara. "Context Versus Isolation: Another Look at Beginning Readers." *Reading Research Quarterly* 19 (Summer, 1984), 461–467.

20. Paris, S. G.; Newman, R. S.; and McVey, K. A. "Learning the Functional Significance of Mnemonic Actions: A Microgenetic Study of Strategy Acquisition." *Journal of Experimental Child Psychology* 34 (December, 1982), 490–509.

21. Pillar, Arlene M. "Individualizing Book Reviews." *Elementary English* 52 (April, 1975), 467–469.

22. Rash, Judy; Johnson, Terry D.; and Gleadow, Norman. "Acquisition and Retention of Written Words by Kindergarten Children under Varying Learning Conditions." *Reading Research Quarterly* 19 (Summer, 1984), 452–460.

23. Richek, Margaret. "Readiness Skills That Predict Initial Word Learning Using Two Different Methods of Instruction." *Reading Research Quarterly* 13 (1977–78, No. 2), 200–222.

24. Rodenborn, Leo V., and Washburn, Earlene. "Some Implications of the New Basal Readers." *Elementary English* 51 (September, 1974), 885–888.

25. Rosenshine, Barak. "Teaching Functions in Instructional Programs." *Elementary School Journal* 83 (March, 1983), 335–351.

26. Samuels, S. Jay. "Automatic Decoding and Reading Comprehension." *Language Arts* 53 (March, 1976), 323–325.

27. Samuels, S. J.; Begy, Gerald; and Chen, Chaur Ching. "Comparison of Word Recognition Speed and Strategies of Less Skilled and More Highly Skilled Readers." *Reading Research Quarterly* 11 (1975–1976, No. 1), 72–86.

28. Wolfram, Walter. "Sociolinguistic Alternatives in Teaching Reading to Non-

Standard Speakers." *Reading Research Quarterly* 6 (Fall, 1970), 9–33.
29. Wolfram, Walter. *A Sociolinguistic Description of Negro Speech*. Washington, D.C.: Center for Applied Linguistics, 1969.
30. Yatvin, Joanne. "Recreational Reading for the Whole School." *Reading Teacher* 31 (November, 1977), 185–188.

CHAPTER 8

Contexts

Even though this book espouses the use of whole word methodology as the best way to get reading vocabularies started, it does not support its continued use as the sole means for keeping those vocabularies growing. To do so would ignore the common sense of Ausubel's conception of readiness, which suggests the need for variety (as well as quality) in instructional methodology to ensure that every child has maximum opportunity to be successful.

To be noted, too, is that a prolonged, exclusive use of whole word methodology ignores the obvious: If unknown words are always named for children, they are not too likely to acquire the strategies required to cope with new or forgotten words. The desirability of independence, therefore, is a second reason for complementing whole word methodology with instruction that will equip children to cope on their own with new or forgotten words. The need for such independence has been emphasized in a study done by William Nagy and Richard Anderson entitled "How Many Words Are There in Printed English?" (11). One of the researchers' recommendations follows:

> A basic implication of our study is that, because of the sheer volume of vocabulary that students will encounter in their reading, any approach to vocabulary instruction must include some methods or activities that will increase children's ability to learn words on their own. (p. 325)

One way to foster independence is by making explicit how the known words in a piece of text provide help with other words that are not known. The use of known words for this purpose goes under the heading "Using Contexts." The alphabetic writing system of English allows for a second source of help that promotes independence. This source is rooted in the connection between spellings and pronunciations. The fact that English words have particular types of structure accounts for another source of help.

All this can be summed up by stating that like good parents, good teachers do whatever they can to foster independence in children—in this case, independence in coping with unknown words. To attain that goal, such teachers provide instruction about contextual, graphophonic, and structural cues. The first kind can be thought of as external, beyond-word cues; the second and third as internal or within-word cues. The details of this instruction are the content for this chapter, Chapter 8, as well as for Chapters 9 through 11. Fostering independence, then, is the central theme of the next four chapters.

The term *context* has both a variety of referents and a great deal of significance when the topic is reading. It is unlikely, for example, that the meaning of *This is the season when we want our pasts forgotten and our presents remembered* would have been as readily apparent as it was had the sentence appeared in a newspaper in July rather than in December. Nor might the warning *Watch It or Wear It* be immediately clear were it not for the smell of the paint and the sight of the painters nearby. Not to be omitted is the interesting effect of context on the message of the bumper sticker that said *I hope we don't meet by accident*. And then there was the T-shirt attached to a board in a gymnasium that boasted *Body by Effort*.

What these few examples make clear is that contexts have great impact on both the meaning of text and the ease with which the meaning can be constructed. The same examples further illustrate that contexts with significance for reading are nonverbal as well as verbal.

VERBAL CONTEXTS

The concern of this chapter is verbal contexts, which were discussed in Chapter 7 when whole word methodology was the focus. You will recall such recommendations in that chapter as "New function words should be introduced in contexts" and "Homonyms and homographs require contexts, in the case of the former to reveal the intended meaning and in the case of the latter to indicate the pronunciation and, with that, the meaning." The present discussion of verbal contexts divides them into the categories "general" and "local."

GENERAL CONTEXTS

A *general context* may be thought of as a pervasive theme suggested by something like a title. Themes help readers because they establish expectations for both content and vocabulary. The fact that a section of a newspaper, for instance, is classified as "Sports" allows readers to anticipate the subject matter of articles. In turn, the expectations help them cope with the content of the articles as well as with words that communicate it.

To be more specific, let's take a headline as an example. Finding *Hawks Crush Eagles* on a sports page prompts a reader (who is knowledgeable about sports) not to think of birds killing other birds but of one team badly beating another. Stated differently, the general context in this instance helps a reader make correct inferences about the referents for *Hawks* and *Eagles* and to interpret *Crush* figuratively rather than literally.

To reinforce what is relevant for this chapter, let's stay with sports, in particular, with golf. Students who might otherwise have difficulty recognizing *stroke, handicap, shaft,* and *iron* might experience no problems when these words are in an article in *Golf Digest*. In this case, the general theme (plus the reader's knowledge of golf) allows for contextual information (or cues) that help with vocabulary.

What this underscores for teachers is the importance of preparing children for assigned reading by establishing expectations for the selection that will help not only in comprehending the text as a whole but also in recognizing individual words. One way to do this with expository material is to discuss headings and subheadings. With stories, expectations can be established with references to the setting (e.g., town by the sea) or, for instance, to one or more characters (e.g., a blind girl attending school for the first time).

LOCAL CONTEXTS

For unknown words, the information, or cues, that local contexts offer is more specifically helpful than what derives from general contexts. For that reason, the former are the main topic of this chapter. Exactly what constitutes local contexts will be clarified as the two kinds of cues that they provide are discussed.

The first type of cue is referred to as *syntactic*; the second, as *semantic*. Even though each type is discussed separately at first, it is important to remember that a skilled reader takes advantage of the two so rapidly that syntactic and semantic cues appear to function jointly, not separately.

Syntactic Cues

Syntactic cues contribute to independence in coping with troublesome words in any language that is *positional*. A positional language, such as English, is one in which (a) words are arranged, or ordered, in certain patterned ways, and (b) the patterns determine meaning. How word order affects meaning is illustrated below:

> They are painting the house yellow.
> They are painting the yellow house.

The fact that words can be sequenced only in certain ways if meaning is to be preserved is illustrated next:

> They are painting yellow house the

Because *syntax* refers to the order in which words are arranged in an utterance, the help with unknown words that is rooted in order is called a syntactic cue. (*Syntax* comes from the Latin word *syntaxis*, which means "to arrange.") Although syntactic cues are generally thought of in relation to sentences, the patterned word order of clauses and phrases also makes them available in text that is less than a sentence. Syntactic cues, then, are intrasentence sources of help.

The assistance that syntactic cues offer is indirect. That is, their use apart from other kinds of help will not reveal the identity of an unknown word, but it *will* place constraints on what the word can be by indicating its grammatical function. Take a sentence like *Three boys climbed the fence* as an example. If *climbed* is not in a child's reading vocabulary, its position in the sentence clearly indicates it is a verb. Knowledge of the kinds of words that belong at given points in sentences also allows for concluding with certainty that the missing word in *Many _____ were at the game* is a plural noun. Knowing that pronouns and their referents agree in gender as well as in number leads to the conclusion that the missing word in *The _____ took his book back* is a singular, masculine noun. All this is to say that by narrowing down possibilities, syntactic cues offer considerable assistance with unknown words when used in conjunction with other kinds of help.

Semantic Cues

A second kind of contextual help goes under the heading *semantic cue*. As the name may suggest, a semantic cue is rooted in the meaning of the words in a context that are familiar. (Semantics is a branch of linguistics concerned with the study of meaning.) Whereas syntactic cues are confined to a sentence or less, semantic cues are not similarly restricted. The fact that semantic cues may be either intrasentence or intersentence sources of help is shown in the three contexts below, in which blanks indicate the positions of words presumed to be unfamiliar.

1. I want a _____ of milk.
2. It's time to _____. Here's the needle and thread.
3. Marie was very tired when she got home. She went to _____ right away.

Because the essence of language, whether written or spoken, has to do with "making sense," what the omitted words can be in the three illustrative contexts is constrained by the meaning of the other words. Use of semantic cues in the first sentence, for instance, indicates that the omitted word may be *glass, cup, mug,* or some other kind of container, but it cannot be nouns like *glue, car,* or *mop*. (The fact that the omitted word is a noun derives from syntactic information, which is to say that even though syntactic and semantic cues can be discussed separately, they function jointly.) In the case of the second illustrative text shown above, help with the problematic word in the first sentence is in the sentence that follows. Like the second illustration, the third also demonstrates intersentence semantic help.

As is true of the general contexts discussed earlier in the chapter, relevant world knowledge maximizes the productivity of semantic cues. In some cases, in fact, world knowledge may be enough to eliminate everything but the correct word. This is exemplified below:

> All four _____ on the car were flat.
> The American flag is red, white, and _____.

The possibility that world knowledge may turn "making sense" into something more subjective than it is commonly thought to be was recently demonstrated in a second-grade classroom in which the teacher had spent time earlier stressing the fact that reading is making sense out of print. Consequently, when a child read *The man went into the house* as "The man went into the horse," it was not surprising to hear the teacher ask, "Eric, does it make sense to say that a man went into a horse?" *Unexpected* was Eric's defense: "Once on TV, I saw a whole bunch of men marching into a wooden horse to hide there."

ADDITIONAL COMMENTS ABOUT LOCAL CONTEXTUAL CUES

In addition to demonstrating that making sense is not entirely objective, Eric's response showed that the value of contextual cues for acquiring independence in coping with unfamiliar words should not overshadow the need to consider their spellings. The best of readers, then, use all available sources of help—internal (within-word) cues, external (beyond-word) cues, and world knowledge—when they encounter an unknown word that seems to be important. Even for these readers, it should be emphasized, deciding what a word is by using all available cues is word recognition, not word identification. That this *is* the case implies the following for classroom practices related to new vocabulary. (Since work with new words is often done to prepare for reading a basal reader selection, that framework is used for illustrative purposes.)

NEW VOCABULARY: GUIDELINES FOR TEACHERS

1. Assuming that time has been spent on how to use contextual cues to decide what unknown words say, examine the sentences in which new words first appear in the selection.

2. Do not spend prereading time on any new word (whose meaning is likely to be known) that appears initially in a context that provides a generous amount of information about the word.

3. During postreading activities, show the helpful contexts one at a time. Having underlined the new words, ask the children to (a) read each context silently; (b) read aloud the underlined word; and (c) tell how they decided what that word was.

4. Remind the children, if this seems necessary, of the earlier work with contexts.

5. Provide practice for all the new vocabulary, including words that were in helpful contexts. (Many suggestions for word practice, you recall, are in Chapter 7.)

The procedures just described will be effective with most children, but slower ones may need prereading help even with words in helpful contexts. This should not be surprising when it is remembered that, first, such children often have limited sight vocabularies and, second, words from those vocabularies constitute contexts. This means that what appears to be a helpful context may be no context at all for some children. It also means that teachers must do whatever is possible from the beginning to foster sight vocabularies of maximum size. To attain this goal requires what is sometimes missing from classrooms: sufficient amounts of word practice.

Before attention shifts to instruction with contexts, one further comment is necessary. It pertains to the question, Should such terms as *noun*, *syntax*, and *singular* enter into a teacher's efforts to get children to understand and use contextual information? To respond, a distinction must be made between younger and older children.

To younger children, such terms are totally unfamiliar. What is very familiar, on the other hand, is using contexts, because they do that routinely (but unconsciously) whenever they attend to, or produce, spoken language. This means that encouraging them to use written contexts for help with unfamiliar words is not asking them to do something completely foreign; nor does it require terms like *noun* or *syntax* or *context*.

As children progress to second and third grades, language lessons begin to teach the meaning of terms related to grammar. Only when children thoroughly understand them should they figure in instruction with contextual cues. At that point, they will be helpful, as they allow for more precise communication between teacher and child—for instance, for probing like, "Is that word you don't know going to be a singular or a plural noun? . . . How do you know? . . . Can you think of a singular noun that makes sense?"

INSTRUCTION ABOUT CONTEXTUAL CUES

Instruction in the use of contextual cues can get started before children are able to read. (The presence of senseless responses to words in middle- and upper-grade classrooms suggests that, in some instances, such instruction should go on for a longer time than it does.)

Spoken Contexts

By using spoken language, teachers can initiate explicit attention to contexts very early, because children's tacit knowledge of language—including the fact that it makes sense—allows for discussions like the following, in which twelve kindergartners are involved.

Teacher: Does anyone know what a detective is?

Jimmy: I do. He catches robbers.

Mary: Sometimes he gets shot, too.

Teacher: Yes, that's true. Jimmy, how is he able to catch a robber?

Jimmy: If somebody knows him, they can tell the police.

Teacher: But what if nobody does? Maybe he's wearing a mask and nobody knows who he is. What then? Might he do something in the store he's robbing that will help a detective find him?

Vivian: The other night on television a robber had wet shoes and left puddles in the store. That's how come he was caught.

Teacher: What do we call something like puddles—or maybe fingerprints? What do you call what a detective uses to catch a thief?

Jerry: I know. They're clues. He uses clues.

Teacher: Good for you, Jerry. Have any of you ever heard the word *clue* before?

Mark: I have. I have a detective game at home.

Teacher: Good detectives know how to use clues, don't they?

Jerry: They use them to find people who kill people, too.

Teacher: Yes, they do. Today, I want to find out if you'd make good detectives. I'm going to give you a clue by saying something. I won't say everything, though. I'll leave out a word at the end; and, if you listen, you'll be able to tell me the word I'm thinking of but don't say. Listen now. See if you can tell me the word at the end that I don't say. In our room we have fifteen girls and only nine—who can finish it for me?

Group: Boys!

Teacher: Say, you really are good detectives. You certainly know how to use clues. I'll have to make it a little harder. This time, if you think you know the word I don't say, raise your hand. Here goes. When we draw pictures, we use crayons or _____.

Correctly, this kindergarten teacher started with brief sentences with familiar content. In addition, she provided maximum contextual help by omitting a word at the end of a statement. Finally, she used *clue* rather than *cue*, since *clue* is a word the children understand.

On another day, both to shift the position of the target word and to provide a different framework for using spoken contexts, the same teacher begins by observing:

Sometimes, parents know so much about us that it seems they know what we're thinking even before we say it. They can almost read our minds, can't they? Let's see whether you can read my mind. I'll say something, but I'll leave out one word. I'll think of the word, but I won't say it. When I come to the word that I'm thinking of, I'll raise my hand. Listen. Every Monday morning at ten, Mrs. _____ comes to our room to help us with art.

Other work with spoken contexts makes use of pictured objects. Now, instead of suggesting appropriate words, children select displayed pictures to complete sentences spoken by the teacher. To illustrate:

Pretty flowers are in the _____. (picture of a garden)
To keep our hands warm, we wear _____. (picture of mittens)
The _____ of a bicycle are round. (picture of two bicycle wheels)
My favorite pet is a _____. (picture of a dog, a cat, and a bird)

The last example above allows for attention to the guideline that should be used in evaluating children's responses: Any response is acceptable as long as it is syntactically and semantically consistent with the rest of the context. The emphasis (as in reading) is on the fact that language makes sense.

What should follow activities with spoken contexts depends on what the children have been learning while those activities have been progressing. If they have acquired the beginning of a reading vocabulary, brief written contexts with omitted words can replace the spoken ones. On the other hand, if the children's reading vocabulary is still too limited to allow for such a replacement but a few letter-sound relationships have been learned, the next activities can use spoken sentences and the initial letters of words for the purpose of showing how contextual cues, now combined with others that derive from spellings, allow for independence in coping with unfamiliar words.

Spoken Contexts and Minimal Graphophonic Cues

To illustrate early work with spoken contexts and minimal graphophonic cues (letter-sound relationships), let's assume that an instructional group knows the name of *t* and the sound it records. This makes the following instruction possible.

> *Teacher:* [Holds up card showing *t*.] You know the sound that goes with this letter. Tell me some words that begin with that sound.
>
> *John:* *Tell* starts with it.
>
> *Maria:* So does *two* and *ten* and *tall*.
>
> *Teacher:* Well, you certainly know lots of words that begin with the sound that goes with *t*. I wonder, though, if you can think of one certain word that starts with *t*. I'll think of it but won't say it. See if you can tell me what it is. Listen. Right now we have two pets in our room. One is a _____. Which of our pets am I thinking of? . . . How did you know I was thinking of the turtle? . . . Why did you know I wasn't thinking of our gerbil? . . .

As children learn more sounds, a teacher can provide some variation by showing letters whose sounds suggest answers to riddles. Holding up *p*, for instance, a teacher might ask: "Who can think of something that is little and soft and furry, and its name starts with the sound that goes with this letter? . . . What made you think the answer was 'puppy'? . . . Why couldn't it be 'kitten'? After all, a kitten is little and soft and furry."

Probing like that used at the end is essential, as the purpose of the activity is to get children to use constraints that come from contexts *and* graphophonic cues.

Written Contexts

Because the reason for attending to contexts is to improve word recognition abilities, written language should replace spoken language as soon as existing reading vocabularies allow for the switch. When they do, explicit attention should go to the significance of "making sense" for reading. Such attention can be given in a variety of ways. For example, one teacher may decide to write on the board strings of words like the following:

> We are in first grade
>
> We are in purple grade
>
> We first grade in are

Having children read and discuss the lines of text allows this teacher to make comments like: "When we talk, we don't say silly things, do we? We don't say

'We are in purple grade' or 'We first grade in are'. We say things that make sense. We say something like 'We are in first grade' or maybe we'll say 'We go to Smith School,' because that makes sense. It's the same with reading. What we read should make sense. If it doesn't, something's wrong. Maybe we're mixing up some words."

This same teacher might also decide to give an assignment in which the children's job is to read each line of text in order to decide whether it makes sense. Finished sheets look like Figure 8.1.

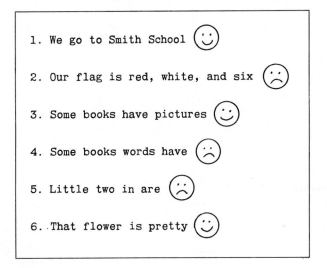

Figure 8.1

To clarify "makes sense" still further, the same teacher might choose to distribute small word cards to members of the instructional group. Now the request is to put them together in ways that say something meaningful. Acceptable combinations include:

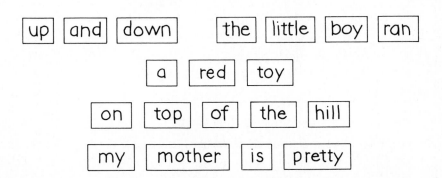

To discourage word-by-word reading and, at the same time, to give further meaning to "makes sense," phrases and clauses might be joined to produce something meaningful. Or, partial sentences might be listed on an assignment sheet so they can be connected to make sentences:

They couldn't carry	the beautiful garden.
I don't know	were on the wall.
They walked through	the heavy chair.
The three pictures	went too fast.
All the cars	how to make this.
In the winter	I like to eat something.
When I get home	it gets very cold.

Knowing the meaning of "makes sense," children are ready for other written assignments. With sentences such as the following, they print in the blank the word that produces a meaningful statement:

I want to _____ the horse.
        look   see

Jack _____ Sue are playing.
   and   are

For a variation of the same procedure, children can underline all the words that are both syntactically and semantically acceptable:

        girls
The boxes are on their way to school.
        boys

                us
                up
They are now on the school.
                in
                at

Crossing out the word that keeps a string of words from making sense is another possibility:

The little big boy is tall.
I cannot fix five that.
The rug is on the flower floor.

Once children acquire some ability in spelling, they are ready to generate words themselves. To be remembered in this case is that what makes sense is the concern, not perfect spellings:

The children _____ to the store.

Can you _____ this afternoon?

It is possible that you recognize <u>filling in blanks with words that make sense as a testing procedure</u>. In that case, it is a method for assessing comprehension and is referred to as the *cloze* procedure. (Cloze comes from the word *closure*, a term associated with Gestalt psychologists, who maintain that human behavior is motivated by the need for wholeness and completeness.) The cloze procedure can be used in a variety of ways when the constraints that contextual cues put on words are the concern. One teacher I know relies on old basal readers to provide material. She separates individual stories, makes booklets, then inks out certain words in each. When she is teaching about nouns, for instance, only nouns might be covered. Children read the stories; list one possibility for each covered word; then compare and discuss their choices, always in the framework of, Does that make sense? This type of assignment is especially valuable in demonstrating that a context may be comprised of more than a sentence.

To encourage children to use more than a single sentence to get help with a word, text like the following is useful, especially when reasons for choices are discussed:

Where did you put the cookies? I can't find _____.

It rained, but I didn't wear my rubbers. Now my feet are _____.

The most important point to make about all these exercises is the need to help children see the <u>connection between omitted and unknown words</u>. That is, they should understand that just as they are using available words to decide on a sensible one to put in a blank, they also should use in their reading known words to get help with any words they might not know or cannot recall. Not to make the connection explicit runs the risk of turning exercises like those discussed into ends in themselves. (For a sample of an exercise in a basal reader workbook, see Figure 8.2 and the commentary about it.)

Written Contexts and Graphophonic Cues

Earlier, the use of spoken contexts and minimal graphophonic cues was illustrated. Now let's consider how one teacher initiated work with graphophonic cues and written contexts. She began as follows:

As you can see, one word is missing from the sentence on the board. [I can open the _____ with my key.] Who would like to suggest what the

Figure 8.2

Figure 8.2 shows a workbook exercise in which the stated purpose is "Using Letter Sounds and Context." The inclusion of pictures, however, makes it an exercise in word recognition, as the pictures provide prompts for the correct words. None of the sentences, therefore, really needs to be read.

    The brevity of the practice shown in Figure 8.2 is typical of commercially prepared workbooks, which provide an abundance of practice but fail to offer what is often needed: extensive, concentrated practice. Whenever a workbook page provides useful but limited practice, teachers should supplement the page with additional work of a similar kind.

Read each sentence. Find the word that makes sense in the sentence and goes with the picture. Print that word on the line.

1. I am going to put on my new __blouse__ today.

   gloves   blouse   blend

2. My little sister is asleep in her __crib__.

   carriage   crisp   crib

3. The ball is over by the __fence__.

   fence   lake   fetch

4. How many __eggs__ are left in the bowl?

   crackers   edge   eggs

5. The silly __clown__ made us laugh.

   joke   cloud   clown

6. Jim played the __trumpet__ for his friends.

   piano   trumpet   tropical

7. We can put our things in this __wagon__.

   ways   wagon   desk

From TOWERS, Level H, Houghton Mifflin Reading Program, Teacher's Annotated Edition by William K. Durr, Jean M. LePere, and John J. Pikulski. Copyright © 1983 by Houghton Mifflin Company. Used with permission.

word might be? . . . Okay. Tom thinks it's *door*. Does anyone think it might be something else? . . . Let's see now. There have been five very good suggestions—*door*, *safe*, *box*, *luggage*, and *drawer*. They're good because they make sense. However, the letter with which the missing word begins is on the back of this card that I'm holding. What letter is this? . . . Since it's *b*, which of your suggestions is the missing word? . . . Right. It must be *box* because *box* starts with *b*, and it makes sense because some boxes have locks. I'll write *box* where it belongs, and then you can read the whole sentence.

After providing additional illustrations of how both help and constraints come from contexts and spellings, this teacher might decide to prepare a list of written sentences similar to those shown below. (Blanks of a single length avoid suggesting that an unfinished word is short or long.) Beginning letters are confined to consonants, as the sound that a vowel records is affected by other letters in the same syllable.

> A clown is supposed to be f_____.
>
> When you get to the corner, t_____ right.
>
> Fill the gl_____ with milk.

If instruction in phonics is concentrating on the sound that a certain letter records—for instance, *f*—written assignments can use sentences like these:

> She had a big smile on her f_____.
>
> Don't go too f_____ on your bike.
>
> A f_____ runs around our yard.

To demonstrate even more spelling constraints, contexts such as the following are useful:

> They are too f_____t to walk on thin ice.
>
> This l_____p doesn't give any light.
>
> Th_____k you for helping me.

When children know that words are decoded syllable by syllable, they are ready for exercises in which word fragments are initial syllables. For instance:

> I'm glad the ti_____ is in a cage.
>
> The children are too lit_____ to go to school.
>
> If you don't water the flow_____ , it will die.

Sentences like those shown provide an opportunity to remind children that contexts may provide so much information about an unfamiliar word that only the spelling of its first syllable requires detailed attention. This is important for children to know, since spending excessive time with individual words hardly facilitates comprehending.

It is important for teachers to remember that with all these exercises, both correct and incorrect answers should be followed with questions. With the last sentence listed, such probes as the following are important: What word or words in the sentence made you think that the word is *flower*? . . . There's an important word that tells you the word is singular. What is that word?

As soon as possible, instruction and practice should concentrate on contexts plus complete graphophonic cues. These might be initiated by showing an unfamiliar word on a card—for instance, *straight*. With the help of a teacher's questions about the spelling, children try to read it. If none can, the teacher shows a sentence card, in this case one displaying something like *Draw a straight line.* After the children read the three known words silently, the teacher again asks them to read *straight*. Once they do, they discuss how the context helped, both syntactically and semantically. Now they are ready to work with other unknown words placed in contexts such as the following:

> They are too <u>heavy</u> to walk on that ice.
>
> It takes <u>practice</u> to be a good swimmer.
>
> Their clothes are different because their <u>climate</u> is different.

At the beginning, figuring out unknown words should be guided by a teacher's comments and questions—for instance, "Read all the words you know. Think what they mean. What do they suggest the unknown word might be? Now look at how the unknown word is spelled. With that spelling, what do you think it says? Does that make sense? Read the whole sentence. Now, who wants to read the sentence aloud?"

Eventually, children can work alone. To provide evidence of their success, they can be asked to write a sentence for each word they figured out independently. Eventually, too, work with unknown words should be in the context of connected sentences—a paragraph, for instance. In all cases, such work is providing children with the combination of cues that should always be considered whenever new or forgotten words are encountered.

PRACTICE IN USING CONTEXTUAL CUES

As the previous pages have shown, a close connection exists between instruction about contextual cues and practice in using them. It is hoped that the same pages also succeeded in reminding you that unexplained practice is not the kind that makes maximum contributions to reading abilities. To achieve that end, children need to understand how what they are doing has value for those times when they come across in their reading a word that is visually unfamiliar. One second-grade teacher who remembered to make explicit the value of practice for reading wrote the following journal entry.

> In my first entry, I explained that I often listen to children read individually in a private area of the room for diagnostic purposes. When doing this recently, I noticed that many of them were stopping when they came to an unknown word and immediately began using phonics rather than reading the rest of the sentence first. Failure to read to the end of the sentence indicates they are not using contextual cues. I would not be overly concerned if their decoding skills were fast and efficient, but the majority of children are slow at decoding and, as a consequence, have comprehension problems. The following is a discussion of a lesson designed to help students become aware of the help that contextual cues give, and to provide practice.
>
> Sentences written on strips were prepared ahead of time. Each had a blank where a word was omitted. The sentence offered both syntactic and semantic cues. I put many of the blanks near the beginning of the sentence so that I could stress the importance of reading the latter part of the sentence to find help. When I introduced the lesson, I did not use the words "syntactic" and "semantic" because, as pointed out in class, terms like these can be confusing. This is especially true if a teacher uses them before the children have adequate understanding of the parts of speech. Instead, I simply explained that the words near an unknown word often give clues about the unknown word, and all good detectives use them.
>
> The sentence strips were placed in a word chart, one at a time. The children were directed to read a sentence silently and to think of a word that would make sense in the blank. All answers that made sense were accepted. I then pointed out that when reading, unknown words are like the blanks and the sentence can give clues about what that word may be.
>
> To provide additional practice, the children played a board game that required them to draw a card showing an incomplete sentence. If the child could name a word for the sentence that made sense, he moved the number of spaces rolled on the dice. The first one to the finish line won. The children seemed to enjoy the game.
>
> The main benefit I derived from our class discussion of contextual cues was a realization of the importance of explaining and showing children the relationship between the practice they do and the application of the skill when reading. In other words, children should realize that all practice is a means to an end.

How work with the use of contextual and graphophonic cues should develop over time is summarized in Figure 8.3.

PROGRESSION IN USING CONTEXTS

Spoken contexts
1. Word omitted at end of sentence.
2. Word omitted anywhere in sentence.

Spoken Contexts/Minimal Graphophonic Cues
3. First letter of omitted word is named or shown.

Written Contexts
4. Sentence with omitted word. Children select suitable word from listed possibilities.
5. Sentence with omitted word. Children fill in blank with any suitable word.

Written Contexts/Incomplete Graphophonic Cues
6. Sentence with omitted word whose first letter is indicated.
7. Sentence with omitted word whose first and last letters are indicated.
8. Sentence with omitted word whose first syllable is indicated.

Written Contexts/Complete Graphophonic Cues
9. Sentence with an unknown word.

Figure 8.3

CONTEXTS AND WORD MEANINGS

How to help children acquire the ability to recognize a word that is known in its spoken form but not in its written form has been the topic of concern thus far. A number of times, and rightly so, credit for such ability was given to experiences, world knowledge, and oral vocabularies as well as to the use of contextual and graphophonic cues. Now it is time to ask, What about occasions when children encounter words that are totally unfamiliar in the sense that they are not in their reading vocabulary or in their oral vocabulary? Will contextual and graphophonic cues help in these cases?

To begin, even maximum skill in using graphophonic cues does not result in help with the meaning of totally unknown words. This reflects the fact that the pronunciation of a word triggers meaning only if the word is known in its spoken form. Consequently, if the totally unfamiliar word *ibis* appears either alone (which is unlikely) or in a context such as *You will not find an ibis in this state*, use of the spelling will yield its pronunciation but will not suggest anything about its meaning. Nor will help come from the context cited above.

In that context, syntactic cues do indicate that *ibis* is a noun; semantic cues, however, are virtually nonexistent. In contrast, semantic cues provide varying amounts of help in the contexts that follow.

1. An ibis is in the same family as the stork.
2. Since it likes to wade in warm water, you will not find an ibis in this state.
3. An ibis, a large wading bird that looks like a stork, lives near warm water. You will not find an ibis in this state.

For readers who know about storks, the first context has semantic cues that provide information about the meaning of *ibis*. If the reader knows that some birds wade in water, the second context may be helpful, too. (What needs to be kept in mind in this discussion is that text about an ibis is apt to be at least a paragraph in length, perhaps accompanied by a picture.) Clearly, the third context listed above provides the greatest amount of semantic help, assuming the meanings of *wade* and *stork* are known.

Let's consider more examples of unknown words embedded in contexts in order to clarify still further the roles of contextual and graphophonic cues (and experiences) in facilitating the comprehension of connected text.

> *Word:*   *eye* (in oral vocabulary but not in reading vocabulary)
> *Context:*   *Some dust was in his eye, making it hard to see.*
> *Comment:*   Even though graphophonic cues will not help with the pronunciation of an irregularly spelled word like *eye*, the context (plus the child's experiences) should allow for recognizing *eye*.

> *Word:*   *pleasant* (not in oral or reading vocabularies)
> *Context:*   *The day was pleasant. It was warm and sunny.*
> *Comment:*   It is possible that the use of graphophonic cues will not result in a correct pronunciation for *pleasant*. Even if it did, nothing would be revealed about the meaning of *pleasant*. Contextual information, however, does offer an approximate meaning, which, in this instance, is enough to allow for understanding the author's message.

> *Word:*   *papaya* (not in oral or reading vocabularies)
> *Context:*   *Instead of having grapefruit for breakfast, they had papaya.*
> *Comment:*   Again, a pronunciation is not likely to be achieved by using the spelling of *papaya*. In this case, the context is such as to indicate that papaya refers to some kind of fruit, which is likely to be sufficient information under most circumstances.

> *Word:*   *ladle* (in oral vocabulary but not in reading vocabulary)
> *Context:*   *He used the ladle.*

Comment: Since the context offers minimal help, it is fortunate that the use of graphophonic cues can result in the pronunciation of *ladle*. In turn, that will suggest its meaning since *ladle* is in the reader's oral vocabulary. (If the reader is not skillful enough to figure out the pronunciation of *ladle* and, second, if recognizing *ladle* is important in relation to the reader's purpose, then a dictionary should be consulted.)

With the help of the examples just discussed, the meaning of the following observations should be clear.

1. If a word is not in a reader's oral vocabulary, contexts will provide maximum assistance with meaning when that word is the only one that is unknown. The context *An ibis is in the same family as the stork* illustrated this.
2. If a word is in a reader's oral vocabulary and has a highly irregular spelling, a context plus experience may combine to provide enough help to reach correct conclusions about the word. This was demonstrated in the sentence *Some dust was in his eye, making it hard to see.*
3. Many times, an approximate meaning for a word is sufficient for comprehension. To be remembered, too, is that comprehension is not necessarily impeded by the failure to know the pronunciation of a word. The adequacy of approximate meanings was illustrated in the contexts *The day was pleasant. It was warm and sunny;* and *Instead of having grapefruit for breakfast, they had papaya.* The latter context also demonstrated that failure to know the pronunciation of a word does not always interfere with comprehension.
4. In contrast, knowing the pronunciation of a written word is the sole source of help with comprehension under the following conditions: (a) the word is in the reader's oral vocabulary, and (b) the word is in a context that is minimally helpful. All this was illustrated in the example *He used a ladle.*

To keep the discussion realistic, it is important to remember that even though contexts determine the meaning of a word, they do not always reveal it. This point underscores the need to do whatever is possible to add to children's oral vocabularies. How to augment them is the topic of Chapter 12.

TEACHING ABOUT CONTEXTS AS A HELP WITH WORD MEANINGS

Given the fundamental importance of word meanings for comprehending, an instructional program should always allot time for attention to how contexts may help with meanings. Since what teachers do with contexts for that purpose should relate to whatever their students are reading, subject matter for instruction ought to originate in that source. Or, stated differently, of what value is it to teach that appositives and clauses often define words if those constructions are not in the material children are able to read? What follows, therefore, are six brief contexts taken from primary-grade readers. Each sample is followed by other contexts teachers might compose to serve as additional examples. (Underlined words are those whose meanings are unknown.) Also listed is what can be emphasized during instruction with the help of the contexts.

Sample Contexts and Instructional Possibilities

1. Bobby lives on Black Mesa. A mesa is a hill that is flat on the top.
   The man was riding on a burro. A burro is a donkey.
   They heard a coyote cry out in the night. A coyote is a wild animal that looks like a dog.
   The kind of sailboat that my uncle has is called a sloop.

   What can be emphasized: Sometimes, authors explain the meaning of a word directly.

2. The car swerved off the road to keep from running over the cat.
   Amy fell down. She injured her leg.
   The ice was too frigid to hold in my hand.
   He ignited the paper with the match.

   What can be emphasized: Experiences and world knowledge help with the meaning of an unknown word.

3. The top of Rachel's dress is aqua and yellow. The bottom is white.
   A banana, orange, and mango were in the fruit bowl.
   The two chairs and sofa will seat five people.
   The band still needs someone to play the drums and the saxophone.

   What can be emphasized: Commonly, similar things are discussed together. Knowing the words that name some often suggests a general meaning or classification for what the unknown word names.

4. That summer, there was a drought. Day after day went by without any rain.
   Be thrifty. Don't spend your money on silly things.
   Leo asked, "Do you have any siblings?" "Yes," said Kate. "I have one sister and two brothers."
   The water in the dog's dish was solid. It had turned into ice.

   What can be emphasized: Authors sometimes use a word in one sentence, then help with its meaning in the sentence that follows.

5. The horse was just a week old. He was a beautiful foal.
   Van began to yell and stamp his feet. He was furious.

Give a short talk. Be concise.
He always tries hard. He gets an *A* for effort.

What can be emphasized: Sometimes, help with the meaning of a word is suggested in the previous sentence.

6. I need a box that is strong enough to hold my books. This one is too flimsy.
Keep the papers you want and discard the others.
At first, the man walked rapidly. Then he began to walk more slowly.
They got an enormous piece of pie, but I only got a small one.

What can be emphasized: A known word that means the opposite of an unknown one may help define the latter.

A Sample Lesson

Two kinds of words, homonyms and homographs, are especially helpful in teaching children that the meaning of a word is suggested by other words in the same context. Since homonyms are more common than homographs, the illustrative lesson that follows focuses on them. The objectives of the lesson are to help children understand, first, that a word often has more than one meaning and, second, that the intended meaning derives from the context in which the word occurs.

To start this lesson, the teacher prints *hand* on the board and asks the group she is instructing to read it. A request to hold up one hand follows. The teacher then shows a picture of a clock and asks, "Does anyone know what the part of a clock that points to the numbers is called?" Immediately, all respond, "The hand!" Instruction then progresses as follows:

Teacher: We have a hand and so does a clock. I've put two sentences on this card. Both have the word *hand*. Would you read the first sentence, Jack?

Jack: The big hand is on ten and the small hand is on eight.

Teacher: What about the word *hand* in the sentence that Jack just read? Who can tell us what *hand* means in that sentence? It's used twice. Kim?

Kim: It means the hands on a clock or watch.

Teacher: Yes, we mustn't forget watches because they have hands, too. What about the word *hand* in this second sentence? [*She has a dime in her hand.*] Read this second sentence so that you'll know what *hand* means. . . . What does the word *hand* mean now, Melissa?

Melissa: It means the hand that we have.

Teacher: How do you know?

Melissa: Well, we hold money in our hand. And, besides, we don't call a clock "she."

Teacher: Good for you. Again, the other words in this sentence told us what to think of when we read *hand*. What about this sentence? [Writes on the board *Hand me the dime.*] Read this to yourself and pretend that I'm saying it. Who will pretend to do what this sentence says? Okay. George wants to try. [George pretends to give a dime to the teacher.] As you can see, George used the other words in the sentence to tell him what *hand* means now. We have had one word and three different meanings. If I wrote *hand* all by itself, you wouldn't know for sure what it meant; but when I put it in a sentence, the other words give you a clue about its meaning.

The teacher continues, using a similar procedure with *cut* and *rock*. Afterward, each child is given a paper that lists groups of sentences followed by definitions. The first group (with answers) is as follows:

---

1. We <u>play</u> after school.
2. We'll have a <u>play</u> on Friday.
3. I can <u>play</u> the piano.

   (2) like a story   (3) make music   (1) have fun

To allow for immediate corrective feedback, the teacher works with the children as they make decisions about what number (and why) to put in each parenthesis. The children are then asked to work alone on two more sheets dealing with the same task.

When the teacher meets with this group the next day, they check and discuss answers, after which the teacher has the children look at specified sentences in their basal reader in order to make more decisions about the meanings of homonyms. (words spelled same – different meanings)

The next lesson deals with homonyms whose meanings are not likely to be known but can be inferred from the sentences in which the homonyms are found. For instance:

The dog stood on the high <u>bank</u> of snow.

She's mixing the <u>batter</u> for the pancakes now.

They were down at the <u>foot</u> of the hill.

As the children progress with these various lessons, they should be learning that words, like people, are affected by the company they keep. That is what using contextual information is all about.

SUMMARY

The importance of helping children acquire the ability to solve their own reading problems was acknowledged in Chapter 8 as it pointed up the value of contextual information for developing independence. Although helpful information is available in both nonverbal and verbal contexts, the latter were the focus of the chapter.

Initially, verbal contexts were discussed as sources of help with words that are familiar in their spoken form but not in their written form. In such cases, the need for readers is to decide what a written word says, as its pronunciation will indicate what it means. Achieving pronunciations is accomplished with the help of cues, which include those rooted in the context in which the unknown word occurs.

In English, there are two types of contextual cues, syntactic and semantic. Syntactic cues are available to help with unknown words because in a positional language such as English, where a word occurs in a sentence indicates its grammatical function. Consequently, syntactic cues offer indirect help with unknown words by indicating the part of speech they are. In a sentence like *The _____ went fast*, the position of the omitted word points to the fact that it is a noun.

Further constraints are put on unknown words by what the known words in the same context mean. Because this source of help derives from meaning, it is referred to as a semantic cue. Syntactic cues are confined to sentences; semantic cues are not. This is illustrated in the text *I didn't have lunch. Now I am very _____.* The syntax of the second sentence reveals that the missing word is an adjective. On the other hand, it is the meaning of the entire text that makes a descriptive word like *hungry* acceptable but one like *rainy* unacceptable.

To make the discussion of contextual cues realistic, the descriptions of instruction and practice in Chapter 8 also gave attention to the help with pronunciations that comes from spellings. To make sure that children do not have to cope with too many unknown words and, further, to ensure that contexts will in fact exist, the need to develop sizable sight vocabularies was stressed again.

The concluding sections in Chapter 8 switched the focus to possible sources of help for a word that is unknown both in its written and its spoken forms. Since, in this case, meaning is of primary importance, how children can ascertain the meaning of a word from contextual information was discussed. At the end, a sample lesson with homonyms was described, along with practice done first under a teacher's supervision in order to provide immediate feedback, and then by the children working alone. As ought to be true of all lessons, the illustrative one made explicit how what was being taught and practiced functions for readers.

REVIEW

1. At one point in Chapter 8, it was said that "Exactly what constitutes local contexts will be clarified as the two kinds of cues that they provide are discussed."

   a. What are the two kinds of cues?
   b. What are local contexts?

2. Respond to the questions below in relation to the discussion of contexts in Chapter 8:

   a. Why are sizable sight vocabularies so important?
   b. Why are sizable oral vocabularies so important?

3. Explain why using contextual cues to learn what a word says results in word recognition, not word identification. Next, explain the significance of this limitation for instructional programs.

4. Let's say that children's responses to *trot* in the sentence *See the horse trot down the road* include *gallop, throat, travel, trot, trudge, try,* and *turn.* List the seven responses from the best to the worst. What are the reasons for your classifications?

5. Why is the following wise advice for children: Once you decide what a troublesome word says, return to the start of the sentence and read the whole of it. *Helps to be sure they picked right word make sense in context*

6. Why is the following wise advice for teachers: Make certain that children understand the connection between doing exercises and becoming a better reader.

7. During a classroom observation, a teacher wrote on the board *The children were idle.* Subsequently, the following dialogue was heard:

   — Write on board show difference

   > *Teacher:* What does "idle" mean?
   >
   > *Anna:* It means a statue.
   >
   > *Teacher:* No, that's another word. Who can tell me what "idle" means?

   Based on Chapter 8, describe better teacher responses.

REFERENCES

1. Artley, A. Sterl. "Words, Words, Words." *Language Arts* 52 (November/ December, 1975), 1067–1072.
2. Barr, Rebecca C. "The Influence of Instructional Conditions on Word Recognition Errors." *Reading Research Quarterly* 7 (Spring, 1972), 509–529.
3. Carnine, Douglas; Kameenui, Edward J.; and Coyle, Gayle. "Utilization of Contextual Information in Determining the Meaning of Unfamiliar Words." *Reading Research Quarterly* 19 (Winter, 1984), 188–204.
4. Durkin, Dolores. *Strategies for Identifying Words*, 2nd ed. Boston: Allyn and Bacon, Inc., 1981.
5. Durkin, Dolores. "Listen to Your Children." *Instructor* 81 (February, 1972), 87–88.
6. Gomberg, Adeline W. "Freeing Children to Take a Chance." *Reading Teacher* 29 (February, 1976), 455–457.
7. Johnson, Dale D., and Pearson, P. David. *Teaching Reading Vocabulary*, 2nd ed. New York: Holt, Rinehart and Winston, 1984.
8. Jongsma, Eugene. *The Cloze Procedure as a Teaching Technique*. Newark, Del.: The International Reading Association, 1971.
9. Juel, Connie. "Comparison of Word Identification Strategies with Varying Context, Word Type, and Reader Skill." *Reading Research Quarterly* 15 (1980, No. 3), 358–376.
10. MacGinitie, Walter H. "Contextual Constraint in English Prose Paragraphs." *Journal of Psychology* 51 (January, 1961), 121–130.
11. Nagy, William E., and Anderson, Richard C. "How Many Words Are There in Printed English?" *Reading Research Quarterly* 19 (Spring, 1984), 304–330.
12. Pflaum, Susanna W., and Bryan, Tanis H. "Oral Reading Behaviors in the Learning Disabled." *Journal of Educational Research* 73 (May/June, 1980), 252–258.
13. Samuels, S. Jay; Dahl, Patricia; and Archwamety, Teara. "Effect of Hypothesis/ Test Training on Reading Skill." *Journal of Educational Psychology* 56 (December, 1974), 835–844.
14. Sternberg, R., and Powell, J. "Comprehending Verbal Comprehension." *American Psychologist* 38 (August, 1983), 878–893.
15. Watson, Dorothy J., and Stansell, John G. "Miscues We Have Known and Loved." *Reading Psychology* 1 (Spring, 1980), 127–132.
16. West, Richard F.; Stanovich, Keith E.; Feeman, Dorothy J.; and Cunningham, Anne E. "The Effect of Sentence Context on Word Recognition in Second- and Sixth-Grade Children." *Reading Research Quarterly* 19 (Fall, 1983), 6–15.

CHAPTER 9

Phonics:
At the Start

PREVIEW

The acquisition of beginning literacy confronts children with what has been called "the written language puzzle" (10). And, as Anne Dyson correctly points out, ". . . as with most puzzles, children cannot solve it by being given only one piece at a time" (10, p. 838).

To help very young children view pieces of the written language puzzle in relation to the whole, it is highly advisable to read to them often. By occasionally pointing out sentences or less, which, for one reason or another, are important or of interest, the reader is able to call attention to pieces in the framework of the whole.

Whenever teachers or others write, and then read aloud, what children say about an experience or a picture they have drawn, they, too, are allowing for a look at the whole. When they subsequently select one or more child-generated words for special attention, they are also showing pieces in meaningful ways.

Teachers who make explicit the availability of contextual cues with procedures like those described in the previous chapter are continuing to help children see pieces as they relate to the whole. The same can be said about teachers who show children the usefulness of graphophonic cues in the way recommended in the same chapter.

Whereas Chapter 8 focused on the early use of graphophonic cues, this chapter steps back, as it were, to concentrate on how to teach them. Because such instruction at the beginning is a natural extension of teaching children how to print, the two kinds of instruction are considered here in Chapter 9. Since the two feature letters occurring in words, they continue the practice of helping children see how a piece, in this case, a letter, relates to the whole, in this case, a word.

Because children who are both learning to print and learning about letter-sound correspondences often move on to produce their own words, Chapter 9 includes a brief section on composing. Chapter 15 also looks at the reading-writing relationship.

The kinds of cues, or prompts, that have the potential to help children cope on their own with troublesome words stem from the nature of the language they are learning to read. Syntactic cues are available to readers of English because, as the previous chapter explained, English is a positional language. On the other hand, semantic cues exist because, like all languages, English makes sense. Of relevance now is that the writing system of English is alphabetic, which allows for prompts in the form of graphophonic cues. These cues are rooted in the connection between spellings (*grapho*) and pronunciations (*phonic*). Using graphophonic cues to work out the pronunciation of words is called *decoding*.

Obviously, decoding English words would be easier than it sometimes is if a perfectly consistent correspondence existed between letters and speech sounds. Since that hardly is the case, what is taught about letter-sound relationships must be viewed by children (and teachers) not as something that inevitably provides correct answers but only as a starting point in the decoding process. Nonetheless, when what is taught about graphophonic cues is applied with flexibility and used jointly with contextual help, the amount of independence a child can develop for dealing successfully with unfamiliar words is great. When the importance of such independence is kept in mind, what is done with phonics will be done well.

SEQUENCE FOR BEGINNING PHONICS

Even though there is no one, universally accepted way to provide beginning instruction in phonics, the focus of such instruction is always the same: speech sounds that letters represent. Because consonant letters are more consistent than vowels in the sounds they stand for, beginning phonics instruction typically attends to some consonants first.

Teachers who rely on commercially prepared manuals usually work with letter-sound relationships in the order the manuals suggest. More flexible teachers, on the other hand, use different criteria for deciding when any given letter will get attention. As illustrated in Chapter 4, one teacher might decide to teach about a sound that *s* records because she has students named *Sam, Steven*, and *Sandy*. (See page 79 for the earlier description of how the three names functioned in beginning phonics.) In another case, a teacher decides it is an opportune time to deal with *v* because, during art, the children will be making vases and violets. (See pages 107–108 to review how an art project contributed to beginning phonics.) In another classroom, the word *door* takes on significance because of the excessive noise of slamming doors. In this instance, a teacher decides to use what started out as a problem to call attention to *door*, to *d*, and to the sound *d* stands for with the help of the bulletin-board display shown in Figure 9.1. (The display suggests that such displays can improve instruction by maximizing children's attention.)

Figure 9.1. *Teaching the Sound Recorded by D*

This bulletin board display was used to highlight the sound that *d* stands for in *door*. The board shows the outline of two doors, each with a doorknob. After printing *door* on the chalkboard next to the bulletin board, the teacher and children discussed *doorknob*, which was printed directly under *door*. In a second column, the names of three students were printed: *Don, Derek*, and *Donna*. All five words were read aloud by the children in response to the teacher's request, "Please read these words. They begin with the same letter. See if you can hear how they also begin with the same sound." Subsequently, objects on the board were named and discussed. Each label was added to a column on the chalkboard. Finally, all the words were read with the teacher's help, after which she summarized by saying, "Remember, capital *D* and lower-case *d* both stand for the sound you hear at the beginning of *door, doorknob, Don, Derek*, and *Donna*."

What the three illustrations point up is the desirability of flexible rather than predetermined sequences for teaching letter-sound correspondences, since that allows for taking advantage of both current interests and unexpected opportunities. The same three illustrations further show that teaching children to read some words allows for phonics instruction that deals with letter-sound relationships, not as isolated bits of information, but in the meaningful context of words.

Much more will be said in the following chapter about the use of known words to teach phonics. Right now, how printing instruction helps with beginning phonics is the main concern.

BEGINNING PHONICS AND PRINTING

Why printing instruction merits the spotlight in a chapter on beginning phonics is explained below:

WHAT CHILDREN CAN ACQUIRE FROM PRINTING INSTRUCTION

1. Understanding of *same* and *different* applied to letters.
2. Ability in visual discrimination.
3. Knowledge of letter names.
4. Awareness that words are composed of letters.
5. Understanding of the left-to-right orientation of print.
6. Awareness that letters stand for sounds.
7. Awareness that the writing (spelling) of a word is related to its pronunciation.
8. Understanding of "beginning of a word."
9. Understanding of "beginning sound."
10. Knowledge of some letter-sound correspondences.

As the list shows, the use of printing—in the ways subsequently described—can make major contributions to developing prerequisites for success with beginning phonics. This will become clear as the chapter shows the natural connection between printing, sometimes called *manuscript writing*, and learning about the sounds that letters record.

How to teach printing is discussed first. Afterward, how printing and beginning phonics can be linked is explained with a number of examples.

PRINTING INSTRUCTION

The description of printing instruction starts with a consideration of pre-instruction decisions.

Initial Decisions

One of the first questions to answer is which manuscript system to use. Many are available, one of which is shown in Figure 9.2. Since research has nothing to say about which system is easiest to teach, choices usually are based on such factors as familiarity and convenience. They also are commonly made by individuals other than a teacher. (If you teach nursery school and are making a selection yourself, find out which system is used in the local schools, because choosing what they use will allow for continuity.)

Regardless of how the decision is made, what is important is that teachers have some system and that they use it with consistency and facility. The same directive is relevant for parents, which suggests the wisdom of providing them with a copy of whatever system is used in school. At a meeting held in the spring for parents of prospective kindergartners, they could be taught manuscript writing and also be reminded that lowercase letters are much more important than the capital forms.*

Sequence for Instruction

When consideration is given to a sequence for attending to the various letters, a number of factors need to be kept in mind. One is difficulty. This suggests starting with more easily made letters such as *i, l, t,* or *x.* Mentioning *x* points up a second factor meriting attention, namely, usefulness. Because learning to print is a means to an end—in this case, writing words and learning letter-sound correspondences—attention to less frequently used letters like *x, q,* and *z* can be postponed.

Likelihood of confusion is another factor to think about when the sequence for printing instruction is the concern. Here, the notorious problem with *b* and *d* comes immediately to mind, suggesting that attention to each be separated by time. The same guideline applies to pairs like *p* and *q.*

The last factor to be mentioned may be the most important. I refer to interest and to the observable fact that some letters are more appealing than others. Those in a child's name, for example, are naturally special, but others can be made special. I recall a nursery school class in which the letter *s*, often

---

*The terms *capital* and *lowercase* (not *small* and *big*) should be used for the simple reason that some "small" letters are as big as capital letters. *Capital* rather than *uppercase* is recommended since it is useful later when capitalization is the focus of instruction.

difficult to make, presented no problems when introduced on the day that brought winter's first snow.

The kind of paper to use is another practical concern. At the start, when children's efforts result more in scribbling than in printing, large unlined paper is suitable. Soon, though, a shift should be made to manuscript paper, which has uniformly spaced lines that make demands pertaining to placement and size. (If children print on chalkboards, they should be lined, too.) For manuscript writing, paper is placed squarely in front of the child with its lower edge parallel to the edge of the desk or table. The child's nonwriting hand is placed at the top to keep the paper from moving. Nothing should be done to try to change the left-handed writer.

In the beginning, help should be given in how to hold a pencil correctly: between the thumb and first finger, resting on the other fingers. Even though educators in earlier decades had much to say about the need for oversize pencils with young children—this was one outgrowth of the exaggerated attention given to maturation—observation indicates they are more awkward, not easier, to handle. Regular size pencils, then, should be used. They ought to be reasonably long, which is to say not like the stubs sometimes seen when classrooms are visited.*

One other question about printing instruction has to do with its pace. The only sensible guideline is to teach the letters as quickly as the children are comfortably able to learn them—but no faster. What turns out to be a comfortable pace will be affected not only by the children's motor coordination and interest but also by the amount of time allotted to printing instruction. In a nursery school—should the teacher decide to teach some printing—the time might be as limited as one or two weekly periods of about fifteen minutes' duration. In first grade, on the other hand, it would probably be daily periods of varying length.

Getting Children Ready for Printing

Whether you teach (or plan to teach) nursery school, kindergarten, or first grade, remember that individual children might have done some printing before coming to school. For the most part, they will only know about capital letters (unless their parents were informed about the importance of lowercase letters) and often will be using incorrect strokes. Nonetheless, they have begun and usually do not require the preparation essential for other children.

The other children often need such basic information as how to hold a

---

*A finding from the research with preschool readers referred to in Chapter 5 is relevant here. The children routinely used regular pencils before starting school; then, in first grade, they were expected to use extra large ones because official school policy said they were unready for the regular size (7). Isn't it unfortunate that so little attention is paid to the children when decisions about them are being made?

D'Nealian™ Manuscript Alphabet

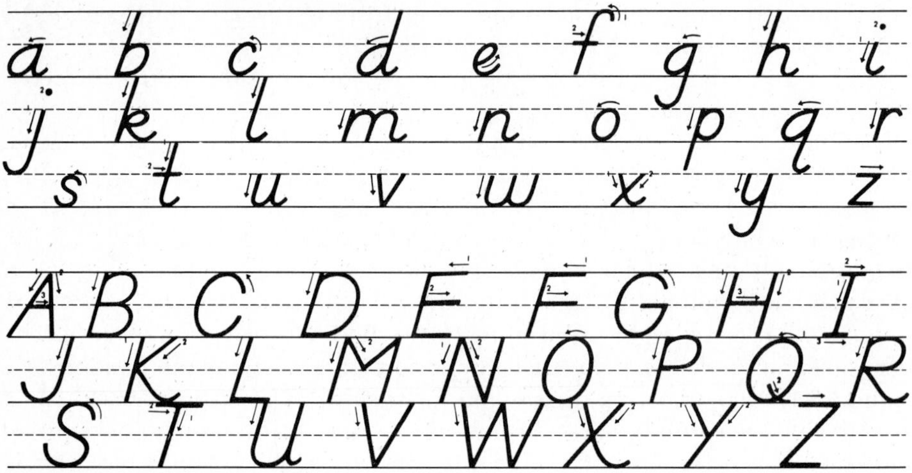

Figure 9.2. *A Manuscript Writing System*

From D'NEALIAN™ HANDWRITING by Donald Thurber. Copyright © 1981 by Scott, Foresman and Company. Reprinted by permission.

This manuscript system is different from most, as the letters are slanted rather than straight. The difference is said by the publisher to facilitate the change from manuscript to cursive writing. Such a claim, however, is not supported by research.

Choosing a manuscript system that is different from others may create problems if children are also using materials in which a more conventional kind of printing is found (see Figure 9.3).

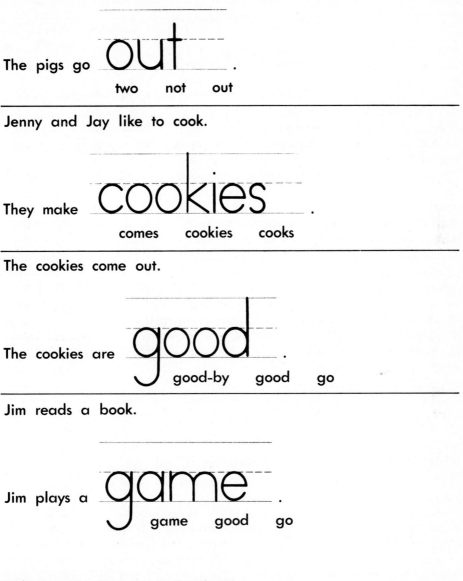

The wolf comes in.

The pigs go out .

two   not   out

Jenny and Jay like to cook.

They make cookies .

comes   cookies   cooks

The cookies come out.

The cookies are good .

good-by   good   go

Jim reads a book.

Jim plays a game .

game   good   go

Level 4: "Jenny and Jay Cook," pp. 16–23. (Comprehension)
Objective: To acquire a basic reading vocabulary. To understand the direct, literal meaning of a sentence.
Directions: Read each pair of sentences. Choose the word that best completes the second sentence of each pair. Write the word in the space.

51

Figure 9.3. *Word and Printing Practice*

From the HOLT BASIC READING SERIES: WORKBOOK, LEVELS 3–6, Teacher's Edition by Weiss, Evertts and Steuer. Copyright © 1983 by Holt, Rinehart and Winston, Publishers. Used with permission.

pencil and how to keep paper from moving. (Without some guidance, children who have had no experience with pencils may hold them as if they were going to stir rather than print.) They may also have to learn the referents for *top* and *bottom*, and for *left side* and *right side*. If experiences at home did not include the chance to use pencils, crayons, and paper, these children will also need to do some scribbling to get a feel for the materials and to experience what might be called "pencil power." Once it is experienced and some control is achieved, the scribbling can be channeled somewhat. I recall one kindergarten teacher who, by having children color the spaces resulting from a limited amount of scribbling, turned their papers into interesting mosaics – or as one child aptly described them, "windows like my church has."

Following the aimless scribbling, beginners should next be encouraged to try to copy or make objects. Of special relevance for manuscript writing are round or oval shapes such as are found in wheels, doughnuts, pumpkins, snowmen, eyes, and eggs. Straight lines can be practiced when children make doors, windows, fences, ladders, and so on.

Thus far, attention has gone to physical preparations, but this is not meant to overshadow the psychological, because getting children interested in learning to print is of major importance. Some children, of course, are already interested, having watched parents or perhaps older siblings write at home. When the interest has not been acquired, probably the quickest way to foster it is to entice the children with the prospect of learning to print their names, always a favorite not only with the young but, as Dale Carnegie tells it, with adults, too (3).

Finding occasions to call attention to names is no problem. The combination of a teacher's taking attendance (done with cards held by her) and signing first names to the children's papers and possessions (e.g., pictures, crayon boxes, and coat hooks) is enough to highlight them. Before long, the children will want to print their names themselves; thus, it isn't long, either, before instruction with printing can get under way.

Initial Lessons

Selecting a letter is the first step. One of the many ways this might be done is explained with a description of an effective kindergarten teacher.

She did nothing with printing until November. Earlier, the children had become accustomed to using pencils and paper and had made both straight lines (fences, houses, tepees) and circles (faces, suns, clocks). Meanwhile, the teacher had decided to get writing started by giving attention to *T* and *t*. This is how the instruction began.

On the first Tuesday in November, as had become the daily practice, the morning started with comments about the weather, what day it was, and so on. Although a card showing *Tuesday* ordinarily would have been on a bulletin board, it was not there in order to give the teacher a reason to say, "I forgot to put up Tuesday," and to print it on the chalkboard as the children watched. Then came the question, "Does anyone know the name of the first letter that I made in order to write Tuesday?" Nobody did, so the teacher answered her own question. She also mentioned it was a capital *T* because *Tuesday* was the name of a day and, like the children's names, began with a capital letter.

She next printed and named lowercase *t* and asked whether anyone could find a word in the room that started with that. (About a week earlier, a small chart showing *one* and *two* written beneath *1* and *2* had been displayed and discussed.) Several children immediately pointed to the number chart, after which the teacher printed *two*. Next she mentioned the possibility of everyone's learning to make *T* and *t*. The children were enthusiastic, which made it the perfect time for the first writing lesson.

The lesson started with the teacher's suggestion to try some "skywriting." (This led to comments about airplanes that write messages in the sky.) The children stood and held up their writing hands; the teacher faced them and demonstrated the correct way to make *T*. Then, as she made it again, the children followed along making their own *T*'s in the air. As they did this, the teacher watched to make sure that the direction of their strokes was correct.

Following the air writing, the children sat down and each received a pencil and a sheet of unlined paper. After some reminders about how to hold the pencil and where to place the paper, they proceeded to make *T*'s wherever they chose but only on one side of the paper. The teacher circulated among them, correcting strokes that were being made in the wrong sequence or direction. Subsequently, the same procedure was followed for lowercase *t*, made on the other side of the paper.

The next day, the kindergartners were taken to visit in a first-grade room where, as had been planned, the children were having a printing lesson using lined manuscript paper. The visit created enough interest in writing for the kindergarten teacher to suggest, after they had returned to their own room, that she get some of the special paper used by the first graders. On the following morning, it was available, and "big kid" writing lessons began, the first dealing only with capital *T*.

As before, words beginning with *T* were named and written on the chalkboard:

Instruction began with skywriting, after which pencils and half sheets of manuscript paper (Figure 9.4) were distributed.

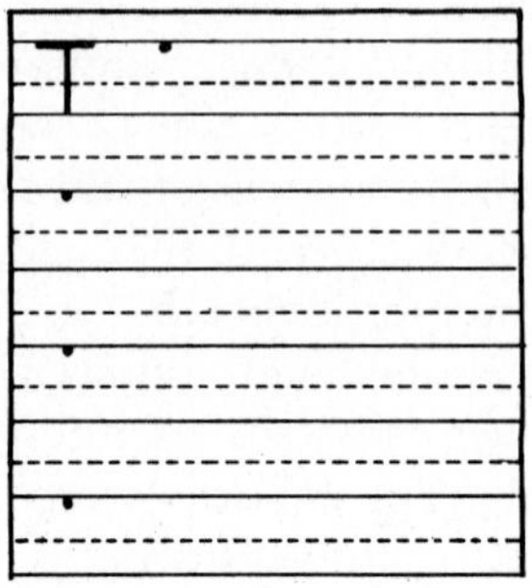

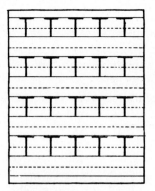

Figure 9.4

One *T* had been printed on each sheet so the children would have a close-at-hand model to follow. (Copying from something as far away as a chalkboard can be difficult for young children.) Dots were added to show where to make the first *T* and where each new row of *T*'s was to begin. (Half sheets of paper were used because past experiences had revealed that a whole sheet was discouraging for some children; too many letters were needed to fill it up.) Finally, a model of a completed paper was hung up for all to see (Figure 9.5). The completed paper had been prepared because the teacher had also learned from earlier experiences that a completed model, like a picture, is better than a thousand words for explaining a task.

Figure 9.5

As soon as pencils and paper were ready, the children began their first attempt to use lined paper. By providing the dot, the teacher made sure everyone started the first *T* at the right place. She also offered reminders for making each of the other *T*'s in the first row. When the children started the second row, another dot showed the children where to begin. And so the practice proceeded.

Several days later, after the children had been talking about Thanksgiving and turkeys, the next writing lesson occurred. The word *turkey* was used to initiate work on lowercase *t* and to remind the children that once they knew how to make other letters they would be able to write their own words. To show words that started with *T* and *t*, the teacher listed:

Before rereading the four words, the teacher casually mentioned that they started not only with the same letter but also with the same sound. (Knowing that she would be calling attention to the beginning sound, she did not include words like *Thursday* and *Thanksgiving*.)

The lesson with lowercase *t* was similar to the one for capital *T*. It began with air writing; a finished paper was displayed; and one *t* plus the helpful dots were on the children's sheets. And so another writing lesson was begun.

IMPORTANT FEATURES OF PRINTING INSTRUCTION

Even though not every teacher initiates printing instruction in the way described, the illustrations in the preceding section exemplify seven practices important for any printing instruction. These practices are specified below.

1. Special effort should be made to ensure that early experiences with printing are pleasurable, successful, and purposeful. In the illustrative lessons, the teacher had the children observe first graders, then gave them the "privilege" of using the paper the older children had. To help make initial efforts successful, the teacher chose *T* because it is easy to make. Although the lowercase and capital forms were introduced together, writing on the manuscript paper dealt with one at a time, again to promote success. To establish a purpose for the printing, the teacher explained that the ability to make letters would soon allow for writing words.

2. Young children need a certain amount of physical activity, thus

skywriting was used both to get them out of their chairs and to allow for immediate corrective feedback. Because the skywriting was compared to the writing airplanes do, it added to the children's enjoyment of the lesson.

3. Distractions should be avoided, which explains why the teacher did not distribute pencils and paper until it was time to use them.

4. Correct terminology should be used. The age of the children in the illustration did not keep the teacher from using the terms *capital letter* and *lowercase letter*. She also made sure the name of the letter being taught was mentioned many times.

5. When printing is demonstrated to children, it should be done with special care. That is why the *T*'s on the completed model, plus the sample printed on the children's papers, were perfectly formed. When the teacher was skywriting and facing the children, she was careful to make her strokes in a way that displayed them correctly from the children's perspective.

6. Precautions should be taken to minimize problems. In the illustration, a page of letters was prepared ahead of time to clarify the job at hand. It was then hung up to serve as a continuous reminder of that job. In addition, half sheets of paper were used to prevent the discouragement that can develop when children view a task as being too extensive. Because deciding where to start a letter and a new row can be a problem for beginners, dots were printed on the papers to provide guidelines.

7. When printing instruction is a means for easing children into phonics, certain steps should be added. In the illustration, words that began with *t* were highlighted because the teacher wanted to refer to the beginning sound. (Generally, the initial sound in a short word is the easiest to perceive as a distinct sound. It makes sense, therefore, to start with that.) Although the attention given sounds was casual during the early lessons, it would gradually become more direct and concentrated as time passed.

BEGINNING INSTRUCTION IN PHONICS

As just mentioned, when children acquire some facility in making letters, printing instruction can do more with letter-sound correspondences. For example, after calling the children's attention to the fact that all the *f* words in a given list start with the same sound (all are read aloud to emphasize this feature), a teacher might ask, "Can *you* think of words that begin with the sound you hear at the beginning of *fast, food, fish*, and *fun*?" In some cases, the children might not yet be ready to respond; that is, they still do not have sufficient ability in auditory discrimination or, perhaps, do not understand the meaning of "begin with the same sound." In other cases, however, teachers are in for a pleasant surprise. I recall one nursery school group for which the teacher had been providing printing instruction much like that described earlier. In the spring, I encouraged her to see whether the children could give examples of words beginning with a certain sound, but even then she was hesitant, doubting that they could. Nonetheless, she gave it a try and soon found herself facing children who just about fell off their chairs in their eagerness to name words, in this case words beginning with the sound that *b* records. The first contribution? *Bourbon*.

While observing other groups of young children, I have seen similar auditory ability displayed. Samples of their contributions follow, along with comments about what was done when the designated letter received attention.

As was her practice, the teacher printed and named *M* and *m*, then printed and read some words that started with the letters. (All this naturally prompted comments about *M & M* candy.) An added attraction was a tray of objects (mask, mitten, magnet, map, picture of a man, table mat) covered with a cloth. The teacher said she was a magician—*magician* was dramatically added to the list of words on the chalkboard—and was about to make some things appear whose names started with *m*. The objects were uncovered, after which the children named them with much enthusiasm. As each object was identified, its name was added to the now extensive list on the board. An especially interesting comment from a boy pertained to the table mat, which was decorated with a picture of Donald Duck. He complained, saying, "For *M*, it should be Mickey Mouse."

Following the board work and the effective use of the magic tray, the kindergartners were able to contribute *medicine, milk, monster,* and *magic* as additional words that began with the same letter and sound as *magician*.

L

When *L* and *l* were introduced in another classroom, words named by the children were numerous and quickly offered. They included *laugh, lamp, look, lap, lawn, ladder, lemon, lantern, leaf, letter, lettuce,* and *Lee*. The children (like others seen in different classrooms) took special delight in the fact that the teacher was running out of space on the chalkboard because they could name so many words that began with the same sound as her original examples: *love, lollipop, Larry,* and *Lincoln*.

Later, art time provided the chance to make lemon lollipops. For this project, small circles were cut out of yellow construction paper. Since these were to be the lollipops, *L* was printed on one side and *l* on the other, as this was the first letter in *lollipop*. (That point was made explicit to ensure that the children understood the connection between *L, l*, and the lollipops. Without the direct explanation, some might never see the connection.) Afterward, each child received a straw through which a piece of pipe cleaner has been pushed to make it firm. (The teacher did not distribute "sticks" until it was time to use them. Had they been handed out earlier, some children would have played with them when they were supposed to be printing *L* and *l*.) Quickly, the teacher stapled each child's stick to his lollipop; the result was a group of very happy children, with one exception. This was a boy who strenuously objected to calling what he made a "lollipop." He insisted it was a sucker. The teacher acknowledged the correctness of his suggestion, then wrote *lollipop* and *sucker* on the board. She identified each and asked, "Does anyone know why we're using 'lollipop' today even though some of you do call what we made a sucker?" Immediately, one child rementioned the connection between *lollipop* and *l*. The teacher continued, "Can anyone think of a reason why I didn't ask you to write the whole word *lollipop* on the circles?" Two responses came quickly. One child said she didn't know how to make all the letters. Another said it was too fat to fit. And so an interesting and productive printing-phonics-art lesson came to an end.

H

When *H* and *h* were being introduced, another teacher drew the outline of a large house on the board and asked the children what it was. They answered promptly, after which the teacher carefully printed *house* next to the outline and named the letter *h*. She then inquired, "What else can we call this house? The word I'm thinking of also begins with *h*." Nobody responded. The teacher continued, "Let's play detective. I'll give you a clue. When you leave school, you don't say, 'I'm going house.' You say, 'I'm going ____.'" And, of course, everyone called out "home." That was printed under *house* and *h* was named again.

Following this, the teacher suggested it might be a good idea to write other *h* words inside rather than outside the house in order to keep them warm. (It was January.) Everyone agreed. Eventually, the following were contributed by the children and printed within the outline: *hammer, hat, Halloween* (this word gave the teacher the chance to identify capital *H* and to explain why *Halloween* started with a capital letter), *hunt, harness, hot* ("hot dog" was the suggestion, so the teacher explained why only *hot* could be printed), *hand, head*, and *heart*. To stress the similarity of their beginning sounds, the teacher concluded the phonics part of the lesson by reading all the words named. Then practice in printing *H* and *h* began.

T

One teacher's work with *T* and *t* is described earlier. Here is what another teacher chose to do. In this case, much more was done with the sound that *t* records because the lesson came later in the year.

As was her custom, this teacher began by writing a capital *T*. She identified it and immediately heard from Tommy that it was the first letter in his name. Consequently, under *T* went *Tommy*. She then said she knew another name starting with *T*. She explained it was not a child's name but, instead, the name of a tuba. This prompted questions about a tuba, all of which were answered with the help of a picture of one. The children next tried to guess its proper name but were unsuccessful. The teacher told them as she printed it. The board now showed:

This lesson also had a special surprise, a recording of the song "Tubby the Tuba." After it was played and obviously enjoyed, the teacher asked for additional words that started like *Tommy, Tubby,* and *tuba*. The following were offered and printed on the board: *television, telephone, table, turkey, tea, teeth, tongue, train, tiny, trick, tent, tonsils, towel,* and *truck*. To summarize the phonics part of the lesson, the teacher read the words, commenting again about how they all began with the same sound. Then printing instruction began.

How a commercially prepared reading program combines phonics and printing is illustrated in Figure 9.6. How one first-grade teacher combined the two is described in the journal entry that follows.

> In the chapter on teaching manuscript writing, I found several recommendations that I already follow including the use of a dot on the paper to show the children where to begin to print their first letter on a line. I, too, have found that children do better with half sheets of paper and, in addition, that the letters are clearer when they skip a line. The same holds true for giving them a model of what their paper should look like when they're finished.
>
> To start my writing lesson today, I printed the capital and lowercase forms of *n* on the board. We reviewed the sound that *n* stands for and how to print it in both forms. I next asked for words that start with *n*. The children's suggestions included *nickel, number, nail, nest, name, Nat, nibble,* and *newspaper*. I then distributed copies of a ditto sheet on which I had traced a large necklace. Some said it was a pair of beads, which I acknowledged as being correct. I went on to explain that I called the drawing a "necklace" because we were working on the letter *n* and the sound it stands for in a word like *necklace*.

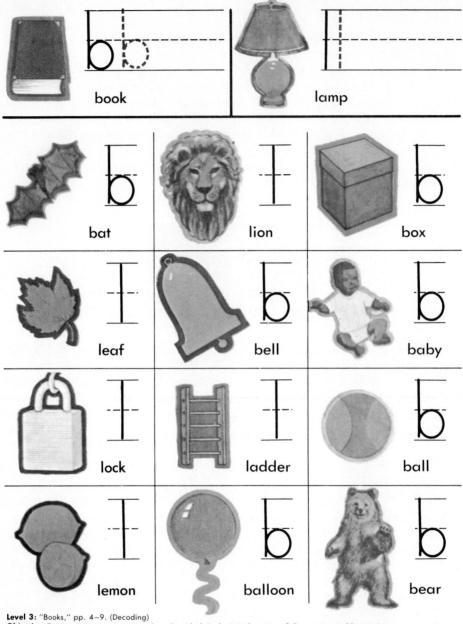

book   lamp

bat   lion   box

leaf   bell   baby

lock   ladder   ball

lemon   balloon   bear

Level 3: "Books," pp. 4–9. (Decoding)
Objective: To associate consonant sounds and symbols in the initial position: /b/b as in *book*, /l/l as in *lamp*.
Directions: Say the words *book* and *lamp*. Then practice writing *b* and *l* at the top of the page. Name each picture below. Write *b* beside each one whose name begins with the same sound as *book*. Write *l* beside each one whose name begins with the same sound as *lamp*.

3

Figure 9.6. *Combining Phonics and Printing*

From the HOLT BASIC READING SERIES: WORKBOOK, LEVELS 3–6, Teacher's Edition by Weiss, Evertts and Steuer. Copyright © 1983 by Holt, Rinehart and Winston, Publishers. Used with permission.

240

Following the discussion of the title (*Necklace*), I asked the children to print each word listed on the board on a bead of their necklace, using their best letters. Afterward, they cut out the necklace and wore it until it was time for lunch. (I thought a more prolonged wearing might create some discipline problems.)

During this activity, I was able to combine printing, phonics, and art in a way that the children seemed to enjoy.

Whether early work with phonics is or is not linked to printing, the following reminders are important.

GUIDELINES FOR BEGINNING
INSTRUCTION IN PHONICS

1. Work done with auditory discrimination should make use of words, not musical or environmental sounds.
2. Perceiving similarities and differences in speech sounds is difficult for many children, which means that slow-paced instruction and generous amounts of practice are often required to ensure the development of auditory discrimination ability.
3. Beginning sounds in words should be featured initially. Later, attention can shift to the same sounds in final position.

PRINTING WORDS

Whether printing and beginning phonics instruction do or do not proceed as complementary activities, children should be helped to understand from the start that learning to form letters is a means for writing their own words and thoughts. One teacher's initial efforts to demonstrate the reason for printing took advantage of the children's perpetual self-interest; she thus started with the word *me*. She first printed *me* on the board, which some children spontaneously identified. Then, at the request of the teacher, all the children named the two letters. (Each had been identified and practiced in an earlier printing lesson.) Next, the teacher suggested it might be a good idea to practice printing *me* because self-portraits (a present for parents) were to be made at art time, and *me* would be a good label.

After practicing *m* and *e* in the air, each child received paper (Figure 9.7).

To specify the task and to serve as a reminder of it, a finished model was displayed in the front of the room (Figure 9.8).

The directions were to print *me* five times. When art began, the children selected their best *m* and *e*, cut them out, and pasted the two rectangular pieces close together (to emphasize the wholeness of the word) at the bottom

Figure 9.7

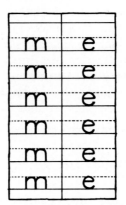

Figure 9.8

of their self-portraits. Motivation and enthusiasm were high; in addition, each letter had been introduced and practiced earlier. The result was a first attempt at writing a word that brought both enjoyment and success.

The ability to print their own names is always a source of enjoyment for young children. (See Figure 9.9.) Even teachers who bypass other printing instruction would be wise to allow time for practice with names if for no other reason than the enjoyment children experience.

Instruction in printing first names can begin with attention to initial letters. One teacher started with the first letter plus a period, explaining that the period would take the place of the remaining letters until all could be made. What she was doing, of course, was paving the way to an understanding of *abbreviation*.

Figure 9.9. *Eight Samples of Name Writing at Mid-Year in Kindergarten*

Practice with initial letters in names can be carried on much like the writing practice already described. Now, though, a teacher will be printing different letters on papers, all of which serve as close-at-hand models when the children attempt their own versions. To replace air writing, impossible now because of the variety of letters, the teacher will move from child to child, offering suggestions and, whenever necessary, helping to correct formations.

Soon the children can practice the first two letters and, before long, all of them. As the various letters are being added, the children can also get some practice in noting their sequence. For this, a small name card can be given to each child, plus an envelope containing all the letters in the name. A more permanent name card might also be attached to each child's desk. Covered with contact paper, its letters can be traced.

As time passes and children routinely sign their names to many papers, they often get careless in forming letters. That is why it is a good idea to schedule time periodically for attention to more careful efforts. For this, the name cards can serve as models, even though they might not have been used for some time. Very helpful, too, are samples of the children's earlier attempts at name writing, done with greater care.

COMPOSING

When both printing and composing skills are limited, children's writing might be as brief as one- or two-word captions for pictures they have drawn. Figure 9.10 shows the efforts of two kindergartners. The first captioned her picture of a sea serpent; the second child listed what she planned to pack for the trip her family was going to take when school ended for the year. Independent writing efforts like these are most apt to occur in classrooms where, earlier, the teacher took the time to print what children dictated. Samples of such dictation were presented earlier (see Figure 5.2) in the discussion of how to show that spoken language has a written counterpart.

Until some independence in printing and spelling is acquired, material that is more extensive than a few words (e.g., invitations, thank-you notes, messages for greeting cards) can be dictated by the children, printed by the teacher, then copied by the children (1).

Once writing skills improve somewhat, a special place can be set aside for writing. Separated from the rest of the classroom by a mobile bulletin board, a table, or bookshelves, the writing center should allow for self-selected, uninterrupted opportunities to do some composing. With this as the goal, a writing center ought to have pencils, pens, and crayons; various sizes of lined and unlined paper; models of the alphabet; and picture dictionaries to help with spelling. To make it an inviting place, other materials should be available, too. Interesting pictures, for instance, often prompt equally interesting writing. Papers with titles or unfinished sentences can also serve as starters.

For children who might choose the writing center as a place to practice their printing, copies of writing workbooks should be available. Occasionally, covers of large boxes can be filled with sand to provide for a special kind of practice. Children also find small, portable chalkboards attractive. A few short papers, carefully printed by the teacher, might be displayed, eventually to be replaced by the children's own work. (Samples of children's illustrated composing efforts constitute Figures 9.11 and 9.12.) Since children doing the composing are providing others with something to read, this is a meaningful time to call attention to requirements like carefully printed letters and ample space between words.

Figure 9.10. *Samples of Beginning Efforts in Composing*

it was a antalope it lived
in a field it had a baby.
The End

Amy AD A Dragon
A Dragon is by big.
My Dragon is Sik.
My Dragon is very very,
tall?

Figure 9.11. *Children's Early Composing Efforts*

What is a friend?

A friend is some one who is
fun.
My friend are Connie
Paula Julie Kataleen
Jana Angela
Rebecca

I saw a red spiter and
it had perpple spots he looked
sille. and it had babys all
difrot colrs. and thay looked
sille too. Kathleen

Figure 9.12. *Samples of More Advanced Writing*

SUMMARY

Written English is alphabetic. As a result, children can be helped to work out pronunciations of words that are unfamiliar in their written form by teaching them letter-sound relationships. Teaching about those relationships goes under the heading *phonics*. Using the relationships to learn what an unknown word says is called *decoding*.

As with any other kind of teaching, phonics instruction proceeds one step at a time, each one building on the previous step. Since consonant letters are more consistent than the vowels in the speech sounds they record, the first steps in phonics instruction are typically concerned with consonants.

The position in Chapter 9 is that, at the start, no need exists to abide by a pre-established sequence for teaching consonant sounds. Instead, a flexible approach to selecting subject matter for instruction was recommended, as this will allow for the use both of what interests children and of "teachable moments." Inherent in such a stance is the belief that before first grade, no given number of letter-sound correspondences *has* to be taught. Also inherent in Chapter 9 is the belief that young children should be eased into work with letter-sound relationships in ways that make them meaningful.

To help make the relationships meaningful, Chapter 9 recommended that they be taught at the start in the context of words. The more specific recommendation was to use words that share the same initial letter and sound. This recommendation is based on the fact that in short words, the easiest sound to perceive as a distinct sound is the one in the initial position. Words such as *bat, ball, Ben, and Bart*, therefore, serve well in illustrating the sound that *b* (and *B*) represents.

Combining beginning phonics instruction with what is done to teach children to print was recommended in the chapter for two reasons. The first has to do with the importance assigned to making phonics instruction maximally meaningful from the start. The second reason is that some young children are more interested in learning to print than in learning to read (4, 7, 8, 13). Because help with printing, sometimes referred to as *manuscript writing*, provides both natural and numerous opportunities to attend to the sounds that letters stand for, Chapter 9 showed, with many examples taken from classrooms, how to link printing instruction with early work with phonics. Since the combination of knowing about letters and sounds, and knowing how to print, sometimes prompts children to do some composing, Chapter 9 closed with that topic.

Even though Chapter 9 focused on kinds of phonics instruction that ought to be much more productive and meaningful than instruction and drill that come straight from workbooks, it still must be remembered that for some young children, letter-sound correspondences are difficult to master and remain fairly meaningless no matter what teachers do to relate instruction to meaningful words. This point is emphasized because of the growing trend at the kindergarten level to treat phonics instruction as if it were the only means for turning nonreaders into readers. When such a stance is taken, some children *will* fail. And since nobody wants a child as young as five to conclude that he is unable to succeed in school, a beginning program must be as eclectic in its approach to reading as is possible. Again, Ausubel's concept of readiness should not be overlooked by teachers even though it seems to be ignored among authors of so-called reading readiness workbooks, which, currently, lay aside almost everything to concentrate on phonics.

REVIEW

1. As was true of Chapter 8, the underlying theme of Chapter 9 is "Promoting Independence." To what does "independence" refer?

2. Explain with specificity the exact meaning of the following statement:

    The kinds of cues, or prompts, available to help children cope on their own with words not in their reading vocabulary depend on the nature of the language they are learning to read.

3. Chapter 9 treats beginning instruction in phonics by linking it to printing instruction; however, not all teachers choose to do that. For such teachers, what suggestions or guidelines does Chapter 9 offer for teaching beginning phonics? What reasons are given for the suggestions made?

4. You have been reminded many times and in many ways that reading and comprehending are synonymous. Keeping that fact in mind, explain the meaning of this sentence:

    The use of graphophonic cues helps readers with words that are orally familiar but visually unfamiliar.

5. Let's say you are teaching children to print *S* and *s* in a way that follows the recommendations of Chapter 9. As a result, your chalkboard shows:

snow	Sue
six	Saturday
seven	September
salt	

    Having read the seven words to an instructional group in order to highlight the similarity of the beginning sounds, you ask, "Can you think of another word that starts with the sound you hear at the beginning of all these words?" One child replies, "Cynthia." How should *you* respond?

REFERENCES

1. Askov, Eunice N., and Greff, Kasper N., "Handwriting: Copying Versus Tracing as the Most Effective Type of Practice." *Journal of Educational Research* 69 (November, 1975), 96–98.
2. Blatt, Gloria T. "Playing with Language." *Reading Teacher* 31 (February, 1978), 487–491.
3. Carnegie, Dale. *How to Win Friends and Influence People*. New York: Simon and Schuster, 1936.
4. Chomsky, Carol. "Write First, Read Later." *Childhood Education* 47 (March, 1971), 296–299.
5. Cutts, Warren. "Does the Teacher Really Matter?" *Reading Teaching* 28 (February, 1975), 449–452.
6. DiStefano, Philip P., and Hagerty, Patricia J. "Teaching Spelling at the Elementary Level: A Realistic Perspective." *Reading Teacher* 38 (January, 1985), 373–377.
7. Durkin, Dolores. *Children Who Read Early*. New York: Teachers College Press, Columbia University, 1966.
8. Durkin, Dolores. "A Language Arts Program for Pre-First Grade Children: Two-Year Achievement Report." *Reading Research Quarterly*, 5 (Summer, 1970), 534–565.
9. Dyson, Anne H. "N Spell My Grandmama: Fostering Early Thinking about Print." *Reading Teacher* 38 (December, 1984), 262–271.
10. Dyson, Anne H. "Reading, Writing, and Language: Young Children Solving the Written Language Puzzle." *Language Arts* 59 (November/December, 1982), 829–839.
11. Ehri, Linnea C. "Movement into Reading: Is the First Sign of Printed Word Learning Visual or Phonetic?" *Reading Research Quarterly* 20 (Winter, 1985), 163–179.
12. Enstrom, E. A. "But How Soon Can We *Really* Write?" *Elementary English* 45 (March, 1968), 360–363.
13. Hall, Mary Ann; Moretz, Sara A.; and Statom, Jodellano. "Writing Before Grade One – A Study of Early Writers." *Language Arts* 53 (May, 1976), 582–585.
14. Hall, Susan, and Hall, Chris. "It Takes a Lot of Letters to Spell 'Erz'." *Language Arts* 61 (December, 1984), 822–827.
15. Heald-Taylor, B. Gail. "Scribble in First Grade Writing." *Reading Teacher* 38 (October, 1984), 4–8.
16. Juel, Connie. "The Influence of Basal Readers on First Grade Reading." *Reading Research Quarterly* 20 (Winter, 1985), 134–152.
17. Lado, Robert. "The Learning-Assimilation-Facility (LAF) Hypothesis in Preschool Literacy." *Reading Teacher* 38 (February, 1985), 548–553.
18. Paradis, Edward, and Peterson, Joseph. "Readiness Training Implications from Research." *Reading Teacher* 28 (February, 1975), 445–448.

19. Read, Charles. "Pre-school Children's Knowledge of English Phonology." *Harvard Educational Review* 41 (February, 1971), 1–34.

20. Richek, Margaret Ann. "Readiness Skills That Predict Initial Word Learning Using Two Different Methods of Instruction." *Reading Research Quarterly* 13 (1977–78, No. 2), 200–222.

21. Temple, Charles A.; Nathan, Ruth G.; and Burris, Nancy A. *The Beginnings of Writing*. Boston: Allyn and Bacon, Inc., 1982.

CHAPTER 10

Phonics: Later On

PREVIEW

Influenced by Ausubel's conception of readiness (2), which points to the need for variety in methodology, previous chapters show how children can start to be readers with instruction that focuses on whole words, contextual cues, printing, and letter-sound relationships. How this eclecticism (as well as small-group instruction) can be realized in classrooms occupied by young children is explained with a sample schedule in Chapter 5. Now, as a result of studying Chapter 5 and Chapters 7 through 9, anyone with responsibility for initiating reading instruction with four-, five-, or six-year-olds should have adequate knowledge of what to do at the beginning. Admittedly, knowledge plus experience is still better. Nonetheless, experience that is not grounded in, and guided by, essential knowledge can result as easily in nonproductive routines as in interesting, successful instruction.

This chapter, which continues the discussion of phonics begun in the previous chapter, is for teachers whose present or future students are beyond beginning phonics. It starts by covering essential subject matter, then moves to a consideration of how the subject matter can be taught to make its usefulness for readers maximally apparent.

Because my own experiences in teaching both preservice and inservice methods courses have shown phonics to be one topic about which the two groups of students are the least informed, it is strongly recommended that you study Chapter 10 with care. As terms are introduced and definitions offered, commit the latter to memory. When generalizations are stated and illustrated, be sure you understand both the statements and how the illustrative words match their content. (Illustrative words show that the generalizations apply to words in both easy and more difficult text.) Again, commit the statements to memory once they are understood.

Finally, since the silent medium of print is not the best vehicle for communicating about speech sounds, make up for the deficiency by reading words aloud whenever they function to illustrate particular sounds.

The goal of phonics instruction, whether at a beginning or an advanced level, is to teach children systematic procedures for using the spellings of words to learn how they are pronounced. If the words are in the reader's oral vocabulary, pronunciations will automatically suggest meanings.

Even though this approach seems positive and productive, words with irregular spellings do present problems. However, contextual cues may provide a resolution. In the case of an irregularly spelled word, such as *one*, for example, the sentence *One and five are six* transforms what, by itself, is a difficult word to recognize into one that is easy. But, again, this is optimistic, since contexts are not always as generous with help as is the sentence just cited.

Because of irregular spellings, children need to understand right from the beginning that the subject matter for phonics instruction provides a starting point for decoding that may or may not result in success. This means that applying what has been taught should be viewed as a type of problem solving in which the first "answer" is not necessarily correct. It thus means that flexible application of generalizations is mandatory.

NATURE OF PHONICS GENERALIZATIONS

As the content of phonics is discussed in this chapter, its basic nature should not be forgotten. That is, when the content is stated in the form of generalizations, keep in mind that they are not "rules" but only descriptions of what has been observed as being generally characteristic of written English. To point out, for instance, that a short vowel sound usually occurs in syllables that have a consonant-vowel-consonant pattern (e.g., *ran*, *disc*) is not the same as saying that is always the case (e.g., *bind*, *tall*). Rather, it is a way of supplying a starting point when children have to decode an unknown word with one or more syllables of that pattern (e.g., *cactus*, *mascot*, *picnic*).

The need for flexibility and a problem-solving stance is stressed at the start of the chapter because classroom visits sometimes reveal that phonics is taught as if it provided direct, inevitably correct answers. That may be one reason it is not as productive as it might otherwise be.

WHAT IS TAUGHT IN PHONICS

Subject matter for phonics pertains to (a) letter-sound relationships, (b) factors that affect them, and (c) syllabication. At the beginning, as the previous chapter shows, the concern is letter-sound correspondences. As pointed out earlier when contextual cues are discussed, instruction in just a few correspondences allows for the use of contextual plus minimal graphophonic cues for recognizing words.

Once additional letter-sound relationships are introduced, attention has to go to factors that affect them. Subsequent pages show that most of this instruction pertains to vowels. Since syllables, not words, are the unit for decoding, phonics instruction also covers how spellings function in getting unknown words divided into syllables.

FOCUS OF THE CHAPTER

This chapter deals with both content and instruction. Content is covered first because, after all, one cannot teach what one does not know. Since the overview is for adults who are somewhat familiar with phonics, it proceeds deductively. It thus is a telling rather than a reasoning process. In no sense, therefore, should the discussion be thought of as a model for teaching children.

Just as the overview of content starts with consonants, so, too, is it recommended that instruction with children start there. This recommendation, as explained earlier, is made for two reasons. First, consonant letters are more consistent than vowels in the sounds they record; and, second, consonant sounds show considerably less dialect variation than do vowel sounds.

CONSONANTS

The quickest way to identify the consonants is to say they are all the letters in the alphabet with the exception of *a, e, i, o,* and *u.* The speech sounds that the consonant letters record are the concern now.

Single Consonants

Sounds commonly recorded by consonant letters can be heard in initial position in the following words.

bat	he	leg	pen	ten	yes
dig	jam	my	red	vest	zoo
fun	kite	no	see	we	

Before dealing with the consonant letters not listed, let me comment just briefly on some that are.

Note first that the initial sound in *kite,* although associated with *k,* is spelled in a variety of ways:

kite   car   chord   brick

When *s* starts a word, it stands for /s/, as in *see* and *sun*.* At other times, *s* records /s/ or /z/, as is illustrated in *bus*, *miss*, *his*, *nose*, and *music*. Such variation means that children should try /z/ whenever /s/ does not produce a recognizable pronunciation – that is, a recognizable word. (This recommendation exemplifies the need for flexibility, which is underscored earlier.)

The letter *v* records the sound heard initially in *vest*. In final position, /v/ is recorded with *v* plus *e* (*cave*, *solve*).

Functioning as consonants, *y* and *w* record the sounds heard at the beginning of *yes* and *we*, respectively. They function as consonants only when they are the first letter in a syllable (*year*, *canyon*; *well*, *away*). In other positions, *y* and *w* serve as vowels.

Additional Consonants

Because *x* appears infrequently in words, it need not be dealt with as early as other consonants. The sounds that *x* stands for are illustrated below:

Sounds	*Examples*
/gz/	exact
/ks/	fix
/z/	xylophone

If you have played Scrabble, you know the special characteristic of another consonant: *q* is always followed by *u*. Children, therefore, should be taught to view *qu* as if it were a single consonant. *Qu* stands for the sounds illustrated below, the first of which is more common.

Sounds	*Examples*
/kw/	queen
/k/	plaque

Since *qu* functions as a single consonant, words like *quick* and *quote* have the same spelling pattern as *sick* and *note*.

If the letters *gu* are in a syllable in which there is another vowel (e.g., *guess*, *guide*, *guard*), that pair also functions as a single consonant. If *u*, on the other hand, is the only vowel in a syllable (e.g., *gum*, *gust*), *g* records one sound and *u* stands for another.

Consonant Clusters

Certain consonants appear with some regularity as adjacent letters in a syllable. They are called *consonant clusters*. Since dealing with more than one

---

*Slash marks are used when the referent is a sound. Consequently, *s* refers to a letter, whereas the referent for /s/ is the sound heard initially in *see*.

letter at a time speeds up decoding, instruction with clusters can contribute to efficiency. Examples are listed below.

Consonant Clusters

bl	fl	sc	st
br	fr	sk	sw
cl	gl	sl	tr
cr	gr	sm	tw
dr	pl	sn	scr
dw	pr	sp	str

As seen in the list, many clusters combine another consonant with *l* or *r*. Others are a combination of *s* and some other consonant(s).

It is important to note that each letter in a cluster records a sound. This means that every cluster stands for a *blend* (or synthesis) of sounds. The cluster *bl*, for instance, records two sounds; *str* stands for three.

Consonant Digraphs

Other pairs of consonants, referred to as *digraphs*, are essentially different from clusters, because the two letters stand for one sound. And that sound is different from the sound associated with either letter. Consonant digraphs are listed below, along with words indicating the sounds they represent.

Consonant Digraphs

ph (phone)	ch (chap; chef)
gh (rough)	th (the; thin)
sh (shell)	ng (rang)

As the illustrative words indicate, *th* stands for two different, but closely similar, sounds. Reading aloud pairs of words like the following should help you hear the difference.

Voiced Sound	*Voiceless Sound*
thy	thigh
bathe	bath
clothe	cloth
either	ether
breathe	breath

Many children are not consciously aware of the difference between the voiced and voiceless sounds associated with *th*, but teachers need to know about it to avoid using less-than-perfect examples. More specifically, if words like *the* and *there* are used as illustrations when the focus of instruction is *th*, other words like *thin* and *thumb* should not be used. Avoiding them will ensure that children who do hear the difference between the voiced and voiceless sounds are not confused by the examples. Later, words like *thin* and *thumb* can be considered.

The nasal sound represented by the digraph *ng* cannot be pronounced in isolation. Since *ng* always follows vowels (e.g., *sing, length*), its sound can be indirectly identified by pronouncing *-ang, -eng, -ing, -ong,* and *-ung.* (Pronounceable units spelled with a vowel followed by one or more consonants are called *phonograms* or, more recently, *graphemic bases.* Additional ones are *-ine, -ake,* and *-ell.*)

Factors Affecting Consonant Sounds

Compared to the vowels, consonant letters are fairly stable in the sounds they represent. The only consonants singled out to call attention to variability are *c* and *g.*

C and *g* are each associated with two different sounds, traditionally referred to as "hard" and "soft" sounds:

c		*g*	
Hard Sound	*Soft Sound*	*Hard Sound*	*Soft Sound*
/k/, as in *car*	/s/, as in *cent*	/g/, as in *go*	/j/, as in *gym*

When children know about the hard and soft sounds, they are ready to learn when each is likely to be present in a syllable. That is, they are ready to consider the visual cues (letters and their sequence) that suggest when each sound is likely to occur. Before presenting generalizations that specify those visual features, reminders for all the generalizations that are cited in the chapter need to be summarized:

1. The unit for decoding is syllables, not words. Therefore, the syllable is the focus of any generalization about letter-sound relationships or about factors that affect them.
2. Generalizations must feature visual (not auditory) cues because when a word is unknown in its written form, only visual features are available to assist with its pronunciation.
3. Generalizations underscore the importance of letter patterns (as opposed to individual letters) for decoding. The importance means that children should scan all of a syllable before making decisions about likely sounds for the individual letters.

On the assumption that you have the hard and soft sounds for *c* and *g* clearly in mind, generalizations that indicate when each is likely to be present in a syllable are stated in Table 10.1. (All the generalizations discussed in this and the subsequent chapter are listed at the end of Chapter 11.)

Table 10.1 *Hard and Soft Sounds: C and G*

When *c* is followed in a syllable by *e*, *i*, or *y*, it usually records the soft sound. Otherwise, the hard sound is common. For instance:

cent	cite	cool	act
cyst	voice	sac	caucus

When *g* is followed in a syllable by *e*, *i*, or *y*, it usually records the soft sound. Otherwise, the hard sound is common. For instance:

gem	gist	go	gust
gym	wage	grill	tag

The fact that the predictions for *c* are more reliable than those for *g* is something children should know. Remembering that difference will help them recall that flexibility (if not one sound for *g*, then try the other) may be necessary when *g* occurs in an unfamiliar word.

VOWELS

Eventually, fifteen vowel sounds are dealt with in phonics. They are recorded by both single letters and pairs of letters.

Vowel Sounds

To identify the fifteen sounds, the following words are listed. Underlined letters represent the sounds.

1. aid	6. at	11. tool
2. eat	7. end	12. took
3. ice	8. if	13. auto (awful)
4. ode	9. odd	14. out (owl)
5. use	10. up	15. oil (oyster)

Long Vowel Sounds. The five sounds heard initially in *aid, eat, ice, ode,* and *use* are the names of the letters *a, e, i, o,* and *u*. It has been customary to call them the *long vowel sounds*, even though the referent is sounds, not their duration in a word.

Short Vowel Sounds. Paralleling the description "long" is the description "short," which is used in reference to the five sounds heard initially in *at*, *end*, *if*, *odd*, and *up*.* Typically, the five short sounds are difficult for children to distinguish and remember; thus, extra practice is commonly needed.

Schwa Sound. One of the most common speech sounds in English is the *schwa sound*, symbolized by /ə/. This sound is mentioned now because one way to describe it is to say it is like an unstressed short *u* sound.

The schwa sound, which occurs routinely in unstressed syllables, is spelled in various ways. In the following words, it is represented by the underlined letters.

> arena   spíral   ómen   divíde   políte   paráde   sýmbol

Vowel sounds in unstressed syllables are reduced to the schwa sound with such regularity that children will be right more often than they are wrong if they assume that the vowel sound in one or more syllables in a multisyllabic word is /ə/.

Factors Affecting Vowel Sounds

When long and short vowel sounds are likely to occur is described in Table 10.2.

Table 10.2. *Generalizations for Vowel Sounds*

When there is one vowel in a syllable and it is not the final letter, it usually records its short sound. For instance:

> and   script   contact   public   index

When there is one vowel and it is the last letter in a syllable, it usually records its long sound. For instance:

> she   halo   banjo   momentum   silent

When there are two adjacent vowels in a syllable, they usually record the long sound of the first one. For instance:

> boat   peach   waif   sleek   maintain

When there are two vowels in a syllable, one of which is final *e*, and they are

---

*To indicate vowel sounds (and vowel letters that stand for no sound), diacritical marks may be used:

> nŏt
> nōté

separated by one consonant, they usually record the long sound of the first vowel. For instance:

use   while   ace   stroke   mete

When there are two vowels in a syllable, one of which is final *e*, and they are separated by two consonants, they usually record the short sound of the first vowel. For instance:

edge   dance   bronze   expense   valve

All the generalizations in Table 10.2 re-emphasize the need for decoders to consider patterns of letters, not single letters. The significance of patterns for pronunciations is highlighted below, where the same generalizations are summarized with spelling patterns. (C = consonant, V = vowel. Whenever *C* is enclosed in a parenthesis, it means the consonant is not an essential part of the pattern.) Be sure you see the relationships between the generalizations, the patterns, and the examples.

Spelling Patterns	*Examples*
(C)VC	in, and, crust
(C)V	I, hi, so, silo
(C)VV(C)	tea, eel, throat
(C)VCe	ice, whole, cube
(C)VCCe	solve, pulse, prance

Remaining Vowel Sounds

Thus far, ten vowel sounds have been identified. The other five are recorded by pairs of letters, referred to as *digraphs*. Thus, there are both consonant and vowel digraphs. The vowel digraphs are underlined in the words below, in which you should be able to hear five different vowel sounds:

Vowel Digraphs

tool   oil (oyster)
took   out (owl)
auto (awful)

As the list indicates, seven digraphs (*oo, au, aw, oi, oy, ou, ow*) represent the five sounds.

The two sounds that double-*o* records are referred to as the long sound (as in *tool*) and the short sound (as in *took*). Because the long sound occurs more frequently, children should try it first whenever an unknown word has two successive *o*'s in a syllable.

Also note that the vowel sounds in *ouch* and *oil* (and in *owl* and *boy*) are each a blend of two sounds. (These particular blends are called *diphthongs*.) Since what children hear is one sound, *ou*, *oi*, *ow*, and *oy* are treated in phonics as if each stands for a single sound. Teachers should be familiar with the term *diphthong*, but there is no reason to use it in instruction (16).

One final comment has to do with *ow*. As just mentioned, *ow* records a diphthong in *owl* and *now*. However, this digraph also adheres to a pattern referred to earlier. (When two successive vowels occur in a syllable, the first often stands for its long sound whereas the second vowel is silent.) Adherence to the pattern is illustrated in *own*, *low*, and *window*. Again, the variation suggests the need for flexibility. More specifically, whenever a decoder encounters a new word in which *o* and *w* are adjacent letters in a syllable, each sound just referred to should be tried to see which produces a recognizable word that makes sense in the given context. In the case of *pillow*, one sound produces a recognizable pronunciation; in the case of *allow*, the diphthong does the job.

Y Functioning as a Vowel

As the earlier list of vowel digraphs demonstrates, *y* may function as a vowel (*oy*). In fact, it assumes that role so often that there are generalizations to describe the vowel sounds it records: /ĭ/, /ē/, and /ī/. The generalizations are listed in Table 10.3.

Table 10.3. Y *Functioning as a Vowel*

When *y* is in medial position in a syllable that contains no vowel letter, it usually stands for the short *i* sound. For instance:

gym   myth   cyst   hymn   system   gypsy

When *y* records the final sound in a multisyllabic word, it usually stands for the long *e* sound. For instance:

hurry   trophy   candy   holy   autopsy   fancy

Otherwise, *y* generally records the long *i* sound. For instance:

try   dye   cycle   asylum   tyrant   dynamo

R-Controlled Vowel Sounds

When a vowel is followed by *r* within a syllable, the result is a blend of sounds in which no attempt should be made to identify the vowel sound. (This point is made because many commercially prepared materials suggest having children listen for vowel sounds in words like *fur*, *car*, and *nor*, even though most adults do not know what the vowel sounds are.) How *r* affects what vowel letters stand for is illustrated in words like *art*, *her*, and *for*. These three words include the different blends that a vowel plus *r* represent—when the vowel and *r* are adjacent letters in a syllable. (What is being discussed, therefore, has no relevance for words like *irate* and *erode* since, in these cases, the vowel is in the first syllable, whereas *r* occurs in the second.) The three blends recorded by vowels plus *r* are further illustrated below:

Words with R-Controlled Vowel Sounds

collar	for	car
her	war	
dirt		
word		
hurl		

Whenever children are examining a syllable, they need to notice when vowels are followed by *re* as well as by *r*. The effect *re* has on vowel sounds is illustrated with contrasts, which are helpful when instructing children:

car	her	fir	for	cur
care	here	fire	fore	cure

SYLLABICATION

By now, the significance of syllables for decoding should be apparent. Before generalizations for dividing unknown words into syllables are stated, a few comments about syllables themselves can be made.

Syllables

Although some instructional materials define *syllable* as "part of a word," that is neither precise nor helpful. After all, a letter is part of a word, too. (Why the same materials suggest having children clap out syllables is something I have never understood, since syllables of unknown words have to be determined by visual features.) The correct definition of a syllable is that it is a vowel sound to which consonant sounds are usually added. Because a vowel sound is the nucleus of a syllable, children are not ready to learn about syllables until they are familiar with some vowel sounds. What to do in the meantime?

Until children are equipped to understand the basic nature of a syllable and, further, that it is syllables that are decoded, a distinction need not be made between *word* and *syllable*. This distinction can easily be avoided by using single-syllable (monosyllabic) words to teach generalizations. Or, if the concern is for a certain letter-sound relationship, only the beginning of words need be the concern. To teach about a sound for *u*, for instance, *us*, *up* and *under* can be used with no attention to syllables. Once children understand what a syllable is, the importance of starting the decoding process by considering the likely syllabication of the unknown word (with the help of its spelling) must be made explicit.

Parts of a Syllable

Although a syllable may be composed of only one letter (*u nite*; *i dol*), it typically has more. This accounts for references to various parts of a syllable. To pinpoint the parts, the following syllables will serve as illustrations:

> a   ac   ack   tack   stack

The examples show that syllables may, but need not, have sounds in *initial*, *medial*, and *final* positions. With *ac*, for instance, *a* records the initial sound, and the final one is represented by *c*. In *tack*, *t* represents the initial sound, *a* the medial sound, and *ck* the final sound. With a syllable like *stack*, *st* stands for the initial sounds, *a* the medial sound, and *ck* the final sound. (Please notice that the three positions refer to syllables, not to words. This means that in both *am* and *symbol* (*sym bol*), *m* records a final sound.)

Generalizations about Syllabication

Of fundamental importance for decoding is the following fact:

> Every syllable has a vowel sound.

This statement indicates that words like *he*, *end*, *bath* and also longer words like *thrust*, *strength*, and *splash* could be no more than one syllable, because each word has only one letter that records vowel sounds. The same statement indicates that a word as short as *arena* may have, and in fact does have, three syllables. (Note that the statement does not say that every syllable has one vowel; rather, that every syllable has one vowel sound. Consequently, words like *age*, *meet*, *voice*, and *squeeze* are also monosyllabic words—though containing more than one vowel letter—because each word has only one vowel sound.)

Other generalizations for syllabication specify visual cues—letters and their sequence—that suggest syllable boundaries. They are listed in Table 10.4.

TABLE 10.4. *Generalizations for Syllabicating Unfamiliar Words*

When two consonants (which are not special digraphs) are between two vowels, a syllabic division often occurs between the two consonants. For instance:

bot tom   pen cil   ban dan na   ad ven ture

When a consonant is between two vowels, the first vowel is often in one syllable and the consonant and the vowel following it are in another. For instance:

mo tel   pa per   e lect   si lent   a re na

When x is preceded and followed by vowels, the preceding vowel and the x are in one syllable and the following vowel is in another. For instance:

ex it   tox ic   Tex as   ax is   tax i

When a word ends in a consonant followed by *le*, the consonant and *le* form a syllable.* For instance:

i dle   bu gle   thim ble   ar ti cle

---

*The schwa sound (unstressed /ŭ/) occurs in such syllables. For instance:

idle (i dəl)   thimble (thim bəl)

Review of Syllabication Generalizations

Children do not have to be able to state generalizations (16); teachers do. This is to ensure that they can communicate the content to students. (What is essential for children is the ability to understand a generalization and to apply it whenever it is appropriate to do so.) Using the following spelling patterns and examples as prompts, see whether you can verbalize the four generalizations about syllabication.

Spelling Pattern	Syllabication	Examples
VCCV	VC CV	window, inferno
VCV	V CV	final, aroma
VxV	Vx V	axis, exit
Cle	Cle	purple, fable

You should now be ready to understand why what is often done with syllabication in commercial materials is not helpful for decoders (see Figure 10.1).

STRESSED SYLLABLES

The fact that stress is important for pronunciations has already been stated: Vowel sounds in unstressed syllables are often reduced to the schwa sound. Shifts in stress also account for different words that have identical spellings:

rébel   cónduct   dígest   cóntract
rebél   condúct   digést   contráct

Since stress *is* significant for pronunciations, how should it be dealt with in words that are unfamiliar in their written form? Usually, working out the sounds of syllables in multisyllabic words suggests which one is stressed. With the help of the generalizations cited, for example, children should be able to decode each syllable in *public*. Pronouncing each syllable in succession should suggest what the word is and therefore which of its syllables is stressed (públic). Assumed in all this, of course, is that *public* is in the children's oral vocabularies. Just how important those vocabularies are for successful decoding is underscored effectively and clearly by linguist Roger Brown (4):

> The usefulness of being able to sound a new word depends on the state of the reader's speaking vocabulary. If the word that is unfamiliar in printed form is also unfamiliar in spoken form the reader who can sound it out will not understand the word any better than the reader who cannot sound it. . . . The real advantage in being able to sound a word that is unfamiliar in print, only appears when the word is familiar in speech. The child's letter-by-letter pronunciation, put together by spelling recipe, will, with the aid of context, call to mind the spoken form. There will be a click of recognition, pronunciation will smooth out, and meaning will transfer to the printed form. The ability to sound out new words is not simply a pronunciation skill; it is a technique for expanding reading comprehension vocabulary to the size of speaking comprehension vocabulary. This is a considerable help since speaking vocabulary is likely to be ten times the size of reading vocabulary for the primary child. (p. 69)

Since English words are not characterized by consistent stress patterns, children should be taught to assign stress to each syllable in a word (beginning with the first) until there is that "click of recognition" to which Brown refers. How to manipulate stress until a recognizable pronunciation results is something teachers should model. That is, they should make visible (by thinking out loud) an invisible mental process.

TEACHING PHONICS: SOME REMINDERS

How instruction in phonics can get started was discussed earlier in connection with contextual cues (Chapter 8) and printing (Chapter 9). Before this chapter continues the discussion, we can review three reminders for any instruction in phonics:

1. In a number of ways, successful decoding depends on children's oral vocabularies. It is those vocabularies, for example, that facilitate shifts

Figure 10.1

A common practice in basal reader programs is to have children work with
words they can read. (Notice the directions in Figure 10.1: "Say each
word . . . .") It *is* correct to use familiar words when children are first learning
about syllables. However, continuing to use them is a waste of time, because
unknown words require the use of spellings to make decisions about their
syllabication.

Exercises like the one in Figure 10.1 have been characteristic of basal programs for decades. (Probably every reader of this textbook can recall doing
some.) All that have changed are the formats in which the exercises are presented.

Unit 1, *Towers* (Guide pp. 13–14)   Decoding: Vowel Sounds and Syllables   (Review)
Say: Read all that is said at the top of the page, and do what you are asked to do. **You may wish to suggest**
that children put a check beside a word before they print it. This will help them keep track of the words
they use.

Say each word below to yourself. Listen

for the number of vowel sounds in each word.

cross	umbrella	flower	brother	children
ball	dress	elephant	high	beautiful

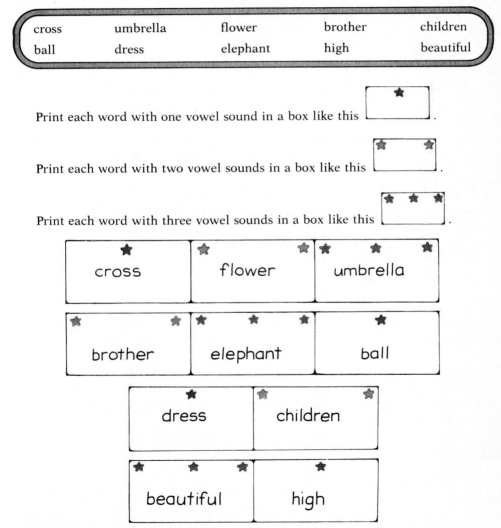

Print each word with one vowel sound in a box like this ⭐.

Print each word with two vowel sounds in a box like this ⭐ ⭐.

Print each word with three vowel sounds in a box like this ⭐ ⭐ ⭐.

⭐ cross	⭐ ⭐ flower	⭐ ⭐ ⭐ umbrella

⭐ ⭐ brother	⭐ ⭐ ⭐ elephant	⭐ ball

⭐ dress	⭐ ⭐ children

⭐ ⭐ ⭐ beautiful	⭐ high

from approximately correct pronunciations to exactly correct pronunciations. And, of course, correctly pronounced words contribute to reading only if their meanings are known.

2. Successful decoding is also facilitated when contextual as well as graphophonic cues are used. Even though this chapter singles out the latter for attention, the importance of a reader's using all available cues should not be forgotten.

3. What is taught in phonics should be determined not only by the readiness of the children to understand it but also by a consideration of usefulness. More specifically, to teach the sounds that x represents, when x is not in any of the words the children are being asked to learn, is senseless. Such practices—which are common in commercially prepared materials—make the content of phonics an end in itself.

Having considered some important reminders for anyone teaching phonics, let's look now at two ways in which the instruction can be offered.

INDUCTIVE VERSUS DEDUCTIVE INSTRUCTION

Whether what is being taught pertains to letter-sound relationships, factors that affect them, or syllabication, phonics instruction can proceed inductively or deductively. The two possibilities are illustrated with lessons about a letter-sound relationship.

An Inductive Lesson

Best Approach

Inductive instruction uses a reasoning process that moves from particular instances to a conclusion about them. With phonics, inductive instruction promotes reasoning from selected words to a conclusion about a visual-auditory feature that is common to them all. If a teacher elects to use inductive instruction to teach the association between p and /p/, the lesson might proceed as follows.

After writing p on the board, the teacher asks, "What's the name of this letter? ['P.'] That's right. I'll write some words you know that begin with p. You can read each one as I write it, but don't say anything until I finish writing a word because, as you learned yesterday, changing just one letter can change what a word says. Okay. Here's the first."

Eventually the board displays:

put

pig

play

pet

The teacher continues: "Let's read the four words again. . . . If you look at each word, you'll see something that's the same at the beginning of each one. What is it? ['They all have *p* at the first.'] Right. Each word begins with the letter *p*. There's something else that's the same. It's something you hear. Say all these words again to see if you can tell me something about the beginning sound of each one. . . . Did you hear something that's the same at the beginning of all these words? ['They start with the same letter.'] Letter? We don't hear a letter. We see a letter, but we hear a sound. Let's read the words again. As you say them, listen to the *sound* at the beginning of each one. It's the same sound. Let's see if you'll be able to tell me what that sound is. . . . Can someone tell us the sound that's at the beginning of *put*, *pig*, *play*, and *pet*? ['Puh.']* Right. Please read these four words again. As you do, listen for that sound at the beginning of each one. . . . Since you're learning about the sound that *p* stands for, I brought some pictures of things whose names start with that sound. ['Mrs. J____, 'picture' starts with that sound.'] Good for you! You're certainly listening. I'm going to show you some pictures one at a time. Think of a name for whatever you see. If you can think of a word that starts with /p/, raise your hand."

A Deductive Lesson

Inductive instruction uses a reasoning process to reach a conclusion; deductive teaching starts with the conclusion. The difference is illustrated in the next lesson, also focusing on the sound that the letter *p* represents.

The teacher starts by writing *p* on the board and saying, "This is the letter *p*, and it stands for /p/. What is the sound for *p*? . . . You'll hear that sound when I say some words that begin with the letter *p*: *pay*, *pin*, *put*, *pond*, *peek*. I'll write those words so that you'll see they all begin with *p*. As I write each one, I'll tell you again what it says. . . . Can you think of words that begin with the same sound as *pay*, *pin*, *put*, *pond*, and *peek*? If you can, I'll write them on the board, too."

Responses come in the following order: *pants*, *pumpkin*, *penny*, *nickel*, *play*. The board thus shows:

pay	pants	~~nickel~~
pin	pumpkin	
put	penny	
pond	play	
peek		

---

*The advisability of explicit identifications of speech sounds is discussed later.

After naming all the words, the teacher moves beyond the deductive lesson in order to use a combination of contextual and graphophonic cues, much as described earlier in Chapter 8. She thus continues: "I'm going to read some sentences, but I'm not going to tell you what the last word is. It will begin with the letter *p*, so that tells you what its beginning sound is. Here's the first sentence. The name of a color is _____ ['Purple.'] Correct. I know another color that starts with *p*. Do you? ['Pink?'] Very good. Here's a different sentence. Tell me what the last word is. It starts with the letter *p*. We call a dog's foot a _____ ['Paw.'] Right again. . . ." Remembering that reading is visual as well as cognitive, this teacher prints each response on the board.

Inductive or Deductive Instruction: Which to Use?

As the illustrative lessons indicated, the key difference between deductive and inductive instruction applied to a letter-sound relationship is that deductive instruction begins with an identification of the sound by the teacher, whereas in inductive instruction it is reasoned out from selected words by the students. However, if children are unable to perceive a sound in the context of words, it will have to be directly identified for them. In such instances, less of a distinction is found between deductive and inductive instruction than might otherwise be the case. Nonetheless, sufficiently important differences between the two procedures exist as to warrant asking, Which to use? The differences are discussed first.

One difference is that inductive instruction, whether applied to letter-sound relationships, factors affecting them, or syllabication, gives children a better opportunity to arrive at an understanding of the alphabetic nature of our writing system. Also, inductive instruction gives them a strategy for learning, which may allow some children to discover phonics content on their own. Further, it makes the idea of "letters standing for sounds" more meaningful, since letters and sounds are dealt with through the vehicle of words. In contrast, deductive instruction commonly attends to isolated sounds before children even know that a word is composed of more than one sound.

With such differences in mind, the recommendation is to introduce letter-sound relationships with inductive instruction. Once children seem to understand what is going on, a combination of inductive and deductive methods is advisable. When should each be used? Words recently spoken by a teacher provide an answer: "If you look at a child, and his eyes tell you he doesn't know what in the world you're talking about, have enough sense to try something else."

Isolating Sounds from Words

Even though research and classroom observations (6, 8) both confirm that some children are unable to hear a given sound in the context of words that contain it, many educators still object to direct identifications. Apparently, authors of basal reader programs believe that such educators are sizable in number, as most of these materials deal with sounds in very obscure, indirect ways (3). In spite of that, one time when teachers tend to disregard basal manual recommendations is when sounds are taught (6). Knowing that most children require explicit identifications, they commonly pronounce sounds for them. ("Yes, the sound that *p* stands for is /p/.")

Why some educators object to isolating sounds from words is explained clearly by D. H. Stott (15):

> It is part of the very essence of language that sounds are uttered in very rapid sequences which become words. Each sound has such a fleeting existence that it is not truly reproducible outside the context of a word. Wresting it out of its natural place makes it something different, altering its length and the amount of breath put into it, and sometimes making it into a syllable by the addition of another sound. (p. 11)

What is the meaning of these observations for anyone teaching phonics? To begin, it should be remembered that its goal is a practical one: to help children decode words that are visually unfamiliar. Although words do flow from one to another, that flow stops whenever an unknown one is encountered in print. When it is, the reader must stop and "wrest it out of its natural place." Once it has been "wrested," a way to figure it out is to consider its letters, their sequence, and the meaning all this has for its likely pronunciation.

With these points in mind, I can accept the idea that "each sound has such a fleeting existence that it is not truly reproducible outside the context of a word" but still be aware of the need to isolate sounds for any child who seems to require at least one explicit identification. This identification can be made carefully to minimize the addition of /ŭ/. Such care, by the way, is especially necessary for what are called *stop sounds* (/b/, /d/, /g/, /p/, /t/, /k/). The special care is required because stop sounds cannot be produced apart from words without adding the extraneous vowel sound.

To take the position that some children require direct identifications of sounds is not to condone what has been heard in classrooms. Here I refer to day-by-day drills with *puh, puh, puh,* even after children have demonstrated that they know the sound that *p* records. I also refer to the times I have heard teachers pronounce (mispronounce) the sounds represented by *r* as "*er,*" by *dr* as "*der,*" and by *cl* as "*cul.*" What also must be questioned are commercial materials that isolate sounds but, in the process, suggest having children do what is impossible—for instance, pronounce /ng/ and /ks/.

MORE ADVANCED INSTRUCTION

Among the most important content taught in phonics are generalizations that describe factors that affect letter-sound relationships. (E.g., when *c* and *g* are followed in a syllable by *e*, *i*, or *y*, they commonly record their soft sounds. Otherwise, the hard sounds are common.) Effective instruction with these generalizations adds substantially to children's self-reliance in coping success-fully with new or forgotten words.

As soon as multisyllabic (polysyllabic) words become common in what-ever materials children are expected to read, generalizations about ways to divide unfamiliar words into syllables must get attention, too. What follow, then, are lessons that deal with the two types of generalizations.

Factors Affecting Letter-Sound Relationships: A Lesson

The lesson described next is inductive and deals with this generalization: When there is one vowel and it comes at the end, it is likely to stand for its long sound. (With beginners, one-syllable words are used; therefore, it is unnecessary at this time to differentiate between a word and a syllable.) It is assumed that the children making up the instructional group know the long and short vowel sounds and thus are ready to learn about their likely occurrence. With this objective, the lesson begins with a review of ten vowel sounds, which I would not hesitate to identify apart from words. (I have never known a child who developed problems because of questions like, "What is the short sound of *e*?" On the other hand, I have known many who had problems because sounds were not reviewed sufficiently.) Following the review, the teacher writes *known* words on the board:

we

no

she

hi

go

The instruction begins by having the children read the words. Then, to highlight the relevant visual-auditory features, question-asking starts: "Let's look at each of these words. How many vowel letters does each word have? ['One.'] What sound does *e* stand for in *we*? ['E.'] Well, yes, it says its own name, but what do we call that sound? ['The long sound.'] Good. Look at *no*. You said there's one vowel in *no*—an *o*. What sound does *o* stand for in *no*? ['The long sound.'] Right again. What about the *e* in *she*? What sound does that stand for? ['The long sound.'] Yes. You can really hear that *e* sound in *she*, can't you? What about *hi*? There's only one vowel in *hi*—an *i*. What sound does *i* make in *hi*? ['I.'] Yes, it says its own name. It has the long sound. What about the last word? What sound does *o* stand for in *go*? ['The long sound.'] You've told me two things that are the same about these words. First, you said they have just one vowel letter. Then you said that each vowel stands for its long sound. Can you tell me something else that's the same about all these words? ['They have two letters.']* Do they? What about *she*? How many letters in *she*? Let's count. ['One-two-three.'] Yes, *she* has three letters. There's something else that's the same about the five words, about the vowel in each one. ['I know. They come at the end.'] Right. In each word, the vowel is at the end. Now you've told me three things that are the same about all these words. You told me they have one vowel letter, the vowel is at the end, and the vowel stands for its long sound. The reason we're talking about all this is that knowing those things will help you figure out new words all by yourself. Now, whenever you come across a new word that has one vowel and it's at the end, you'll know that it will have the long sound—at least most of the time it will have the long sound. Remember. When a word has one vowel and it's at the end, the vowel usually stands for the long sound. I'm going to write all those things on the board to help you remember them."

As the teacher writes, she reads:

1. One vowel
2. At the end
3. Long sound

Pointing to each of the three details, she helps the children verbalize the generalization.

To learn whether they are able to use it to decode syllables, the teacher next shows the following, which are on chart paper:

si	mo	ti	mu
ba	te	ho	la
fa	fi	ro	fu

Explaining that these are not words, the teacher concludes the lesson by asking the children to pronounce each pair of letters. Whenever a child cannot arrive at a pronunciation directly, she outlines steps for blending sounds— steps that are discussed later:

$$\bar{\text{i}} \qquad \bar{\text{a}}$$
$$\bar{\text{si}} \qquad \bar{\text{ba}}$$

What is being done is relevant for decoding initial syllables in words like *silo*, *bacon*, *fable*, *motor*, *tepee*, *final*, *title*, *hotel*, *rotate*, *music*, *lady*, and *future*.

---

*This response demonstrates the importance of having something other than two-letter words, as the number of letters is irrelevant.

On a different day, both to prepare for teaching another generalization and to review the meaning and usefulness of the present one, this same teacher pairs, and asks questions about, known words like:

no	me	hi	go	be
not	men	him	got	bed

As before, questions call attention to relevant visual features – in this case, the number of vowels and their placement in the syllable. Through contrasts (*no–not; me–men*), the children can be helped to see the significance of both for assigning sounds to vowel letters.

Syllabication: A Lesson

The illustrative lesson for syllabication is deductive. It is characterized, therefore, by telling rather than by reasoning. It also exemplifies essential guidelines:

GUIDELINES FOR INSTRUCTION AND APPLICATIONS

When teaching something new ⎫ use words familiar to the children.

When learning whether children can apply what has been taught ⎬ use words they cannot read.

The objective of the deductive lesson is to teach the generalization: When two consonants are preceded and followed by vowels, a syllabic division generally occurs between the consonants. To get started, known words with the described pattern are written on the board:

> window
>
> after
>
> picnic
>
> under

After the children read the list, the teacher asks them to read the words again so they can listen for the number of syllables in each word. Once it is agreed that all have two syllables, the teacher's next question is, "Can you tell me where each of these words divides into syllables?" Since the children know the words, they have no trouble responding. A new list can be written in either of two ways:

win	dow	win	dow
af	ter	af	ter
pic	nic	pic	nic
un	der	un	der

Proceeding deductively, the teacher tells the children, "I want to show you something about these four words, because it will help you read other words when you see them for the very first time. To begin, notice that the first syllable in each word ends with a consonant. Now look at the second syllable. In all these words, it begins with a consonant. And there's something else to know about the words. In each one, a vowel [points to the *i* in *window*, to the *a* in *after*, etc.] comes before the two consonants, and another vowel [points to the *o* in *window*, etc.] comes after them. I've asked you to look at lots of things in these words, haven't I? Let's see if I can put everything together, and then we'll see how it can help you divide words you can't read so that you can get them figured out. I've said that if there are two consonants in a word [points to the appropriate letters in each of the four words], and a vowel comes before the first consonant and another vowel comes after the second consonant [again points to the appropriate letters], then there usually is a syllable break between the consonants. I'll write everything I just said this short way:

VCCV

VC CV

"I want to show you now how all this will help you to divide words you don't know so that you can figure out each syllable." A list of *un*known words is written next:

kidnap

accent

album

succeed

"Can anybody read any of these words? . . . I didn't think that you could, but what you just learned should held you pronounce them. If someone can tell us where the words divide into syllables, that will help you know how to pronounce them. Remember, I've just said that when a word has two consonants and a vowel comes before and after the consonants, there usually is a syllable break between the consonants. Where do you think the first word up here divides into syllables? . . . That's exactly right, between *d* and *n*. . . ."

Eventually the board shows:

kid   nap

ac   cent

al   bum

suc   ceed

The teacher continues, "Now that you've divided these words into syllables, let's see how they're pronounced." As the pronunciation of each is worked out, attention also goes to meanings.

EARLY USE OF PHONICS

Just as all teachers should strive to provide the best instruction, they must also make certain that children see its practical value. Even when only a few letter-sound relationships are known, children can—and should—begin using a combination of graphophonic and contextual cues to recognize words. How such use progresses is summarized earlier in Figure 8.3. (This is an appropriate time to review the content of Figure 8.3, since commercially produced workbooks for kindergarten often teach many letter-sound correspondences without ever showing their value for recognizing unknown words.)

Children's knowledge of a few letter-sound relationships can also be put to use with whole word methodology. If one new word in a basal reader selection is *sat*, a teacher might say something like the following after writing two unfamiliar words:

1. run

2. sat

"One new word in the story you'll be reading today is *sat*. The children sat on the floor. If you think about the sounds of letters that you've been learning, I think you'll know which word on the board is 'sat.' Please keep your hands down until you think about *sat*. Of the two words on the board, which is the only one that could be *sat*? . . . Brian, why do you think the second word is *sat*?"

If members of the instructional group have been listening for speech sounds at the end as well as the beginning of words, the same teacher might have written *sad* instead of *run*. This would allow for a review of the sounds that *s, t*, and *d* represent and of instructional language like "beginning sound" and "last sound."

Because children ought to understand the reason for phonics right from the beginning, one more example of an early use of consonant sounds is described. In this case, the word *dot* is of interest because of a discussion of polka dots; so the teacher suggests: "Let me show you what the word *dot* looks like when it's written. You can help me write it if you listen to the sounds in *dot*. Say 'dot.' . . . What letter stands for the sound you hear at the beginning of *dot*? . . . Right. I'll print *d*. . . . Listen again. This time listen for the last sound in *dot*. *Dot*. . . . Right again. I'm going to leave a space between *d* and *t*. The letter that goes in between—I'll write it now—is *o*. These three letters spell *dot*. What is this word? . . . Spell it. . . . What does this word say?

"I'm going to write another word under *dot* that looks just like it except it starts with *h* instead of *d*. . . . Think of the sound of *h*. You've heard that sound at the beginning of words like *he, how, help*, and *her*. What is the sound for *h*? . . . What do you think *h, o, t* spells? The first word is *dot*. What is this second word? . . . Nobody knows? I'll give you a hint. This second word tells how you feel when you've been outside playing a long time on a very warm day and. . . . Yes, the second word is *hot*. Look up here, please. Say both words and see if you can hear how they sound the very same except at the beginning. . . ."

What was just described illustrates a common pattern, namely, that when a procedure is first introduced—in this case, substituting sounds—a teacher often has to answer questions as well as ask them. In doing so, she is clarifying the meaning of her requests.

LATER USE OF LETTER-SOUND RELATIONSHIPS

What one teacher chose to do with *dot* and *hot* is preparation for uses of letter-sound correspondences that can be categorized as *substitutions* and *additions*. All such uses start slowly—as with *dot* and *hot*—and proceed with whatever amount of practice is necessary. Further practice using *dot* as a starting point, for example, might use the following:

<u>*dot*</u>

I am <u>hot</u> now.

I am <u>not</u> little.

I have a <u>lot</u> of toys.

Examples of more substitutions, and also additions, comprise Table 10.5.

Blending sounds to produce syllables, a topic still to be discussed, has its roots in the addition process illustrated in Table 10.5. Because both adding and substituting sounds are important for fast decoding, what one teacher did to help with the two processes is described next.

Table 10.5. *Using Substitutions and Additions for Decoding*

Substitutions: Initial Sounds

Known words	cat	in	top
Known sounds	/f/	/ă/	/ch/
Decoded words	fat	an	chop

Substitutions: Final Sounds

Known words	feel	he	cat
Known sounds	/d/	/i/	/sh/
Decoded words	feed	hi	cash

Substitutions: Medial Sounds

Known words	lip	ant	dirt
Known sounds	/ă/	/k/	/ar/
Decoded words	lap	act	dart

Additions: Initial Sounds

Known words	all	and	in
Known sounds	/b/	/st/	/th/
Decoded words	ball	stand	thin

Additions: Final Sounds

Known words	star	in	fir
Known sounds	/t/	/ch/	/st/
Decoded words	start	inch	first

ADDING AND SUBSTITUTING SOUNDS

To prepare for work with adding and substituting sounds, two columns of unlabeled pictures had been thumbtacked to a bulletin board. The nine children in the instructional group were asked to name all the objects in the pictures. (Explicit naming is usually necessary in order to make certain the children are assigning the same name to a picture. A picture of a woman, for example, might be named "woman," "lady," "mom," or "teacher.") In the column at the left side of the board were pictures of a wagon, a web, a woman, and a walrus. The column at the right displayed four other pictures showing waves, a wallet, some wood, and a window. The teacher then inquired, "Can someone tell us with what letter all those words begin?" The entire group responded, "W." After complimenting the children for remembering, the teacher attached a capital *W* and a lowercase *w* to the top of the board and said, "Nothing can go on this board unless it starts with *w*." (One boy suggested putting a child whose name was *Wayne* on the board.)

The teacher next attached a strip of heavy paper just under the *W* and *w*.

Willie Worm was printed on it. Since "What do these two words say?" was followed by silence, the children were asked to look at the chalkboard, where the teacher wrote the familiar words *work* and *word*, which were quickly identified. Under the two words went *worm*:

work

word

worm

After the children reread *work* and *word*, the teacher asked, "Can someone read the next word?" Since nobody could, responses to the following words and parts of words were elicited:

wor

work

wor

word

wor

worm

"What's this last word?" the teacher asked. Its identification was immediately followed by a spontaneous discussion of worms. It ended when the teacher commented, "Now, don't forget what this word says [pointing to *worm*]. What is it?" One child was heard to say "worms," so the teacher added to what was on the board:

work   worm

word   worms

worm

After the children reread all the words, their attention was directed back to the bulletin board, where they reidentified *Worm* but still could not read *Willie*. Consequently, the teacher told them it said "Willie" and that it was a special worm's name. At that point, a sectioned worm cut from construction paper was added to the board just beneath his name. Word cards were attached to each of Willie's sections. Once the children quieted down—Willie was an exciting attraction—they read all the word cards. Then came the promise that more words could be fed to Willie on the following day so he could grow even bigger.

| want | with | walk | was | we | went | would | were | won't | wait | wouldn't |

The next day, known words (*big, gave, day, hide,* and *get*), coupled with initial consonant substitutions, were used to identify five new words: *wig, wave, way, wide,* and *wet.* Once they were recognized, the five words were displayed in sentences so they could be read in a variety of contexts. After that, five additional word cards were added to Willie, who was then so long he extended beyond the edge of the bulletin board. For the rest of the week, all the words were reviewed both in isolation and in contexts. At the end, a story about a worm was read to the children, after which they were asked to draw a picture of Willie and to write something about him.

USE OF GENERALIZATIONS

When children are relative beginners in reading, using what they are learning might progress no further than substitutions and additions such as those just described. Eventually, however, they need to be able to use generalizations about factors that affect sounds—for instance: When there is one vowel in a syllable and it is not at the end, it generally stands for its short sound. Before application is discussed, it should first be pointed out that for the sake of efficiency, some words to which such generalizations apply should be decoded with the help of known words plus additions or substitutions. (It is correct *and* quick decoding that makes maximum contributions to comprehension.) To illustrate, the generalization just stated is relevant for a word like *man;* yet if children can read *an* and know the sound that *m* stands for, adding /m/ to the beginning of *an* is the desirable decoding procedure. Other words to which the same generalization applies (*pan, ant, in*) can also be figured out efficiently in such ways as the following:

Known Word	Unknown Word	Decoding Procedure
an	pan	Initial consonant addition
an	ant	Final consonant addition
an	in	Initial vowel substitution

Even though these procedures are quicker than a letter-by-letter, sound-by-sound analysis of *pan, ant,* and *in,* it is not always possible for children to use them, because related words (e.g., *an*) may not be known or are not recalled when needed. These two reasons explain why children should learn to use generalizations such as: When there is one vowel and it is not at the end, it usually stands for its short sound.

To illustrate how its usefulness can be taught, let's consider the word *fast.* (The assumption is that neither *fast* nor related words like *last* and *past* are known.) An effective teacher begins with a review of the sounds recorded by *f, s,* and *t* (or the cluster *st,* if that received attention), and of the short sound for *a.* Taught earlier, the generalization itself is also reviewed with words that reflect its content. Then comes attention to the way the generalization functions with unfamiliar words.

The teacher begins by writing *fast* on the chalkboard—not as part of a sentence because, in this case, the objective is to demonstrate how a generalization, not a context, helps with unknown words. (Times when contexts *should* be used are explained later.) The teacher next poses questions about *fast*: "How many vowels are in this new word? . . . Is that vowel at the end of the word? . . . What do you know about the sound a vowel usually stands for when it is the only vowel and it is not at the end of a word? . . . What *is* the short sound of *a*? . . . Can anyone tell us what this word is?"

Let's assume that nobody can. This is realistic; in addition, it provides an opportunity to discuss blending.* With *fast*, blending is guided by a teacher's questions:

1. What is the sound of short *a*? [ă]
2. Let's put the sound of *f* before /ă/. What are the sounds of *fa*? [fă]
3. Say "fă" again. . . . Now say it once more, but this time add the sound of *s* to the end of it. [făs]
4. Say "făs" again and add /t/. [făst]
5. Yes, fast. This new word is fast. What does it mean to go fast?

At the same time that the questions are being asked and answered, the teacher writes the following to add the necessary visual dimension:

ă

fă

făs

făst

Had the children been taught to deal with clusters (*st*), one less question and one less step would be necessary:

ă

fă

făst

Either way, notice that the first step in the blending is to produce the vowel sound, even though the first letter in *fast* is *f*. This procedure is followed in order to avoid isolating /f/ and, in turn, to avoid an "answer" that might sound

---

*Children may know the sounds that compose words but still not know how to pronounce them. Nonetheless, most available reading series omit help for teaching children how to blend sounds to produce syllables and words (1, 3, 9, 18).

something like "fu-ast." Had the unknown word started with a vowel (*end*, for instance), the blending sequence would parallel the left-to-right sequence of the letters:

ĕ

ĕn

ĕnd

To sum up, blending sounds to form syllables follows letter progression, except when the initial letter is a consonant. In those cases, the first vowel sound is produced, and the initial consonant sound is then affixed to it. Subsequently, the sequence for blending follows the sequence of the letters. More illustrations of this recommended procedure (and of the use of other generalizations) are shown below:

Unknown Word	*Blending Sequence*
hot	ŏ ⟶ hŏ ⟶ hŏt
stop	ŏ ⟶ stŏ ⟶ stŏp
champ	ă ⟶ chă ⟶ chăm ⟶ chămp
wait	ā ⟶ wā ⟶ wāit
owl	ow ⟶ owl
ade	ā ⟶ ādé

To be noted: When blending is taught or practiced, decisions about the likely sounds in the word are made first. (At the beginning, using diacritical marks is helpful.) Following that, the sequence for blending should be displayed:

hŏt	stŏp	chămp	āim
ŏ	ŏ	ă	āi
hŏ	stŏ	chă	āim
hŏt	stŏp	chăm	
		chămp	

Whenever multisyllabic words require a letter-by-letter, sound-by-sound analysis, similar blending procedures are followed, once the word is divided into syllables. Now, each syllable is considered separately. Because treating syllables separately makes each one sound like a word (más cot; cá blé), putting multisyllabic words in contexts is recommended. The help they offer allows children to convert approximately correct pronunciation into precisely correct ones. Such changes often require adjustments in stressed syllables (aú tó ⟶ aú to) and in vowel sounds (sí lĕnt′ ⟶ sí lənt).

PRACTICE: SOME
INTRODUCTORY COMMENTS

As mentioned, one characteristic of successful comprehenders is the ability to decode unknown words both correctly *and* quickly (10, 11, 12, 13, 14). To achieve that end, all available cues are used. The desirability of a balanced use of every source of help is the reason the earlier chapter on contexts recommends practice that includes exercises like the following:

Contexts and Minimal Graphophonic Cues

> The m_____ in the car is running.
> We camped out and slept in a t_____t.

Contexts and Initial Syllables

> We're going to the cir_____ to see the lions.

Contexts and Closely Similar Words

> I have a _____ in my finger.
>   silver   sliver

You should also recall from the earlier chapter on contexts the reminder about making sure children see the connection between filling in blanks and coping with new words.

SAMPLES OF PHONICS PRACTICE

Without question, using spellings – plus whatever other help is available – to figure out unfamiliar words encountered in a story, chapter, or newspaper is the best kind of practice. In fact, such use of spellings is the only reason for teaching phonics. In addition to this natural practice, more contrived kinds are often necessary. The additional practice is usually in the form of assignments. Samples of such practice follow, organized according to subject matter dealt with in phonics instruction.

Letter-Sound Relationships

Even though commercially prepared materials persist for a long time in having children listen for certain sounds in words, auditory discrimination enters into phonics only when children are required – as happens when letter-sound correspondences are taught inductively – to perceive a sound in given words (8). Instead of spending so much time on auditory exercises, therefore, teachers should provide practice that helps children automatically associate certain letters with certain sounds. This will help them move, as decoders must, from spellings to pronunciations.

What busy teachers must do is use materials for a variety of objectives. To illustrate one kind of adaptation, a suggestion made in Chapter 7 for whole word practice is repeated below.

> Cut out baby ghosts from white construction paper and print a word on each. Place the ghosts in a trick-or-treat bag (ordinary grocery bag). Children can pull them out one at a time and identify the displayed word.

To adapt the suggestion for phonics, a letter or digraph can be printed on each ghost; the tasks for the children are to think of its sound and to name a word that starts (ends) with it.

Since a number of ideas for practice with letter-sound correspondences are described in the previous chapter, only a few are offered now.

For practice with short vowel sounds, a ladder like one in Figure 10.2 can be drawn on the chalkboard. To climb each rung, children must think of the letter, then its sound, then name a word that starts with that sound. For variation, letters can be printed around the edge of a paper plate, now a race track.

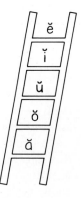

Figure 10.2

For more variation, something like the picture in Figure 10.3 can be drawn on the board. To go from home to the swimming pool, children name words beginning with the sounds suggested by the letters.

At times, children's own art work can provide practice in associating certain letters with certain sounds. (See the suggestions following Figure 10.3.)

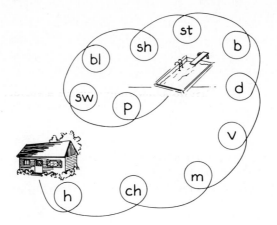

Figure 10.3

- To call attention each week to one letter-sound relationship, have children draw a page of objects whose names begin with the designated letter and sound. (Capital and lowercase forms of the letter are printed at the bottom.) Eventually, pages can be assembled into phonics books to serve for review.
- With a sheet like the one in Figure 10.4, children can be asked to draw in each box a picture of something whose name starts with the letter(s) printed there.

s	st
sl	sh
sn	sw
sp	sm

Figure 10.4

- To reinforce the connection between *f* and /f/, paper fans with fairly wide folds can be made. To prepare for decorating them, dittoed pictures of objects whose names begin with *f* (e.g., face, fence, flower, foot, frog, fountain, feather, flag, fire, fan) can be named, colored, cut out, and pasted in the folds. (In using something like this for phonics practice or review, it is essential that children understand the connection between the fan, the names of the pictures, and the sound recorded by *f*. Otherwise, the instructional potential of the activity will not be realized.)

Just as displays on bulletin boards can be used to teach letter-sound associations (see Figure 9.1), they can also function in making the associations automatic. How some observed teachers used bulletin boards for practice is described next.

- To reinforce the connection between *u* and /ŭ/, one board displayed the outline of a large umbrella, under which appeared the word *umbrella*. Also on this board were cutouts of *U* and *u*. Lacking pictures of objects whose names start with /ŭ/, the teacher used words the children could read (*us, up, under, upon*), which were printed on small, umbrella-shaped cards attached to the board. Later, the children made their own umbrella outlines. An added attraction was the chance to select "fabric" for their umbrellas from an old book of wallpaper samples.
- A board in another classroom was entitled "Oscar the Octopus." The children had been working on medial short sounds; consequently, pictures they had drawn showed objects like clocks, dolls, pots, mops, rocks, and blocks.
- "Helping Hands" was the title of another board in another room. Large outlines of two paper hands formed the background. Attached to one hand were pictures of objects whose names begin with /h/. Attached to the other were cards showing familiar words beginning with *h*.
- Interest in telephone numbers suggested the theme for another phonics display. Because there were twenty-three children, twenty-three outlines of a telephone appeared in rows. On each, a child had carefully printed his name and number. At the top of the board, *telephone* appeared in large lowercase letters. At the bottom, capital *T* and lowercase *t* were displayed.
- A colorful picture of a farm (commercially drawn) hung on one board. Cutout letters whose sounds had been taught were thumbtacked beneath it. To provide for review, individual children were directed to name a letter, think of its sound, then name something in the picture whose name began (ended) with it.
- Another board showed rows of cutout flowers, each with a letter printed on its center. Two paper bees appeared at the top, next to which was printed:

> The bees want to fly.
> You can play with them.

Initially, this board was used under the direction of the teacher; later, pairs of children used it on their own at free-choice time. In either case, a child became a bee (by holding a paper bee) and flew from flower to flower naming words that started with the letter printed on the flower. (Each flower could be picked up like a flap, under which was a list of familiar words beginning with the letter printed on the flower.)

Adding and Substituting Sounds

Bulletin board displays can also provide practice in adding and substituting sounds. Descriptions of three displays follow.

- One board, called "Iceberg Hop," allowed for practice in adding initial sounds to blends recorded by graphemic bases. To realize that objective, the board showed icebergs on which bases like *-ake, -ell*, and *-ight* had been printed. Children held a paper penguin that displayed a letter and hopped from iceberg to iceberg naming the words that resulted when the sound recorded by the letter was added to the beginning of the blends recorded by the graphemic bases. (To highlight the wholeness of the words, they were later printed by the teacher on a chalkboard.)
- Graphemic bases figured in a display that featured a paper clown who was holding four balloons (circular paper of different colors) attached to the end of string. On each balloon, one of these letters appeared: *d, f, n, l*. The teacher displayed cards showing graphemic bases; the job for the children was to name words comprised of the letters followed by the bases. For instance, if the teacher placed *-ine* after each letter, a child would say: *dine, fine, nine, line*. Every time this was done, the teacher wrote the words on a nearby chalkboard so what had been said could be seen.

Figure 10.5 shows a bulletin board used for practice in substituting sounds.

Decoding Unknown Words

The various kinds of practice that prepare children to cope correctly and quickly with unfamiliar words that are embedded in helpful contexts are discussed in Chapter 8. Realistically, children also need practice in using only spellings, as helpful contexts are not always present. Use of spellings to reach conclusions about pronunciations requires:

Figure 10.5. *Substituting Sounds*

To encourage use of letter-sound associations, one teacher wrote the following ▶
on a chalkboard:

get

met

bet

let

jet

Consonant sounds were reviewed first, then *get* was read. (A list like the one above begins with a known word and continues with unknown ones.) Next, individual children were given the chance to decode the other words by using *get* and the sounds recorded by *m, b, l,* and *j.* Meanings of the words were discussed.

To add interest to the practice, flowers were attached to a bulletin board. Graphemic bases were printed on the stamens. The petals, which were cut in one piece and were movable, displayed consonant letters. By rotating the petals to align the letters with the graphemic bases, further practice with initial consonant substitutions was available.

For practice with medial and final substitutions, monosyllabic words serve well. For example:

cat	ant	cat	bus
cot	act	can	but
cut		cap	bun

291

1. Knowing letter-sound correspondences at the level of automaticity.
2. Ability to add and substitute sounds.
3. Ability to apply generalizations having to do with:
   a. syllabication.
   b. factors that affect letter-sound correspondences.

How these prerequisites enter into the decoding of a word like *fifteen* is outlined below. Teachers can use similar outlines and sequences when they model decoding for students. In turn, the children can use them as they practice what they have seen and heard their teachers do.

fifteen

Syllabication:

When two consonants (that are not special digraphs) are preceded and followed by vowels, a division usually occurs between the consonants.

fif   teen

When there are two successive vowels in a syllable (that are not special digraphs), the first usually stands for its long sound and the second is silent.

fif   tn

Every syllable must have a vowel sound; this is two syllables.

Sounds of Syllables:

fif

When there is one vowel in a syllable and it is not in final position, it generally stands for its short sound.

ĭ
fĭ
fĭf

The likelihood of *fifteen* being in the children's oral vocabularies will make the product of this decoding effort a recognizable pronunciation—that is, a recognizable word, even when it is not in a context.

More details about decoding are in the next chapter, which looks at one further kind of relevant cue: word structure.

SUMMARY

Like good parents, good teachers do whatever they can to help children grow in independence. The specific concern of Chapter 10 is independence in decoding unfamiliar words, which the use of graphophonic cues makes possible. These cues are available to readers of English because of its alphabetic writing system.

Developing decoding ability is the goal of phonics instruction. To realize that end, the subject matter taught covers letter-sound relationships, factors that affect those relationships, and syllabication. Syllabication is an essential topic, as the syllable is the unit of pronunciation in the decoding process.

Phonics instruction often deals with generalizations about the way English is recorded. Statements of the generalizations specify visual cues that signal information about syllabication and pronunciations. Highlighting the visual is mandatory, because that is all that is available when a word is not in a child's reading vocabulary. For decoding, the significant visual features are letters and their sequence.

Although important, teaching about those features is not enough. What must be added is instruction that will help children use relevant features to figure out unfamiliar words. At first, teachers should model (act out) the use of what has been taught. Such demonstrations will be especially helpful when the concern is for flexible use. Flexibility is essential, since symbols for words do not always display perfect consistency in letter-sound relationships. (More is said about flexibility in the next chapter.)

To promote flexibility, words to be decoded should be placed in contexts, except when teachers want to learn what children can do with spellings only. Contexts allow for the combined use of contextual and graphophonic cues and for the question, Does this pronunciation make sense in this context?

Making sense, of course, is what reading is all about. While, at best, a phonic analysis of a word only yields its pronunciation, that pronunciation will signal a meaning if the word in question is in the reader's oral vocabulary. Once again, therefore, the fundamental importance of those vocabularies for reading is established. Recognizing it is especially important for nursery school and kindergarten teachers, some of whom are now spending more time on phonics than on oral language—thanks mostly to the availability of commercial materials that equate beginning reading instruction with phonics instruction. Everything said in Chapter 10 underscores the wisdom of doing whatever is possible to extend children's oral vocabularies. In the end, that is bound to be more helpful for reading than premature instruction in phonics.

REVIEW

1. The Preview for Chapter 10 recommends giving close attention to the terms that would be introduced and defined. It seems appropriate, therefore, to start a review with requests (a) to place each term listed below under the heading *Letter* or *Sound*, and (b) to explain why you think the terms placed under *Letter* pertain to letters and why those listed under *Sound* have to do with sounds.

blend	graphemic base
cluster	phonogram
consonant digraph	schwa
diphthong	vowel digraph

2. Having classified the terms listed above, you should be ready to specify errors in the following comments, all of which were either heard in classrooms or found in commercially prepared workbooks.
   a. "Underline the blends in the following words."
   b. "A digraph is one sound spelled with two letters."
   c. "Print the diphthongs on cards."
   d. "This page is designed to help children hear digraphs."

3. Having identified the errors in the above statements, you should be able to generalize about them all. In general, what is wrong with the statements?

4. With examples, explain why all the following statements are correct.
   a. The less prediction allowed for by the text, the more do the visual features of an unfamiliar word have to be relied on to learn what it says.
   b. The likelihood of children acquiring proficiency in decoding is determined by many factors, one of which is the size of their oral vocabularies.

   c. Using what is taught in phonics with flexibility reduces the amount of phonics content that needs to be taught.

5. A recent talk I gave to a group of teachers emphasized the uselessness of phonics practice that has children apply what they learned in phonics to known words. During the question period, a teacher defended the use of familiar words with the comment, "I need to keep some children busy so I'll be free to help others. To keep them busy, I have to give them something they know how to do." How would you respond to this teacher?

6. Starting toward the end of grade three and continuing until the end of elementary school, classroom observations identify a common practice: If a student has trouble reading a word, the teacher says, "Look it up in the glossary" or "Look it up in the dictionary." This is the case even in school systems that spend a great deal of time teaching phonics as early as kindergarten. What do you think about this practice?

7. Critique the following generalizations, both found in commercial materials.
   a. When a single consonant comes between two vowels in a word, the word is usually divided after the consonant if the first vowel is short.
   b. If a word has two successive consonants that are not special digraphs, divide the word between the consonants.

REFERENCES

1. Anderson, Richard C.; Hiebert, Elfrieda H.; Scott, Judith A.; and Wilkinson, Ian A. G. *Becoming a Nation of Readers.* Washington, D.C.: The National Institute of Education, 1985.
2. Ausubel, David P. "Viewpoints from Related Disciplines: Human Growth and Development." *Teachers College Record* 60 (February, 1959), 245–254.
3. Beck, Isabel L., and McCaslin, Ellen S. *An Analysis of Dimensions That Affect the Development of Code-Breaking Ability in Eight Beginning Reading Programs.* Pittsburgh: University of Pittsburgh, Learning Research and Development Center, 1978.
4. Brown, Roger. *Words and Things.* New York: The Free Press, 1958.
5. Durkin, Dolores. *The Decoding Ability of Elementary School Students*, Reading Education Report No. 49. Urbana: University of Illinois, Center for the Study of Reading, May, 1984.
6. Durkin, Dolores. "Is There a Match between What Elementary Teachers Do and What Basal Reader Manuals Recommend?" *Reading Teacher* 37 (April, 1984), 734–744.
7. Durkin, Dolores. *Strategies for Identifying Words*, 2nd ed. Boston: Allyn and Bacon, Inc., 1981.

8. Eeds-Kniep, Maryann. "The Frenetic Fanatic Phonic Backlash." *Language Arts* 56 (November/December, 1979), 909–917.

9. Haddock, Maryann. "Teaching Blending in Beginning Reading Instruction *Is* Important." *Reading Teacher* 31 (March, 1978), 654–658.

10. Lesgold, Alan M., and Resnick, Lauren B. *How Reading Difficulties Develop: Perspectives from a Longitudinal Study.* Pittsburgh: University of Pittsburgh, Learning Research and Development Center, 1981.

11. Perfetti, Charles A. "Language Comprehension and Fast Decoding: Some Psycholinguistic Prerequisites for Skilled Reading Comprehension." In John T. Guthrie (Ed.), *Cognition, Curriculum, and Comprehension.* Newark, Del.: International Reading Association, 1977.

12. Samuels, S. Jay. "Comparison of Word Recognition Speed and Strategies of Less Skilled and More Highly Skilled Readers." *Reading Research Quarterly* 11 (1975–76, No. 1), 72–86.

13. Stanovich, Keith E. "Toward an Interactive-Compensatory Model of Individual Differences in the Development of Reading Fluency." *Reading Research Quarterly* 16 (1980, No. 1), 32–71.

14. Stanovich, Keith E.; Cunningham, Anne E.; and Feeman, Dorothy J. "Intelligence, Cognitive Skills, and Early Reading Progress." *Reading Research Quarterly* 19 (Spring, 1984), 278–303.

15. Stott, D. H. Manual for "Programmed Reading Kits 1 and 2." Toronto: Gage Educational Publishing Limited, 1970.

16. Tovey, Duane R. "Children's Grasp of Phonics Terms vs. Sound-Symbol Relationships." *Reading Teacher* 33 (January, 1980), 431–437.

17. Weaver, Phyllis, and Shonkoff, Fredi. *Research within Reach.* Washington, D.C.: The National Institute of Education, 1978.

18. Williams, Joanna P. "Teaching Decoding with an Emphasis on Phoneme Analysis and Phoneme Blending." *Journal of Educational Psychology* 72 (February, 1980), 1–15.

CHAPTER 11

Structural Analysis

PREVIEW

How to advance children's ability to cope successfully, quickly, and independently with new or forgotten words continues to be the central theme as Chapter 11 considers structural analysis. You may have noticed in the two phonics chapters that all the illustrative words were roots. That was not accidental, since phonics instruction is concerned with the spellings of roots. In contrast, it is spellings (and meanings) of prefixes (e.g., *un-*, *mis-*) and suffixes (e.g., *-able*, *-ed*) that teachers attend to for structural analysis. Combined, the two kinds of instruction are a means for developing the ability to decode words like *unworkable* and *miscounted*. For children whose oral vocabularies include *work* and *count*, a knowledge of the prefixes *un-* and *mis-* and of the suffixes *-able* and *-ed* also makes apparent the meanings of *unworkable* and *miscounted*. Given the importance of meanings for comprehending, structural analysis should never be viewed as a minor part of an instructional program.

One way to help yourself comprehend Chapter 11 is to commit to memory any definition below that is unfamiliar.

Word Family: Words having the same origin.* (Sometimes the origin, or root, is a self-sustaining word, as in the family composed of such members as *read*, *reader*, *readable*, *unreadable*, and *reread*. At other times, the origin is not an English word, as in the family that includes *auditory*, *auditorium*, *audience*, and *audition*.)

Root: The origin of a word family. (If the root is a word, it cannot be reduced (e.g., *peach* to *each*) and still remain a member of the family.) *Base* is a synonym for *root*.

*Commonly, basal materials erroneously assign the description "family" to a group of words like *sun*, *fun*, *run*, and *bun*.

Prefix: A unit of one or more letters placed before a root. (Prefixes alter the meaning of roots, as illustrated in *retie*, *foretell*, and *amoral*.)

Suffix: A unit of one or more letters placed at the end of a root.

Derivational Suffix: A unit of one or more letters placed at the end of a root that alters its meaning. (Examples of derivational suffixes affixed to roots are care*ful*, care*less*, and care*free*.)

Derived Word: Composed of a root and a prefix (*react*); a root and a derivational suffix (*actor*); or a root, a prefix, and a derivational suffix (*reactor*).

Inflectional Suffix: A unit of one or more letters placed at the end of a root for grammatical purposes. (Examples of inflectional suffixes, sometimes called *inflections*, affixed to roots are want*s*, boxe*s*, tall*er*, and slow*ly*.)

Inflected Word: Composed of a root to which an inflectional suffix is added. (Examples of inflected words are *doing*, *girls*, *richest*, and *curly*.)

Affix: Refers to a prefix, a derivational suffix, or an inflectional suffix.

word family according to Durkin
┌ un winding
└ wind

phonograms - sound/parts
  — ake \ lake \ bake

Root - <u>wind</u>   roots derived from Latin
              ped (foot)
Base pedal ←

prefix put in front
Suffix = inflectional — added on — to verb s, er ing ly ed est ┌ grammatical purposes
        = derivational   └ taught in primary
        — change word meaning

As the Preview for this chapter indicates, decoders must be able to deal with the structure of words, since many are composed not just of roots but also of other meaning-bearing parts called prefixes and suffixes. Because meaning takes precedence over everything else, any dismantling of these more complex words must keep roots, prefixes, and suffixes intact. To illustrate, should *redrawing* be an unfamiliar word, a correct segmentation and synthesis of its components for the purpose of decoding are as follows:

redrawing

drawing

draw

drawing

redrawing

This analysis is based on structural parts; the analysis below, which obscures two of the three meaningful components, is based on phonological divisions:

redrawing

red   raw   ing

The main thrust of these introductory comments is that the importance of keeping roots and affixes intact in order to preserve meaning accounts for the need to consider structure whenever a word has to be figured out.

How phonic and structural analyses function together to get words decoded is clarified later in the chapter. Now, two basic, related questions are considered: (a) When should instruction about word structure begin? (b) Does attention go to prefixes first or to suffixes? The two questions assume that some instruction in phonics precedes initial attention to word structure, since instruction with prefixes and suffixes makes use of roots known to the children either because they were taught directly or because they were decoded and then practiced. Prior instruction in phonics will also allow for decoding roots whenever they are unfamiliar.

INITIAL INSTRUCTION

As with any topic covered in reading instruction, whatever is done with word structure should make its value for reading apparent. Applied to word structure specifically, the guideline means that children should have a clear understanding of how knowing about structure helps with both the pronunciation and the meaning of derived and inflected words.

The importance of children seeing the practical value of what they are asked to learn and practice points to the answer about when initial instruction with word structure should take place: When text that children are expected to read contains words other than roots. If a piece of text has plural nouns, for instance, it is time to deal with inflectional suffixes.

Admittedly, specifying *need* as a criterion for making decisions about the timing of instruction may seem like stating the obvious. Nonetheless, the explicit identification is made because the most frequently used instructional materials—basal reader programs—routinely teach what is not needed at the time it is taught. One recently examined basal lesson, for example, included a brief section labeled "Instruction" that dealt with the prefixes *re-* and *un-*. Why these two prefixes were introduced together was unclear; but why they were covered at all was equally unclear, since the selection that students would soon be assigned to read did not include any word that had either prefix.

When need for the instruction is kept in mind, whether to teach prefixes or suffixes first is no longer a dilemma. Again, what children are being asked to read makes it clear that inflected words (e.g., plural nouns, and present-tense and past-tense verbs) show up earlier than derived words. Hence, work with word structure gets under way by attending to common inflectional suffixes.

Before a lesson dealing with one such suffix is described, a more encompassing look at lessons serves as an introduction. So, too, should Table 11.1.

Table 11.1. *Inflected Words*

Nouns	*Verbs*	*Adjectives*	*Adverbs*
books	plays	tall*er*	quick*ly*
tax*es*	bless*es*	slow*est*	
ox*en*	look*ed*	snow*y*	
bird*'s*	read*ing*		
plants*'*	hard*en*		

OBJECTIVES OF LESSONS FOR WORD STRUCTURE

Regardless of the specific focus, four objectives for all instruction with affixes can be generalized as follows:

1. Children will be able to spell the affix being taught. (This allows them to recognize it when they scan the letters in an unknown word.)
2. Children will be able to pronounce the affix. (Even though a knowl-

edge of letter-sound correspondences leads to correct pronunciations for most affixes, knowing how to pronounce them "on the spot" not only speeds up decoding but also frees the reader to attend to meaning.)

3. Children will be able to describe how the affix affects the meaning of roots. (Even though the need to realize this objective is obvious, knowing about the semantic effect of affixes is productive only when the meaning of roots is also known. To be knowledgeable about the prefix *un-*, for instance, is of little practical value for dealing with *untidy* if the meaning of *tidy* isn't known. Once again, then, the dependence of reading on oral vocabularies is made clear.)

4. Children will be able to use what they learn about an affix when it is found in a derived or an inflected word that did not figure in the lesson. (This objective reflects the fact that learning that has no transfer value is of little consequence.)

BEGINNING LESSON: PLURAL NOUNS

Often, reasons to teach plural nouns exist long before children are ready for formal lessons with prefixes and suffixes. Early in kindergarten, for example, a teacher may decide it would be of practical value to have the children learn to read *Girls* and *Boys*. While she may choose to mention that adding *s* to *girl* makes it say "girls" and that adding *s* to *boy* makes it say "boys," the additional comments are unnecessary. *Girls* and *Boys* can both be taught as whole words.

Eventually, children do need instruction about the plural marker *-s*; a description of a lesson that illustrates such instruction follows. As you read it, keep in mind the four objectives that should be realized whenever a prefix or suffix is taught. (What *are* the four objectives?)

Since, in this case, members of the instructional group can read *the*, *is*, *top*, and *green*, the teacher starts the lesson about the plural marker *-s* by writing the following sentence:

The top is green.

After the children read the sentence, silently first, then aloud, their attention is called to a picture of three green tops. Once they have discussed and counted the tops, the teacher suggests, "Read the sentence on the board again. . . . How many tops does it tell us about? . . . It doesn't tell us about this picture, then, does it? . . . What do I have to write to tell about the picture? . . . Correct. Let me write what you just said."

The top is green.

The tops are green.

Next the teacher explains how the addition of *s* to a word that is the name of something makes it mean more than one. Using singular nouns that the children can read, she writes and discusses such contrasts as these:

girl	boy	hat	car
girls	boys	hats	cars

Subsequently, copies of sentences like the following are distributed for a reading-writing assignment:

1. The _____ are going fast.
   car cars
2. The girl has a blue_____.
   hat hats

Combined, the various procedures serve to introduce word structure and, with the above assignment, to make further use of contextual help.

Before describing a second lesson, let me discuss a few details about the one just referred to. Probably the most important detail is the connection between oral language and instruction about inflections. Dealing with the formation of plurals through the addition of *s*, the teacher evoked oral language with the help of a picture. She asked, "What do I have to write to tell about the picture?" The children responded, "The tops are green." In this way, in order to introduce a new learning in reading, the teacher made a natural shift from spoken to written language.*

Spoken language entered the scene again, though covertly, when the children moved from a plural like *tops* to one like *girls*. In this case, their tacit knowledge of language allowed them (unconsciously) to assign /z/ to the *s* in *girls* even though they had assigned /s/ to the *s* in *tops*. Although no need exists for children to have a conscious, verbalized understanding of what they do "without thinking," the following pattern may be of interest to you.

When the final sound in a singular noun is /p/, /t/, /k/, or /f/, the inflection *s* records /s/. Otherwise, it stands for /z/. For instance:

tops	cats	tacks	puffs	coughs
days	toys	dads	rags	bells

This generalization also applies to a verb inflection. That is, *s* stands for /s/ in verbs like *stops*, *wants*, *picks*, and *laughs*, but for /z/ in verbs like *plays*, *runs*, and *tells*.

---

*Nonstandard English will be considered later.

ANOTHER LESSON: PAST-TENSE VERBS

The objective of the next lesson to be described is to teach the tense marker *-ed*. Again, the teacher makes use of oral language, plus words the children can read. Known words are combined as follows:

> Today is Wednesday.
> We will look at books.

After the children read the two sentences, the teacher inquires, "If today is Wednesday, what day was yesterday? . . . I'll write Tuesday to see what we can say about that:

> Today is Wednesday.
> We will look at books.
> On Tuesday we

"If we want to tell about looking at books yesterday, on Tuesday, what do we have to say? . . . Yes, we have to say, 'On Tuesday we *looked* at books.' I'll write that:

> Today is Wednesday.
> We will look at books.
> On Tuesday we looked at books too.

"Who can read all three sentences? . . . Please take a close look at what I did to *look* to make it say 'looked'." Now the teacher extracts *look* and *looked* from their contexts to allow close scrutiny of both:

> look
> looked

"See how I added *e* and *d* to the end of *look* to make it say 'looked'. Whenever that's done to words, the words tell us what happened not today, but yesterday or maybe last week or even last year. Let me show you how that works with some words you know. . . ." At the end, the board displays:

jump	call	laugh	show
jumped	called	laughed	showed
talk	walk	work	play
talked	walked	worked	played

With words like those shown, further unconscious behavior will be observed. That is, children will automatically shift from assigning /t/ to *ed* (*looked, jumped*) to assigning /d/ (*called, showed, played*). Again, no need exists for them to be able to verbalize what they know intuitively:

When the sound preceding *ed* is /p/, /k/, /f/, or /s/, the *ed* records /t/. Otherwise it stands for /d/. For instance:

tapped	asked	puffed	passed
tagged	flowed	stayed	peeled

Another pattern, one that *does* require explicit attention in a lesson, is described below:

When the inflectional suffix *-ed* is added to a verb ending with *t* or *d*, it is a separate syllable ("əd"). Otherwise, it adds a sound but not a syllable.*
For instance:

want ed	paint ed	need ed	land ed
played	cleaned	wished	helped

This generalization points out that *want* is one syllable, whereas *wanted* is two. It further suggests that the verb *play* is composed of one syllable and three sounds, and the inflected form *played* is one syllable that has four sounds.

MORE ADVANCED INSTRUCTION WITH INFLECTIONAL SUFFIXES

When children know roots like *top* and *look*, seeing them in *tops* and *looked* is usually easy. The same cannot be said when the spellings of roots are altered as they are in *ponies* and *skated*. For some children, known roots may even be obscure in inflected words like *canned* and *rubbed*.

To help children sort out roots in systematic ways so they can see the connection between what is familiar (root) and what is not (inflected word), spelling generalizations should be taught in ways that show their relevance for that task. For example, children who know the generalizations should be able to expose roots in words like the following:

---

*This generalization only describes verbs, thus does not pertain to adjectives like *wicked*, *ragged*, and *crooked*.

babies	making	hummed	pleases	liked	laziest	beginner
baby	make	hum	please	like	lazy	begin

Spelling generalizations that help children see roots in both inflected and derived words comprise Table 11.2.

Table 11.2. *Spelling Generalizations*

The plural of nouns ending in s, ss, ch, and sh is formed by adding *es*. The *[handwritten: Sound the es words the add]* pronunciation of this inflectional suffix is /əz/. For instance:

buses   passes   churches   wishes

The plural of nouns ending in *f* is formed by changing *f* to *v* and adding *es*. For instance:

leaf   leaves   loaf   loaves

When a verb ends in a consonant that is preceded by a single vowel, the consonant usually is doubled before inflectional suffixes like *ed* or *ing* are added. For instance: *[handwritten: add consonant to keep vowel short]*

wrap   wrapped   rub   rubbing

When a root ends in *y* and it is preceded by a consonant, *y* is changed to *i* before adding *es, ed, er, est, ly, ful, less,* or *ous*. For instance: *[handwritten: Change y to i and add es]*

lady	ladies	carry	carried	tiny	tinier
pretty	prettiest	merry	merrily	plenty	plentiful
penny	penniless	melody	melodious		

When a root ends in "silent" *e*, the *e* usually is omitted when either an inflectional or a derivational suffix beginning with a vowel is added. For instance:

make	dance	rate	excite	strange	create
making	dancer	rated	excitable	stranger	creation

NONSTANDARD ENGLISH AND INFLECTIONAL SUFFIXES

Whether instruction with inflectional suffixes is just beginning or is more advanced, what is taught relates directly to spoken language. You can recall that the relationship is both apparent and useful in the lessons dealing with the plural of *top* and the past tense of *look*. It calls for two guidelines for instruction offered to nonstandard English speakers:

1. When standard English speakers are being instructed, a reference ought to be made to spoken language ("If we want to tell about

something that happened yesterday, what do we have to say? . . . Yes, we'd say 'looked' instead of 'look'."); however, a similar reference could confuse nonstandard speakers who do not pronounce the inflectional suffix -ed when they talk. With such individuals, instruction about written inflections ought to proceed deductively: "When you're reading about something that has already happened—maybe it happened yesterday or even last year—you'll find the letters e and d at the end of the word. That's why I added e and d to the end of look. I wanted the letters to show we did that yesterday, on Tuesday. Who can give me another sentence that starts with the word 'Yesterday'?" Eventually, the board shows three contributions from the children:

> Yesterday I walked home from school.
>
> Last week I stayed home.
>
> Last night I burned my hand.

2. How nonstandard English speakers respond aloud to *walked* (whether with "walk" or "walked") is less important for reading than is their understanding of the function of -ed (or whatever the inflectional suffix might be). The fact that understanding is the key issue reflects the essence of reading, which is comprehension.

Samples of nonstandard deviations that have relevance for instruction with inflectional suffixes follow (1, 4):

Written Language	*Nonstandard Speech*
He looks.	"He look."
I dropped it.	"I drop it."
She turned around.	"She turnt around."
She is coming.	"She is come."
They let us do it.	"They lets us do it."
He started crying.	"He stard crying."

INSTRUCTION FOR DERIVED WORDS

While instruction is proceeding with common inflectional suffixes, a few derivatives will begin to show up in what the children are reading. This is the time, then, for initiating instruction with derivational suffixes. By now, finding special letters at the end of familiar roots will not be new because of the earlier attention to inflectional suffixes.

Starting with derivational suffixes (e.g., -*ful*) as opposed to prefixes (e.g., *re-*) makes sense not only because of the previous attention to inflectional suffixes but also because what is familiar (e.g., *play*) will precede what is new (*-ful*) in the more complex word (*playful*). This contrasts with a derived word like *replay* in which the familiar base is less obvious.

Even though the guidelines just stated are logical and defensible, need for the instruction remains the most important of all criteria. Its importance means that if derived words with prefixes are in text that children are expected to read, instruction with prefixes takes precedence over any concerned with derivational suffixes, whether or not commercially prepared materials suggest this. (Because teachers sometimes have to put together their own lessons, samples are included in this and other chapters.)

Before lessons dealing with derivational suffixes are described, it might be useful to examine the prefixes and derivational suffixes listed in Table 11.3.

BEGINNING LESSONS: DERIVATIONAL SUFFIXES

How one teacher initiated instruction with the derivational suffix *-er* is described in Chapter 2. What another teacher did with *-less* is described here.

In this case, the teacher used the cleaning-up activities that follow art to teach about it. Consequently, after the classroom had been tidied up one afternoon, she commented about the cleanliness, then deliberately added, "This room is absolutely spotless. Does anyone know what *spotless* means?" Nobody did, so the teacher continued, "It means there isn't one dirty spot in this room, thanks to your help. Let me write the word *spot*. You know how to read that already, but under it I'm going to write the word I just used—the word *spotless*. [The experience of cleaning up provided a context, making a verbal one unnecessary.]

spot

spotless

"Let's take a look at the new part. How would you expect it to sound? . . . Yes, with a short *e*. But when this part is at the end of a word, we say it so fast it sounds more like 'luss' than 'less'. Listen. 'Spotless.'* How do you spell this new part? . . . Remember, this new part comes at the end of words and it means 'without'. *Spotless* means 'without a spot'—like this room right now.

---

*If the children knew about the schwa sound, teaching the derivational suffix *-less* would be a time to remind them of the occurrence of that sound in unstressed syllables.

Table 11.3. *Some Common Prefixes and Suffixes*

Prefix	Meaning	Example
ir	not	irregular
il		illegal
im		impatient
in		inactive
a		atypical
non		nonhuman
un	opposite of	unlock, unkind
dis	not	disobey
	remove	disarm
re	again	remake
	back	recall
mis	wrongly	miscount
pre	before	preschool
fore	before	forewarn
	in front	foreward
co	with	co-author
counter	against	counteract
anti		antiwar
under	below	underage
semi	half	semicircle
	partly	semitropical
	coming twice	semiannual

Suffix	Meaning	Example
-er	one who; doer of action	teacher
-or		actor
-eer		auctioneer
-less	without	spotless
-able	capable of being	readable
-ful	full; characterized by	careful
-y		oily
-ous		dangerous
-ful	amount that fills	cupful
-ic (ical)	connected with	poetic, historical
-ist		humorist
-ness	state of	softness
-hood		childhood
-ship		friendship
-ance		tolerance
-ence		dependence
-tion (ation)		action, starvation
-ment		enjoyment
-ward	in the direction of	homeward
-age	act of	marriage
	amount of	mileage
	home of	orphanage
-ee	object of action	employee

"I'll write some other words you know to see what happens when *l, e, s, s,* is added:

mother	shoe	home
motherless	shoeless	homeless
pain	belt	boot
painless	beltless	bootless

"What's this first word? . . . What does it say when I add the new part to it? . . . Who can tell us what *motherless* means? . . . Will someone use it in a sentence? . . . Okay. What's this next word?" And so the lesson about the new derivational suffix continues.

As subsequent lessons concentrate on other derivational suffixes, they should offer children considerable help with word meanings. Soon, for instance, lessons will allow for attention to antonyms in a form such as the following:

careless	useless	painless	hopeless	colorless	fruitless
careful	useful	painful	hopeful	colorful	fruitful

Systematic and frequent attention to word meanings through the vehicle of derivatives is especially important for the following reason. Although derived words appear frequently in written material, they are much less common in spoken language. This means that although authors can be expected to use descriptions like *treeless* and *mournful*, speakers—even well-educated speakers—are more apt to say something like "bare" and "sad." The difference means that children may have problems with derived words, since oral language will not be as helpful as it commonly is. Knowing this, teachers should devote ample time to derivatives.

PREFIXES

Why instruction should not cover a large number of derivational suffixes before a switch is made to prefixes is suggested in Table 11.3. As that table shows, the semantic effect many derivational suffixes have on roots is difficult to verbalize in a way that is meaningful for young children. I am reminded here of a visit to a second grade in which the derivational suffix *-ness* had been introduced. Rather than try to deal explicitly with the meaning of *-ness*, the teacher chose instead to have the children use words like *softness*, *darkness*, and *goodness* in oral sentences. When she requested a sentence for *sameness*, my immediate thought was, "I hope she doesn't call on me!" Fortunately, she called on a girl who quickly offered, "People who have sameness are twins." In spite of this delightful use of *sameness* by a second grader, difficult-to-explain derivational suffixes are a sufficient reason to move away from them (to return to these suffixes later) to deal with common, easily understood prefixes.

At one time, prefixes were obvious, because they were commonly separated from roots with hyphens. As the use of hyphens becomes much less common, recognizing certain letters as being prefixes is more difficult. Again, this suggests the need for more attention to prefixes than is sometimes given.

SAMPLE LESSON WITH A PREFIX

For illustrative purposes, let's assume that an instructional group needs to be able to deal with *un-*, since several adjectives in what they will soon be reading start with this prefix. Let's further assume that the teacher has decided to teach about it in connection with a discussion of safety. (*Safe* is a root the children can read.) Together, the teacher and children talk about staying away from dangerous things: buildings under construction, traffic, hot stoves and irons, matches, and so on. Summarizing, the teacher says: "There's a word that describes all these things. It means 'dangerous.' It means 'not safe,' and yet the word *safe* is part of it. Does anyone know the word I'm thinking of? [Scary?] No, it can't be 'scary' because I said that the word has the word *safe* in it, yet it means 'not safe.' I think I'll tell you. The word I'm thinking of is *unsafe*. Have you ever heard that word? ['No'.] Well, now you know a new word. What is it? ['Unsafe'.] I'll write it so that you can see what it looks like:

safe

unsafe

"The new word I just used—*unsafe*—looks exactly like *safe* except for *u* and *n* at the beginning. Together, *u* and *n* say 'un.' When we put *u* and *n* at the beginning of a word like *safe*, it means 'not'; in this case, 'not safe.' I'll write some other words you know, and I'll put *u* and *n* at the beginning of them, too. How do you pronounce *u* and *n*? ['Un'.] What does it mean? ['Not'.] First I'll write a word you can read. Then I'll write *u* and *n* and write the word again. . . ." Soon the board shows:

| safe | happy | kind | like |
| unsafe | unhappy | unkind | unlike |

While calling the children's attention to each derived word, the teacher remembers the four essential outcomes of every lesson dealing with structure. She thus emphasizes the spelling and pronunciation of *un-* as well as its semantic effect on adjectives like *safe* and *happy*. To make sure the children can apply what was taught to roots not used in the lesson, she distributes copies of a list of sentences that starts as follows:

The <u>unspent</u> money went into her bank.

Do not say anything that is <u>untrue</u>.

The <u>uncut</u> flowers will last a long time.

I'm <u>unsure</u> of what day it is.

Each sentence is read silently first, then orally by individuals. Following that, the meaning of the derived word is discussed.

Sometime later, when members of the instructional group have additional roots in their reading vocabularies, this same teacher will focus on the second meaning of *un-* (to do the opposite of), this time using verbs like *dress, pin, tie,* and *pack.** All this instruction is designed to enable children to cope successfully not only with derivatives like *unfair* and *unlock* but also with more difficult ones such as *unwanted, unlawful,* and *unobjectionable*.

ADDITIONAL COMMENTS ABOUT
DERIVED WORDS

As mentioned earlier, some of the most difficult words for children to cope with are derivatives. This is not only because derivatives are relatively uncommon in spoken language but also because the many letters often required to record them result in their looking undecipherable—as is illustrated in *undecipherable*. Such words, however, need not be threatening if, right from the start, ample, explicit attention goes to word relationships.

New Vocabulary and Word Families

One suitable time to attend to relationships is when a new word is being taught. This is not to say that word families should be featured every time a word is introduced; that would be too much of a good thing. But it is to suggest that relationships deserve more instructional time than is typically allotted them.

---

*This teacher obviously knows more about prefixes than does the author of a recently examined basal lesson. The manual contained a brief segment for teaching about *un-*, "as meaning 'not'." Only two derivatives were used in the illustrations (*unhappy* and *unhurt*), but at least they were correct. The same cannot be said for the subsequent workbook page assignment, which included such incorrect examples as *unfold, unload,* and *unwrap*. Clearly, this was a time when a Teacher A was needed.

To illustrate, should new words include *coarsely*, a teacher might begin by writing, naming, and discussing *coarse*. Next, a sentence in which *coarsely* is found in whatever it is that the instructional group is about to read will be added to the chalkboard:

The grain was *coarsely* ground.

After the sentence is read and discussed and *coarsely* is renamed, *coarse* and *coarsely* can be written in a way that highlights the common root:

coarse

coarsely

Another teacher might decide to work with the new word *roll* as follows. To start, she writes a sentence in order to make a distinction between *roll* and *role*, both of which are displayed:

The <u>roll</u> of paper was almost gone.   roll

role

A little later, after *roll* has been discussed, this teacher calls attention to related words, writing them in a way that makes apparent what they share:

roll

unroll

roller

Next comes a discussion of roller skates that brings out the reason for their being called "roller." Since previous lessons dealt with the prefixes *re-* and *un-*, the instruction proceeds with attention to the meanings of *unroll* and *reroll*. To make certain that the difference in meaning is clear, a volunteer demonstrates unrolling and rerolling paper.

Let's take one more illustration. If the suffix *-er* has been taught and a new word is *over*, this is a time not only to review that suffix but also to make distinctions among words ending in *er* with the help of columns of words like:

over	work<u>er</u>	tall<u>er</u>
under	read<u>er</u>	rich<u>er</u>
after	teach<u>er</u>	loud<u>er</u>
paper	spell<u>er</u>	round<u>er</u>

Help with Troublesome Derivatives

Times when children have trouble recognizing derived or inflected words that they ought to be able to figure out are other occasions for calling attention to structural components. Specifically, if the root *want*, the prefix *un-*, and the inflectional suffix *-ed* have all been taught, yet one or more children are unable to recognize *unwanted*, it is time to offer visual help that follows a pattern meriting explicit instruction. The pattern is described below.

COPING WITH DERIVED AND INFLECTED WORDS

1. Remove the prefix first.
2. Next remove the suffix(es).
3. If the root is unfamiliar, decode it.
4. Add the suffix(es).
5. Add the prefix.

In the case of the inflected derivative *unwanted*, visual help that adheres to the sequence of steps just listed is as follows:

unwanted

wanted

want

wanted

unwanted

The need to adhere to the suggested sequence lies in the fact that prefixes are sometimes affixed to inflected and derived words (*wanted-unwanted; lawful-unlawful*) but not to their roots (*want-unwant; law-unlaw*). To avoid nonwords (*unwant, unlaw*) in the decoding process, the suggested sequence should be taught, frequently modeled by teachers, and routinely used by children.

To specify still further the sequence recommended for dealing systematically with the meaning-bearing units of derived and inflected words, additional examples follow. They show what a teacher would display (and, eventually, what the children themselves should do, at first in writing and later mentally) whenever inflected or derived words need to be decoded. The same examples illustrate the help that comes from the spelling generalizations listed earlier in Table 11.2.

miscounted	easiest	rewrapped	displeased	carefully
counted	easy	wrapped	pleased	careful
count	easiest	wrap	please	care
counted		wrapped	pleased	careful
miscounted		rewrapped	displeased	carefully

Finding workbook pages like the one in Figure 11.1 suggests the need to emphasize that (a) segmenting inflected and derived words into prefixes, roots, and suffixes, and (b) dividing roots into syllables in the ways discussed in the previous chapter are both essentialy different from looking randomly for short words in longer words. This is not to say that using known words (e.g., *us*) to decode unknown words (e.g., *must*) should be avoided. But it *is* to say that students need to know the precautions that must be taken when seeking such help, none of which were taken into account in the commercially prepared page in Figure 11.1.

The precautions are stated and illustrated below.

Precautions	*Acceptable*	*Unacceptable*
1. Only roots should be examined to see if they contain shorter known words.	notice	nonexample
2. All letters in the shorter word must be in the same syllable in the longer root.	amuse	amuse
3. The shorter word must include all the vowel letters in a syllable.	heat	heat
4. The shorter word must have the same spelling pattern as the syllable in which it occurs.	snail	met

Even when these four guidelines are followed, children should not take it for granted that the pronunciation of the short word will be retained in the longer one. For example:

(a) crisp   (b) organ   (c) laundry

Proficient decoders will know, of course, (a) that *s* record /s/ as well as /z/; (b) that vowel letters occurring in unstressed syllables are often reduced to /ə/; and (c) that when *y* records the final sound in a multisyllabic word, it is likely to stand for /ē/.

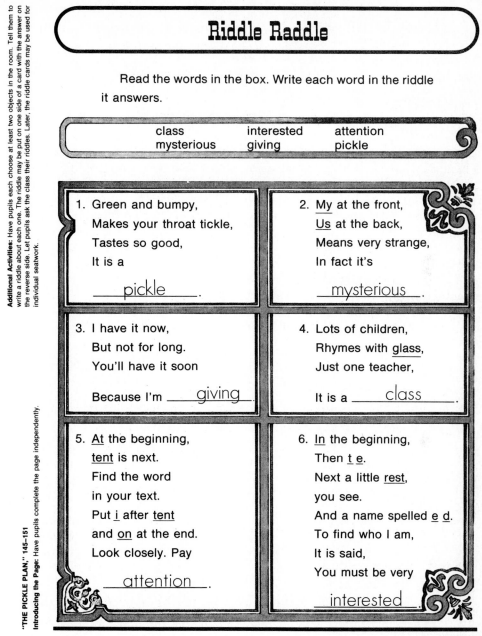

Riddle Raddle

Read the words in the box. Write each word in the riddle it answers.

class	interested	attention
mysterious	giving	pickle

1. Green and bumpy,
   Makes your throat tickle,
   Tastes so good,
   It is a
   ___pickle___ .

2. <u>My</u> at the front,
   <u>Us</u> at the back,
   Means very strange,
   In fact it's
   ___mysterious___ .

3. I have it now,
   But not for long.
   You'll have it soon
   Because I'm ___giving___ .

4. Lots of children,
   Rhymes with <u>glass</u>,
   Just one teacher,
   It is a ___class___ .

5. <u>At</u> the beginning,
   <u>tent</u> is next.
   Find the word
   in your text.
   Put <u>i</u> after <u>tent</u>
   and <u>on</u> at the end.
   Look closely. Pay
   ___attention___ .

6. <u>In</u> the beginning,
   Then <u>t e</u>.
   Next a little <u>rest</u>,
   you see.
   And a name spelled <u>e d</u>.
   To find who I am,
   It is said,
   You must be very
   ___interested___ .

Vocabulary: word identification   **63**

Figure 11.1

From Teacher's Edition of Studybook for *Give Me a Clue* of the GINN READING PROGRAM by Theodore Clymer and others. © Copyright, 1985, 1982, by Ginn and Company. Used with permission.

Regardless of a decoder's ability, using what has been taught is facilitated when words are in contexts (e.g., *crisp lettuce*). It is appropriate to bring the discussion of decoding to a close, therefore, with a look at how contextual, graphophonic, and structural cues function jointly.

MORE ADVANCED DECODING

Roots were the concern when phonics was discussed in the two previous chapters. Now, to portray what children need to know and be able to do when the possibility exists that an unknown word is composed of more than a root, the thoughts of one decoder will be made explicit. This is not done on the assumption that mental processes that occur virtually simultaneously can be duplicated in writing. Rather, the purpose is to approximate what *may* go on in order to allow for attention to procedures discussed in several chapters. A second purpose is to illustrate how teachers can model decoding.

To look at one decoder's strategies, let's say that *unhurt* is an unknown word found in the following context:

The boy fell off his horse but was unhurt.

> unhurt

Context: It tells something about the boy when he fell off the horse.

Syllables: Those first two letters could be a prefix. If it is, it would mean "not" or "to do the opposite of." I'll put that aside for the time being. Let's see about the end of this word. There's nothing there that looks like a suffix. Probably *h, u, r, t* is the root. There's only one vowel, so it's one syllable.

Sounds: h: Probably sounds as it does in words like *home* and *house*.
ur: Those two letters go together because when *r* follows a vowel in a syllable, the two have special sounds. *Ur* probably sounds like *er*.
t: Probably sounds like it does in *top*.

Blending: I'll start with *u* and *r* because the root begins with a consonant. The blending would be: *ur* ⟶ *hur* ⟶ *hurt*. Oh sure, I know that word—*unhurt*. Not hurt. The boy didn't get hurt when he fell off the horse.

Even though the strategies of decoders are not likely to be identical—some take tiny steps (as did the one above) whereas others move in leaps and bounds—let me use the thoughts just described to underscore some prerequisites for coping with unfamiliar words.

As suggested in the earlier chapter on phonics, once a context has been examined for possible help, decoding begins with a consideration of syllables, since the syllable is the unit of pronunciation. With the generalization stated below in mind, a decoder's initial thoughts about an unfamiliar word ought to be something like, "Does this word have an affix?" This is the case because:

Usually, affixes are syllables.* For instance:

un tie	spot less	do ing	want ed
dis trust	teach er	safe ly	tall er

If a decoder concludes (at least tentatively) that the unknown word does have one or more affixes, he mentally lays them aside in order to consider the root. In the case of *unhurt*, for example, the prefix *un* was temporarily separated from *hurt*.

Still considering syllabication, the decoder just described saw the single vowel in *hurt* and correctly concluded it was a one-syllable root. That made him ready to assign sounds to the letters composing it.

Once decisions were made about the likely sounds, they were blended into a syllable. As suggested, blending began with the vowel sound, in this case with the blend recorded by *ur*. The result was a recognizable root.

Then the decoder was ready to affix *un* to the root. Since previous instruction had taught both the pronunciation of *un* and the effect it has on the meaning of adjectives, the result was a derived word with a known meaning and a correct pronunciation: *unhúrt*. The pronunciation exemplified the following generalization:

In inflected and derived words, primary stress falls on or within the root.
For instance:

cárefully   sínging   disobéy   miscoúnted

It is highly likely that what any particular decoder does or uses varies tremendously. Factors that account for the variability include:

1. The amount of contextual help available.
2. The decoder's oral vocabulary.
3. The decoder's reading vocabulary. (Had *curt* been known, an initial consonant substitution would have resulted in the pronunciation of *hurt*. If *hurl* was familiar, a final consonant substitution would get the job done.)
4. The decoder's prior experiences in figuring out unfamiliar words.
5. How well the decoder has been taught.

---

*One atypical pattern pertains to roots ending in *t* to which *ion* is added. In these cases (e.g., *elect, election; direct, direction*), *tion* is a syllable even though *t* is part of the root.

In spite of the likelihood of variability, the possible thoughts of one more decoder are described to pinpoint with more specificity the prerequisites for successful decoding, thereby indicating the objectives of instruction. As the thoughts of this second decoder are outlined, notice how they reflect a strategy guided by the following questions:

	Concerns	*Focus*
1.	What do the words I know tell about the one I don't know?	Context
2.	Are there any prefixes or suffixes?	Word
3.	What are the syllables in the root?	Root
4.	What are the sounds?	Syllable(s)
5.	How should I blend the sounds?	Syllable(s)
6.	Which syllable is stressed?	Word
7.	Does this make sense?	Context

In the following depiction of a decoder's efforts, the unknown word is *staple* embedded in the sentence *She needs a staple for the papers.**

$$\boxed{\text{staple}}$$

Context: This word tells what she needs for the papers.

Syllables: There's nothing at the beginning that looks like a prefix and nothing at the end that spells a suffix. This must be a root. It ends with a consonant followed by *le*. That's one syllable. That leaves *s*, *t*, and *a*, and that's one syllable because it has only one vowel.

Sounds: sta: I know the sounds for the cluster *st*. I remember learning that blend in words like *story* and *star*. Let's see—the *a*. Oh sure. There's only one vowel and it's at the end. That will probably be a long sound for *a*.

Blending: I'll start with /ā/, so it goes: ā ⟶ stā. That takes care of that syllable.

Sounds: ple: This kind of syllable has the schwa sound. And I know the sounds for *p* and *l*.

---

*It is possible that the decoder would recognize the similarity between *staple* and a word he knows—*stable*. He then should be able to substitute /p/ for /b/ and quickly know the pronunciation of *staple*. In order to allow for the detailed analysis of an unfamiliar word, however, let's assume that the decoder does not make the connection or, perhaps, that *stable* is unfamiliar, too.

Blending: I'd better start with the schwa sound: ə ──➤ *pəl.*

Stress: Stáple. I never heard that word before, and I know the second syllable isn't stressed. Stáple? I wonder what that means. I wonder why someone would need whatever this is for papers. Maybe I'd better look it up in the dictionary.

This decoder's efforts allow for further review:

1. Once a context has been scrutinized for possible help, decoding should begin with thoughts about syllables. Since affixes usually are syllables, the possibility of their being part of the unknown word is the initial consideration. If present, they should be mentally separated from the root so the latter can be identified or, if unknown, decoded.
2. Even advanced decoding skills are not always sufficient. An example of their inadequacy was revealed by the decoder who had little trouble figuring out the pronunciation of *staple*, yet knew nothing about its meaning. This suggests two additional points. The first is the fundamental importance of oral vocabularies for decoding. The second is that a dictionary sometimes needs to be consulted but only when a word cannot be decoded or when its meaning is obscure or unknown. Since dictionaries list roots, the systematic sorting-out process that has been recommended for decoding will contribute to a child's skillful use of dictionaries.

It should be noted that recommending the use of dictionaries (or glossaries) at specified times is different from the practices of basal reader programs. As mentioned, even though all their manuals attend to letter-sound correspondences as early as kindergarten and then persist relentlessly until grade three with phonics (plus a little work with affixes), the arrival of grade four (or the second half of grade three) ushers in a sudden switch to another source of help. Now, "Look it up in the glossary (or dictionary)" is the typical advice whenever a new word is in a piece of text that needs to be read. This practice, as stated before, seems indefensible given the amount of time and, therefore, money that were spent earlier on phonics.

CONTRACTIONS

The amount of time these same materials give to contractions—another type of word having a special structure—is also puzzling. (See Figure 11.2 and the comments about it.) The puzzlement is rooted in the fact that in the normal development of speech, contractions enter into oral vocabularies quite early. Children can be expected to use "I won't," for example, long before they ever

Figure 11.2

This workbook page is characteristic of many such pages. To begin, the part
called "Contraction Tic-Tac-Toe" is unrelated to anything a reader needs to do.
The reader's job is to construct meaning from sentences like *I've done this
page* and *We've done it many times before.* As far as the contractions *I've* and
We've are concerned, the need is to be familiar with their written forms, as their
spoken versions will have been used long before pages like this one are assigned.

The bottom half of the page also fails to deal with the requirements of reading. Specifically, the task of the reader is to be able to deal with *hopping*,
which may or may not require dismantling it to expose the root. The exercise
thus proceeds backward by supplying the root and requesting the spelling of
the inflected word.

The value of the bottom half of the page must be questioned for another
reason: The repetition of one process (double the consonant and add the inflections) engenders mindless kinds of responses that have little impact on the
ability to deal with unfamiliar inflected words when a child is reading.

Contraction Tic-Tac-Toe

Write the contraction for each pair of words.

I have I've	we have we've	they have they've
it is it's	FREE SPACE	I am I'm
we will we'll	you have you've	we are we're

Add an Ending

Add the endings -ing and -ed to each word below.

1. hop	hopping	hopped
2. pat	patting	patted
3. clip	clipping	clipped
4. knit	knitting	knitted
5. nod	nodding	nodded
6. plan	planning	planned

(handwritten note in left margin: better to do it in Reverse hopping decide base word from it)

Additional Activities: Have pupils use the words with contractions in sentences. Have pupils think of other words in which the consonant is doubled before -ing and -ed and make up -ing or -ed tic-tac-toe games using those words.

14   Decoding: contractions with *have;* double consonants before *-ing, -ed* (review)

From Teacher's Edition of Studybook for *Give Me a Clue* of the GINN READING PROGRAM by Theodore Clymer and others, © Copyright, 1985, 1982, by Ginn and Company. Used with permission.

say "I will not." Early proficiency with contractions indicates, therefore, that young readers need only to learn their visual counterparts. This means that contractions can and should be taught early (with whole word methodology) not only because they are familiar but also because they allow for text composed of natural language—for instance, *I haven't seen that* as opposed to *I have not seen that.* Natural constructions are important, as they allow children to use their considerable knowledge of oral language to help with their reading.

Although these recommendations for contractions seem difficult to dispute, basal series have traditionally used sentences like *I did not run* before one like *I didn't run.* When they finally do introduce contractions, another traditional practice is to make much to-do about their construction. For as many as three years, numerous pages in workbooks have children write the words for which a contraction stands and the letters that the apostrophe replaces. This means that teachers who heed manual suggestions waste instructional time and, on occasion, unintentionally frustrate children. Why I suggest this can be explained with a reference to one third grade.

On the morning I observed in this room, the teacher was working with three boys for whom learning to read was anything but easy. The lesson dealt with contractions. Presumably, its objective was ability to identify and understand the meanings of eight contractions listed on the board. The boys seemed able to identify most of them; however, when an error occurred, the teacher corrected and discussed it in a pleasant, nonpunitive way. Once all the contractions appeared to be known, the teacher next showed sentences printed on cards, each containing one of the eight contractions. For every sentence, her directions were to read it silently, then tell what it means "in your own words." The boys did all this with success and obvious pride.

Unfortunately, the next part of the lesson put a damper on both the success and the pride, for it required the boys to name the words for which each of the eight contractions substituted and to name the letters that each apostrophe replaced. Now, guessing, erroneous answers, and much fidgeting were characteristic. Clearly the lesson had become too demanding, but what needs to be especially emphasized is that it went beyond what reading requires: identification of contractions coupled with an understanding of their meanings. Since the boys in question appeared to meet the two requirements, why did their teacher go beyond them and, in the process, unintentionally cause frustration and discouragement? "That's what their workbook does with contractions" was her explanation.

The detailed consideration of contractions exemplified in this lesson is warranted only when the word *contraction* is being taught. Here, it is important to remember that when it *is* taught, children may understand the concept well enough without knowing exactly what is being substituted for what in every example of a contraction. This suggests that with children who have to struggle to attain even modest ability in reading, it is essential to separate what is necessary from what is not. Even with more able children, relevant goals should always take precedence over nonessentials.

This brings us back to a point stressed many times – the importance of teachers' habitually asking themselves, *Why* am I doing what I'm doing?

SAMPLES OF PRACTICE

When instruction for word structure was described, practice was depicted, too. To conclude the chapter, additional kinds of practice are listed.

- An assignment sheet that begins like the one in Figure 11.3 provides practice in exposing roots whose spellings are altered. A supplement to the assignment could request written sentences for the words in the first column to see whether their meanings are understood.

Figure 11.3

- Another assignment sheet divides as in Figure 11.4 to allow for illustrations of the three forms of an adjective. (In one room, a child drew a window with a small smudge on the glass for *dirty*, and one with many smudges for *dirtiest*. Another child illustrated *sweet* with one piece of candy; *sweetest*, with many pieces.)

| dirty |
| dirtier |
| dirtiest |

Figure 11.4

- Another possibility for an assignment would have children draw a line from each word in one column (e.g., *bold, quiet, wrong, different, cool*) to the derivative in a second column that has a similar meaning (e.g., *disobedient, inactive, incorrect, unlike, unheated*). One column should be longer than the other to discourage guessing.
- The start of another assignment is shown in Figure 11.5. It not only brings children into contact with superlative forms of adjectives but also fosters thoughtful reading. Discussions of answers are likely to reveal interesting reasons for choices.

```
Underline the right answer.
1. Which is the smallest?   puppy  kitten  bird
2. Which is the hottest?    summer day  lighted match  oven
3. Which is the heaviest?   nail  hammer  pencil
```

Figure 11.5

- To discourage overgeneralizing about words ending in *er*, an assignment like the one in Figure 11.6 is useful.

```
After each sentence, write the root of the
underlined word.
1. Fill the vase with water. _____
2. Have the mover pack the dishes. _____
3. He was a gunner on a war plane. _____
4. Ask the waiter for a spoon. _____
5. Use the butter for the rolls. _____
```

Figure 11.6

Once *-or* is taught, the assignment can be adapted for that suffix.
- For practice with contractions, children can make something like apple-shaped books whose pages have incomplete captions. For example:

An apple can't _____.

An apple isn't _____.

An apple didn't _____.

The children complete and illustrate each caption.

Card games can also provide practice in using word structure. Some possibilities follow:

- Each player holds a different root card (e.g., *act*). The deck is composed of cards on which related words are printed; for example, *actor, overact, action, react.* (Related words are restricted to four so all families are of equal size.) Players take turns selecting cards from the deck, keeping only those that are related to their root. The first child to collect a complete family is the winner, assuming the requested pronunciations and meanings of the five words are correct.
- A bingo-like game uses cards with different roots at the top of each. One such card might look like this:

open	quick	work
un-	-er	-able
-ing	-ly	re-
-ed	-est	-er

- Cards for the caller show derived and inflected words. Should *unopen* be called, the child holding the above card covers the box directly under *open*. The first child to cover all the boxes on a card is the winner, if the three roots and the nine derived and inflected words can be read.
- Prefix cards are distributed to players. The deck is composed of root cards. Children take turns selecting a card from the deck. If they choose one that forms a derivative with a card they hold, and if they can define the root and the derivative, they lay the two cards down. Otherwise, the root card is returned to the bottom of the deck. The first child out of cards is the winner.
- The final game to be described uses a deck consisting of pairs of words (one word per card) with identical beginnings and endings (e.g., *uncle, uncut; her, doer; undo, under; sing, seeing; rest, restart; slowed, sled*). All the cards are shuffled, then dealt to players. Each studies his or her cards, then lays down those that are roots. A correct choice merits a point;

wrong choices subtract points. The child with the most points is the winner.

SUMMARY

In this and the four previous chapters, detailed attention went to ways for developing reading vocabularies. Chapter 7 first considered direct identifications as it discussed whole word methodology. Following that, Chapter 8 illustrated how contextual cues assist with unknown words. Chapters 9 and 10 explained how children can be taught to recognize roots with the help of generalizations about letter-sound relationships, factors that affect them, and syllabication. Finally, the present chapter shifted to more complex words and showed how children can be taught to deal with affixes systematically in order to get help with both pronunciations and meanings.* Now it might be useful to synthesize the five chapters by considering a question for which teachers must have an answer: What should I do with these new words?

Because of the importance of independence in coping with new words, the first guideline is: Identify such words only when there is no alternative. The lack of an alternative is determined by considering three factors: (a) the nature of the new word, which includes the relationship between its spelling and pronunciation as well as its structure; (b) the children's ability in phonic and structural analyses; and (c) the context in which the new word is embedded. Each factor is dealt with in the discussion that follows.

At the start, when reading instruction is still in its early stages, whole word methodology ("This word says 'me'.") is used routinely because children are unequipped to decode on their own. At that point, then, the nature of the new word has little relevance. Regularly spelled (*me*) or irregularly spelled (*they*), all words are directly identified.

Gradually, as more instruction in phonics is provided, the relationship between how a word is spelled and how it is pronounced takes on significance. Now, regularly spelled roots like *just* and *brake* might not have to be identified. Instead, children can apply what they have been learning and figure them out themselves. Even irregularly spelled words such as *would* and *should* might not have to be identified, assuming *could* had been taught earlier with whole word methodology.

Once instruction begins to deal with affixes, more independence is possible; now, children become increasingly able to figure out not only the pronunciations of inflected and derived words but also the meanings.

As the various decoding skills are increasing, so are the contexts in which new words appear. Instead of simple sentences like *The girl has a bike*, longer

---

*See the end of this summary for a list of generalizations that pertain to roots and to derived and inflected words.

strings of connected words gradually become common. As they do, they offer the perceptive, well-taught reader further help with new vocabulary in the form of syntactic and semantic cues. Combined, then, the instruction featured in this and the four preceding chapters make whole word methodology much less frequent, though never nonexistent. Words like *indict*, *quay*, *suite*, and *chamois* keep it in existence.

Now, what is the significance of all this for teaching the new vocabulary in something like a basal reader selection? It means a distinction must be made between words that will be identified for children and words that they should be able to figure out themselves. At some time, however, either before the reading begins or afterward, a check should be made to see that all words in the second group were in fact decoded correctly and are understood in the given contexts.

Whether a word was identified by a teacher or decoded with the help of contextual, graphophonic, and structural cues, it must be practiced to ensure that it gets into the children's sight vocabularies. Knowledge of cues does reduce substantially the amount of practice that will be required, but some is necessary. This is important for teachers at all grade levels to remember, since the only kind of word that facilitates comprehension is the one read both correctly and instantaneously.

GENERALIZATIONS FOR DECODING

SYLLABICATION

Structural Divisions

Most prefixes and suffixes are syllables (un lock; care less; play ing).

When the suffix *-ed* is added to a verb ending in *d* or *t*, it is a syllable (need ed; dent ed). Otherwise, it adds a sound to the verb but not a syllable (marched, pulled).

When the suffix *-ion* is added to a root ending in *t*, the letters *tion* form a syllable (act, ac tion).

Phonological Divisions

When two consonants are preceded and followed by vowels, a syllabic division usually occurs between the consonants (win dow).

When a vowel precedes and follows a consonant, a syllabic division usually occurs after the first vowel (si lent).

When *x* is preceded and followed by vowels, the first vowel and *x* are in the same syllable (tax i).

When a root ends in a consonant followed by *le*, the consonant and *le* are the final syllable (pur ple).

When a root ends in *ture* or *tion*, these letters constitute a syllable (punc ture; na tion).

For purposes of syllabication, each consonant and vowel digraph functions as one unit (ath lete, au thor).

VOWEL SOUNDS

When a syllable has one vowel that is in final position, it commonly stands for its long sound (silo).

When a syllable has one vowel that is not in final position, it commonly stands for its short sound (album).

When a syllable has two vowels, the long sound of the first is common (meet, mete).

When a syllable has two vowels, one of which is final *e*, and the two are separated by two or more consonants, the short sound of the first vowel is common (pulse).

Vowel sounds in unstressed syllables are often reduced to the schwa sound (random).

The digraph *oo* has both long and short sounds (cool, cook).

The digraph *ow* stands for a diphthong and the long *o* sound (owl, own).

When a vowel is followed by *r* in a syllable, three different sounds are possible (art, her, for).

When a vowel is followed by *re* in a syllable, five different sounds are possible (care, mere, hire, bore, pure).

Y FUNCTIONING AS A VOWEL

When *y* is in medial position in a syllable that has no vowel, it commonly stands for the short *i* sound (myth).

When *y* stands for the final sound in a multisyllabic word, it usually records the long *e* sound (fancy, hurry).

Otherwise, *y* is likely to stand for the long *i* sound (try, dye, cycle).

CONSONANT SOUNDS

When *c* and *g* are followed in a syllable by *e, i,* or *y,* they commonly stand for their soft sounds (cell, cinder, cyst; gem, gin, gypsy). Otherwise, the hard sounds are common (can, talc, act; glad, pig, wagon).

The letter s stands for either /s/ or /z/ (see, has).

The digraph th records a voiced and a voiceless sound (the, thin).

The digraph ch commonly records the sound heard initially in chop. It may also stand for the sounds heard initially in chef and chord.

Together, q and u stand for either /kw/ or /k/ (quit, plaque).

The letter x stands for /z/, /ks/ or /gz/ (xylophone, sox, exact).

REVIEW

1. How does the subject matter taught in phonics enter into attempts to decode unfamiliar derived and inflected words?

2. In Chapter 11, four objectives were named that should be realized in any lesson that deals with affixes.
   a. What are the four objectives?
   b. Explain the importance of each one.
   c. Keeping the objectives in mind, enumerate what ought to be accomplished when the prefix anti- is taught.

3. In Chapter 11, a strategy for dismantling and reassembling the structural parts of derived and inflected words was explained and illustrated. If you wanted to display the strategy on a chalkboard, list what you would write for each word below:

   reassembling   impolitely   forewarned   carelessness

   Explain the rationale for the recommended strategy.

4. Sometimes a short known word is visible in a longer unknown word. Unfortunately, using such words to get the longer one decoded can create more pronunciation problems than it solves – unless certain precautions are taken. With examples, explain the precautions.

5. A segment in one basal reader manual, called "Syllabication," describes a procedure for teaching the following generalization: When there are two consonants in a word and the two are preceded and followed by vowels, a syllabic division generally occurs between the consonants. It recommends that the following words be used to illustrate the generalization. (The examples are said to be words the children can read.)

   | fluffy | pillow | summer | biggest |
   | berries | written | bottom | manners |

   just use base word entirely – no ending

   Are the illustrative words good choices? Why or why not?

6. Explain why all the following statements are false.

    a. Teachers should not spend time showing students the connection between contractions and the words they replace.

    b. When a child comes across a word he does not know, he should consult a dictionary for help.

    c. Once students have acquired proficiency in using contextual, structural, and graphophonic cues, word practice is no longer required.

7. In several chapters, including Chapter 11, modeling was recommended as an effective mode of teaching. With an example, explain exactly what modeling is.

REFERENCES

1. DeStefano, Johanna S. *Language, Society, and Education: A Profile of Black English*. Worthington, Oh.: Charles A. Jones Publishing Company, 1973.
2. Durkin, Dolores. *Strategies for Identifying Words*, 2nd ed. Boston: Allyn and Bacon, Inc., 1981.
3. Johnson, Dale D., and Pearson, P. David. *Teaching Reading Vocabulary*, 2nd ed. New York: Holt, Rinehart and Winston, 1984.
4. Morgan, Argiro L. "A New Orleans Oral Language Study." *Elementary English* 51 (February, 1974), 222–229.
5. Nagy, William E., and Anderson, Richard C. "How Many Words Are There in Printed School English?" *Reading Research Quarterly* 19 (Spring, 1984), 304–330.

CHAPTER 12

Oral Vocabularies

PREVIEW

Helping children become competent users of language has many dimensions. The one in this chapter is word meanings, viewed as being the product of experiences, concept development, instruction, and knowledge acquistion. Underlying the chapter, therefore, is the fact that vocabulary knowledge allows children to communicate and share what they know and understand.

That children sometimes use words whose meaning for them is limited or confused is well known. A kindergarten teacher reminds us of this when she recalls how quickly her children named an anchor upon seeing a picture of a ship; yet, "when questioned about the function of an anchor, individual children said it was used to catch big fish, drag things out of the ocean, clean the bay, stop the ship, start the ship, catch crabs" (17, pp. 18–19).

Teachers themselves have to be on guard lest they become so textbook-bound that they, too, are involved more with naming than with understanding. Research reveals, for example, that in middle- and upper-grade classrooms, noticeable amounts of empty verbalization go on when content subjects like social studies are taught (5). Witness one conversation in a fourth grade:

Teacher: Who can tell us what a continent is?
Child 1: A really big place with states and countries and stuff.
Teacher: Could anybody give us another description?
Child 2: It's a large land mass.
Teacher: Fine. Good.

What teachers also have to guard against is discouraging children from doing exactly what they should do: Use what they know and have experienced to reach conclusions about vocabulary. Again, listen in on a conversation in which students were being prepared for a chapter in a social studies textbook that had a sociological-anthropological orientation:

Teacher: Who can give us an example of a group?

Child 1: A fight.

Teacher: When we find out the four reasons that make a group, you'll see that a fight isn't a group.

Child 2: When you're on a bus in Chicago.

Teacher: Once we read about the rules of a group, that will fit.

If nothing else, Chapter 12 should help you see that the most productive *and* interesting ways for expanding oral vocabularies derive not from textbooks but from teachers' heads and noncommercial materials. Reading the Summary will help you see more generally what Chapter 12 covers.

Certain facts and guidelines are stated more than once in previous chapters because of their fundamental importance. Although no attempt was made to calculate the frequency of the repetitions, it seems safe to conclude that the dependence of reading ability on oral vocabularies is what has been emphasized and reemphasized most often. This is as it ought to be, for the dependence is very pervasive. Let me remind you of the pervasiveness with a few illustrations.

ORAL VOCABULARIES AND READING

Two points made when discussing whole word methodology in Chapter 7 clearly point up the significance of oral vocabularies for reading. One is the fact that children can learn to name any word but that they can only learn to *read* words that are meaningful in their spoken form. The same chapter also emphasizes that words with special meaning are the easiest to remember and thus require the least practice.

When Chapter 8 discusses contexts as sources of help for recognizing unknown words, it shows that semantic cues are useful only when the unknown words are familiar orally. For example, in the sentence *Use the _____ to color your picture*, syntactic cues indicate the omitted word is a noun. Deciding which noun it is, however, depends not only on the spelling of the word and the semantic cues in the context, but also on the nouns in the reader's oral vocabulary. After all, those are the only words that can come to mind no matter how helpful a context may be.

The dependence of decoding ability on oral vocabularies is demonstrated in several ways in the chapters dealing with phonics and structural analysis. It is pointed out in Chapter 10, for instance, that the most knowledgeable use of graphophonic cues may yield only approximately correct pronunciations. They are enough, however, if the words are in the reader's oral vocabulary. Such is the case because knowing a word in its spoken form allows for shifts from the approximately correct pronunciation ("law yer") to the correct one ("loi yer"). Even when decoding efforts do result in a correct pronunciation, it is of no value if the pronunciation fails to suggest a meaning. This is illustrated in Chapter 11, when a decoder achieved the correct pronunciation for *staple* but did not know its meaning. In such cases, asking "Does this make sense?" is irrelevant, for that question can only be answered when the pronunciation of a word gives access to its meaning.

When the previous chapter covers structural cues, it further reinforces the significance of oral vocabularies for reading. It states, for instance, that it is pointless to know about the semantic effect of affixes on roots if the meanings of the roots themselves are unknown. The same chapter also reminds you that learning to read contractions is relatively easy, for they are in children's oral vocabularies at an early age.

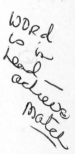

word to in head — achieve matel

337

Since reading *is* comprehending, the fact that one word whose meaning is unknown impedes understanding as little as a sentence must not be overlooked. Can *you*, for example, understand *They are experienced spelunkers*?

All this is to say that enlarging students' oral vocabularies will have a major impact on their chances of becoming able readers. This makes the topic of the present chapter a very important one.

TWO COMPONENTS OF ORAL VOCABULARIES

Although this chapter continues to use "oral vocabularies" when ways for adding to the number of words that children understand are discussed, it should be kept in mind that such vocabularies divide as follows:

> *Listening Vocabulary*
> All the words an individual understands when they are used by other people.

> *Speaking Vocabulary*
> All the words an individual can pronounce and, in addition, understands well enough to be able to use herself or himself.

For reading, listening vocabularies are adequate. Speaking vocabularies, however, are more helpful, since – other things being equal – words in a reader's speaking vocabulary are decoded and understood more quickly. This is important, because both the accuracy and the speed are necessary for comprehending connected text (2, 16).

NATURE OF INSTRUCTIONAL TASKS FOR VOCABULARY DEVELOPMENT

Before various ways for augmenting oral vocabularies are considered, some preliminary comments will be made that have to do with the kinds of tasks involved in extending vocabulary knowledge.

Multiple Meanings

The first two points meriting immediate attention are that most words are polysemous (have multiple meanings) and, second, that which meaning these words have is determined by context. The "simple" word *see* is useful in demonstrating the two points:

I see them over there.
See to it that nothing gets lost.
Please see to the children while I'm at the store.
Do you see the point he's trying to make?
She'll see them in her office at 3:15 tomorrow.
The bishop's see is a large one, isn't it?
They're trying to see what the problem is.
All the men will soon see service overseas.
Let me see you to the front door.
Let me see, how many more meanings are there?

The fact that, like people, words are affected by the company they keep is not always reflected in classroom practices. Evidence of this is as common as the dictionary assignments all of us received in elementary school and that continue to be found on chalkboards in forms like the following:

1. Write each word three times.
2. Look up its meaning in the dictionary.
3. Write that meaning.
4. Write a sentence using each word

Disregard for the facts that most words have multiple meanings and that the meaning that should be accessed depends on context also shows up in children's responses. To illustrate:

An instructional group was discussing the protagonist in a story they had just read. Summing up all the good things that had been said about her, the teacher commented, "Abigail certainly was a patient person, wasn't she?" Everyone agreed. The teacher then asked, "What does 'patient' mean?" In response she heard: "If you go to the doctor and he tells you you're real sick, then you go to the hospital and you're a patient."

In addition to enjoying what could only come from the mouths of babes, teachers should see in a response like the one just cited the need to help children understand that the meaning they assign a word must fit the context, which may be less than a phrase or as long as a story.

Literal Versus Figurative Meanings

Another point to keep in mind when instructional needs are considered is that authors commonly use language figuratively, even in text that relative beginners in reading are assigned. This means that fairly early, children need to realize that words do not always mean what they seem to mean. Contrasting sentences like those below, coupled with discussions of meanings, can provide a helpful introduction to literal versus figurative uses of language:

> Her paper was glued to the board.
> Her eyes were glued to the board.
>
> Each child said something different.
> Each clock said something different.
>
> Don't look for Jim.
> Don't look for trouble.
>
> I've got my hand on you.
> I've got my eye on you.

The fact that contexts may help with the meaning of figurative language is something else that children need to be aware of. With examples and discussions, the help can be specified:

> She had never felt so happy. She was grinning from ear to ear.
>
> The sun is too bright. Draw the drapes so that it won't get hot in here.
>
> Sean is a real bookworm. Whenever you see him, he's reading something.
>
> Everybody thought that Charlie would easily win the race. Instead, he won by a hair.

Once instructional time has gone to figurative expressions, books that highlight them in stories are appealing (15). So, too, are other books that feature the history behind curious expressions (18). Depending on the children's reading abilities, such books can either be read to, or read by, them.

Additional Facets of Vocabulary Instruction

Distinctions other than the one of literal and figurative language are important for teachers to keep in the foreground for they, too, define instructional tasks. Four distinctions that pertain to unfamiliar words will be discussed. They are listed below in a form that emphasizes what teachers need to do when, for instance, they are attending to new vocabulary in preparation for an assignment in a basal reader:

1. Expand a referent.
2. Teach a name for a familiar referent.

3. Teach an additional name for a familiar referent.
4. Teach a new referent and a name for it.

Expanding a Referent.   Just as life's experiences expand our knowledge of the world, so, too, do they expand what words mean. It is no exaggeration to say, in fact, that the meanings of many words change as life's experiences change us.

How one kindergarten teacher in a rural community went about enlarging the meanings of "brush" is instructive; it is described in the journal entry that follows:

For Sharing Time this week, I asked each child to bring in a brush. (A note was sent home earlier that explained the reason for the request.) Recalling our discussion in class about the usefulness of common objects for vocabulary development, I decided to use brushes this week. My hope was that enough different brushes would be brought in that any child who had but one notion of "brush" would have many by the time we finished.

Luckily, a variety of brushes *was* brought to school this morning. Since I have a fairly small class, allowing each child to say something about his or her brush was no problem. Following the comments, we talked about how the brushes were alike and how they were different. (Earlier, one of the children had seen a janitor sweeping the halls, which created the need to discuss whether a broom is a brush.) From time to time, I posed questions to bring out the various functions that the brushes served. In the end, the available brushes were divided into three groups based on use. One was for cleaning houses; the second was for animals; and the third group was for what I ended up calling "personal use." (The word "personal" took some explaining on my part. Fortunately, one child helped by saying it sounded like "person," so "Those brushes must be for persons.")

Once the brushes were grouped and counted, we recorded the results in the form of a simple graph. Before I printed *Brushes* at the top, we reviewed what a title is and the fact that the first letter is printed in its capital form.

I always feel special satisfaction when what I plan allows not only for realizing the pre-established objective but also for using what we have been learning.

Teaching a Name for a Familiar Referent.   One of the easiest ways to enlarge oral vocabularies occurs whenever the referent for a word is known but the word itself is not. If children, for instance, have experienced green things but do not know the word "green," all a teacher has to do is inform them that the name of the color they have been seeing is "green." (Later—as with "brush"—experiences with various shades of green should be provided in order to expand the meaning of "green.")

The need to give a name to a color that had been experienced was identified in one first-grade classroom when the teacher and children were developing a chart called "Eye Coloring":

Eye Coloring			
brown	blue	gray	hazel

In this case, all the colors of the children's eyes were known with the exception of "hazel." At the time of the observation, the children were busy drawing and coloring pictures of their own faces, which would be cut out and glued in the appropriate column on the large chart. Teaching "hazel," the teacher explained later, had not been an original objective, but the need to teach it became clear very soon. What she had originally planned to do was to use *eye* to reinforce the fact that words do not always sound the way they are spelled and, second, to show and discuss some members of the word family whose root is *color*. All that was still done, along with the attention that went to "hazel."

Teaching an Additional Name for a Familiar Referent. As children's ability to read increases, so, too, does the need to help them learn new names for familiar referents. To specify this responsibility, words that may be familiar and that have familiar referents, plus synonyms that may require a teacher's time and help, are listed below:

Teaching Synonyms

Familiar Word with Familiar Referent	Unfamiliar Word with Familiar Referent
car	automobile
elevator	lift
fat	obese
crown	diadem
buffalo	bison
spying	espionage
argument	altercation

It should be noted that teaching a synonym for a familiar word whose referent is familiar is essentially different from explaining one word that is not understood with another that is only poorly understood—something that often happens when children are directed to use glossaries and dictionaries to learn what a word means. Some time ago, Albert Harris effectively described the hazards of this all-too-common practice:

> One difficulty with this procedure is the danger of relying on superficial verbalizations. Meanings that are clear to the teacher may be quite hazy to the child. Many of the classical boners are due to superficial and inadequate grasp of word meanings. It is not sufficient to tell a child that *frantic* means *wild*, or that *athletic* means *strong*; he may try to pick *frantic flowers* and pour *athletic vinegar* into a salad dressing. (8, p. 409)

One way to minimize superficial verbalizations is to let children have their say when words are being explained. I recall one classroom in which the teacher was talking about the meaning of "freedom." Among other things, she said that children "are not free to do bad things, such as take somebody else's coat." Immediately, one of the children objected with, "Sometimes it's okay to take a coat. When you have company you say to them, 'May I take your coat?'"

Teaching a New Referent and a Name for It. The most difficult instructional task involves words that need to be understood when neither the words nor their referents are familiar. (Middle- and upper-grade teachers face this task routinely with social studies and science textbooks.) Words that fall into such a category for young children could include *beach, skyscraper*, and *bridge*, all of whose referents can be clarified with pictures, filmstrips, or movies. In the case of other words that might be in the same category—for instance, *bitter, smooth*, and *sip*—direct experience with the referent may be not only helpful but also necessary. As Edward Dolch pointed out, even a word like *snake* may require direct experiences if children are to be clear about the referent:

> The average adult tries again and again to tell children with words what things are. . . . The child asks, "What is a snake?" The adult says, "An animal that crawls along the ground." The child imagines such an animal and asks, "But his legs will be in the way." The adult says, "Oh, he hasn't any legs." So the child takes off the legs and sees a legless body lying there. "But how does he crawl around without legs?" "He wiggles," says the adult. The child tries to make the legless body wiggle. "How does that get him to go forward?" The adult loses his temper. The peculiar way in which part of the snake pushes the other cannot be described. It has to be seen. Let us go to the zoo. (4, p. 309)

The effectiveness of this quote may have one drawback. It could prompt the conclusion that "providing children with experiences" means taking them on a trip or doing something exotic in the classroom. That is hardly the case, however. Should clarification of the meaning of "pair" be the objective, teaching procedures might begin with a brief verbal explanation, coupled with a reference to the children's shoes, eyes, ears, and so on. Subsequently, a simple activity could provide an experience to solidify the meaning of "pair":

- Fill two boxes with identical collections of small objects (e.g., earrings, dice, socks, bracelets, shoelaces, knitting needles). Have children take turns selecting an object from one of the boxes. Each child names his object, finds the same object in the second box, then places the two side by side on a table. The eventual results are labeled displays of pairs of objects and, hopefully, an understanding of "pair."

Some of the experiences that one kindergarten teacher provided for unfamiliar words with unfamiliar referents are reflected in the pages shown in Figure 12.1. (The two pages, plus others, developed into a book called *Water*.) The experiences were simple, carefully planned experiments that gave the kindergartners opportunities to acquire specific understandings for words like *liquid, freeze, solid, boil, steam, evaporate,* and *chill*.

INSTRUCTIONAL MATERIALS

As the discussion in this chapter ought to have made clear by now, purchasing materials is unnecessary when extending oral vocabularies is the objective. One of the richest (and cheapest) sources of help, as a matter of fact, is the text that surrounds us on all sides. Environmental text is valuable not only in the subject matter it so generously provides but also because it is attractive to children. A few samples of such text, plus descriptions of their potential for instruction, follow:

Environmental Text

Source	Text	Can Help With
Poster	"Don't clown at the wheel." (Caption under picture of clown driving a car)	Figurative language
Garbage truck	"We refuse no refuse."	Homographs
Contractor's sign	"Home being reborn. Quiet, please."	Semantic effect of prefixes on roots
Sign at athletic club	"A Self-Contained World of Sports"	Semantic effect of prefixes on roots

| Sign on lot where bank is being constructed | "Don't bank it in your sock. Sock it in the bank." | Polysemous words |
| Advertisement | "The maximum for the minimum" | Extending vocabularies through contrasts |

Float and Sink

Some things float.

Some things sink.

Some things float and sink.

Things heavier than water sink.

Things lighter than water float.

Ice

1. We put water into the freezer.

2. The water is a liquid.

3. The water is freezing.

4. The water is a solid.

5. The water is ice.

Figure 12.1. *Some Kindergarten Science Experiments*

One teacher who did not go beyond her own classroom to find suitable material for instruction merits a description. In this case, the objective of the instruction was clarification of the meanings of "fact" and "opinion." To prepare for the lesson, the teacher had written three questions on a large piece of posterboard:

> How many windows are in our room? _____
>
> How many bulletin boards are there? _____
>
> What color are the shades? _____

The lesson began by having the children read each question silently, then aloud, after which answers were requested. The teacher next pointed out that all three answers were facts (both *fact* and *facts* were printed on the board) because their correctness could be checked by counting and looking. She then continued, "Sometimes, answers to questions are opinions. An opinion, unlike a fact, is neither right nor wrong. It's just the way somebody feels about something." At that point, *opinion* was written. To illustrate opinions, the teacher posed other questions: "Do you like the color of the shades? . . . Do you think we have enough windows in our room? . . . Is there a better place for the bulletin boards? . . . "

To sum up, the teacher asked volunteers to define "fact" and "opinion." She then offered an example of a sentence that stated a fact, after which the children contributed other examples. The same procedure was followed for opinions.

In order to see what her students had learned, the teacher distributed two small cards to each child. One card had *fact* printed on it; the other displayed *opinion*. She explained that she would show larger cards with sentences, which were to be read silently. When she said "Now," the children were to hold up one of their two cards to indicate whether the sentence stated a fact or expressed an opinion. Finally, the assignment sheet shown in Figure 12.2 was distributed.

The lesson just described illustrates not only instruction but also supervised and independent practice plus evaluation. Work for the next day allows for application: the teacher will read a factual account of opossums, after which the children will read a story about an opossum in order to check the accuracy of the fictional account.

Another commendable feature of the same lesson is its concentration on two terms that inevitably enter into critical reading. It could thus be viewed as readiness instruction for that. Not to be forgotten, either, was the teacher's use of sentences that related to the children. Had she chosen to do so, other personalized sentences could have helped explain why opinions often differ. For example:

Read each sentence below. If a sentence states a fact, write
<u>fact</u> after it. If a sentence tells an opinion, write
<u>opinion</u> after it. Think before you write anything.

1. There are 13 girls in this room right now and 12
   boys. _____

2. Too many children are in our class. _____

3. Our class is the best class in the school. _____

4. The clock in our room is close to the door. _____

5. One plant in the room is about to die. _____

6. After lunch we have spelling. _____

7. Yesterday was the coldest day of the year so far. _____

8. Our school is on Rice Street. _____

9. The story we heard yesterday was the best one our teacher
   has read to us. _____

10. Our science book has a cover that is blue, green, and
    white. _____

On the other side of this sheet, write two sentences that
state a fact. Write two other sentences that give an opinion
about something.

Figure 12.2. *An Assignment for Facts and Opinions*

> Children like to have a big classroom.
> The men who clean schools like small classrooms.
>
> I think this is a cold day.
> An Eskimo would think it is a warm day.

The final attempt to show that special, commercially prepared materials are not a requirement for enlarging vocabularies focuses on bulletin board displays. Only four of the many that have been seen (and admired) in classrooms are described.

- Divided into four sections, a bulletin board in a kindergarten was called "Shades of Colors." Names of colors (*Blue, Yellow, Green, Brown*) were titles for the sections. In each section, the teacher had arranged rows of the small, plastic squares that decorators use to help customers select paint colors. This board was highly effective in demonstrating that a word like "blue" hardly refers to one color.
- A first-grade teacher had been working on the names of animal homes, mostly by reading to children from colorfully illustrated books. To summarize, she prepared a bulletin board showing pictures of a cage,

nest, bowl, stream, barn, jungle, cave, and pen. A pocket had been made at the bottom of each picture by stapling to it three sides of a rectangular piece of construction paper. The teacher also had a collection of animal pictures. The display was used by having individual children name an animal shown by the teacher. After it was identified, the child named its home and then placed the animal's picture in the correct pocket. (Later, playing with the display could be selected by any two children at free-choice time.)

- Another first-grade teacher had been working on homophones. (Homophones are words that are pronounced the same but have different spellings and meanings.) They were introduced with a bulletin board showing two paper trees labeled, "A Pair of Pear Trees." A picture of a pear was pasted to one while the other held a picture of two shoes. Nothing more was done with the board while homophones were receiving attention, although the children knew that at some time they would fill up both trees with pictures. At the conclusion of the instruction, the bulletin board was used again to summarize. Now the trees showed pictures depicting *one, won; sea, see; break, brake; blue, blew; Mary, merry.* (In this dialect area, *merry* and *Mary* were pronounced the same, thus were homophones. In other areas, pronunciations are different.)

- In another classroom, bulletin boards that changed every month were used to teach the names of the months, to practice naming numerals and colors, and to teach word meanings. During April, the board showed a large tree in the background and flowers and bushes in the foreground. For this display, the teacher had cut out thirty tiny birds. Before the display was assembled, spring had been discussed in order to introduce "migrate," a term used frequently during April. As each of its days passed, one bird was added to the board, attached either to the tree or a bush. Daily, the birds were counted and "migrate" was mentioned. (Unexpectedly, the children became very interested in birds; consequently, April turned out to be a month for bird watching and naming. Books about birds were read, too.)

Now that a number of instructional materials have been described, let's move to another important topic: preplanned lessons for developing vocabularies.

PREPLANNED LESSONS: SOME COMMENTS

To give support to careful planning as a prerequisite for successful instruction is one purpose this book is meant to serve. Even so, it is not assumed that planning inevitably results in effective teaching. Why such an assumption is rejected can be explained with a reference to a classroom observation.

The visit was in a first grade, and I was there at the teacher's request. She wanted me to see, and react to, one of her initial conscious efforts to extend oral vocabularies. The attempt focused on "happy" and "joy." (The selection of an adjective and a noun created problems that became apparent when the children later suggested sentences using the two words.) The method chosen to teach "joy" ("happy" was familiar) was a minilecture to which the children responded with almost no interest except for a boy who insisted that "joy" was the name of soap.

As it happened, I remained in the room for the rest of the afternoon and was glad I did because of what occurred during art. It was fall, so leaves were to be traced. In preparation, the teacher distributed a real leaf to each child — enough to create noticeable excitement. The children were encouraged to feel it and, as they did, the teacher talked about its veins and theirs, and also about the stem. But all this was done quickly in order to get to the tracing.

Since I knew this teacher was genuinely interested in helping with word meanings, I was naturally surprised that the potential of the artwork was overlooked. Because it was, only a few of the children probably acquired new words for their vocabularies (vein, stem, trace, outline) when, in fact, the opportunity was available to teach them to all the children because they were so interested in the leaves.

As a result of this and many additional observations, it seems necessary to underscore two points. First, when instruction for vocabulary development is preplanned, both the words selected and the means chosen to teach them should be appropriate for the children being instructed. Neither "joy" nor a minilecture were suitable for the first graders just referred to. The second point of equal importance is that unexpected opportunities to extend vocabulary knowledge should be taken advantage of whenever possible, especially when the words are of obvious interest.

EXAMPLES OF
PREPLANNED INSTRUCTION

Some of what a kindergarten teacher did in the course of a year to add to oral vocabularies starts the specific treatment of planned instruction, since the procedures allow for the enumeration of characteristics of instruction for young children. Brief descriptions of this teacher's efforts constitute Figure 12.3. Comments about the procedures, which are listed at the top of page 357, suggest guidelines for working with young children.

Figure 12.3. *Kindergarten Activities*

Some Ways for Adding to Oral Vocabularies

OBJECTIVES	PROCEDURES
To teach the meaning of "fall" and "autumn." To introduce the sequence of the seasons.*	1. Used first day of autumn to introduce "fall." Wrote it on board and pronounced it. Mentioned names of other seasons too. Also talked about another meaning for "fall" with help of sentences like, "Don't fall off your chair" and "Try not to fall when you play." 2. The next day, introduced "autumn" as a word that can be used in place of "fall." Read a story about the fall as a time of changing colors in leaves. 3. On the following day, took children to the park to collect leaves. Upon return to school, used the leaves to remention "fall" and "autumn," and to provide practice in counting and in naming colors. (Learned

---

*The teacher attended to the second objective because of one of her more

sophisticated kindergartners. Asked, "When does spring come?" the child

responded, "In the fall."

OBJECTIVES	PROCEDURES
	children are confused both about colors and counting.)
	4. A week later, read story about squirrels gathering nuts to prepare for winter. (Showed children some nuts.) Used story to review "fall" and "autumn" and to introduce the fall season as one that is followed by winter. Also mentioned that summer comes before fall. Showed this sequence with time line on the board.
To call attention to words related to homes: door, window, stairs, porch, roof, chimney, TV antenna, gutter, drain pipe.	1. Used magazine pictures to name parts of house. Discussed reasons for chimney, gutter, and drain pipe.
	2. Children drew pictures of their own homes or apartment buildings.
	3. The next day, children were taken for a walk to look at different parts of houses.
To call attention to names of materials from which homes are often built: wood, brick, and stone.	4. The following day, story about a wooden house was read. Explained that other houses may be brick or stone.

OBJECTIVES	PROCEDURES
	5. After the story, children were taken for a walk to find wood, brick, and stone buildings.
To give meaning to "measure," "ruler," and "inch."	1. Introduced measurement by asking, "If I wanted to learn how tall you are, how could I find out?" This led to idea of measuring. Tape measure was used to demonstrate how child might be measured. The word "inch" was introduced and printed on the board. Under it, a one-inch line was drawn. Used a 12-inch ruler to measure length of comb, pencil, and sheet of paper.
	2. Later, reviewed "measure," "ruler," and "inch" by demonstrating measurement of toy car. Distributed sheets on which simple outlines of a comb, pencil, straw, and crayon were drawn. Children were to measure each and write the number of inches it measured beside the picture. (Comb was measured with much guidance to make sure

OBJECTIVES	PROCEDURES
	children understood the task. Major problem: tendency to put ruler to edge of paper rather than to edge of picture being measured.) Answers were checked later.
	3. For several weeks, rulers were kept in a box on a table. Whenever there was free time, children could measure various objects in the room.
To teach the meaning of: orchestra, orchestra leader, baton, violin, trumpet, flute, trombone, clarinet, saxaphone.	1. Once children were accustomed to their own band instruments, used pictures of orchestral instruments to introduce them to names of others. During three-week period, gave attention to each with the help of pictures and a musical recording that highlighted it. Summarized with bulletin-board display of labeled pictures.
	2. High school orchestra leader visited classroom, bringing with him students who played the instruments that had been

OBJECTIVES	PROCEDURES
	discussed. The leader also explained and demonstrated use of the baton.
	3. Children visited high school when orchestra was practicing. One selection was played especially for them. Upon returning to the classroom, children played their own selections with the help of triangles, sticks, bells, and tambourines.
To teach names of baby animals: calf, colt, chick, piglet, duckling.	1. Showed picture of a woman holding a baby. Talked about it, mentioning that animals also have babies and that each has a special name. Talked about the familiar names "puppy" and "kitten." Read a story that told about other baby animals. Discussed each picture and counted the number of animals shown. Repeated their names.
	2. Prepared bulletin-board display of animals, each labeled. Talked about pictures to

OBJECTIVES	PROCEDURES
	introduce art project, which was to make clay figures of a mother animal and her baby. Later, each was labeled and put on a table for display.
	3. Periodically, read a story about the animals that had been discussed. Later, to provide review, reread the story used to introduce the baby animal terms.
To teach the concept "circle."	1. Began by asking, "Who knows what a circle is?" Showed circular objects: bracelet, clock face, penny, button, jar cover. Printed circle on board, read it, then showed children a small paper circle on which the word circle had been printed. Said each would receive a circle to take home to serve as a reminder to look for circular objects or pictures of them. They were discussed the next day.
	2. For the day circular objects and pictures were to be discussed, prepared bulletin-board display

OBJECTIVES	PROCEDURES

showing paper circles of different sizes and colors. Each was labeled <u>circle</u>. Used display for practice in counting and naming colors and, with the help of questions and paper squares, to teach that the concept "circle" encompasses variation in size and color but not shape.

3. For the next day's art project, children were given paper circles of different sizes and colors, which were to be pasted on black paper to make a design.

4. Pictures of circular objects brought in earlier by the children were assembled in a scrapbook cut in the shape of a circle. Each page was shown to them. Later, it was added to the collection of books that children can select at free-choice time. (Similar procedures were used later to teach the concepts "rectangle," "triangle," and "square.")

Reminders

1. Like all instruction, plans for teaching word meanings begin with the selection of a specific objective having to do with words whose meanings are unfamiliar but not overly abstract or obscure.
2. Sometimes, objectives other than the preselected one can be realized with the same instruction. When *fall* and *autumn* were the concern in the instruction just described, attention went to counting and identifying colors. Objectives related to meanings also provided many opportunities to expose the children to written words, thus giving them the chance to learn to read them.
3. Teachers must consider prerequisites. If children cannot identify numerals, for example, they are not ready to use rulers to measure.
4. Procedures should incorporate use of the familiar to get to the less familiar. This guideline was followed when *puppy* and *kitten* were discussed before *calf* and *duckling*.
5. Generally, combinations of teaching procedures are necessary to realize an objective. (They also allow for variety.) Combinations in the illustrations included explanations, discussions, objects, stories, recordings, pictures, walks, and bulletin-board displays.
6. Even with young children, word study can make use of homonyms such as "fall," even though the term *homonym* is not used. (Homonyms, referred to earlier as polysemous words, are words that are spelled and pronounced the same but have different origins and meanings.)
7. Teaching word meanings should not be confined to a specified period in a day's schedule. In one procedure just described, time set aside for art allowed for reinforcement of the names of baby animals.

ANOTHER PLANNED LESSON

To provide background information for the next instruction to be described, terms that identify and help organize instructional needs are listed, defined, and illustrated below (19):

Synonyms: Words of similar meaning (*big, large; dad, father*).

Antonyms: Words of opposite meaning (*tall, short; poor, rich*).

Homonyms: Words that have the same pronunciation and spelling but that have different origins and meanings (*fall; cobbler*).

Homographs: Words that share a spelling but have different pronunciations and meanings (*row; lead*).

Homophones: Words that have the same pronunciation but different spellings and meanings (*boy, buoy; plane, plain*).

As the definitions indicate, homonyms and homographs are text-dependent words. Their identity, therefore,can be established only in context (*fall down* vs. *fall season*). This means that if new vocabulary in something like a basal reader selection includes homonyms or homographs, they should be introduced in contexts from which the intended words and meanings can be inferred.

Homophones have the same pronunciation but can be distinguished by their spellings. Children,therefore,should have a chance to see homophones whenever they enter into a discussion.

One possible way to introduce the concept *homophone* is described below. The description is meant to portray a lesson more advanced and structured than the lessons offered by the kindergarten teacher referred to earlier. The detailed plan for this lesson is written in a way that (a) illustrates specific objectives; (b) shows the significance of prior learnings (prerequisites) for realizing the objectives; (c) points up the need for teacher preparation; and (d) includes practice.

HOMOPHONES

Objectives
a. Children will know that some words, called "homophones," are pronounced the same but have different spellings and meanings.
b. Children will be able to explain the meaning of such words with appropriate pictures.

Prerequisites
a. Ability to read *a, ate, be, child, come, comes, did, eight, first, get, going, Halloween, I'm, in, is, on, prize, the, to, too, two, which, will, witch.*
b. Understand the function of a question mark and the meaning of "title."
c. Know that underlining often signals the need to stress the underscored word.
d. Ability to learn the pronunciations and meanings of words from a dictionary.

Teacher Preparations
a. Bulletin board, covered with orange paper, entitled "Which is Witch?"*

*In most dialect areas, *witch* and *which* are pronounced the same, thus are homophones.

b. Two sentences, each printed on a tagboard strip: *Which child comes in first will get the prize,* and *Which child <u>did</u> come in first?*

c. Sheets of black construction paper cut in the shape of a witch.

d. Smaller sheets of white paper cut in the same shape.

e. Picture of a witch drawn on white paper, under which is written *I'm going to be a witch on Halloween.* The picture and sentence are pasted to one of the sheets of black paper cut in the shape of a witch.

f. As many lists of paired homophones as there are children in the instructional group.

Instruction

Standing next to a bulletin board that displays the title, *Which Is Witch?* the teacher begins:

Teacher: What does this title say?

Group: Which is Witch?

Teacher: (Pointing to *Which* and then to *Witch*) Two words in this title are pronounced the same. Name both words.

Group: Which and witch.

Teacher: Are they spelled the same?

Group: No.

Teacher: Spell the word that often starts a question, Colleen.

Colleen: W, h, i, c, h.

Teacher: Who will spell the word that names somebody who always gets talked about when it's Halloween? Would you spell that word, Ted?

Ted: W, i, t, c, h.

Teacher: Ted, is a witch something that could be pictured?

Ted: Sure. I could draw one.

Teacher: Can anybody think of a way to draw a picture of the other word that says "which"—the one that's spelled *w, h, i, c, h?* . . . Nobody? *I* can't think of a way to draw a picture of it, either, but I do have a sentence for *which.* (Shows the sentence strip *Which child comes in first will get the prize.*) Please read this silently. . . . Now let's read it together aloud.

Group: Which child comes in first will get the prize.

Teacher: I wrote this sentence to show that *which* often starts a question, but not always. (Next shows the sentence, *Which child did come in first?*) Read this second sentence with your eyes. . . . Okay. Let's read it aloud together.

Group: Which child *did* come in first?

Teacher: Good. I was glad to hear you give special stress to *did.* That's why I drew a line under it. Now let's get back to the two words we were talking about (points to *Which* and *Witch*). What do they say?

Group: Which, witch.

Teacher: Are these two words spelled the same?

Group: No.

Teacher: They're not spelled the same, they don't have the same meaning, but they *are* pronounced the same. Words like this are called homophones. What are they called?

Group: Homophones.

Teacher: What are words like *which* and *witch* called, Fran?

Fran: Homophones.

Teacher: Look up here, please. (Waits, then prints *homophones* on the chalkboard next to the bulletin board.) What does this word say, everybody?

Group: Homophones.

Teacher: Let me write some other homophones you know. (Quickly prints *two, too,* and *to*.) Read these words, please.

Group: Two, too, to.

Teacher: These are homophones because they're pronounced the same, but they have different spellings and meanings. Look at the word spelled *t, w, o.* Can anyone think of a picture you could draw that tells what *t, w, o* means? Jean?

Jean: I have twin sisters, so I'd draw a picture of them.

Teacher: Wonderful! And you could write under the picture something like *The two sisters are twins.* How about the word that says *to,* but it's spelled *t, o.* Can anyone think of a picture that would tell its meaning? . . . Nobody? Let me remind you of what it means by using it in a sentence—or, better yet, *you* give me some sentences that have the word *t, o* in them.

Prillie:	I came to school.
Teacher:	Fine. One more sentence?
Bridget:	I'm going to a birthday party this Saturday.
Teacher:	Okay. What about the word spelled *t, o, o*? Who can think of a sentence for that word, meaning "also"?
Anne:	One and one are two.
Teacher:	That word, Anne, is a number word – like twins are two children. The word I'm talking about now is spelled *t, o, o* and it means "also." How about a sentence for the word *t, o, o*?
Anne:	I have twin sisters, too.
Teacher:	That's better. Now let's see if we remember what we call words like *to* and *two*, and words like *which* and *witch*. (Points to *homophones.*) What does this say?
Group:	Homophones.
Teacher:	I've given you examples of homophones. Can anybody tell me what homophones are? If someone asked, "What are homophones?" how would you answer? Think of all the things we said about the words *which* and *witch*.
Ronnie:	They're. . . .
Teacher:	Ronnie, why don't you start with the word you're telling us about so that we don't forget.
Ronnie:	Homophones are words that are pronounced the same way, but they mean different things.
Teacher:	Anything else? . . . Erin?
Erin:	They aren't spelled the same either.
Teacher:	Correct. (Points to *homophones*). Homophones are words that are pronounced the same, but they have different meanings and different spellings. I'm going to give each of you a list of homophones, some of which you might not know. If you don't, use your dictionaries. When you know the pronunciations and meanings of your homophones – for example (writes *ate* and *eight* on the board), "ate" and "eight," draw a picture on white paper – it's on the table – and write a sentence under the picture that shows you know what the word means. Paste the drawings with the sentences on the sheets of paper cut to look like the outline of a witch. (As a model, the teacher

(continued)

shows a picture of a witch, under which the sentence, *I'm going to be a witch on Halloween* is written. This is pasted on a sheet of black paper cut in the shape of a witch.) When you're done, we'll put some of the witches on the bulletin board and some in a book we'll call *Which Is Witch?* Any questions about what you're to do?

Homophones that might appear on lists include:

pain	pane	muscle	mussel	
paws	pause	cereal	serial	
hair	hare	heal	heel	
chilly	chili	sale	sail	
tea	tee	rain	reign	
one	won	pear	pair	pare
fair	fare	meet	meat	mete

When time permits, the pictures, the sentences, and the homophones themselves will be discussed. To show the value of knowing about homophones, examples in basal reader selections and whatever else is being read will be brought to the children's attention.

Should a teacher decide that further practice with homophones is necessary, a written sheet that starts as follows can be prepared. Under each sentence, empty space would be left to accommodate a definition for the underlined homophone.

Write a definition under each sentence for the underlined word.

1. An <u>ant</u> walked under our kitchen door.

2. We're going to visit my <u>aunt</u> Sunday.

3. Stay away from the <u>bear</u>.

4. He was walking in his <u>bare</u> feet.

Another assignment might request definitions for each of the two homophones found in sentences like:

I read the red book last night.
Pare the pear with this knife.
During the night, the knight left the castle.

PROVIDING EXPERIENCES

Preplanned lessons can be highly productive for vocabulary growth; experiences — direct or vicarious — are also especially helpful for young children. Sometimes, experiences may even be required for a reason mentioned earlier: Neither a referent nor the name for it are known. Because of the value of experiences, what some teachers have done to provide them is described.

In one instance, a teacher invited a police officer to come to school. Always careful about preparations, she had read a story to her class about police officers in which the words *crest* (for the badge on their hat) and *uniform* were especially highlighted. She mentioned this to the policeman before his visit, so he used those words several times as he talked. An interesting thing then happened in connection with his use of *crest*. The word reminded a child of the name of her toothpaste, which, of course, she mentioned. Others spontaneously named theirs. To the amusement of the adults (the children went right on naming brands), one girl said her toothpaste was "sex appeal."

This particular experience, in addition to reminding us that life with young children is never dull, offers another reminder: Potentially rich experiences can be fruitless if a teacher does not see to it that certain words receive explicit attention — sometimes before, during, and following the experience. This same point has been made effectively by Alexander Frazier (6), who put it this way:

> Experience may be said to have been fully experienced only when it has been worked through in terms of language. The meaning of experience has to be extracted, clarified, and codified, so to speak. Perhaps, then, one of our chief challenges is to attend more carefully to the development of vocabulary from whatever experiences [children] are having. (p. 176)

Since experiences do have great potential for producing vocabulary growth, teachers ought to keep in mind that elaborate ones are unnecessary. A walk through the community, after all, might be the best dictionary for *shingle*, *dormer*, *cupola*, *shutter*, and *eaves* — or *drainpipe*, *gutter*, *chimney*, and even *satellite dish*. A walk anywhere allows for scavenger hunts, which, in turn, can result in collaborative collages back in the classroom. Arrangements of items attached to a board in the order in which they were found allow for labels like *first*, *next*, *later*, and *at the end*. Depending on what was found, neatly printed cards might display such descriptions as *small*, *smaller*, *smallest*, or *big*, *bigger*, *biggest*.

Seeing in the ordinary great possibilities for developing vocabularies is not the same as saying that special trips should never be taken. A trip to an airport, after all, is effective in changing the meaning of *airplane* from a noisy spot in the sky to a structure of unexpected size, and a trip to the zoo can change *snake* from an unbelievable creature into something starkly simple. Probably the most generally useful reminder in this regard is that the productivity of an experience is not dependent on its elaborateness or exotic quality but on what a teacher does to ensure that concepts and words are clarified as a result of the experience.

Another reminder is found in the description of the police officer's visit: It is essential to plan ahead of time with the people who are involved in an experience. With the police officer, planning merely required asking him to talk about his uniform and, more specifically, the crest on his hat. With other resource people, preplanning may take different forms. Why some type is necessary is explained well by a teacher:

> The first year I taught I knew it was important to provide children with experiences, and I guess I assumed they would automatically result in better vocabularies. I remember very well the first trip I planned. It was to a greenhouse and, other than to get permission from the owner to come, I made no special preparations. The result was a tedious tour that seemed more appropriate for botanists than my first graders. It was sufficiently disappointing that I didn't do anything else with trips that year.
>
> By my second year of teaching – thanks to some things I had read – I was more aware that the good that comes from excursions is not an accidental happening. What results, I learned, comes from planning. For that reason, at the start of the second year I spent some time with the florist before I took my new group to see his greenhouses. Because of the time we spent together, this second tour was most productive. It started in the classroom by calling the children's attention to the word *greenhouse* by writing it on the board. Many of them knew *green*, some recognized *house*, and all seemed to know why it was an appropriate name once we arrived at our destination. On this tour, the florist showed the children how all the plants were kept warm in winter and how each one was individually watered by a tiny hose connected to a larger one. At the end of the discussion, he turned on the entire sprinkling system. Need I mention how much this delighted the children?
>
> They were also delighted when each received a small bag of crocus bulbs at the end of the tour. Earlier, the florist had demonstrated some planting and had shown pictures of what their bulbs would look like in the spring.
>
> The end result of all of this, combined with some discussion and showing of pictures when we got back to school, was new or more specific

meanings for *greenhouse, florist, sprinkle, hose, bulb, temperature, mum,* and *chrysanthemum*. (The connection between the last two words was brought out during the tour. At first the florist used *chrysanthemum*, then switched to *mum*. One of the boys picked this up immediately, commenting, "That's not what you called it before." Very nicely the florist explained the connection. Fortunately, when we got back to school, I remembered to write both on the board so that the children could see how *chrysanthemum* included *mum*.)

Encouraged by the successful trip to the greenhouse, this teacher followed it up with one to the post office. Out of class, preparation began by talking with the worker who was to be the guide; in class, by having the children compose a thank you letter to the florist. The teacher later typed it and showed and reread it to the children. She then addressed and stamped an envelope, after which everyone went to the post office to mail the letter.

At the post office, the group was met by the guide. The tour itself began by dropping the letter in the "City" slot. It proceeded by tracing what would be done with the letter in order to get it to its destination.

Preparation for the next trip, this one to a firehouse, began when the children learned to read *red*. In talking about it, fire trucks naturally were mentioned. This reference was followed by some stories about fire trucks and firefighters. Then it was time to ask the children, "Would you like to go to the firehouse some day?" They soon went and not only learned about a variety of equipment but also got to stand on the rear of the trucks. The climax came when the firefighter who was acting as guide let all the sirens ring.

As it happened, the trip offered many opportunities not only for vocabulary development (*firefighter, firehouse, fire truck, axe, pick, siren, ladder, hose*) but also for attention to other goals. While discussing the trip, the teacher wrote *red* and all identified it. She also wrote *fire* and then showed how it was part of *firehouse* and *firefighter*. The children had already learned the correspondence between *f* and /f/; consequently, the same words were used to review that. Later, at art time, each child received a copy of a typed, two-sentence caption:

> Look and see the boys and girls.
>
> See the fire truck.

The children read the sentences, then drew pictures to go with them.

This trip and others (newspaper office, lumber yard, pharmacy, jewelry store, hatchery, grocery store) effectively demonstrated how different objectives can be worked on simultaneously. This is an important point to remember because, in talking or writing about teaching, only one thing can be mentioned at a time. Consequently, it is possible to give the incorrect impression that a teacher does this *or* that—for instance, works on word meanings *or* reviews words *or* uses phonics. What the descriptions of the trips correctly point out is that most of the time a teacher meshes objectives and works on more than one. With the trip to the firehouse, for example, the pre-established objective was vocabulary development. Yet, in both the preparation and follow-up periods, the children learned to read *red*; were exposed many times to *fire*; were introduced to compound words (*firehouse, firefighter*); and reviewed what they had learned earlier about the sound that *f* records. Because teaching requires attention to so many objectives, it should be a consolation to know that more than one can often be dealt with at the same time.

READING TO CHILDREN

Next to providing experiences, reading to children is one of the best sources of help with vocabulary. In fact, it has so many valuable by-products that teachers should view it as an indispensable, daily activity. As emphasized in earlier chapters, reading to children who are unable to read themselves is one way to get them to want to learn. It also is a means for bringing children into contact with book language, for giving them a sense of "story," and for adding to their knowledge of the world. Of concern now is that it can also add to their knowledge of words.

The various ways in which reading to children entered into one kindergarten teacher's efforts to teach concepts and the words that name them was described earlier in Figure 12.3. How another kindergarten teacher concentrated on just one word is told in a journal entry:

> This week, I'm reading some of the *Curious George* books. They were very popular last year; now I hope to make them both more enjoyable and more productive for developing vocabularies.
>
> I began today by showing the children a monkey puppet, introducing him as George. We talked about the puppet for a while, after which I said that George was an especially curious monkey. Naturally I asked, "What does 'curious' mean?" Although a number of the children were eager to answer, it soon became clear that nobody knew. George then announced he would visit classrooms of older children to see if *they* knew. He promised to return later.
>
> Through the work and play periods, I used "curious" as many times as possible – for instance, "I'm curious about George. I wonder where he is now" and "So many are raising their hands today. I'm curious to see who can tell me the right number."
>
> At story time, George reappeared. I told the children he returned because today's story was about him. I showed them the word *George* on the cover of the book I was about to read and then printed it on the chalkboard. After the story was finished, George asked whether anybody

had learned what "curious" meant while he was gone. By this time, most had a pretty good idea of the meaning, responding with answers like "trying to learn about something" and "being nosy."

The next day I read *Curious George Learns the Alphabet* to reinforce the meaning of "curious" and to motivate the children to learn about letters.

Curious George—the children renamed the puppet—is now in our library corner, along with a few other puppets who were also introduced in connection with books I read. The children enjoy using all the puppets for dramatic play, for acting out stories I've read, and for pretending they are reading to the puppets.

ORGANIZING WHAT IS BEING LEARNED

Combined, the various sections in the chapter have now pointed up the many different ways in which vocabulary acquisition can be realized. Such acquisition is very important, as is retention. Recognizing that, teachers should not overlook the fact that organizing in some meaningful way what is being acquired helps with retention. Making apparent connections between known and new vocabulary, for instance, or clarifying what certain words have in common can facilitate—sometimes greatly—both understanding and recall.

The widespread attention given in relatively recent years to what is called at different times "conceptual networks," "semantic mapping," and "semantic feature analysis" (10, 12) may account for the increased appearance of word displays in classrooms. Examples are in Figure 12.4. Whatever the reason, all such displays should be the product of discussions and decisions in which children are active participants. At times, they should also be the ones who prepare the displays.

Like other instructional materials, word displays ought to serve not as classroom decorations but as helpful tools for learning. This means that as soon as their pedagogical value approaches zero, they should be taken down, perhaps to be replaced by something reflecting more current work with concepts and vocabulary.

TIMES FOR ATTENDING TO WORD MEANINGS

Some of you may have started this chapter wondering what can be done to produce vocabulary growth; perhaps even more of you now wonder how teachers can find time to do all that *can* be done to realize that objective. Given the fundamental importance of oral vocabularies for reading, it seems safe to say that the best teachers allot as much time to vocabulary development as is humanly possible. Minimally, all teachers should feel obligated to

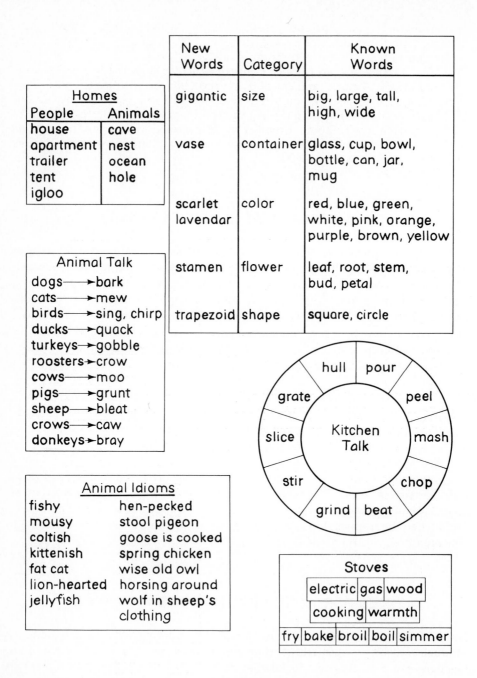

New Words	Category	Known Words
gigantic	size	big, large, tall, high, wide
vase	container	glass, cup, bowl, bottle, can, jar, mug
scarlet lavendar	color	red, blue, green, white, pink, orange, purple, brown, yellow
stamen	flower	leaf, root, **stem**, bud, petal
trapezoid	shape	**square**, circle

Homes

People	Animals
house	cave
apartment	nest
trailer	ocean
tent	hole
igloo	

Animal Talk

dogs→bark
cats→mew
birds→sing, chirp
ducks→quack
turkeys→gobble
roosters→crow
cows→moo
pigs→grunt
sheep→bleat
crows→caw
donkeys→bray

Animal Idioms

fishy	hen-pecked
mousy	stool pigeon
coltish	goose is cooked
kittenish	spring chicken
fat cat	wise old owl
lion-hearted	horsing around
jellyfish	wolf in sheep's clothing

Kitchen Talk: hull, pour, peel, mash, chop, beat, grind, stir, slice, grate

Stoves

electric	gas	wood
cooking	warmth	

| fry | bake | broil | boil | simmer |

Figure 12.4. *Visual Displays of Word Relationships*

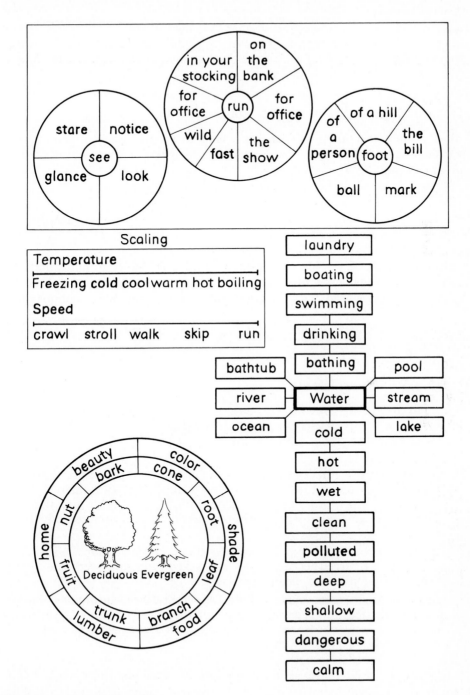

Scaling

Temperature

Freezing **cold** cool warm hot boiling

Speed

crawl   stroll   walk   skip   run

laundry

boating

swimming

drinking

bathing

bathtub	bathing	pool
river	**Water**	stream
ocean		lake

cold

hot

wet

clean

polluted

deep

shallow

dangerous

calm

Figure 12.4 *(continued)*

attend to word meanings (a) whenever children are being prepared for assigned reading that contains unknown words; (b) whenever children are confused about words; and (c) whenever they fail to select meanings for words that fit specific contexts. Each of the three mandatory times for attending to the meanings of words is discussed below.

Unknown Words in Assigned Reading

Most of the selections children are asked to read in school contain new vocabulary. In fact, one common reason for assigned reading is to use it as a means for adding to vocabularies.

Since it hardly is fair to expect children to succeed in comprehending a piece of text if key words are not in their oral vocabularies, one necessary time for dealing with word meanings is when children are being prepared to read that text. (An exception is when contexts or the structure of words provide ample help.)

What should be done with new words insofar as their pronunciations are concerned is considered in Chapter 11. There, the assumption is that the words in question are familiar orally; thus, achieving their pronunciation would suggest their meaning. This chapter described the many procedures that can be used with words that are totally new: unknown both visually *and* orally.

Confusion among Words

A second mandatory time for attending to word meanings is when children's answers, or use of words, provide evidence of confusion. Let me describe a few occasions when help with meanings was clearly needed.

> In a third grade, the approach of Veteran's Day made it natural for the teacher to ask about the meaning of "veteran." One child explained, "It's a person who works on animals." Seeing from the teacher's expression that this explanation was unacceptable, a second child volunteered, "It's a person who doesn't eat meat."
>
> In another room, a group was talking about various occupations. When the teacher referred to carpenters and asked what they did, she heard, "They are people who clean carpets."
>
> In still another room, "synonym" had apparently been introduced earlier, because the teacher asked an instructional group, "Does anyone remember what we call words that have just about the same meaning?" One child immediately suggested "Cinnamons."

What all three of these incidents shared was not only evidence of children's confusion about words but also their teachers' failure to deal with the confusion by writing responses on the board so that what was heard could be seen and then compared with what should have been offered. Instead of doing anything like that, each teacher either called on additional children until a correct response was given, or else provided the answer herself and moved on to something else.

To provide an instructive contrast, let me refer to one third-grade class. In this class, the teacher and students were discussing a newspaper article that related the details of an accident in which one of the children had been involved the previous afternoon. Among other things, the reporter said that their classmate "was suffering from internal bleeding." When the teacher inquired what 'internal bleeding' was, one child said, "It's bleeding that goes on forever."

Recognizing the source of the confusion, the teacher responded, "I can see why you might think that, because there are two words that sound very much alike. Let's take a careful look at both." She then went to the board and wrote:

internal

eternal

This teacher continued: "The first word – 'internal' – describes where Billy was bleeding following the accident. '*In*ternal' means 'inside.' Apparently, Billy didn't look as if anything had been cut because the bleeding was inside his body where it couldn't be seen. It was *in*ternal bleeding. The second word that I wrote – '*e*ternal' – means 'forever.' Sometimes when we have bad pains like Billy must be having now, we think they will be eternal. We think they will go on forever. If we wanted to use both of these words, we could say that Billy has – or at least had – internal bleeding and we hope that if he's in pain, it won't be eternal."

Inappropriate Meanings for Given Contexts

A third time when attention to word meanings is essential occurs whenever children fail to access word meanings that make sense in given contexts. Earlier in the chapter, examples of this problem are described. Let me cite one further illustration, this time to allow for a discussion of what can be done when proposed meanings do not fit contexts.

In this instance, a group was talking about a film that dealt with reptiles. In the course of the discussion, the teacher observed, "At one point in the film, the person who was doing the talking used the word 'viper.' What *is* a viper anyway?" Since a child's response was, "It's what takes the water off the front window of a car," it is time to ask, What to do?

First of all, it should be kept in mind – and this point is made in an earlier chapter – that for some children, it is more appealing to respond in any way to a teacher's question (including the wrong way) than not to respond at all. Given this fact, teachers should consciously develop the habit of not calling on the first children to raise their hands. Instead, a reminder like, "Let's think for a few minutes" should precede calling on anyone.

When an erroneous response is given, it is important for teachers to try to understand what lies behind the error. Sometimes, the correct pronunciation of a new word was never really heard—"synonyms" may, in fact, have been heard as "cinnamons," in which case "cinnamons" is not as wrong as it may at first appear to be. The message that such "boners" clearly convey is: *Use the chalkboard! Show the word!!* Showing *cinnamons* and *synonyms* was certainly called for, but not done, in one of the illustrations cited earlier.

But let's take the case of "viper," obviously defined as if it were the word "wiper." What to do in this situation? Again, the initial step is to write the words being confused:

viper

wiper

After both words are pronounced, a teacher might say to the child who responded incorrectly, "What you suggested for the meaning of 'viper'—the first word up here—was an excellent description of the second word, the word 'wiper.' But, remember, the film that we saw had nothing to say about cars. It was about reptiles—about lizards and snakes, and the like. So if the person speaking in the film used the word 'viper,' it probably had something to do with reptiles, not cars. Does anyone think they know what a viper might be? . . . No? Why don't we find out in the dictionary. I think you'll see that its meaning has something to do with a reptile that we saw in the film."

No one best way can be cited for dealing with every instance of erroneous responses concerning word meanings, but some general guidelines for teachers do exist. For instance:

1. When words are discussed, and certainly when they are introduced for the first time, they ought to be written so children can see what they look like.
2. If children offer erroneous explanations or definitions, they should always end up understanding *why* they are incorrect.
3. If the meaning offered for a word is incorrect because it does not match a given context, that should be explained with specificity.
4. If a response is incorrect because one word is being confused with another, both words should be written, examined, and their different meanings clarified.
5. In listening to children's responses, the focus of a teacher's attention should not be exclusively on, Is that right or is that wrong? The reason

that may lie behind a response, right *or* wrong, is of equal importance for instructional purposes.

SUMMARY

Chapter 12 began by reviewing specific ways in which reading ability is dependent on oral vocabularies. It also stressed the difference between empty verbalization—for instance, memorized synonyms or definitions—and a genuine understanding of words.

The chapter went on to make distinctions among unfamiliar words that allowed for identifying corresponding distinctions among instructional needs. Viewed from a teacher's perspective, the needs are four in number: (a) expanding referents; (b) teaching a name for a familiar referent; (c) teaching an additional name for a familiar referent; and (d) teaching a new referent and a name for it. These differences among unfamiliar words merit attention whenever decisions are being made about what to do with new vocabulary. At these times, too, the importance of encouraging children to work out word meanings themselves should be kept in mind. Such independence derives from ability to use contextual cues (Chapter 8) and from a knowledge of affixes (Chapter 11).

To provide further help in sorting out instructional needs and in organizing instruction itself, the chapter discussed literal and figurative language and also catalogued words as being synonyms, antonyms, homonyms, homographs, and homophones. Definitions of the five categories showed that homonyms and homographs are text-dependent words, making it necessary to present them in context so the intended words and their meanings can be inferred. The need in general for teachers to let children *see* words more often than is sometimes the case was underscored with a number of examples of children's erroneous and confused responses related to both the pronunciation and the meaning of words.

Chapter 12 naturally discussed ways available to expand children's knowledge of vocabulary. It assigned special importance to such sources of help as experiences, reading to children, and both planned and "on-the-spot" lessons. Knowing how to plan lessons is a necessary ability, as many of the frequently used commercially prepared materials do less with meanings than their importance warrants. What is missing must be supplied by teachers.

Because of flaws and omissions in commercial materials, Chapter 12 showed with many illustrations that materials need not be purchased—that, in fact, the world is literally filled with objects and texts that are rich with subject matter for instruction. Fortunately, these close-at-hand materials have the added feature of being of interest to children.

Chapter 12 also showed some ways for organizing what children are learning about concepts and the words that name them. This was done because some type of meaningful organization fosters both understanding and retention.

Recognizing all the demands made of a teacher's time, the chapter ended by pointing out when attention *must* go to word meanings no matter how busy teachers are. New words in assigned reading, confusion about words, and failure to access the meaning of a word that a given context requires were the three occasions singled out as requiring attention to vocabulary.

REVIEW

1. As acknowledged at the start of Chapter 12, a number of points (including the dependence of reading on oral vocabularies) are made more than once in Chapters 1 through 11. What are some of the suggestions made repeatedly in this textbook because of their significance for effective instructional programs?

2. Early in Chapter 12, a common (and persistent) type of dictionary assignment was criticized.   *might cloose wrong meaning*
   a. Describe the criticism and the reasons for it.
   b. Tell how the criticized assignment can be improved.

3. Chapter 12 pinpoints how unfamiliar words are unfamiliar in different ways. What *are* the four differences and, second, what are the implications of the differences for instruction?

4. Explain the following statements with examples:
   a. Homophones must be seen to be understood unless they are in contexts.
   b. Homographs and homonyms must be in contexts if the intended meanings are to be correctly inferred.

5. In Chapter 12, it was stated that figurative language occurs fairly frequently in easy text. It was also said that textbooks are not essential for helping children cope with word meanings. Keeping the two assertions in mind, bring to class some headlines from sports sections of various newspapers that illustrate the use of figurative language.

REFERENCES

1. Beck, Isabel L., and McKeown, Margaret G. "Learning Words Well—A Program to Enhance Vocabulary and Comprehension." *Reading Teacher* 36 (March, 1983), 622–625.
2. Beck, Isabel L.; Perfetti, Charles A.; and McKeown, Margaret G. "Effects of Long-Term Vocabulary Instruction on Lexical Access and Reading Comprehension." *Journal of Educational Psychology* 74 (August, 1982), 506–521.

3. Berry, Kathleen S. "Talking to Learn Subject Matter/Learning Subject Matter Talk." *Language Arts* 62 (January, 1985), 34–42.

4. Dolch, Edward W. *Psychology and the Teaching of Reading*. Champaign, Ill.: Garrard Press, 1951.

5. Durkin, Dolores. "What Classroom Observations Reveal about Comprehension Instruction." *Reading Research Quarterly* 14 (1978–79, No. 4), 481–533.

6. Frazier, Alexander. "Developing a Vocabulary of the Senses." *Elementary English* 47 (February, 1970), 176–184.

7. Gipe, Joan P. "Investigating Techniques for Teaching Word Meanings." *Reading Research Quarterly* 14 (1978–79, No. 4), 624–644.

8. Harris, Albert J. *How to Increase Reading Ability*. New York: Longmans, Green and Co., 1961.

9. Jenkins, Joseph R.; Stein, Marcy L.; and Wysocki, Katherine. "Learning Vocabulary through Reading." *American Educational Research Journal* 21 (Winter, 1984), 767–787.

10. Johnson, Dale D., and Pearson, P. David. *Teaching Reading Vocabulary*, 2d ed. New York: Holt, Rinehart and Winston, 1984.

11. Kameenui, Edward J.; Carnine, Douglas W.; and Freschi, Roger. "Effects of Text Construction and Instructional Procedures for Teaching Word Meanings on Comprehension and Recall." *Reading Research Quarterly* 17 (1982, No. 3), 367–388.

12. McNeil, John D. "Teaching Vocabulary from an Interactive View of Reading Comprehension." In *Reading Comprehension*. Glenview, Ill.: Scott, Foresman and Company, 1984, 96–113.

13. Nagy, William E., and Anderson, Richard C. "How Many Words Are There in Printed School English?" *Reading Research Quarterly* 19 (Spring, 1984), 304–330.

14. Nagy, William E.; Herman, Patricia A.; and Anderson, Richard C. "Learning Words from Context." *Reading Research Quarterly* 20 (Winter, 1985), 233–253.

15. Parish, Peggy. *Good Work, Amelia Bedelia*. New York: William Morrow and Co., Inc., 1976.

16. Perfetti, Charles A., and Hogaboam, Thomas. "The Relationship between Single Word Decoding and Reading Comprehension Skill." *Journal of Educational Psychology* 67 (August, 1975), 461–469.

17. Robinson, Violet B.; Strickland, Dorothy S.; and Cullinan, Bernice. "The Child: Ready or Not?" In Lloyd O. Ollila (Ed.), *The Kindergarten Child and Reading*. Newark, Del.: International Reading Association, 1977, 13–39.

18. Sperling, Susan K. *Tenderfeet and Ladyfingers*. New York: Viking Press, 1981.

19. Yelland, H. L.; Jones, J. C.; and Easton, K. S. W. *A Handbook of Literary Terms*. Boston: Writer, 1980.

CHAPTER 13

Comprehension

PREVIEW

Any textbook written to help people who are, or will be, teaching reading is obligated to attend to comprehension almost immediately if only to make the point that reading and comprehending are synonymous. The equation is highlighted in this book in the first chapter by getting you consciously involved with the comprehension process and subsequently by analyzing what was required to comprehend two sentences about girls playing Checkers. The analysis, as you recall, portrays comprehending as an interactive process in which readers use an author's words in conjunction with their own relevant knowledge in order to construct the author's message. Readers emerge, then, as active participants in the comprehension process. Just calling off the words on a page is not enough to get the job done.

Roberta Golinkoff also looked at readers in a review of studies concerned with comprehension (11) and reached conclusions that will surprise nobody who has read earlier chapters in this book. Focusing on a comparison of good and poor comprehenders, the review disclosed that:

> Poor comprehenders:
>   Are less aware of what it means to comprehend
>   Read word by word
>   Are more concerned with pronunciations than with
>   meanings
>   Make more decoding errors
>   Take more time to decode
>   Ignore contextual cues while decoding

These characteristics are of readers; the following related guidelines, also discussed in previous chapters, pertain to instruction:

To discourage children from concluding that reading is a performing art, undue attention should not go to oral reading. From the beginning, the emphasis should be on the conceptual side of reading.

The dependence of comprehending on automatic word identifications assigns great importance to word practice. For the most part, such practice should be carried on with words in brief contexts rather than in lists.

The need for correct, quick decoding also assigns importance to practice in using graphophonic and structural cues. Such practice should be not only with unknown words but also with words in context in order to allow for the combined and balanced use of all available cues.

As can be seen, much of what contributes to children's comprehension abilities has already been discussed. This chapter, therefore, moves the focus to comprehension instruction itself.

To get this chapter under way, let's start with some thoughts about comprehension instruction; specifically, about what it is. Following the advice of earlier chapters in which contrasts are proposed as useful teaching tools, the introductory discussion is of contrasts among (a) facilitating comprehension, (b) testing comprehension, and (c) teaching comprehension. Seeing the latter in relation to the other two responsibilities of teachers should help clarify the meaning of "comprehension instruction."

The sketch in Figure 13.1 provides a setting for the ensuing discussion.

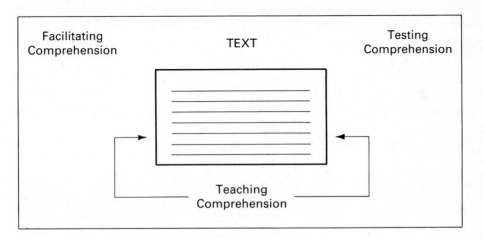

Figure 13.1. *Comprehension: Teacher Responsibilities*

FACILITATING COMPREHENSION

Facilitating comprehension divides into three responsibilities having to do with (a) new vocabulary, (b) essential background information, and (c) purpose(s) for reading. Each responsibility receives only brief attention, since what needs to be done to facilitate comprehension comes up again when the next chapter looks at basal reader lessons.

Teaching New Vocabulary

Typically, not knowing some words in a piece of text is no major obstacle to comprehension unless one or more of them are of central importance to the author's or the reader's purpose. Ideally, all the words in a selection would be in a child's sight vocabulary; what to do when that is not the case is discussed in the two previous chapters. In the summary section of Chapter 11, advice is offered for times when a word is known in its oral form but is unfamiliar

379

visually. Chapter 12 outlines instructional needs when a word is unfamiliar both visually and orally.

Providing Essential Background Information

By this time, why and even how background information facilitates comprehension should require no explanation. What may need attention, however, is the restriction imposed by the word *essential*. That description is meant, first, to discourage anyone from concluding, "The more the better" and, therefore, from turning the imparting of background information into an end in itself; and, second, to allow for making the point that what *is* essential is affected by such variables as purpose for reading. To be more specific, what a reader needs to know about Checkers to draw in color a picture of the content of two sentences about girls playing Checkers clearly exceeds what is necessary when the reason for reading the same text is to be able to answer the question, "What do you suppose Checkers is?"

Establishing Purpose(s) for Reading

The reason(s) something is being read determine(s) what constitutes not only essential background information but also adequate comprehension (8). At times—for instance, when reading a recipe to make muffins—"adequate" means knowing about details related to amount, sequence, temperature, and time. On other occasions—for example, when reading a novel to relax—"adequate" means gleaning just enough about a plot and characters to forget the day's worries and problems. This suggests that having clear purposes in mind makes it easier to comprehend, as purposes define what is important, which, in turn, determines what merits close attention or, on the other hand, little more than a quick look.

To sum up, purpose should keep readers from wandering aimlessly through a piece of text, not knowing what to attend to or what to try to remember. Used to guide reading, purpose clearly facilitates comprehension by turning it into intentional thinking.

TESTING COMPREHENSION

Just as purpose determines what constitutes (a) essential background information, (b) adequate comprehension, and (c) appropriate rates of reading, it should also affect what is tested once the reading has been done. Or, stated differently, if reading is a purposeful pursuit, then assessment should be an effort to learn whether the purpose(s) has been realized. This suggests that the question "Why am I doing what I'm doing?" is as important for persons considering assessment as it is for those planning instruction.

TEACHING COMPREHENSION

Testing comprehension is concerned with the *product* of reading; the *process* of reading is the concern of comprehension instruction. The difference means that the aim of teaching comprehension is to have a positive effect on children's mental activities as they work their way through a piece of text, whereas the aim of testing comprehension is to make a judgment about the outcome of those activities.

As is true for any instruction, procedures for teaching children how to comprehend vary in relation to specific objectives. (This is illustrated later when comprehension lessons are described.) When comprehension instruction is viewed globally, the usual means for accomplishing goals is some combination of imparting information, providing explanations, giving examples and nonexamples, modeling, and asking questions.

As with other instruction, that concerned with comprehension ought to be complemented with practice, both supervised and independent, and with opportunities for children to apply what they learned in something like a basal selection, a trade book, a newspaper article, and so forth. One reason for the application, you recall, is to have children experience the relevance and value of what was taught.

For purposes of summarizing, part of what has been said about comprehension instruction thus far is sketched in Figure 13.2.

As the diagram in Figure 13.2 points up, practice and application allow for opportunities to learn whether instruction was effective. This type of assessment contrasts with what is described earlier under the heading "Testing Comprehension." There, assessment is viewed as a means for learning what readers comprehended in a piece of text.

Although the diagram in Figure 13.2 identifies some topics that are subject matter for comprehension instruction, other topics should at least be mentioned if only to clarify still further what it means to teach children how to comprehend.

SOME TOPICS FOR INSTRUCTION

One way to identify possible subject matter for teaching comprehension is to examine what writers do to communicate. Some of the things they do are named in the sections that follow.

Typographic Signals

What every author does is take advantage of typographic features of written text that help with meaning, most of which fall under the heading "punctuation." This suggests that readers must be able to respond to those signals in

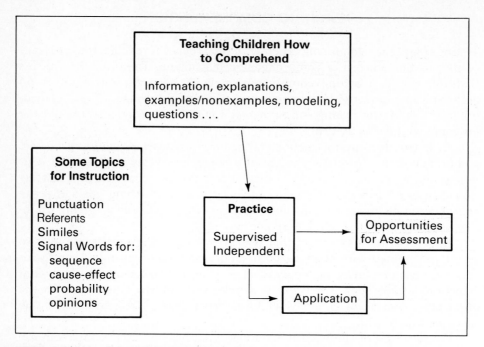

Figure 13.2. *Comprehension Instruction*

appropriate ways. Over a period of time, therefore, children should be taught the following guidelines:

Periods
  signal the end of a thought.
Commas
  signal a pause.
  set off an appositive.
  indicate the person being addressed.
Question Marks
  signal a question.
Exclamation Marks
  indicate emotions.
  suggest emphasis (as do italics and underlining).
Capitalization
  indicates a title, the start of a sentence, or a proper name.
Semicolons
  suggest that what follows is related to what preceded.

Colons
   signal that a series of related items follows.

Paragraph Indentation
   suggests a shift in focus.

Descriptions

Describing is something else that authors often do. What readers need to know is that descriptions come in different forms. For example:

Adjectives
   The *cool* weather was *pleasant*.

Adverbs
   The sun rose *slowly*.

Phrases
   The boy *in the red shirt* stood up.

Clauses
   Our house, *which is on a hill*, stayed dry.

Appositives
   Angela, *the oldest in the family*, has her first job.

For adding variety and color to descriptions, nonliteral uses of language are available to authors. Consequently, other topics for comprehension instruction include:

Idiom
   You need to read between the lines.

Hyperbole
   The tall trees reached to the sky.

Simile
   He's as thin as a twig.

Metaphor
   The sun was a gold coin.

A writer's descriptions may deal with sequence, simultaneous events, or, perhaps, causes and effects. In this case, children need to know that certain words help them comprehend such descriptions:

Some signal words for sequence
   first, next, before, later, after, earlier, eventually, finally

Some signal words for simultaneous events
   while, meanwhile, at the same time, simultaneously

Some signal words for cause-effect relationships
because, hence, therefore, since, as a result, for that reason, that is why

Pronoun and Adverb Referents

To avoid repeating the same words, authors often use pronoun and adverb referents. Even though their use does result in less repetition, it also accounts for some comprehension problems (3, 19). That is why referents like those illustrated in the italicized words below are necessary topics for instruction:

Paul took off quickly on *his* motorcycle.

The girls went to Sharon's home, but *she* wasn't *there*.

The trip to the cottage was long. "Well, *here* we are at last," said Dad.

The elderly man was tired and cold. *That* is why *he* left.

It was a rainy day, but *that* did not keep *him* from working.

Elliptical Sentences

Elliptical sentences like those printed below in italics provide writers with another means for avoiding use of the same words, and also for communicating more briefly. The nature of elliptical sentences and their implied content provide more subject matter for comprehension instruction:

The windows in the garage are dirty. *The car is, too.*

"Are you going to the game?" asked Joel. *"Yes,"* answered Beth.

All the children in the family are sick. *So is their mother.*

Alan may be late. *If so, start the meeting anyway.*

Discussion of, and questions about, abbreviated text like that shown above should clarify (as is the case with pronoun and adverb referents) what is substituting for what.

Cohesive Ties

Topics like pronoun referents, adverb referents, and elliptical sentences are closely linked to another topic that is relevant for comprehension lessons: cohesive ties. The existence of cohesive ties (e.g., It's expensive. Buy it *nonetheless*.) reflects the fact that in connected text, the meaning of one sentence (or more) is related to, and is dependent on, the meaning of another sentence (or more). This suggests that children must understand fairly early that reading is not processing one sentence at a time but, instead, requires integrating information across sentences. A more specific implication for readers is the need to know that the meaning of one or more words may depend on prior text (e.g., Bernard is ill. *For that reason*, the work has not been done.) or on subsequent text (e.g., Turn *it* off. We don't need a fan now.).

As just these few examples should make clear, cohesive ties come in many forms and provide generous amounts of subject matter for comprehension instruction.

Complex Sentences

Often, a long, seemingly complicated sentence causes comprehension problems (13). Instruction, therefore, must help children see that what looks like an incomprehensible sentence may in fact be a simple one that has been embellished:

The cat that Teddy got yesterday scratched
his mother's best furniture.

Agent	***Action***	***Object***
cat	scratched	furniture

Children also need to be vigilant about the possibility that long sentences may be a combination of several short sentences that are easy to understand. For instance:

The man got out of the car, went into the store, and bought roses.

The man got out of the car.

The man went into the store.

The man bought roses.

Inferences

As is amply illustrated in Chapter 1, authors communicate through implication as well as directly. Children, therefore, have to be taught not only about inferences but also about what enables them to make inferences. The sentences below explain why children need to know that an author's words and what they themselves know both help with inferences:

1. *Mark fell. He hurt his knee.*
   [Knowledge-based inference: The fall caused the injury.]
2. *Of the three girls, only Kelli could reach up to the shelf where their mother kept the cookies.*
   [Text-based inferences: The girls are sisters, and Kelli is the tallest.]

[Knowledge-based inference: Mother keeps the cookies on a high shelf (a) to keep them from being eaten right away, and/or (b) to avoid having appetites for regular meals spoiled.]

Fiction

When authors write stories, they bring additional comprehension requirements into existence. As a result, other topics take on significance for instruction. For instance:

> *Quotation Marks*
>   indicate what characters say.
>
> *New Paragraph*
>   indicates a different character is speaking.
>
> *Story Structure*
>   Setting.
>   Time
>   Locale
>   Central character
>   Introduction of problem.
>   Attempt(s) to resolve problem.
>   Resolution.
>
> *Ways for Revealing Traits of Characters*
>   Direct descriptions.
>   What a character says and does.
>   What others say about a character.
>   How others respond to a character.

Now that some requirements for comprehending text (and some of the subject matter for instruction) have been named, let's consider what teachers can do to help with comprehension even before children are able to do any reading.

LISTENING COMPREHENSION

You recall that Chapter 8 shows how spoken language allows teachers of young, nonreaders to attend to contextual cues. How spoken language functions in preparing for comprehending written text is illustrated now. In this case, purposeful listening activities are the focus.*

---

*One more goal can now be added to the list of readiness goals on page 111: Help children to listen purposefully as a way of preparing for reading comprehension.

It should be noted, first of all, that a recommendation to spend time on listening comprehension is not based on the assumption that it is identical to reading comprehension; in fact, the next sections pinpoint differences as well as similarities between the two. Rather, the recommendation stems from the notion that preplanned work with listening may contribute to children's later ability to comprehend written text (7, 17).

Similarity between Listening and Reading

The major similarity between listening and reading is very apparent: Both the listener and reader attend to language for the purpose of getting or constructing a message. The two thus display language-processing behavior.

The fact that the basic similarity between listening and reading is obvious often prompts an oversimplified and, therefore, an erroneous conclusion:

listening comprehension ability + decoding ability = reading comprehension ability *doesn't account for differences*

Why this equation is an oversimplification is clarified as the following section identifies differences between spoken and written language that are relevant for comprehending.

Differences between Spoken and Written Language

Unlike written text, spoken language is fleeting. That is, unless it is recorded on tape, it is not retrievable. In contrast, written language not only makes words a possible subject for study but also permits behaviors like backward checking and forward scanning. For reasons such as these, the reader is more "in charge" than is the listener.

Listeners, however, are not completely at the mercy of speakers. Failing to understand, they can express puzzlement with a facial expression or direct question. Since speakers routinely monitor the success of their communication efforts, such responses typically lead to adjustments that may include a slower rate of speaking, some repetition, more elaboration, additional illustrations, and so on.

The nature of spoken language offers further help for communication. Here, I have in mind characteristics like intonation and stress, which are poorly duplicated in print with underlining, italics, bold type, question marks, and exclamation marks. Of even greater importance for comprehension is the way speakers segment sentences (through pauses) into such meaningful units as a phrase or a clause. Evidently, the commas, semicolons, and periods found in print are not of equal help because research indicates that instead of processing print into conceptual units, poor comprehenders often read as if a page of text were lines of unrelated words (20, 21).

Although spoken language does have built-in features for helping with communication, it commonly lacks the elegance of carefully constructed prose. Just how inelegant it can be is made apparent whenever a conversation or even an interview is recorded, then played back. Too obvious to miss are the hesitations, repetitions, corrections, as well as the abandoned and poorly constructed sentences.

Differences in the kinds of sentences that characterize speech and written text have an important implication for any teacher who decides to spend time on listening comprehension as a way of preparing for reading comprehension. The implication is suggested in Figure 13.3.

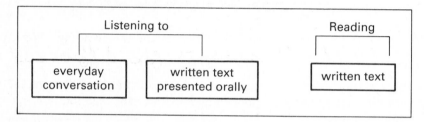

Figure 13.3. *Processing Language*

Since written text is not—as is sometimes claimed—"talk written down," the material most suitable for listening comprehension activities is not everyday conversation but, rather, what is referred to in Figure 13.3 as "written text presented orally." This suggests that reading to children is an appropriate topic with which to start the discussion of listening activities.

LISTENING ACTIVITIES: READING TO CHILDREN

In earlier chapters, reading to children is recommended for numerous reasons: (a) to foster positive attitudes toward books and school; (b) to motivate children to want to become readers; (c) to give them opportunities to hear book language; (d) to communicate information that will help them understand what they themselves will read; (e) to provide a model of good oral reading; and (f) to teach concepts and word meanings. Even though all these goals are of marked importance, nothing should ever be done that will diminish the pleasure children derive from being read to. That always comes first. The same guideline should prevail when teachers read to children as a way of developing comprehension abilities. To specify the guideline, what one kindergarten teacher did who forgot to adhere to it is described.

On the morning her class was observed, this teacher read an animal story that was listened to with rapt attention. (The response was not surprising because of the selection and the effectiveness of the reading.) When the story ended, several children commented simultaneously and could not be understood. Consequently, the teacher reminded everyone of the need to take turns. Eventually, many took a turn. One child said that the animal in the story was like her grandmother's dog. Another said that was impossible because the dog in the story wasn't real. Still another referred to the discrepancy between how the story ended and the way he thought things would turn out. All in all, it was an excellent discussion that revealed excellent comprehension. For that reason, the teacher's next procedure was both unnecessary and unexpected. Perhaps mimicking the practice of basal manuals, she posed a series of questions (How many . . . ? What color was . . . ? Where did . . . ? When did . . . ?). By the time the questions were answered, a group of squirming five-year-olds had replaced the group of wholly engrossed discussants. Afterward, the interrogation was explained in terms of "helping with comprehension."

Whenever that *is* an objective and reading to children is a means chosen to achieve it, procedures other than excessive questioning can be used. Let me describe some; and as I do, please bear in mind an important fact: Any procedure becomes wearisome if used all the time.

Reading Fiction

Typically, much of what is read to young children is fiction; and that's fine because they love stories. In addition to promoting positive attitudes and bringing children into contact with book language, fiction allows for attention to some requirements of reading comprehension. For instance:

Comprehension Requirements	Possible Procedures
Constructing mental images revealed through text	Omit showing illustrations. After the story is read, encourage the children to tell what they think the main character looks like (and *why*). Compare their versions with the author's by showing the illustrations. For another story, the children can draw their own versions.
Following the sequence of events	Stop before the story ends. Ask the

(continued)

children what they think will happen next (and *why*). Afterward, compare their predictions with what did come next.

After discussing the order in which events of a story occurred, show children a scroll-like paper with a division for each important event. Help the children decide what kind of a picture can go in each division so that as the paper is unrolled, the plot is revealed. Volunteers do the illustrations. For another story, use similar procedures, this time pulling the paper through a television screen (box with opening on side). As the pictures are displayed, the children retell the story. (The ability to retell what was heard—or read—is reliable evidence of successful comprehension, especially when children do the retelling in their own language. The translation demonstrates that the listener [or reader] has successfully reconstructed the author's message into a form that is personally meaningful.)

Distinguishing between fact and fancy

After reading a fictional account of an animal, read an encyclopedia article about the same animal to allow for a comparison of the two versions. What was factual and what was make-believe in the story should be emphasized through discussion. If the make-believe account deals with an animal that is familiar to the children, draw on their experiences for the comparison.

Evaluating authenticity

Whenever appropriate, encourage children to think critically about characterizations in stories. Pose questions like, "Is that the way children *really* act? If *your* little sister took something of yours, would *you* smile?" A story about a rabbit might make it natural to inquire, "Would a real rabbit feel sorry for a gardener and not eat his plants?"

Oral Presentation of Other Materials

Material other than storybooks is also suitable for purposeful listening. As mentioned in Chapter 2, if curious children are allowed to examine a school that has been vandalized, they can critique a newspaper account of the event. First, it would be read by the teacher, then analyzed with the help of questions like: When we went outside and walked around the building, were *all* the windows broken? . . . Was *every* room on the first floor a terrible mess?

At another time, books of riddles, which are available in generous numbers (6), can offer help in highlighting details. In this case, wrong conclusions allow for reminders about the need to listen carefully before any conclusion is reached.

Orally presented directions for arranging discs of various colors call attention both to details and to the meanings of place signals like *on, above, below, beneath, beside,* and *next to.* With discs in front of them, children can be asked to carry out directions like, "Put the blue circle beneath the green one."

Read by a teacher, the words of a song can be used to identify pervasive themes—for example, sadness. Once that conclusion is reached, a further consideration might be: "Does the music go with the words? Does it make you feel sad? Listen again."

Having children act out what is portrayed in words is another way to promote attentive, purposeful listening. In fact, the potential of this activity makes it one that ought to be used more often than is typical. The example below, which would be read sentence by sentence to allow two children to act out what each communicates, deals with a type of mental imagery that is helpful for comprehending in general and for solving arithmetic problems in particular:

> Jerry and Mark sat down at the round table. There were four books on the table, so Jerry opened one and began to read. Mark picked up a book, too, but didn't open it. He looked at the other books on the table. How many were there?

Perhaps a sufficient number of listening activities have now been described to make the point that attention to comprehension need not be delayed until children have acquired reading vocabularies. What has been proposed for listening can get started before reading instruction begins and can be continued while the children's reading ability is just coming into existence. It should also be kept in mind that what has been described for listening comprehension can be adapted later to help with comprehending written text.

How one second-grade teacher progressed from listening to reading comprehension is described below in a journal entry:

> Moving from listening comprehension activities to reading comprehension seemed like a suggestion worth trying with my poorest readers. I

wanted to work on how authors reveal characters' feelings, so I started by reading passages from stories that allowed for discussions related to that topic. I did this for about ten minutes on five successive days.

On the sixth, I switched to simply written paragraphs that I composed. I reminded the children that each was to be read to learn how a person or an animal felt about something. The brief passages were distributed one at a time and read silently over a two-day period. A discussion of character feelings followed the reading of each selection, during which the children were always asked to justify their answers. Often, a justification provided valuable diagnostic information. One boy's misinterpretation of a character's feelings, for example, was due to a misunderstanding of the meaning of one word. Justifying answers also helped the children see how the thoughts of others in the group led to a correct (or an incorrect) conclusion.

I felt that using a listening comprehension activity to begin was beneficial, because it allowed the children to experience success at the start. When that occurs, they are more receptive to the rest of the instruction. Since the children in this low reading group are more easily discouraged than most of the others in my class, I was especially happy with that result. I think they also learned about the ways in which authors indicate how characters feel about something.

READING COMPREHENSION: EXAMPLES OF INSTRUCTION

Earlier in this chapter, when some of the topics for comprehension instruction were identified, one was sequence. The comprehension instruction to be described initially deals with that. The description is meant, first, to explain that many objectives of comprehension instruction require attention not just once but over a period of time and, second, to reinforce the fact that some objectives can receive attention before children are able to read.

The objective that guides what is suggested for prereaders has to do with developing an understanding both of sequence and of words that signal the order of events. How the same objective continues to get attention when children have the beginnings of a reading vocabulary is dealt with next. After that, a more structured type of lesson is described.

At the Beginning

Young children's interest in themselves, thus in something like their birthdays, makes it easy and natural to initiate attention to sequence with a birthday time line that begins with August (or whenever school begins). An example is shown in Figure 13.4. Over a period of a school year, the array of birthdays coupled with questions about their occurrence can be used to help children understand sequence itself and to highlight words that provide sequence cues—for example, *first, last, before, after, at the beginning,* and *close to the end.*

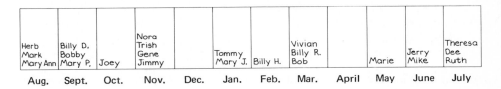

Aug.	Sept.	Oct.	Nov.	Dec.	Jan.	Feb.	Mar.	April	May	June	July
Herb Mark Mary Ann	Billy D. Bobby Mary P.	Joey	Nora Trish Gene Jimmy		Tommy Mary J.	Billy H.	Vivian Billy R. Bob		Marie	Jerry Mike	Theresa Dee Ruth

Figure 13.4

Some of what is read to children offers further opportunities to deal with both sequence and related words. If children know the episodes in *The Three Bears,* for instance, they can act them out after their order has been discussed with teacher-prompts coming from signal words like *first, after that, later on,* and *finally.*

Even pictures can help prereaders think in relation to sequential events (18). After a picture showing children in muddy clothes has been discussed, it can be the focus for the question, "What do you suppose happened before this picture was taken?" Subsequent probing might include: "What do you suppose will happen now that their clothes are dirty? For instance, what do you think will happen when they get home?" Since the concern of the discussion is for sequence, it is important to conclude with the teacher summarizing: "First the children fell in a puddle. When they got up, their clothes were dirty. After they got home, they got a spanking. Then they went in the tub."

As soon as cue words for sequence make their way into children's reading vocabularies, text like the one in Figure 13.5 can highlight them.

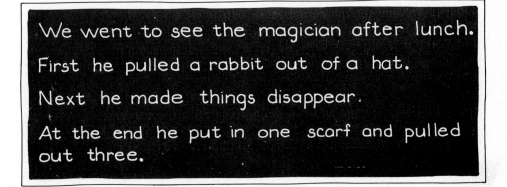

We went to see the magician after lunch.
First he pulled a rabbit out of a hat.
Next he made things disappear.
At the end he put in one scarf and pulled out three.

Figure 13.5

The following questions from the teacher served as prompts for composing the account of the magician's tricks:

When did we go to see the magician?
What was the very first thing he did?
What did he do next?
What did the magician do at the end?

Additional questions like those listed below are necessary, given the reason for composing the text about the magician:

In the first line, what words tell *when* we went?
What word tells *when* the magician pulled the rabbit out of the hat?
What words tells *when* he made things disappear?
What words tell *when* he used the scarves?

Further attention can go to *after lunch*, *first*, *next*, and *at the end* when children illustrate not only what they saw the magician do but also when they saw him do it, with the help of paper sectioned and captioned in the way shown in Figure 13.6.

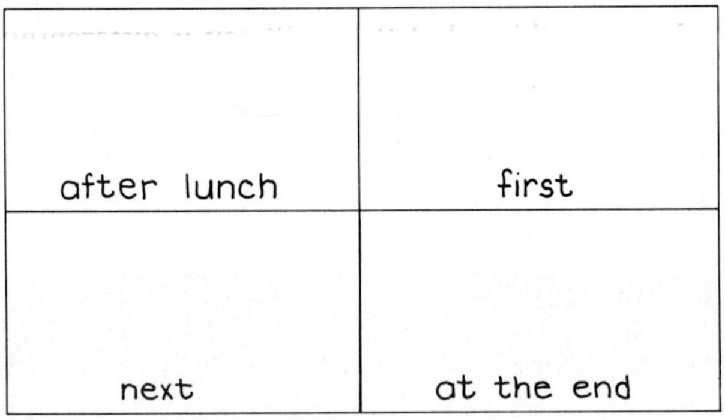

after lunch	first
next	at the end

Figure 13.6

Later On

Once children's reading vocabularies expand, much more can be done to help them keep track of sequence revealed in text. One possibility follows.

LESSON DEALING WITH SEQUENCE

Objective: Children will use what they know as a way of helping themselves follow a sequence of events when what happened first is not stated first. (For the sake of brevity, a limited number of single sentences will be used. In reality, the use of sentences would be followed by the use of paragraphs, since comprehenders have to be able to integrate the meaning of separate sentences even when they are relative beginners.)

Review: Wisely, the teacher starts with a review of what was taught earlier, using sentences like those listed below, in which what happened first appears first. The same two questions (What happened first? What happened next?) are asked for each sentence, after it is read silently by the instructional group and then orally by an individual.

> The children ate their dinner and went to bed.
>
> Blackie ran to the window and barked.
>
> When John came inside, he took off his cap.

Instruction: Following the brief review, instruction begins: "In the three sentences you just read, what happened first came first in the sentence. But that isn't the way it always is. Sometimes, what happened first may be told last. Let me show you that by writing these three sentences in a different way. They will say the same thing, but they will say it differently:

> The children went to bed after eating their dinner.
>
> Blackie barked after running to the window.
>
> John took off his cap when he came inside.

"Read the first sentence silently. . . . What did the children do first? . . . What's mentioned first in the sentence? . . . What word in this sentence helped you to decide what came first? . . . Yes, *after*. In this sentence, *after* is a very important word. It lets you know *when* the two things that the children did happened. It tells you it was *after* eating that they went to bed."

The teacher follows similar procedures for the next two sentences, after which she shifts to using world knowledge for comprehending. She begins: "Sometimes, what you know will tell you when things happened. For instance, I bet all of you at one time or another have gotten sore eyes from watching too much television. Right? . . . I thought so. See how that helps with the sentence I'm going to write:

(continued)

Anne's eyes hurt from watching too much T.V.

"Based on the times when *your* eyes hurt, what came first — the sore eyes or too much television? . . . Sure, watching television, and yet the sore eyes are mentioned first in the sentence."

To sum up, the teacher says, "Remember, when you're reading a sentence that tells about things happening at different times, don't take it for granted that what happened first is mentioned first. Think about what the sentence says *and* what you know before deciding what happened first and what came next."

Supervised Practice: To learn whether the children have profited from the instruction, the teacher continues: "I've written some sentences on this chart [Figure 13.7]. Each sentence tells about two things. Think what the two things are. Then let us know which happened first. Read the first sentence to yourself.

```
1. The bus left before the people came.

2. My picture broke when it fell from the wall.

3. The game started once the children arrived.

4. They ate all the candy and were sick.
```

Figure 13.7

"This sentence tells you two different things. What does it say first? . . . Yes, let me write that. . . . What else does it tell you? . . . I'll write that, too. . . . Now, what came first? Did the bus leave first, or did the people come first? . . . Yes, the bus left *before* the people came."

Now the top of the chart looks like Figure 13.8.

```
1. The bus left before the people came.

   The bus left. ①
   The people came. ②
```

Figure 13.8

Independent Practice: Once the teacher feels fairly confident (based on the guided practice) that the children understand (a) that what happens first may or may not be mentioned first; (b) that words may be available that tell the order in which things happened; and (c) that their experiences may be helpful in deciding what occurred first, it is time for independent, written practice. For this, sentences from something like a basal reader or sentences composed by a teacher can be used. (When·children know that the sentences are from published texts, the value of what they are doing is more apparent.) Again, children will be asked to write under each listed sentence the two things it said and to indicate which of the two occurred first and which came later. Or, a written assignment might have the children underline what a sentence tells and show the sequence with numbers:

The flowers opened when the sun came out.
      ②   ①

Application: The instruction just described for sequence is preparation for later attention to flashback. Natural application, therefore, includes having children themselves read a story that includes a recollection of the past by one or more characters. Two stories include:

Hall, Lynn. *Megan's Mare.* New York: Charles Scribner's Sons, 1983.
Jukes, Mavis, and Bloom, Lloyd. *No One Is Going to Nashville.* New York: Alfred A. Knopf, 1983.

Even though the number of easy books that include a flashback is limited, many are available that younger children can comprehend if the stories are read to them. Some books in the latter category are:

Konigsburg, Elaine L. *Father's Arcane Daughter.* New York: Atheneum, 1976.
Saint-Exupery, Antoine de. *The Little Prince.* New York: Harcourt, Brace and World, 1943.
Voigt, Cynthia. *Building Blocks.* New York: Atheneum, 1984.

A similar type of application is appropriate for many topics covered in comprehension lessons. Attention to exaggeration, for example, may be initiated by using sentences (e.g., *The meal was so filling they didn't want to eat again for a month.*) but can end with tall tales, many of which children with limited reading ability can read themselves. For instance:

(continued)

Rounds, Glen. *Mr. Yowder and the Train Robbers.* New York: Holiday House, 1981.

Rounds, Glen. *Mr. Yowder and the Windwagon.* New York: Holiday House, 1983.

Sleator, William. *Once, Said Darlene.* New York: E. P. Dutton, 1979.

Slightly more difficult tall tales that can be read to younger children include:

Fleischman, Sid. *McBroom the Rainmaker.* New York: Grosset and Dunlap, Inc., 1973.

Fleischman, Sid. *McBroom and the Great Race.* Boston: Little, Brown and Company, 1980.

MORE COMPREHENSION INSTRUCTION

Since authors commonly use pronoun referents in easy text, a lesson focusing on *some* serves as the last example of comprehension instruction.

LESSON DEALING WITH A PRONOUN REFERENT

Objective: Children will know that *some* may stand for one or more words.

Review: Having taught other pronoun referents (*they, she, he,* and *it*), the teacher starts the lesson by reviewing them. (The attention *they* receives illustrates how the other pronouns are reviewed.)

When the instructional group arrives at the reading area, the children see a sentence on the board referring to two classmates:

Scott and Paula aren't in school today.

Once the group reads the sentence silently, a volunteer reads it aloud, after which the teacher comments, "If I wanted to say something else about Scott and Paula, I could write it two different ways." Soon, two more sentences are on the board:

Scott and Paula aren't in school today.

Scott and Paula are sick.

They are sick.

The teacher continues, "Which do you like better? 'Scott and Paula aren't in school today. Scott and Paula are sick' or 'Scott and Paula aren't in school today. They are sick.' " Since the monotony of repetitious words was discussed earlier in connection with other pronouns, one child quickly expresses a preference for the second version and the reason for it. Next the teacher asks, "To whom does the word 'They' refer? . . . Yes, it takes the place of the words 'Scott and Paula.' "

The teacher continues, "We've talked about words other than *they* that can take the place of something else." This is followed by a quick review of *she*, *he*, and *it*.

Instruction: To initiate attention to *some*, the teacher prints it on the board and immediately hears "some" in response to her question, "What does this say?" She continues: "Like the other words we've been talking about this morning, 'some' may stand for other words. You'll see that at times it does and at times it doesn't, with the help of sentences I've written." Dittoed lists of eight paired sentences are distributed, starting with:

> All the children are in school.
> Some shouldn't be here because they have colds.
>
> The lady had a lot of packages.
> We carried some for her.

Each pair of sentences is discussed in ways that show, first, how *some* often means that a word has been omitted and, second, that readers must know what the missing word is if they are going to understand the meaning of a sentence.

To discourage overgeneralizing, the teacher concludes the lesson by demonstrating with sentences written on the second side of the dittoed sheets that the presence of *some* does not always mean a word has been left out (e.g., *Some paper is on the floor.*).

Supervised Practice: To see whether the children understand when *some* stands for one or more other words and when it does not, another sheet with paired sentences is distributed and discussed. The list starts as follows:

> The rain fell hard last night.
> Some got in our basement.
>
> The rain fell hard last night.
> Some basements got wet.

Independent Practice: To see whether the objective of the lesson was realized, an assignment sheet listing further pairs of sentences is distributed and explained. The job for the children to do on their own is illustrated below:

(continued)

I found coins in the parking lot.   The firefighters can't leave.

I also found ~~some~~ in the snow.   Some trees are still burning.
      coins

Application: The lesson just described preceded an assignment to read a basal selection in which *some* appears in three sentences, serving twice as a pronoun referent and once as an adjective. The sentences will be examined in the postreading discussion of the selection, allowing the teacher to make explicit the reason for the earlier work with *some*.

ADDITIONAL COMMENTS ABOUT COMPREHENSION INSTRUCTION

The comprehension lessons described should not only make the content of Figure 13.2 more meaningful but also help differentiate between teaching comprehension and testing comprehension. Achieving the second purpose is particularly necessary because of widespread confusion between the two. It is still thought by some teachers and authors of materials, for example, that asking assessment questions is the way to "develop" comprehension abilities. (See Figure 13.9 and the commentary about it.) While questions typically figure in a comprehension lesson—especially during the instruction and supervised practice components—questions that help teach comprehension and questions that assess it are different. The difference is illustrated below with text that has pronoun referents, since that topic is featured earlier in a lesson.

> A spider must be in the house. It made a web here.

What made the web? . . . [Assessing]

What made the web? . . . The word "house" is closer to "it" than to "spider." How did you know the word "it" was referring to the spider and not to the house? . . . [Instructing]

> Carole and her brother are shopping. She has the money.

Who has the money? . . . [Assessing]

Who has the money? . . . Why do you know that it is Carole and not her brother who has it? . . . [Instructing]

Anyone who wants to use questions in ways that will be instructive avoids what is sometimes found in classrooms (9, 10): Teachers ask a question until someone responds correctly, after which another question is posed and the same procedure follows. Instructors naturally want to know whether a response is right or wrong, but that should be only one of the concerns. At least as <u>important are the reasons that lie behind</u> responses, right *or* wrong.

WHEN SHOULD COMPREHENSION INSTRUCTION BE OFFERED?

As acknowledged in the previous chapter, teachers must plan carefully and work hard to try to do all that can be done to give children every opportunity to become the best readers they are capable of being. In the past, comprehension instruction was uncommon (10) primarily because of the assumption that asking postreading assessment questions was enough to develop comprehension abilities. Now that clearer distinctions have been made between teaching comprehension and assessing it, teachers have a serious responsibility to provide comprehension instruction with both preplanned lessons and on-the-spot help. In either form, only what can be applied in what children are reading merits attention.

Preplanned Lessons

As Figure 13.1 shows, comprehension instruction can be scheduled either before or after children read a selection. Prereading instruction is called for if a feature of the text is likely to cause problems, if something like the use of a flashback occurs for the first time or, for instance, if the selection includes one or more unusual uses of language.

Prereading comprehension instruction seemed to be called for in a recent observation in a second grade when a group was assigned a basal story about a boy from South America whose new North American classmates laughed at him because of his literal interpretation of English idioms. Even though the manual made no such suggestion, this seemed like a perfect time for a prereading lesson on literal versus figurative uses of language like the one described in the previous chapter. (In this case, the importance of essential background information indicated a need for clarifying that non-native speakers usually have problems with idioms; again, however, nothing was said about that in the manual.)

Regardless of what manuals do or do not suggest, postreading comprehension lessons are sometimes preferable, as they allow for learning whether instruction is necessary. A selection about UFO's, for instance, is likely to provide text for a lesson on words that signal facts (e.g., "There is evidence to support. . . .") and words that signal opinions (e.g., "Some believe that. . . .").

Figure 13.9. *Assessment That Is Said to Be Instruction*

This page is from a series of workbooks for grades 1 through 3. Even though
the title of each workbook starts with "Lessons in . . ." and even though the
theme running through the Introduction to all the workbooks is "Teaching Reading Comprehension," the materials only provide a variety of ways for assessing
comprehension. Suggested procedures include requests like:

Write titles for "stories" (paragraphs).
Answer questions about details.
Fill in a word to complete unfinished sentences.
Select the main idea of a "story" from several possibilites listed.
Write endings for "stories."
Number columns of sentences in an order that matches the sequence of
events in "stories."

The page reproduced in Figure 13.9 follows a one-page selection called "The
Three-Legged Chicken" that tells of a girl named Carla who ate three chicken
legs for dinner. Since her mother had bought but one package of chicken,
Carla starts wondering about the number of legs that chickens have. Why a
child would have to seek help from five different sources before learning that
whoever packaged the chicken put in three instead of two legs is puzzling. In
any case, the questions shown in Figure 13.9 are about that quest. For any
who may wonder, the Answer Key states that "Carla solves a three-legged mystery" is the main idea.

402

1. Draw a line from the chicken to the main idea of the story.

Meat packers are not very careful.

Carla solves a three-legged mystery.

Some chickens have three legs.

2. Who was the first person Carla asked about finding a chicken?
_____
_____
_____
_____

3. Where would you go to find a chicken?
_____
_____
_____
_____

4. Who answered Carla's question about three legs?
_____
_____
_____
_____

5. Do you think a chicken could have three legs?   **yes   no**

Knowing that the instructional group understands the meaning of *fact* and *opinion* (as a result of instruction like that referred to in the previous chapter), a teacher may decide to postpone attention to the signal words until evidence shows up in the postreading discussion of the UFO selection that supports either the need, or the lack of need, for a formal lesson. To allow for evidence to surface, the teacher will make certain that some questions she poses can be answered only if the ways in which facts and opinions are indicated are understood. Even if they *are* understood, the instructional group should return to relevant parts of the text at some point in the discussion to examine each use of signal words. Ideally, and as soon as possible after the selection about UFO's was read, one or more additional selections should be assigned in which authors also signal factual statements and opinions with certain expressions. Again, this allows for application that makes the value of what a teacher is doing maximally apparent to students.

On-the-Spot Help

When teachers take the time to probe in order to learn *why* children respond in a given way, the need for help with comprehending may become clear. With children who are relative beginners, assistance is often required for processing as few as one or two sentences. Or, an erroneous response to a question may point to the need for help with adverb referents—for help with sentences like: *Tom's father shoveled the driveway so that Tom could leave his bicycle there.* An answer to another question might identify problems in processing sentences that have a compound subject, or a compound verb, or both.

If prior instruction covered the use of commas to separate words in a series, a teacher might choose to use some postreading time having children read aloud sentences from the selection in order to see whether they pause when a comma signals that a pause is required. If a problem is identified, on-the-spot help may center on the oral reading of paired sentences like those referred to in Chapter 6:

> Joan, Sue Anne, and I walked to school.
>
> Joan, Sue, Anne, and I walked to school.

Once the oral reading is done and the function of commas reviewed, it is time to return to the selection in which the problem was originally identified in order to make certain that the children see the connection between the oral reading of paired sentences and the use of commas in the selection.

The point of all these illustrations is that children's responses may indicate the need for a particular kind of comprehension instruction or, perhaps, for a review of what was taught earlier. On such occasions, there is no better time than the present to try to resolve the problem. This on-the-spot help, coupled with planned lessons for direct, explicit instruction, make a significant contribution to helping children realize their potential insofar as reading is concerned (5).

COMPREHENSION PRACTICE

As mentioned in this and other chapters, preplanned lessons based on specific objectives start with instruction offered in a way that lets children know both what is to be taught and why it is important for reading.

Two kinds of practice ought to follow instruction. The first, guided or teacher-supervised practice, allows for monitoring children's responses and also is the time when a teacher provides feedback so children know how well (or poorly) they are doing.

Children working on their own constitutes the second type of practice. When this independent work is written, a teacher is free to give time to another instructional group or to individuals. For that reason, the samples of practice that follow are almost all of written practice.

Samples of Practice

The fact that time should not be spent on trivial details hardly eliminates the need to comprehend important details. The initial samples of practice, therefore, focus on details.

- For a free-choice activity for beginners, pictures and question cards can be put in an attractively decorated box. Sorting the pictures is done by considering the details of the questions, which might ask: Which pictures show something you can eat? Which pictures show something that is alive? Which pictures are of something you like to do?
- Write paragraphs that describe the content of pictures. (Difficulty should correspond to reading abilities.) Children match each paragraph with the picture it describes.
- Prepare three cards, each with a slightly larger opening (see Figure 13.10). Write a sentence on each that tells something about a detail in a picture.

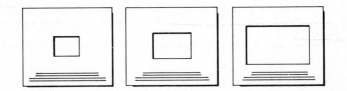

Figure 13.10

Lay the card with the smallest opening over that picture. Direct children to read silently the "hint" printed on the card and to guess what the picture is. If nobody responds correctly, repeat the procedure with the next card, and then with the third one if necessary.

Ideas for practice in recognizing central themes are described next. The first two are for children who know that titles often name themes or subjects.

- Select or write paragraphs, each dealing with a different theme. (Some can be found in old workbooks.) Distribute copies to an instructional group. Give each group member two small cards, one displaying *1*, the other *2*. Have children first read a paragraph silently to see what it is generally about. Afterward, display a card showing two titles, each numbered. (Unlike authors of commercial workbooks and texts, do not make one title so obviously incorrect that the correct one can be chosen through the process of elimination.)
- Attach some fairly short newspaper articles (minus titles) to a sheet of oak tag. Duplicate as many copies as will be needed for a group working on central themes via titles. Clip the directions shown in Figure 13.11 to each copy:

```
Directions:
Read each article so that you can write a title for it.  Write
titles below.  Later, we'll compare your titles with those that
were in the newspaper.
```

Figure 13.11

- Write paragraphs so that each one includes a sentence that does not relate to the topic of the paragraph. Children will be asked to draw a line through all such sentences for the purpose of reminding them that reading is making sense out of written text.

Two facts that are relevant for teachers working with beginners in reading have been illustrated several times: (a) Even easy material may require inferences, and (b) short sentences may be difficult to comprehend because of their implied content. To help children see that sometimes they have to add to what an author writes, a written assignment like the one in Figure 13.12 is beneficial.

Just as short, dense sentences are difficult for beginners to process, so are long, embellished ones. To help with the latter, a practice assignment like the one in Figure 13.13 can be given.

```
I spent the whole day shopping.  My sister did, too.
   Below, tell what the sister did.



One tree was tall.  The other was the opposite.
   Below, tell what the second tree was like.



Mary is quiet.  So is her brother.
   Below, tell what this says about Mary's brother.
```

Figure 13.12

```
That new blue car parked near the truck is mine.

   That _____ is mine.

The boy living in that old house on the hill is sick.

   The _____ is sick.
```

Figure 13.13

Sentences like *The town was flooded by the rain* (passive voice) are more difficult to comprehend than sentences like *The rain flooded the town* (active voice). When instruction focuses on the two types of sentences, practice like that shown in Figure 13.14 is appropriate.

```
The girls were followed home by the dog.

   The _____ followed the _____.

Our barn was struck by lightning.

   _____ struck our _____.
```

Figure 13.14

As stated earlier, reading fiction requires knowing that authors sometimes reveal the traits of characters indirectly. The practice shown in Figure 13.15 relates to that need. As with all practice, the text should be difficult enough to provide challenge but not so difficult that children cannot do the work independently.

```
He wanted the candy, but his sister wanted it, too.  He let
her have it.

                selfish.
This boy is  kind.
                loud.

They kept the dog tied up.  To keep people from getting hurt,
they posted the sign, DOG.  KEEP OUT.

                gentle.
This dog is  friendly.
                fierce.
```

Figure 13.15

Concluding Comments about Practice

The samples of practice just described exemplify what teachers themselves can devise. Additional kinds of practice can be selected from workbooks and other commercially prepared sources.

As with instruction itself, decisions about the nature of practice should be guided by objectives. For practice, answers to two questions identify what needs to be done: What is essential for comprehending? From among the essentials, what do these children need to learn or improve?

When decisions about practice are being made, the most important kind of practice should not be overlooked: uninterrupted reading of self-selected material.

SUMMARY

Since this textbook is for teachers of young children, descriptions of procedures that help with comprehension included the use of purposeful listening. Getting under way before children are able to read, listening activities can be continued while they are acquiring reading ability. Listening activities are even suitable for older children with reading problems, because they allow such children to experience success. The same activities can also be used to emphasize that reading, like listening, has to do with getting and constructing messages. Since all the activities proposed in Chapter 13 for listening comprehension can be adapted for reading, they offer a natural transition between the two.

To help clarify the meaning of "teaching reading comprehension," the chapter divided teachers' responsibilities into three categories: (a) facilitating comprehension, (b) teaching comprehension, and (c) testing comprehension. Such a division neither minimizes the significance of background information for comprehending nor does it question the need for assessment. Instead, the categories were introduced both to make distinctions among the three responsibilities and to underscore the need to *teach* children *how* to comprehend. The latter purpose was chosen because comprehension instruction is offered less frequently and regularly than ought to be the case.

Chapter 13 continued by naming some topics for comprehension lessons. Those topics named were mostly concerned with features of text (e.g., referents, cohesive ties, complex sentence structure) and special uses of language (simile, figurative expression, hyperbole) that may be obstacles to comprehending written discourse.

To specify still further what it means to teach comprehension, several lessons were described. In addition to illustrating instruction, the lessons were meant to remind teachers (a) to let children know what it is that they are trying to teach, and (b) to make sure that the children understand how what is being taught relates to becoming better readers. The lessons were also included to make the point that some topics need to be covered more than once—that is, at different levels of difficulty and complexity—and, in addition, that the most effective lessons include instruction, guided and independent practice, and—last but not least—application.

The chapter's emphasis on teaching comprehension is in no way a denial of the fact that many children learn quite a bit on their own about comprehending. Rather, Chapter 13 is intended to highlight the strong likelihood that if more direct, explicit instruction were provided than is now typical, more children would be successful readers—that is, better comprehenders.

REVIEW

1. As specifically as possible, point out the differences between facilitating comprehension and teaching comprehension.

2. Explain each detail of the following observation:

   When text is familiar lexically, structurally, and experientially, comprehension is likely to occur automatically. Otherwise, effort is required. If too much is unfamiliar, not even effort is likely to help.

3. Research data suggest that poor readers, when compared with better

ones, are less aware of what it means to comprehend. How could a request to children to draw the details of a picture based on the sentence shown below be used to help them understand some of what successful comprehension requires?

He is painting the ceiling.

Before responding, list the details that might be in the requested picture. This will help you to be specific in your response.

4. Explain the following statement: "Reading is a purposeful pursuit." What is the implication of this definition of reading for (a) rate of reading, and (b) comprehension assessment?

5. One essential component of every lesson, regardless of its objective, is application. What *is* "application" and why is it important?

6. Chapter 13 pointed out that referents and cohesive ties are two topics that are suitable for comprehension instruction.
   a. What is meant by "referents"? Pronoun\ Adverbs   They\ That Some
   b. What are "cohesive ties"? meaning one sentence(s)\ closely related to next
   Use the following text to add specificity to your answers:
   The children can hardly wait to get there. It is their favorite park. Now they are getting ready for the picnic. Two are making lemonade, because it is a warm day. Another is looking for games that they can play when they get there.

7. Questions commonly function in assessing comprehension. Questions are often needed, too, for instruction. Give one example of an assessment question for the paragraph about the children going to the park. What is an example of a question about the paragraph that is instructive and thus might be posed during a comprehension lesson?

REFERENCES

1. Baker, Deborah T. "What Happened When?" *Reading Teacher* 36 (November, 1982), 216–218.
2. Baldwin, R. Scott; Luce, Terrence S.; and Readance, John E. "The Impact of Subschemata on Metaphorical Processing." *Reading Research Quarterly* 17 (1982, No. 4), 528–543.
3. Barnitz, John G. "Syntactic Effect on the Reading Comprehension of Pronoun-Referent Structures by Children in Grades Two, Four, and Six." *Reading Research Quarterly* 15 (1980, No. 2), 268–289.
4. Baumann, James F. "The Effectiveness of a Direct Instruction Paradigm for Teaching Main Idea Comprehension." *Reading Research Quarterly* 20 (Fall, 1984), 93–115.
5. Berliner, D. C. "Academic Learning Time and Reading Achievement." In J. T.

Guthrie (Ed.), *Comprehension and Teaching: Research Reviews.* Newark, Del.: International Reading Association, 1981.

6. Blatt, Gloria T. "Playing with Language." *Reading Teacher* 31 (February, 1978), 487–493.

7. Boodt, Gloria M. "Critical Listeners Become Critical Readers in Remedial Reading Class." *Reading Teacher* 37 (January, 1984), 390–394.

8. Brown, Ann L. "Learning How to Learn from Reading." In J. Langer and M. Smith-Burke (Eds.), *Reader Meets Author: Bridging the Gap.* Newark, Del.: International Reading Association, 1982.

9. Durkin, Dolores. "Is There a Match between What Elementary Teachers Do and What Basal Reader Manuals Recommend?" *Reading Teacher* 37 (April, 1984), 734–744.

10. Durkin, Dolores. "What Classroom Observations Reveal about Comprehension Instruction." *Reading Research Quarterly* 14 (1978–79, No. 4), 481–533.

11. Golinkoff, Roberta M. "A Comparison of Reading Comprehension Processes in Good and Poor Comprehenders." *Reading Research Quarterly* 11 (1975–76, No. 4), 623–659.

12. Jorgensen, C. C., and Kintsch, Walter. "The Role of Imagery in the Evaluation of Sentences." *Cognitive Psychology* 4 (January, 1973), 110–116.

13. Kachuck, Beatrice. "Relative Clauses May Cause Confusion for Young Readers." *Reading Teacher* 34 (January, 1981), 372–377.

14. McIntosh, Margaret E. "What Do Practitioners Need to Know about Current Inference Research?" *Reading Teacher* 38 (April, 1985), 755–761.

15. Mathewson, Grover C. "Teaching Forms of Negation in Reading and Reasoning." *Reading Teacher* 37 (January, 1984), 354–358.

16. Morgan, Argiro L. "Context: The Web of Meaning." *Language Arts* 60 (March, 1983), 305–314.

17. Pearson, P. David, and Fielding, Linda. "Research Update: Listening Comprehension." *Language Arts* 59 (September, 1982), 617–619.

18. Policastro, Margaret M. "What's Happening: Predicting before, during, and after the Picture." *Reading Teacher* 38 (May, 1985), 929.

19. Richek, Margaret Ann. "Reading Comprehension of Anaphoric Forms in Varying Linguistic Contexts." *Reading Research Quarterly* 12 (1976–77, No. 2), 145–165.

20. Rode, Sara S. "Development of Phrase and Clause Boundary Reading in Children." *Reading Research Quarterly* 10 (1974–75, No. 1) 124–142.

21. Steiner, Robert; Wiener, Morton; and Cramer, Ward. "Comprehension Training and Identification for Poor and Good Readers." *Journal of Educational Psychology* 62 (December, 1971), 506–513.

22. Strange, Michael. "Instructional Implications of a Conceptual Theory of Reading Comprehension." *Reading Teacher* 33 (January, 1980), 391–397.

23. Wilson, Cathy R. "Teaching Reading Comprehension by Connecting the Known to the New." *Reading Teacher* 36 (January, 1983), 382–390.

PART IV
Instructional Materials

"Too many to count" is one justifiable response to the question, "Thus far in this book, how many references have been made to instructional materials?" In spite of the generous coverage, two points about materials are sufficiently important to warrant their being repeated.

The first has to do with the conception of "instructional material" that underlies the numerous references: anything that displays words. Within this framework, teachers do not allow textbooks to block their view of all kinds of other materials that have instructional value—trade books, newspapers, maps, magazines, bulletin boards, greeting cards, stamps, letters, pamphlets, catalogues, telephone directories, calendars, television commercials, bumper stickers, timetables, pencils, recipes, menus, coupons, road signs, and labeled boxes, packages, bottles, and cans. The use of a wide variety of materials is desirable, first, to allow for the development of the full range of reading abilities; second, to make it easier for students to see the practical value of what occurs in school under the rubric "teaching reading"; and third, to eliminate the boredom that is inevitable when something like a basal reader series is all that is used.

In case the reference to boredom encourages anyone to conclude that variety for the sake of variety has just been endorsed, the second important point about materials is made: Any given material merits being used only if it helps a teacher achieve a maximum of individualized instruction. "Good" materials thus function as a means for attaining objectives that reflect children's needs. The latter may range from "need to acquire an interest in reading" to something like, "need to learn that hyperbole characterizes advertisements."

The means-end relationship between materials and objectives might have brought to mind the contrast made in Chapter 2 between Teacher A and Teacher B. You recall that what makes the two distinctly different is that Teacher A uses materials to achieve pre-established objectives, whereas materials use Teacher B in the sense that she allows them to define not only objectives but also the means for attaining them.

Regardless of how materials do function, they play a sufficiently major role in all instructional programs that two chapters are allotted them. The purpose of the first, Chapter 14, is to provide information about a professional use as opposed to a dependent use of a basal reader series. Chapter 15 covers other kinds of materials. For readers of this book who do not participate in the use of a basal program, Chapter 15 can be considered an extension of Chapter 5, "A Beginning Literacy Program." For those who use, or expect to use, a basal series, Chapter 15 serves to show how other materials can—and should— supplement basal programs.

CHAPTER 14

Basal Reader Materials

PREVIEW

An indisputable fact accounts for allotting an entire chapter to basal materials: They enjoy unique influence over what goes on in elementary classrooms to teach reading. Such influence is hardly new (3, 25), and there is no reason to expect it to decrease in the immediate future.

Since flaws in basal series have been discussed, you may wonder why these materials persist in being—as someone once put it—the big gun in the educational arsenal insofar as reading is concerned. Actually, answers vary, depending on who is responding. Teachers often say, for instance, that principals take the use of basal materials for granted (26). Conversations with administrators, in turn, underscore the belief that a basal program ensures the delivery of instruction, which is an interesting explanation given the fact that studies show that basal manual suggestions deal far more frequently with practice and assessment than with instruction (12, 13). Complementing those studies are others that have identified numerous shortcomings in such sources of practice as basal workbooks and ditto masters (23).

Researchers offer still other explanations for the widespread influence of basal programs. Gerald Duffy, for example, links their popularity with teachers' worries about classroom management and the possibility of "losing control" (10). The proposed connection lies in the fact that basal materials are viewed as an important means for keeping children moving from one activity to another. One unfortunate consequence of the desire for a smooth flow of activities, Duffy says, is that teachers are oriented more toward covering material than teaching children.

What cannot be omitted from the picture drawn thus far is the need for a reading program that is coordinated from grade to grade within a school. Even though the many pieces that constitute each basal series hardly add up to the carefully orchestrated whole that many assume exists (13), school personnel commonly depend on a basal program to provide coordinated efforts if only because they view alternatives to be either nonexistent or out of reach.

Whatever the reasons, basal materials are found practically everywhere. The question that needs to be addressed, therefore, is, "How can they function in the best possible ways?" This question guides the development of Chapter 14.

With the help of Figure 14.1, let's start the chapter with a brief overview of the components of a basal reader series. Additional comments follow.

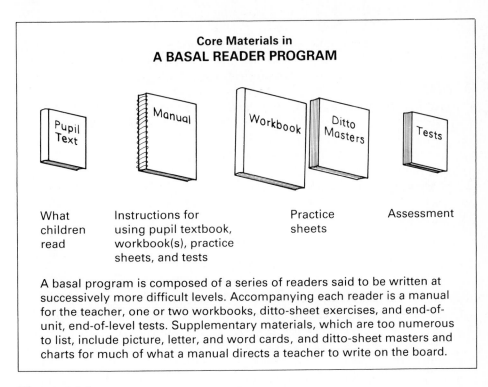

Core Materials in
A BASAL READER PROGRAM

Pupil Text	Manual	Workbook / Ditto Masters	Tests
What children read	Instructions for using pupil textbook, workbook(s), practice sheets, and tests	Practice sheets	Assessment

A basal program is composed of a series of readers said to be written at successively more difficult levels. Accompanying each reader is a manual for the teacher, one or two workbooks, ditto-sheet exercises, and end-of-unit, end-of-level tests. Supplementary materials, which are too numerous to list, include picture, letter, and word cards, and ditto-sheet masters and charts for much of what a manual directs a teacher to write on the board.

Figure 14.1

BASAL READER PROGRAMS: GENERAL COMMENTS

Currently, about seventeen basal reader programs are available. At any given time, three or four will be the best sellers. Careful scrutiny by competitors of the most popular series, along with such factors as worry about being too different, tend to make all the programs look more similar than dissimilar.

Unquestionably, one similarity is the special importance now assigned to assessment. This is a direct consequence of two related factors: (a) vocal critics of the schools, and (b) the tendency of the public in general and of school boards in particular to equate success in reading with high test scores— regardless of the quality of the test. To foster satisfactory scores by the children using their programs, most publishers spend considerable amounts of money and time to learn about the content of the most frequently used reading tests and, in turn, to ensure that their materials cover the same topics.

Because of everybody's interest in assessment instruments that computers can score, it is now difficult to find a test that uses anything but a multiple-choice format. This is the case even though such testing encourages guessing and excludes to a great degree the possibility of assessing what is most significant for successful reading.

Another obvious similarity among basal programs is their publishers' attempts to make the readers maximally attractive. Such efforts reflect the interest of textbook selection committees in this part of a series. Although each selection in a basal reader is commonly thought to be the central focus of a basal lesson, that is not necessarily the case. Instead, a sizable amount of the instruction and practice recommended in manuals has little or nothing to do with what the children are, or will soon be, reading. As a result, the various components of a basal program do not add up to the carefully integrated package that some people assume a program to be (11).

Since it also is a commonly held belief that the difficulty of each reader in a series is controlled in some scientifically reliable way, it is time to deal with the concept *readability*.

READABILITY

Readability, as suggested, refers to the difficulty of a piece of text. Text a beginner can manage has a lower readability level than a passage comprehensible only to an individual with more advanced ability.

Starting as early as the 1920s, formulas have been available to measure readability. Even though the details of each differ, all the formulas assume that: (a) a word is difficult if it has more than one syllable, or does not appear on some list of commonly used words; and (b) the difficulty of comprehending a sentence is directly related to the number of words it contains. (See Figure 14.2 and the commentary about it.)

Because of their interest in having materials that match student abilities, textbook selection committees have traditionally required publishers of basal programs to furnish data derived from a formula that describe the readability levels of samples of selections from each of their readers. (This has been the practice even though studies have shown that the difficulty of the selections that make up a reader varies, sometimes substantially [5, 9].) One effect of requests for readability information is especially apparent in the easiest readers. Wanting to please both the customers who expect good literature and the customers who will reject a series if the difficulty of the selections is not to their liking, those responsible for preparing beginning readers commonly water down good stories by substituting easy words for difficult words and short sentences for long sentences. Even though linguists have demonstrated that such adaptations usually make a selection more, not less, difficult to understand (8), interest in having readability data persists. The persistence is just one of the reasons the customer must assume responsibility for some of the shortcomings in basal programs. The same persistence also underscores the need for textbook selection committees to be composed of knowledgeable individuals who have enough time to use what they know to make the best choice.

Anyone who has read the previous chapter should be sufficiently knowledgeable to understand why counting syllables and words is not the most accurate way to determine the difficulty of text. Factors like the following, which do not lend themselves to being quantified for use in a formula, are of greater significance:

Degree of cohesion in the text
Number and clarity of referents
Number and complexity of required inferences
Amount of background knowledge assumed by the author to be possessed
  by the reader
Amount and kind of figurative language
Complexity and density of ideas

More subjective factors that affect the difficulty of any given passage for any given child cannot be overlooked. For instance:

The child's interest in the content
What the child knows that is relevant
What motivated the child to read the selection

Clearly, the moral for teachers of the sad tale about readability formulas is: For both objective and subjective reasons, do not assume that the difficulty of each selection in a basal reader is the same. Instead, when reading through a selection as part of your preparations for a lesson, be on the lookout for possible sources of difficulty that may have to do with an author's unusual use of words, with text structure, or with required background information. At the same time, be ready to identify selections that are much easier than others and thus require much less preparation and assessment than the manual recommends. In such cases, in fact, the selection might be read strictly for enjoyment, after which time can be allotted to a very informal discussion.

BASAL READER LESSONS: AN OVERVIEW

To provide a referent for this brief, preliminary treatment of basal lessons, Figure 14.3 offers an overview of those parts discussed in subsequent sections of the chapter. Most series include the topics shown in Figure 14.3, even though the recommended sequence for dealing with them differs from one

Figure 14.2. *Fry's Readability Graph*

Those who publish basal programs and tests have always been the most frequent users of readability formulas. The increasing availability of computers in
schools may now add to their use, even though major criticisms of formulas
are circulated repeatedly (7).

To illustrate how a formula works, the one proposed by George Spache is
used (28) since it is intended to function with primary-grade material. His formula requires choosing three to five 100-word passages from a selection, calculating the percentage of uncommon words based on a word list of 1,040
common words, and calculating the average number of words per sentence in
a passage. The two numbers (percentage of uncommon words and the average number of words per sentence) are then used in this formula:

> Reading grade-level = .082 × percentage of uncommon words
> + .121 × average number of words per sentence
> + .659.

Formulas like those of Spache point up the reason the method for assessing
readability that Edward Fry proposed (Figure 14.2) won quick acceptance.

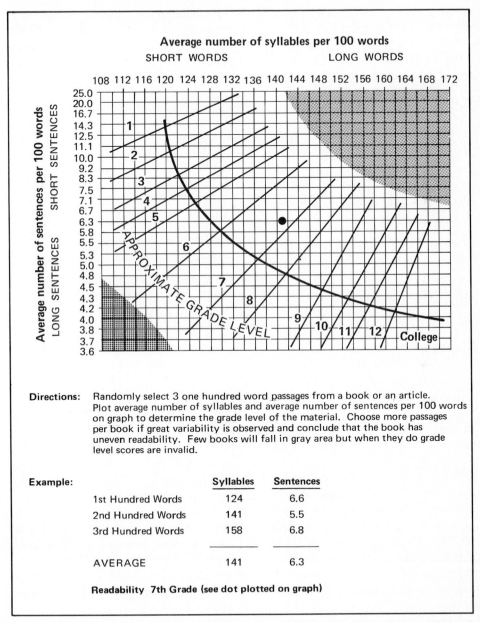

Average number of syllables per 100 words

SHORT WORDS   LONG WORDS

108 112 116 120 124 128 132 136 140 144 148 152 156 160 164 168 172

Average number of sentences per 100 words

SHORT SENTENCES / LONG SENTENCES

25.0 20.0 16.7 14.3 12.5 11.1 10.0 9.2 8.3 7.5 7.1 6.7 6.3 5.8 5.5 5.3 5.0 4.8 4.5 4.3 4.2 4.0 3.8 3.7 3.6

1 2 3 4 5 6 7 8 9 10 11 12 College

APPROXIMATE GRADE LEVEL

Directions: Randomly select 3 one hundred word passages from a book or an article. Plot average number of syllables and average number of sentences per 100 words on graph to determine the grade level of the material. Choose more passages per book if great variability is observed and conclude that the book has uneven readability. Few books will fall in gray area but when they do grade level scores are invalid.

Example:

	Syllables	Sentences
1st Hundred Words	124	6.6
2nd Hundred Words	141	5.5
3rd Hundred Words	158	6.8
AVERAGE	141	6.3

Readability 7th Grade (see dot plotted on graph)

From Edward Fry, *Reading Instruction for Classroom and Clinic* (New York: McGraw-Hill Book Company, 1972), p. 232. Copyright © 1972 by McGraw-Hill Book Company and used with their permission.

program to another. Of greater significance is that once a publisher selects a lesson format, it remains the same throughout the series. The unchanging sequence and routines help account for the monotony of what is done with reading in the classroom of a Teacher B. This is especially true when the only materials that supplement the basal program are ditto-sheet exercises. If for no other reason than to avoid monotony, altering the recommended sequence for activities is one option a Teacher A considers as she examines a manual. Other options pertain to the activities themselves and include the possibility of omitting, changing, or amplifying them.

Basal Reader Lessons

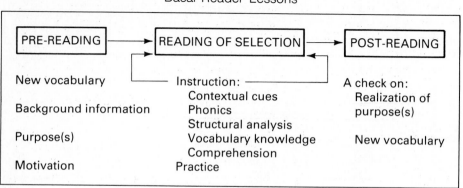

Figure 14.3.

What is said about instruction and practice in Chapters 4 through 13 is intended to assist teachers in making decisions that can change a very ordinary basal lesson into something both productive and of interest to children. It goes without saying that achieving these ends is possible only for teachers who know both the selection that will be read and the children who will do the reading. Familiarity with the illustrations in the text is important, too, because in the easiest readers, pictures often communicate much of the content or else duplicate the message of the text. These characteristics need to be kept in mind when, for example, assessment questions are selected. This is the case because posing questions that for the most part are answered by pictures may cause some children to become confused about what they are supposed to do when they read. With other children, overreliance on pictures may lead to comprehension problems later when basal selections are less profusely illustrated.

Having gone over some general points about basal series, let's consider the various parts of basal lessons.

PREREADING ACTIVITIES

The purposes of prereading activities are to enable children to read a selection silently, independently, and with ease; and to interest them in doing the reading with one or more definite purposes in mind. To realize these goals, it is generally necessary to allot time to (a) teaching new vocabulary, (b) providing essential background information, (c) establishing a purpose(s) for the reading, and (d) motivating the children to want to do the reading.

New Vocabulary

Since Chapter 11 concludes with a fairly comprehensive description of how to deal with new vocabulary, only three points about this responsibility will be made now. The first point is that more usually needs to be done with new words than manuals typically recommend. Watching a Teacher B recently, who spent eight minutes on nine new words, reinforced the correctness of this advice. At the end of the eight minutes, the children seemed to know only two of the words, naming with great hesitation – sometimes incorrectly – the other seven. Nonetheless, the teacher proceeded to the next activity suggested in her manual.

The second point about vocabulary pertains to the need for teachers to look beyond the new words, because how an author chooses to use familiar words may make it necessary to spend time on them, too. An example of such a need was seen in a second grade in which the teacher wisely included in her work with vocabulary such expressions as "a deep sigh," "a low moan," and "a twinkling eye," all found in the story that the children would soon be expected to read.

The third point has to do with the basic reason for attending to new vocabulary: to facilitate comprehension. That a teacher had failed to ask herself, "Why am I doing what I'm doing?" when she attended to new words – assuming that she had – seemed like a strong possibility in one fourth grade. In this instance, the observed teacher was working with nine children described as being the lowest achievers in grades 4 to 6. During all of the observation, nothing was seen except round robin reading, which was very poor because of the inability of child after child to identify a sizable number of words. Asked later why she had spent the time on oral reading, the teacher quickly explained that these children were so immature that the only way she could get them to read was to do it with them. She added that on the previous day, she had asked the same group to read silently the story they were "reading" aloud on the day of the observation. "But," she added, "in less than ten minutes, none were reading."

In cases like this, one has to wonder whether the children had abandoned the assignment because they were "immature," or because they recognized what for them was an impossible task. As said before, it seems a little unfair to expect children to do some reading for which they have not been adequately prepared.

Essential Background Information

Adequate preparation for reading a piece of text includes helping children either recall or acquire information necessary for comprehending it. At times, part or even all of this responsibility can be met in conjunction with the attention given to new words. Should a story take place some time ago and *pioneer* is a new word, differences about life in earlier days (that are essential for understanding the story) can be discussed when *pioneer* is introduced. More specifically, if the pioneer girl who is the protagonist becomes a heroine because of her efforts to warn of an impending disaster by knocking on everyone's door, children need to know that in pioneer times, taken-for-granted items like telephones did not exist. Not having that information could cause some readers to conclude that the girl was a less than efficient heroine.

Some reasons for not going beyond the information essential for comprehension were made clear in one third grade in which the teacher began a basal lesson by announcing, "The story we'll be reading today takes place in Antarctica . . .", after which members of the group spontaneously pretended they were shivering. The teacher continued, "where there are penguins." The additional information prompted one child to call out, "Tom has a penguin on his T-shirt!" Apparently ignoring what the children were telling her about their existing knowledge, this Teacher B continued with the basal manual, thus spent a little time talking about penguins and a great deal of time with a globe for the purpose of showing the location of Antarctica in relation to where the children lived. The inability of this group to visualize the implications of living in a world that is round became clear almost immediately; for the result of the discussion was the comment "Gee, I didn't know the South Pole is under us!"

Two important points were made as a result of this observation. First, if children's information is sufficient for comprehending a selection, there is no need to take the time to add to it; and, second, attending to nonessentials may reduce the time available for essentials. In the case of the observed third grade, so much time was spent on the globe that too little went to new vocabulary. The consequence was obvious as soon as the group began to read the story—again in round robin fashion: Everyone had problems with the new words.

Purpose(s) for Reading

Just as new vocabulary and background information can sometimes be dealt with together, so too will there be occasions when background information and purposes for reading can be covered jointly. To demonstrate this, expository material is considered because increased amounts of informational text are now in basal readers including those for the primary grades. (See Figure 14.4.)

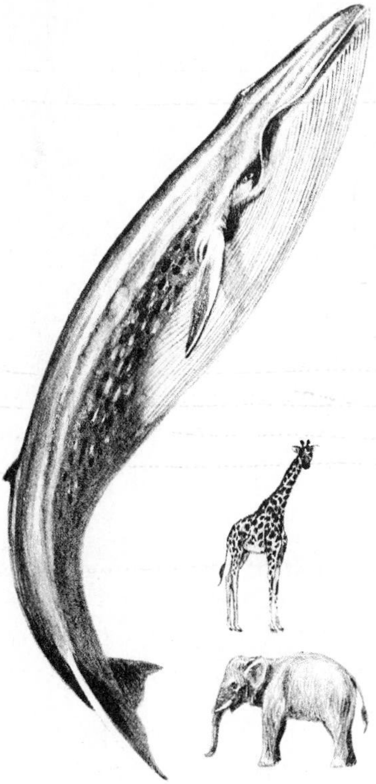

HOW BIG IS BIG?

Animals live in all parts of the world. They come in many sizes. Some animals are so tiny that you can't see them. Some are so huge that it's hard to even picture them in your mind. Find out just how big some animals are.

Figure 14.4

From Houghton Mifflin Reading Program, ADVENTURES, Level G. Copyright © 1986 by Houghton Mifflin Company. Reprinted with permission of the publishers.

A natural way to begin preparing children to read a selection about a given topic—whales, erosion, or airplanes, for example—is to find out what the children already know about it. (Since expository selections in basal readers usually have excellent colored photographs, examining and discussing them with the children is one way to do this.) Attempts to uncover existing knowledge allow teachers to learn not only what is not known that is important but also what is known that is inaccurate. Teachers' awareness of the latter is more critical than is often realized, as studies do show that "young readers who have inaccurate notions . . . are reluctant to relinquish that information in favor of text information. Indeed, they appear more likely to distort the text information to align it with their previous ideas" (18, p. 763). Complementing this conclusion is another from the same research: The children "seemed better able to learn new information when they did not have wrong ideas cluttering up their knowledge structures" (18, p. 762).

These conclusions suggest one three-part procedure that teachers might use with expository material: (a) Discuss with the children what they know about the topic of the material; (b) have them read the selection in order to learn what the author says about it; and (c) compare the two bodies of information once the reading has been done. Charts like the following are helpful for organizing the comparison:

Prereading Chart   *Postreading Chart*

What we know about hummingbirds: 1.

What we knew:	What we learned:

Once children have had the opportunity to compare their own knowledge about a variety of topics with information authors have provided, they are ready for further comparisons:

Postreading Chart

What we knew: 1.	What we learned: 1.	What we knew that was: correct 1.	incorrect 1.

To discourage children from concluding that if it's in print it's correct, what appears to be misinformation on their part can be checked with sources other than the one they read—with an encyclopedia, for instance. At first, comparisons can be made as a teacher reads the encyclopedia passage; later, more advanced ability will allow the children to do the checking themselves.

What about establishing purposes when a basal selection is a story? Manuals usually include "purpose setting" questions for stories; consequently, it is appropriate to look at how carefully selected questions can serve that function for narrative material.

Because attempts to comprehend trivial content are not worth anyone's time, it is assumed that questions designed to let children in on what needs to be comprehended focus on the key elements in a piece of fiction. Since stories, like sentences, have a structure or grammar, the major pieces that make up the whole often suggest the content for such questions.

The structure of a story, in its most elementary form, consists of these components:

Setting   *Problem*   *Attempt(s) to Resolve Problem*   *Resolution*
  Time
  Locale
  Central
    character

With the help of a story summary, let's see how these components can help teachers formulate prereading questions that pertain to essential content:

Peter, the youngest in his pioneer family, wants more than anything else to be as big as his siblings. Recalling that someone once said that by dipping a hand in a certain pool, wishes came true, Peter seeks out the pool, states his wish to grow, dips his hand into the water, and inadvertently falls in. Lying on the nearby grass to allow his clothes to dry, Peter eventually falls asleep. When he wakes up, his clothes, having shrunk considerably from the heat of the sun, make him think his wish came true. Although he is elated at first, the walk home allows Peter to have some unhappy thoughts about the possibility of being too big—too big to get into his own house, for instance. Once Peter arrives home, he is relieved to find that he has not grown. Now he is happy just to be able to still curl up in his mother's lap.

For the story about Peter, the structural components named earlier will be expanded slightly:

[A]	[B]	[C]	[D]	[E]	[F]
		Attempt to Resolve			
Setting	*Problem*	*Problem*	*Resolution*	*New Problem*	*Resolution*
Peter, a pioneer boy, lives in small town.	Wants to be big.	Dips hand in magic pool.	Shrunken clothes suggest growth.	Worries about being excessively big.	Learns clothes have shrunk and he is the same size.

How the six components, labeled A–F, enter into the composition of prereading questions is illustrated below.

A. Deal with when background information is provided.
B. *Question:* What was Peter's wish?
C. *Question:* What did Peter do to get his wish?
D. Discuss after reading is done, as this is clearly shown in several illustrations.
E. *Question:* Was Peter glad that he got his wish? Why (not)?
F. *Question:* How does the story end?

The four suggested questions could be written on a ditto sheet and distributed to members of the instructional group before they start the story. In time, the children should understand that they are expected to keep such questions in mind as they read, and that if they are unable to answer any, rereading—at least certain parts of the story—is called for. This is important because it moves children toward regulating or monitoring their own reading.

In contrast to the four questions just noted, twenty-six could be posed by a Teacher B, since that is the number in the manual for the story about Peter. Teachers knowledgeable about story structure can either compose their own questions in the way just illustrated, or sort out from all the questions suggested in manuals those that merit attention.

Children's Purposes

Even though it is true that relative beginners in reading may not be ready to establish their own reasons for reading, encouraging them to get into the habit of doing that is important, given the significance of purpose for comprehending. (As the previous chapter points out, purpose determines what constitutes both adequate comprehension and an appropriate rate for reading.) With a teacher's help, beginners can often decide what they want to get from their reading when the text deals with something familiar. If an instructional group has information about lightning and thunder, the two topics covered in the selection its members will be assigned next, preparations for the reading can include teacher-questions designed both to make apparent the children's existing knowledge and to help them decide what else they want to learn. The latter, recorded by the teacher in the form of questions, will be the focus in the postreading discussion. At that time, a comparison can be made between what the author said about lightning and thunder that was new to the children and what they had hoped to learn.

It is also possible to get beginners to raise questions about stories, since most of the narrative text in basal readers deals with problems similar to the children's own wishes, needs, feelings, and thoughts. Sometimes, for example, a title plus the illustrations (if they do not reveal too much of the content) are enough to get children to make predictions and ask questions that establish suitable purposes for reading.

Motivation

In many ways, how to interest children in reading a selection has already been covered. Only four reminders, therefore, are offered here:

1. Children are most interested in what is a little, but not too, familiar. This points to the value of making explicit what is in a selection that relates to what they know or have experienced.
2. Interest in reading a selection is heightened when children are actively involved in establishing the purpose(s) for doing the reading.
3. Interest is also increased when teachers display an honest concern for children's ideas and opinions about something that is in a selection.
4. At times, titles and pictures pique children's curiosity. When this occurs, one or the other or both should be used in a way that serves that function.

One final point about motivating children has been made: Do not arouse their interest if prereading preparations are not sufficient to enable the children to comprehend the selection with relative ease.

READING THE SELECTION

When it is time for children to read a basal selection, manuals adhere to a guideline recommended in an earlier chapter: Silent reading should precede oral reading except for diagnosis. Nothing recommended in any chapter, however, supports using the many, many questions they suggest for both silent and oral reading.

The first group of recommended questions in manuals is for the initial silent reading. They begin with one or two purpose-setting questions that are usually stated indirectly (e.g., Have the pupils read the story to find out what the title means.). Although starting this way suggests that the children will read the selection as a whole, it is usual for the purpose-setting questions to be followed immediately by many other questions for each page of text. The page-by-page questions are typically divided into the categories "Before reading" and "After reading."

Once the page-by-page reading and discussions end, it is common but not inevitable to find a reference to the purpose-setting questions. This is customarily followed by another list of questions described as a means for considering the selection as a whole. More questions are in the children's reader; these may or may not duplicate questions in the manual.

Even though it is becoming much less common to find recommendations in manuals that point explicitly in the direction of round robin reading, suggestions for some form of oral reading are inevitable, once the silent reading has been done. Since both acceptable and unacceptable ways to include oral reading in an instructional program are discussed in earlier chapters, there is no need to comment further. Instead, let me conclude this section with a few brief statements about how children ought to read a basal selection.

To begin, prereading preparations should allow children to read the entire selection on their own. (Reading it as a whole is recommended because this keeps intact the cohesiveness of the content.) Ideally, the pre-established purpose(s) for the reading will be kept in mind by the children as they move through the text. If questions were chosen, for instance, they should be written and available to each child while the reading is going on. Ideally, too, children will think of themselves as having finished the reading only when they are ready to show they have achieved the purpose (can answer the questions, can make a comparison between what the author said about a topic and what they hoped they would learn, and so on).

Admittedly, some of you may now be wondering, What about children who, for whatever reasons, are unable to do the kind of independent reading just recommended? How can they be accommodated?

If preparations for the reading were adequate and certain children still seem unable to do what has been recommended, teachers can use a variety of procedures to provide additional help. Examples follow, all of which are based on the assumption that the children are not being asked to read text that is so difficult that even a considerable amount of assistance would not solve their problems. To simplify the descriptions, one further assumption is that questions provide the purpose for reading.

1. Pose aloud the preselected question that is answered first in the text. Have the children read the selection silently until they think they have the answer. Discuss the answer with them; in particular, why it is the

answer. Do this with the other questions until the entire selection is read. (Since carefully selected questions will be relatively few compared to the number found in manuals, this procedure will not chunk the text into so many pieces that the wholeness of the content is lost.)

2. Depending on the children and the text, it may be helpful or even necessary to follow the procedure just described, after which the children will reread the entire selection, this time independently and without interruptions. At this point, the independent reading should be easier because (a) the structure of the text is now familiar, and (b) earlier parts of the text may provide background information that facilitates comprehending subsequent sections.

3. Another procedure is to divide the selection into parts which, if considered separately, do not obscure their connections. Have the children read the first part silently, then pose a question about the content. After the second part is read, let a child ask you a question. Continue taking turns like this until the entire selection is read. Again, it might be of value to have the selection reread without interruptions.

One reason for the recommendations just made originates in classroom studies of poor readers, which inevitably point to the large amounts of time they spend taking turns reading something aloud (1). Because of the number of interruptions, due to the readers' inability to identify words and a teacher's chastisement of children who are not following the text, low achievers spend much less time reading than do more successful children. Researchers conducting these studies consistently conclude that teachers must strive to reduce the use of round robin reading with low achievers and, in its place, allow for as much uninterrupted silent reading as is possible.

POSTREADING ACTIVITIES

As Figure 14.3 suggests, basal manuals vary in the timing of the recommendations they make for instruction and practice. For this reason, instruction and practice are discussed in the next section of the chapter. This section considers two responsibilities that should always be taken care of after children read a selection. The first pertains to new vocabulary; the second, to the purposes established for doing the reading.

Checking on New Vocabulary

One point made repeatedly when prior chapters cover the development of sight vocabularies is the importance of teachers' checking to see (a) whether children remember the new words that were taught with whole word methodology, and (b) whether they were able to use some combination of contextual, graphophonic, and structural cues to decode the other new words on their own. How to do this checking is described earlier. Numerous suggestions for word practice, should the checking show that some is required, are listed at the end of Chapter 7. If the checking also reveals deficiencies in decoding, ways to provide remedies are described at the conclusion of Chapters 8, 10, and 11.

Checking on the Realization of Purposes for Reading

Since questions are the most common means teachers use to bring purposes into existence, how purpose-setting questions should be handled once children have read a selection is dealt with initially.

Purpose-Setting Questions.   The first point that may require explicit attention is that purpose-setting questions need not always be posed with the original wording; however, they should focus on the original content. If this guideline is not followed, children quickly learn not to take prereading questions seriously. How they respond to purpose-setting questions may indicate that additional questions should be raised. On the other hand, it may happen that a child's response to one question allows for omitting others. (It might be necessary to point out, too, that questions should be posed to everyone. Naming a child and then asking a question is a sequence that hardly encourages all members of a group to pay attention.)

Whether a teacher's postreading questions are planned or spontaneous, responding with words taken directly from the text is usually never required. To be kept in mind, in fact, is that when comprehending breaks down, children tend to use an author's words to answer a question. In spite of that, some teachers are too textbound. Witness the following dialogue, for instance, heard in a first grade:

> *Teacher:*   Where did they look for her?
>   *Child:*   All over.
> *Teacher:*   That's not what it said. The story says they looked everywhere.

Textbound expectations are especially noticeable when content subjects like social studies are taught. Two examples of this are quoted in the Preview for Chapter 12.

Other discussions heard in classrooms make apparent the need for teachers to make a distinction between comprehension and retention. Although the two are related, they are also different. The difference makes it important for teachers to decide ahead of time whether postreading assessment efforts should focus on comprehension, or on comprehension plus retention. To be more specific, with a passage whose content deals mainly with the steps for assembling a kite, assessment should only be concerned with whether the children are able to follow the sequence revealed in the text. Committing the steps to memory is unnecessary, just as it is generally unnecessary to memorize a recipe. On the other hand, if the purpose for reading a selection is to learn about the characteristics of living things, then assessment efforts ought to concentrate not only on the children's understanding of those characteristics but also on their ability to recall them. The twofold focus is required because retention of the characteristics will facilitate acquisition of related information later on.

The implication for teaching of the differences just discussed follows. When discussing the procedural passage about kites, children should be allowed to go back into the text if necessary to name the steps in correct order. In contrast, the selection about common characteristics of living things calls for a closed-book discussion—unless, of course, the children's responses indicate problems with the text. In such cases, a teacher-guided discussion of the part of the selection that caused the problem is the procedure to follow. Depending on the nature of the problem, on-the-spot comprehension instruction may be required.

This suggests one final point about postreading, question-answer sessions: They should not be as examlike in nature as they often are. Some give-and-take between teacher and children can still allow for learning about comprehension abilities and shortcomings, which is important for both teacher and child. At the same time, it also allows for real discussion as opposed to what Judith Langer refers to as "an *imitation* of a discussion" (17) in which teachers only pose questions for which they already have answers.

Purpose-Setting Assignments. Although it is true that teachers rely on questions more often than anything else to make reading purposeful, earlier sections in the chapter show that prereading assignments accomplish the same goal. Recall, for instance, the pre- and postreading charts that allow for recorded comparisons of "What I knew" and "What I learned." As early as Chapter 1, you also experienced how asking students to make a drawing of the content of a passage is another means for bringing a purpose into existence and, later, for allowing a teacher to learn what and how much was comprehended. Samples of products of purpose-setting assignments other than drawings follow:

A map that indicates where the major events of a story took place.

A time line that shows when the major events occurred.

A completed assignment sheet composed by a teacher on which the children indicated which characters in a story were most likely to make each comment listed on the sheet.

A brief written version of a first-person story that was read, now supposedly written by a character other than the one who told the story in the basal reader.

A Brief Summary.   Whether questions or assignments serve to make reading purposeful, they should be chosen with care. After all, they also serve the important function of showing children that reading is anything but a single, unchanging behavior. The time spent later on answers and products of assignments is equally important, because children need evidence that what they do when they read is working—or, as the case may be, not working. Although managing a roomful of children sometimes keeps teachers from doing everything at the right time, an effort should be made to attend to the products of children's reading (e.g., answers, written work) as soon after the reading has been done as is possible. Like us all, children's interest in, and recollection of, what they read is keenest immediately after the book is closed.

Now that prereading and postreading responsibilities have been dealt with, let's return to responsibilities for instruction.

MANUAL SUGGESTIONS FOR INSTRUCTION

With all the space devoted to discussions of instruction in earlier chapters, there should be no need now to pursue the topic in any great detail. In fact, since the purpose of this chapter is to promote a professional use of basal materials, decisions about what else to say about instruction are made with only that goal in mind.

Anyone seriously interested in using basal manual suggestions professionally must ask one fundamental question: Should I use the recommendations made for instruction? Depending on the answer, a second question may have to be asked; namely, When should I use them? Why both *should* and *when* are necessary considerations is clarified with summary descriptions of procedures for instruction found in manuals published by a variety of companies including those whose materials are best sellers.

Problems with Suggestions:
Incorrect and Inappropriate

When a teacher is deciding whether to follow an instructional procedure in a manual, two questions that need answers are:

Is the recommended instruction correct?
Is it appropriate, given the age and abilities of my students?

Sample instructional procedures that illustrate why correctness and appropriateness are two criteria requiring immediate attention are cited below.

Incorrect

1. A manual segment recommends introducing the prefix *un-* as meaning *not*. Illustrative derivatives used in the instruction include *unlike* and *unclean* but also *untie* and *unload*.
2. Describing instruction for inflected forms, a manual refers to *shiny* as a base word. In a different series, one manual says that the inflection in words like *baked*, *named*, *wired*, and *liked* is *d*.
3. For instruction with medial sounds, a manual states that /m/ occurs in medial position in *lemon*, *comic*, and *camel*.
4. When introducing the concept *main idea*, a manual uses the following passage to illustrate text that has a main idea:

> Johnny asked Claire to take care of his monkey while he was gone. He asked his father to look after the dog. His mother would feed the bird.

The teacher is directed to write on the board three sentences so that the instructional group can decide which states the main idea:

_____ Johnny is leaving for a vacation.

_____ Johnny is coming home from camp.

_____ All the pets are going away.

(The first statement is said to be the correct answer.)

Inappropriate

1. One kindergarten manual teaches the sounds of all the letters in alphabetical order.
2. To provide instruction about time clues, a first-grade manual suggests having children read a given page in their basal readers, after which the directions to the teacher are: Help pupils see how *once* means long ago and *after a time* means a while later, but is still in the past. Ask pupils if *today* means only the present day or within recent years. Explain that in comparison to thousands of years ago when paper was made from grasses, *today* means since the time the paper was made from wood.
3. Another first-grade manual encourages teachers to provide instruction about contextual cues by repeatedly posing three questions: What is the word? . . . How did you know it wasn't _____? (wrong sounds)

How did you know it wasn't _____? (no sense) One unfinished sentence recommended for instruction is:

> When the lights went out, our house was left in complete _____.

Then the questioning commences:

> What is the word? . . .
>
> How did you know it wasn't *chaos*? (wrong sounds)
>
> How did you know it wasn't *doubtless*? (no sense)

4. In instruction dealing with *r*-controlled vowel sounds, one second-grade manual suggests asking children to listen for the schwa sound in words like *her*, *dirt*, and *curl*.

Another Problem: Questionable Timing

Fairly frequently, a recommended procedure for instruction is both correc. and appropriate for a given age, yet its timing is faulty. Examples o: questionable sequences are listed next.

Questionable Timing

1. On a number of pages in one kindergarten manual, the word *sentence* enters into what is to be said to the children. Much later, a lesson whose objective is to teach the meaning of *sentence* is described.
2. In a third-grade manual, an excellent lesson is depicted for teaching about appositives whose function is to provide information about the subject of a sentence. The fact that appositives are signaled by the use of commas is dealt with, too. Although the instruction is followed by equally good practice, nothing is done with application. That is, no reference is made to any selection in the basal reader that includes appositives. Instead, the manual next covers an entirely different topic: decoding practice.
3. A segment in a manual suggests teaching the prefixes *re-* and *un-*. Although the instruction is skimpy, a more serious flaw is that neither the basal selection just read nor the one to be assigned next contain derivatives that include the two prefixes.
4. A skeletonlike lesson labeled "Details of Description" starts by telling the teacher to have students recall a story covered in the manual 40 pages earlier. The rest of the lesson continues to dwell on that story even though it is likely that some members of the instructional group have not retained a clear picture of its content.
5. After a basal selection has been read, analyzed, and discussed with

many questions, the manual offers ideas for teaching children how to scan to find answers to specific questions. All the questions suggested for practice are about the story just read, which means that most if not all of the children already know the answers.

Still Another Problem: Mislabeled Suggestions

Research has shown that consumers of basal manuals cannot take it for granted that a match exists between the content of a suggested procedure in a manual and the title assigned to it (13). One of the most common kinds of mislabeling is an assessment procedure that is called instruction. Examples of that mismatch, plus others, are listed next.

Mislabeled
1. In one second-grade manual, the label "Study Skills" is assigned to a segment recommending, first, that a teacher write on the board the emergency telephone numbers of the police and fire departments. The next recommendation is to have a discussion for the purpose of identifying circumstances that call for using the numbers. (Since the recommendation bears no relationship to any selection in the reader, the procedure also belongs with those listed earlier to illustrate questionable timing.)
2. Appearing under the general heading "Instruction for Basic Skills" is a recommendation for teachers to read aloud a brief paragraph that describes a boy's efforts to make a dessert for his father's birthday. Although the label indicates the suggestion pertains to instruction for noting correct sequence, all the questions a teacher is supposed to raise following the oral reading are concerned with assessment (e.g., Who can tell us what Martin did first to make the dessert? . . . Then what did he do? . . .). After the questions, the manual shifts to an entirely different topic.
3. Labeled "Teaching Suggestions for Literal Comprehension," one section in a manual encourages teachers to have children retell a story they just read. The stipulation is made that the story must be told in six sentences. Although it is clear that the suggestion has nothing to do with instruction, the reason for requiring a six-sentence summary is unclear.
4. In a segment called "Word Identification," procedures recommended for teaching new words include the following: A teacher reads a sentence, the last word of which is omitted. Children are to finish the sentence by reading one of the new words listed on the board.
5. Another manual segment is referred to as "Instruction for Distinguishing between Realistic Fiction and Fantasy." Exemplifying the tendency of manual authors to equate assessment with instruction—that is, to

assume that children can do what supposedly is being taught – the segment suggests having children read very brief stories in their workbook, each of which is followed by a square. Children are to color the square if the story could really happen.

Useful Suggestions

Although many manual suggestions for instruction are questionable for reasons just named, some highly commendable procedures can be found, too. (A growing trend is the inclusion of brief instruction in the readers themselves. For an example, see Figure 14.5.) Examples of useful suggestions for instruction are described below.

Useful

1. One segment in a manual deals with the concept *probability* as well as with the words authors may use to indicate statements of probability. After listing pairs of contrasting sentences that are to be discussed (e.g., *The soil caused the crop failure* and *The soil may have caused the crop failure*), the manual suggests returning to the basal selection just read so the children can, first, find additional statements of probability and, second, point out the words that suggest probability.

2. The objective of a lesson described in another manual is to inform children about four ways authors reveal the traits of characters. Four brief, simply worded paragraphs about a girl are listed, each to be read by the teacher, then discussed. The teacher is next directed to have the children reread a basal story for the purpose of seeing which of the four devices the author uses to reveal the traits of the protagonist.

3. That commas suggest a brief pause is the topic of another procedure worth using – assuming children need to learn this. Contrasting sentences listed on a ditto sheet are to be read aloud in order to make clear how correct and incorrect pauses alter the meaning of sentences.

4. After an expository selection dealing with UFO's is read, a procedure is described for teaching about words that signal opinions. (On an earlier page in the same manual, a segment dealt effectively with the meanings of *fact* and *opinion*.) After examples of such signal words are written and discussed, the suggestion is made to return to the selection to have the children find sentences that express opinions and, in addition, to explain why they think those sentences are someone's opinion rather than an established fact.

A Brief Summary

Now that various characteristics of manual suggestions for instruction have been identified and illustrated, it is time to summarize the basic components of a professional use of manuals.

Sometimes one or more words in a sentence will stand for one or more words in another sentence. Read these sentences.

Don and Bob could not find Sue's book. **She** forgot to tell **them** where to look.

In these sentences, the word *she* stands for the word *Sue*. The word *them* stands for the words *Don* and *Bob*.

The words *she* and *them* are in one sentence and the words they stand for are in another sentence.

What do the words in heavy black letters mean?

Father bought some eggs at the store. **He** brought **them** home.

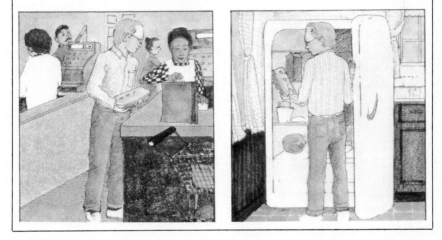

Figure 14.5

Underlying any consideration of commercially produced materials is the assumption that none merits being used unless it stands a chance of adding either to children's interest in reading or to their ability to read. The two criteria mean that a professional use of basal manuals can be equated with a *selective* use of their suggestions that takes into account the particular children being instructed. Since it is teachers who know children, they must assume responsibility for making the choices.

As explained, a selective use of manual recommendations for instruction includes omitting some, either because they are incorrect or inappropriate. Omissions may also be of mislabeled segments because, once the true nature of the recommendations is identified, it may turn out that they fail to deal with the needs of an instructional group. Other omissions will be temporary. That is, a worthwhile recommendation will be followed later than the manual suggests in order to allow children the opportunity to apply what is taught to what they are reading.

Omissions and rearrangements of sequence (both within and across lessons) are not all that constitute a professional use of manuals insofar as instruction is concerned. Other alterations include additions to skeletonlike lessons and, in some instances, adding to, or replacing, examples. Not to be overlooked is that a professional use of manuals sometimes means doing exactly what they recommend at the time they suggest doing it.

MANUAL SUGGESTIONS FOR PRACTICE

Everything that has been said about a professional use of recommendations for instruction applies to those made for practice, which is usually written exercises originating in workbooks and ditto-sheet masters. Since classroom studies show that children may spend up to 70 percent of the time scheduled for reading doing these exercises (2), they are a significant component of basal programs. The same percentage figure suggests why researchers like Duffy (10) concluded that such exercises serve the function of keeping a class under control and, further, why basal reader practice sheets are commonly called busywork.

For our purposes, the most relevant point is that not all of the large number of assignments referred to in basal manuals merit being used. To encourage discriminating use, some of the more pervasive flaws are described and illustrated.

Common Flaws in Basal Reader Practice Assignments

As should now be clear, a basal reader lesson usually extends over two or more days. There are natural interruptions, therefore, caused by the need to stop in order to move on to the next part of a day's schedule. The source of even more interruptions, however, is practice assignments. In fact, adhering to the recommendations for practice found in manuals, Teacher B could end up having children do a little of this, then a little of that, followed by a little of something else, none of which might be related to anything in particular, including the basal selection children are or will be reading. Evidence of this "flitting" (12, 14) has been found by a number of researchers. Jana Mason, for example, began a study of classroom reading instruction with the assumption that introducing, reading, and discussing a selection constitute the key components of a basal lesson (20). Observing what actually occurred, she found that "only 5 instances from 110 lessons" included an unbroken sequence of the three components. The most frequent interruption was assignments of workbook and ditto-sheet exercises, the majority of which were "text-unrelated events." Mason's final conclusion? "Lessons are disconnected by exercises" (20, p. 911).

Even when a recommended exercise does bear some relationship to a selection in the basal reader, a teacher's failure to clarify its purpose may obscure the relationship. An example of this omission was seen in one classroom (12) when the workbook page shown in Figure 14.6 was assigned. Before the basal manual's recommendation to have the children do this page, a segment dealt with a review of reaching unstated conclusions based on what an author does state. Although the workbook page in Figure 14.6 refers at the top to "Drawing Conclusions," that task was never mentioned when the observed teacher assigned the page, perhaps because five other one-page exercises, each dealing with a different topic, were given at the same time. One likely result for many children is that they did all the assignments simply to get them finished (2). If any students thought about the nature of the task on the page shown in Figure 14.6, the most likely conclusion they would reach is that following directions, not reaching conclusions, was what they were doing. This points to the need to reinforce the importance of two guidelines for teachers that have been stated before: Be sure children (a) understand what it is they are being asked to do, and (b) see the connection between what they are doing and becoming a better reader. Any teacher who resolves to follow these guidelines will inevitably learn—and quickly—that it is often impossible to adhere to the second guideline because of the nature of a recommended assignment. Brief descriptions follow of a few assignments that would be difficult to explain as contributors to reading ability (see also Figures 4.2 and 5.4):

Directions at the top of one workbook page are as follows: Read the sentences below. Decide which vowel letter is used the most. Then underline that letter each time it is used.
Directions for another page tell children to circle all the proper nouns in

20

Read each numbered group of sentences.
Then do what you are asked to do.

1. Ellie came to a green park
   bench. She didn't see the sign
   on the bench. She sat down and
   started reading. When Ellie got up,
   her dress had green paint on it.

   Draw a line around the sign
   that was on the bench.

2. Mr. Hill's cat had four kittens.
   Mr. Hill didn't know what to do
   with all the kittens. Then he
   had an idea. He put a sign on
   his door. Soon all the kittens
   were gone.

   Draw a line around the sign
   that was on Mr. Hill's door.

3. David and his little sister Mary
   were walking to school. When
   Mary ran in front of David to
   the street, David called, "Stop
   right there! Read the sign."

   Draw a line around the sign
   David was talking about.

4. Carol wanted to give popcorn
   to the elephants at the zoo.
   But after she read the sign
   on the elephant house, she ate
   the popcorn herself.

   Draw a line around the sign
   on the elephant house.

Figure 14.6

From TOWERS, Level H, Houghton Mifflin Reading Program, Teacher's Annotated Edition by William K. Durr, Jean M. LePere, and John J. Pikulski. Copyright © 1983 by Houghton Mifflin Company. Used with permission.

four paragraphs. (Every word in the paragraphs that starts with a capital letter is a proper noun.)

Another workbook page directs children to read several columns of previously taught words. The task is to divide each word into syllables with slash marks.

One workbook page for second grade has children add the inflectional suffix *-ed* to two columns of roots.

Another second-grade workbook has a page on which children are to arrange twenty-six words in alphabetical order.

Other Flaws in Basal Reader Practice Assignments

The page shown in Figure 14.6 illustrates another common flaw in assignments, which is apparent to anyone who merely skims the pages of a randomly selected workbook. In this instance, it is the skimpiness of the practice provided, even when it is practice worth doing. This particular shortcoming reflects the interest of publishers in demonstrating to prospective buyers that their program covers a wide variety of topics. Fortunately, it is a shortcoming that Teacher A can remedy with additional items of her own.

It is taken for granted that assignments that should be omitted are any that reinforce incorrect information. Falling into this category are erroneous materials like those referred to earlier: practice sheets that encourage children to think (a) that the prefix in derivatives like *untie* and *unroll* means *not*, and (b) that the inflectional suffix in such words as *raced* and *liked* is *d*. Additional incorrect information is communicated on a workbook page entitled "Two Consonants with One Sound." The consonants referred to are *sm, sp, sk*, and *st*.

Other assignments that should be omitted from every teacher's plans are not easy to characterize but are highly questionable. In recently published basal programs, for instance, the following assignments are recommended:

Children are to write any small word they see in recently introduced vocabulary. The answer key indicates, for example, that *my* and *us* should be written after *mysterious*, and that *at* and *tent* should be written next to *attention*. [Refer to Figure 11.1.]

A segment in one manual describes a procedure for teaching about the helpfulness of the spelling pattern VCCV for syllabicating unknown words. The suggested practice assignment uses roots like *window* and *chimney* but also inflected words like *wanted, hurries*, and *written*.

Some Teacher A's automatically eliminate both incorrect and questionable practice like that just listed; others may use it—at least some of the time—for the purpose of contrasting what is correct and what is incorrect. Such contrasts can be a productive experience for children.

Concluding Comments about
Basal Reader Practice Assignments

Because of the importance of good practice for successful, permanent learning, the foregoing treatment of basal reader practice assignments concentrates on flaws. The presence of flaws also explains why previous chapters use a significant amount of space to describe suggestions for practice dealing with a wide variety of topics.

If consumers of basal programs were to become more vocal about the shortcomings that characterize a sizable amount of their practice materials, there is no doubt that improvement would soon follow. The need to improve practice is a major one, because good practice serves a number of valuable functions. To begin, it advances children's ability to read, which, after all, is the basic reason for practice. In addition, good practice provides teachers with feedback that is helpful when they plan future instruction or, as the case may be, remedial procedures. Last but not least is the contribution that independent practice makes to freeing a teacher to work with small groups or individuals.

SUMMARY

Recognizing the unique influence that basal reader programs enjoy, Chapter 14 attempted to show how they can function in ways that maximize the quality of the instruction and practice provided in classrooms. As the chapter demonstrated, achieving that goal requires various combinations of using, omitting, and revising the suggestions that make up each basal reader manual. As also illustrated in the chapter, achieving excellence often calls for altering the sequence of recommended procedures.

The professional use of basal materials just described begins with reading the selection children will be expected to read. This step is essential for making decisions about what needs to be done to prepare the children to do the reading. What ends up requiring attention (e.g., new vocabulary, background information, purpose for reading, motivation) may or may not be covered adequately in the manual. Either way, prereading preparations are always important, as they facilitate comprehension.

If what is done to facilitate comprehension is sufficient, children should be able to read the basal selection silently, independently, and without interruption. The independent reading allows teachers to work with another instructional group or with individuals. At the same time, reading that is not interrupted with page-by-page questions helps children keep together the pieces of what they are reading so they end up with a well-integrated whole.

To learn what they *have* ended up with is the reason for postreading assessment procedures that relate directly to the purpose established for doing the reading. Postreading activities should also provide teachers with opportunities to uncover how well children are able to cope both with individual words and connected text.

Incorporating instruction and practice (other than the practice achieved by reading the selection) into a basal lesson is also essential. When each ought to be provided will vary from lesson to lesson and from one instructional group to another. What does not change, however, is the requirement to provide instruction at a time when the opportunity is available to apply what is learned. Like instruction, practice should also be assigned in a way (and at a time) that clarifies its connection with becoming a better reader. Reasons that some of the recommendations made in basal manuals for both instruction and practice need to be altered or omitted were specified in the chapter.

Now that Chapter 14 has covered basal reader programs, Chapter 15 will consider nonbasal materials that can make important contributions to children's growing abilities to read.

REVIEW

1. Using the two categories "What I Knew" and "What I Learned," state what you now know about basal reader programs that you did not know when you began reading Chapter 14.

2. What is the difference between (a) teaching children and (b) covering material? Are the two ever the same?

3. Starting with a definition of *readability*, explain the following statement:

   Readability formulas are of questionable value not because of the variables they include but because of all the ones they do not include.

4. Return to the section in Chapter 14 entitled "Manual Suggestions for Instructon."

   a. Explain why the four examples listed under "Incorrect" are incorrect.
   b. Explain why the four examples listed under "Inappropriate" are inappropriate.
   c. Explain why the timing of the five examples listed under "Questionable Timing" is questionable.
   d. Explain why the five examples said to be mislabeled are mislabeled.

5. Reread the section in Chapter 14 called "Manual Suggestions for Practice"; then categorize the various flaws in basal reader practice assignments that are described and illustrated.

6. As a way of summarizing the major points made about basal reader materials in the whole of the chapter, write a paragraph that starts as follows:

In using a basal reader series, Teacher A . . . .

REFERENCES

1. Allington, Richard L. "Poor Readers Don't Get to Read Much in Reading Groups." *Language Arts* 57 (November/December, 1980), 872–876.
2. Anderson, Linda. "The Environment of Instruction: The Function of Seatwork in a Commercially Developed Curriculum." In Gerald G. Duffy, Laura R. Roehler, and Jana Mason (Eds.), *Comprehension Instruction*. New York: Longman Inc., 1984, 93–103.
3. Aukerman, Robert C. *The Basal Reader Approach to Reading*. New York: John Wiley, 1981.
4. Beck, Isabel L., and McKeown, Margaret G. "Developing Questions That Promote Comprehension: The Story Map." *Language Arts* 58 (November/December, 1981), 913–918.
5. Bradley, John M., and Ames, Wilbur S. "The Influence of Intrabook Readability Variation on Oral Reading Performance." *Journal of Educational Research* 70 (November/December, 1976), 101–105.
6. Brown, Ann L.; Campione, Joseph C.; and Day, Jeanne D. "Learning to Learn: On Training Students to Learn from Texts." *Educational Researcher* 10 (February, 1981), 14–21.
7. Cullinan, Bernice, and Fitzgerald, Sheila. "IRA–NCTE Joint Statement on Readability." *Reading Today* 2 (December, 1984/January 1985), 1.
8. Davison, Alice, and Kantor, Robert N. "On the Failure of Readability Formulas to Define Readable Texts: A Case Study from Adaptations." *Reading Research Quarterly* 17 (1982, No. 2), 187–209.
9. Duffelmeyer, Frederick A. "A Comparison of Two Noncomputational Readability Techniques." *Reading Teacher* 36 (October, 1982), 4–7.
10. Duffy, Gerald G. *Theory to Practice: How Does It Work in Real Classrooms?* Research Series No. 98. East Lansing, Mich.: The Institute for Research on Teaching, Michigan State University, July, 1981.
11. Durkin, Dolores. "An Attempt to Make Sense Out of a Senseless Basal Reader Lesson." *Illinois Reading Council Journal* 14 (Spring, 1986), 23–31.
12. Durkin, Dolores. "Is There a Match between What Elementary Teachers Do and What Basal Reader Manuals Recommend?" *Reading Teacher* 37 (April, 1984), 734–744.
13. Durkin, Dolores. "Reading Comprehension Instruction in Five Basal Reader Series." *Reading Research Quarterly* 16 (1981, No. 4), 515–544.
14. Durkin, Dolores. "What Classroom Observations Reveal about Reading Comprehension Instruction." *Reading Research Quarterly* 14 (1978–79, No. 4), 481–533.
15. Hansen, Jane, and Hubbard, Ruth. "Poor Readers Can Draw Inferences." *Reading Teacher* 37 (March, 1984), 586–589.

16. Juel, Connie, and Roper, Diane S. "The Influence of Basal Readers on First Grade Reading." *Reading Research Quarterly* 20 (Winter, 1985), 134–152.
17. Langer, Judith A. "Reading, Thinking, Writing . . . and Teaching." *Language Arts* 59 (April, 1982), 336–341.
18. Lipson, Marjorie Y. "Some Unexpected Issues in Prior Knowledge and Comprehension." *Reading Teacher* 37 (April, 1984), 760–764.
19. Marshall, Nancy. "Using Story Grammar to Assess Reading Comprehension." *Reading Teacher* 36 (March, 1983), 616–620.
20. Mason, Jana M. "An Examination of Reading Instruction in Third and Fourth Grades." *Reading Teacher* 36 (May, 1983), 906–913.
21. Moe, Alden J. "Cohesion as a Factor in the Comprehensibility of Connected Discourse." Paper presented at the annual meeting of the National Reading Conference, St. Petersburg, Fla., December 1, 1978.
22. Moldofsky, Penny B. "Teaching Students to Determine the Central Story Problem: A Practical Application of Schema Theory." *Reading Teacher* 36 (April, 1983), 740–745.
23. Osborn, Jean. "Workbooks: Counting, Matching, and Judging." In Jean Osborn, Paul T. Wilson, and Richard C. Anderson (Eds.), *Reading Education: Foundations for a Literate America*. Lexington, Mass.: D.C. Health and Company, 1985, 2–28.
24. Rand, Muriel K. "Story Schema: Theory, Research and Practice." *Reading Teacher* 37 (January, 1984), 377–382.
25. Shannon, Patrick. "A Retrospective Look at Teachers' Reliance on Commercial Reading Materials." *Language Arts* 59 (November/December, 1982), 844–853.
26. Shannon, Patrick. "Some Subjective Reasons for Teachers' Reliance on Commercial Reading Materials." *Reading Teacher* 35 (May, 1982), 884–889.
27. Shapiro, Sheila. "An Analysis of Poetry Teaching Procedures in Sixth-Grade Basal Manuals." *Reading Research Quarterly* 20 (Spring, 1985), 368–381.
28. Spache, George D. *Good Reading for Poor Readers*, 10th ed. Champaign, Ill.: Garrard Press, 1978.

CHAPTER 15

Other Materials

PREVIEW

It seems correct to say that for teachers, instructional materials—whether basal materials or bumper stickers—are the tools of their trade. Viewed this way, materials can be compared to something like a carpenter's tools:

Carpenter	*Teacher*
1. Description of job	1. Identification of objective
2. Selection of appropriate tools	2. Selection of appropriate materials
3. Knowledgeable use of tools	3. Knowledgeable use of materials
4. Completion of job	4. Attainment of objective

Just as a carpenter selects tools in relation to the next job to be done, so should a teacher's choice of materials depend on the objective to be realized. The priority of objectives explains why a selective use of basal manual recommendations is emphasized in the previous chapter. The underlying importance of objectives also explains why this chapter highlights materials other than basal series; for using nothing but the latter excludes objectives that require different kinds of materials. The other reason for a second chapter for instructional materials reflects an almost inevitable consequence when a basal reader program is used exclusively: monotony.

To avoid monotony and, at the same time, to personalize what is done to teach reading, the use of language experience materials is enthusiastically endorsed. This accounts for their being discussed again here in Chapter 15. (They are considered initially in Chapter 5.)

Since language experience materials and children's writing are closely connected, how writing may contribute to reading ability is looked at next. In recognition of the fact that practically every elementary teacher uses one or more basal series, how to complement or extend basal selections with additional material also receives attention. And because elementary school faculties have been known to put old basal programs to good use, that possibility is covered in Chapter 15, too.

Rereading Chapter 5 ("A Beginning Literacy Program") is a good way to prepare for this chapter, as the earlier one illustrates the variety in materials that ought to be the norm for all classrooms. Included in Chapter 5 are references to language experience materials used to achieve various purposes. Additional contributions they are able to make are the current concern.

LANGUAGE EXPERIENCE MATERIALS

Distinctions based on function divide language experience materials into three categories: *contactual, instructional*, and *practice*. The first use is dealt with in Chapter 5 and, as the label suggests, has to do with bringing young nonreaders into contact with print in meaningful, personal ways. Simultaneously, the same contacts allow teachers to demonstrate the meaning of *word*; to show how empty space divides words; and to discuss and illustrate the left-to-right, top-to-bottom orientation of written English. As a result of early contacts with print, some children begin to read; but getting reading started is not the primary goal.

Later uses of language experience materials, which is the focus now, have to do with instruction and practice and aim directly toward the start and continuation of reading ability. Within this framework, language experience materials can function in developing and reviewing reading vocabularies; in illustrating the significance of capitalization and punctuation; and in providing words for teaching about letter-sound relationships and word structure. Directly connected with the children themselves, language experience materials also enhance motivation.

Because they are concerned with particular children and their experiences, the meanings of neither individual words nor sentences cause problems. Nonetheless, these materials can sometimes be used in instruction with topics like homophones, facts and opinions, sequence of events, cause-effect relationships, and important versus unimportant details.

Some Instructional Objectives

As with any other material, objectives establish guidelines for the development and use of language experience materials. This is illustrated in the examples that follow.

Developing Reading Vocabularies. Neither the time nor the need exists to teach every new word through language experience material, but teaching some new words with its help makes learning to read relevant and interesting. This is shown in the procedures one teacher selected when the objective was to teach *red* to nine new first-graders:

Teacher: This really is a beautiful morning, isn't it? It was a good morning to look at things on the way to school. As I was driving, I saw leaves that were the most beautiful colors — green, yellow, red, orange. Did *you* notice anything as you walked to school?

Tonia: My mother drove me.

Annamarie: I saw some noisy motorcycles!

Teacher: What color were they?

Annamarie: I don't know. They were too noisy.

Teacher: What did *you* see, David?

David: I saw Tommy's bike.

Teacher: What color is it?

David: I forget.

Teacher: Let's see if we can think of some things whose colors we remember. When you do think of something, I'll write what you say up here [points to chalkboard]. I'll pick one color to get started. I'll take red. That's a good, bright color for a good, bright morning. Let me show you the word *red* [prints *red* on board]. What does this word say?

Children: Red.

Teacher: To help you remember it, let's spell *red* [points to letters].

Children: R, e, d.

Teacher: What does this word say?

Children: Red.

Teacher: I'll name one thing that's red — or at least the ones in our town are red. A fire truck is red. Watch me print what I just said. Now I'll read it [points to each word]. "A fire truck is red." What does this word say [points to *red*]?

Children: Red.

Teacher: Try to read all the words I just wrote [points to each].

Children: A fire truck is red.

Teacher: Can you tell me something else that's red? George?

George: Chicken pox and measles are red.

Teacher: Wonderful! Watch as I print what George just told us about red things.

Eventually the chalkboard showed the sentences in Figure 15.1.

What else is done with *red* to ensure that it will be a sight word depends on the children, in particular on what they know and on how quickly they

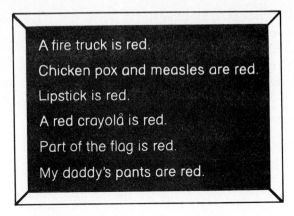

A fire truck is red.

Chicken pox and measles are red.

Lipstick is red.

A red crayola is red.

Part of the flag is red.

My daddy's pants are red.

Figure 15.1

learn. If their entire reading vocabulary is composed of *red, blue,* and *green,* this teacher could use a ditto sheet showing an outline of something like a clown whose clothes are to be colored according to one-word directions: *red, blue, green.* Slightly larger vocabularies allow for practice with more than single words. Now the teacher might show cards like the following:

the green toy	a little red hat	red, white, and blue

After asking the children to read the first card silently, the teacher can pose such questions as:

> Does this tell about something to eat or to play with?
> What is the color of the toy?
> Who wants to read the three words?

Other questions will be asked about the remaining cards, all designed to keep the communicative function of print in the foreground while individual words are receiving attention.

To personalize what is done with *red,* the next step in this lesson is the chance to draw anything, as long as it has some connection with red. All the children start with *Red* printed at the top of their paper. (This offers an opportunity for a brief discussion of titles and capitalization.) Later, as the children finish their drawings, the teacher or aide will print any comments the children want to make.

Additional Instructional Objectives. To show how language experience materials can give attention to a variety of topics, further examples are cited below. Under each, instructional possibilities are listed.

The first example resulted from a discussion of spring in a first-grade classroom. Children's contributions provided the content whereas instructional objectives determined how the teacher transformed the contributions into sentences.

Look for Spring

Look for the sun in the sky.

Look for bugs in trees.

Look for green grass.

Look for robins.

Instructional Possibilities
Reading vocabulary:
  Teach *for.*
  Review *the, in, look.*

Distinction in meaning:
  four (taught previously) and *for*

Way to denote plural:
  bugs, robins, trees

The next sample of text was seen in another first grade in which one student received special attention each week. Written descriptions of that child were dictated by a small group whose members changed weekly. The sentences were printed by the teacher (first on the board, then on primary chart paper); read by everyone; and featured on a bulletin board entitled "The Kid of the Week."

Guess Who?

This is a girl.

She has very long hair.

Sometimes she wears a ribbon in her hair.

She has a new baby sister.

Who is she?

Instructional Possibilities
Reading vocabulary:
  Teach *new, sister.*
  Review *guess, who, girl, has, hair, this, she.*
Punctuation:
  Review function of question mark.

One more sample of text composed by children—in this case, to describe a recent addition to their classroom—follows:

Gold

Gold is a goldfish.

Gold has fins.

Gold has a tail.

Gold has scales.

Gold must be in water.

Gold is orange.

Instructional Possibilities
Reading vocabulary:
  Teach *gold, orange.*
  Review *is, a, has, in.*
Introduce compound words:
  goldfish

Like the other examples, the text about a goldfish shows how language experience material inevitably demonstrates the value of knowing such serviceable (but uninteresting) words as *is, a, has, in, and, are, for,* and *the.*

Steps for Composing Language Experience Material

As illustrated, what children need to learn or review often figures in the composition of language experience material. Regardless of objectives, however, five steps should be followed in developing the text:

  1. Selection of objective(s)
  2. Selection of a topic
  3. Discussion

4. Composing the material
5. Follow-up activities

Comments about each step follow.

Selection of Objective(s).   The basic reason for language experience material is to make learning to read of personal interest to children. In addition to that underlying goal, other more specific objectives should be selected before choosing a topic to talk and write about. This sequence is important because the nature of the objectives generally affects both the choice and development of a topic. More specifically, if one objective is to review that the end of a thought does not always coincide with the end of a line, a teacher has to see to it that some sentences are either longer or shorter than a line. On the other hand, if an objective is to teach words that are in the next basal reader story, the selected topic must be one that allows for the use of those words, ideally more than once.

Even though it is necessary to have objectives at the outset, how material develops may allow for attention to additional needs. If some or all of the children are struggling to remember *and, the,* and *what,* for example, and these words are in the material, it can be used to review them.

Selection of a Topic.   Although teachers often have to work at motivating children to read commercially prepared material, that should not be the case with language experience material. If it is, the wrong topic was selected.

Only if a topic captures everyone's sustained attention should an entire class participate in its development. Even when a whole class is involved, the material may eventually be used in different ways with different children.

Discussion.   Ideally, both the content and sentences for language experience material originate with the children. At times, however, instructional objectives make teachers more active participants. Either way, involving children in the prewriting discussion of the selected topic is important; otherwise, the content may show little relationship to their experiences, observations, and thoughts. Depending on the topic, the children, and the objectives, a discussion may be entirely spontaneous or, on the other hand, structured with questions such as: How did you feel when that happened? How many were there? What did you think when you heard that? What color was it? Did you get a chance to feel it? What happened first? Why do you think they did that? At other times, pictures, objects, a film, or a story might be the best way to get children thinking and talking. Whatever the stimulus, prewriting discussion is always important.

Composing the Material.   Whether a sentence comes directly from a child, comes from a child but is edited, or comes directly from the teacher, it should be printed carefully but quickly while the children watch. Each word and then the sentence itself is read first by the teacher and next by the children with as much help as is necessary. Once the entire account has been printed, the children should read all of it, again with as much prompting as is required.

Follow-up Activities.   The next step varies as much as material, children, and objectives vary. If an entire class has been involved, some members might be asked to copy and illustrate the material, to write their own ideas on the same topic, or to return to their desks or tables to start or finish unrelated work. These possibilities free teachers to use the account with other children in ways that correspond to what they need to learn or review.

If, for whatever reason, material has value for more than a day, it can be transferred to chart paper. If each child needs a copy, the account can be typed and duplicated. Copies can eventually be taken home to allow the children to read the text to family members.

Topics for Language Experience Material

Selecting topics that win children's sustained attention is essential. Some topics that have done that include:

Buttons	Haircuts	At the Hatchery
Melting Snow	Puddles	Mumps
Halloween Masks	When We Grow Up	Crickets
Shade	Something in My	What Happened to Our
Toys with Wheels	Eye	Gerbil?

As all the topics point up, looking for the exotic to write about is not necessary—or desirable; children are most interested in what is near at hand, in what is happening now, and in what relates to themselves.

Perhaps it should be mentioned, too, that interest can be developed. Take the topic "Buttons" as an example. In and of itself, this topic may prompt little response from children. However, having experienced a large and colorful collection of buttons brought by a teacher on the day that the sound for *b* was introduced, children can be counted on to have something to say.

Regardless of the topic, language experience material will often be narration, although other kinds of text result from the need to extend an invitation, to express appreciation, to explain a process, to remember what to bring to school on a certain day, or to summarize. In one classroom, a bulletin board displayed a very effective summary. To the left was a simple bar graph that showed the frequency with which specified colors of cars were seen on a recent walk through the neighborhood. To the right was a group-dictated account of additional observations about the cars. To the right of the account was a long column of photographs of cars taken from dealers' brochures, each labeled with a car's name.

The board effectively demonstrated various ways of communicating; it also illustrated how the real world can enter into efforts to learn to read. Along with all the other examples of language experience material, it should point up how restrictive it is to think of instructional materials only in terms of textbooks, workbooks, and ditto sheets.

CHILDREN'S WRITING

A natural next step for children who have had many opportunities to help compose language experience material is to write their own. What children write provides text they and others can read.

As with group-composed material, writing by individuals does not just happen but, instead, is stimulated and nourished by experiences and the chance to talk about them. This is effectively illustrated in a journal entry written by a second-grade teacher:

> Because children tire of reading basal stories and doing workbook and ditto-sheet pages, my objective this afternoon was to provide variety in the form of writing in which the whole class could participate.
>
> Before the children returned from gym, I taped huge, three-toed footprints on the floor, on top of some desks, and on part of the chalkboard. This was done in such a way that a path could be followed from the door to an open window. When the children came back, they were naturally excited, so it took a little time to calm things down to allow for a discussion.
>
> The discussion that took place was lively. Some children said that a monster had visited the room, so I wrote *monster* on the board. Others suggested it was a magic dragon. That, too, was listed on the board in a column of words that began with *m*. Another list eventually included *Frankenstein, Fang* (a sweet-toothed monster), and *Fat Albert*. Next we talked about the likely size of our visitor. Some immediately said he was big, which I printed by itself on another part of the chalkboard. Under *big*, I later added other contributions: *large, huge, gigantic*, and *enormous*.
>
> I then encouraged the children to tell me what they thought the "thing" looked like. Some said it had only one eye and one foot. Others said it had two feet like us all; otherwise, how could it walk? One child said that the monster had many feet. Still another suggested it stood as tall as the ceiling.
>
> Since one purpose of all these imaginative descriptions was to motivate some writing, I next had the children draw a picture of the monster. Those who finished first began writing stories to go with their drawings.

Individuals who had trouble writing dictated ideas to me, which I printed on other paper so that the children could copy them.

Tomorrow, after all the pictures and stories are finished, we'll listen to volunteers read what they wrote. One child suggested that we put the pictures and stories on the bulletin board, adding that "Mystery Feet" would be a good title for the display.

How unexpected events also provide content for children's writing was illustrated in another second grade. In this case, the description is written by an observer.

Approximately fifteen minutes before I arrived in this classroom, some-one else had come—a little black kitten who walked in with the children after lunch. When I did arrive, the teacher was holding the kitten while all the children sat around watching and talking. Intermittently, the teacher posed questions: How do you suppose this kitten feels when you pet him? Do you think the kitten likes being with us? Would he have any interest in coming to school?

Unexpectedly, one child observed aloud, "What if he belongs to some-body, and they're looking for him?" This altered the focus of the discussion, which now concluded with the decision to bring the kitten to the principal's office.

Before that was done, the kitten was allowed to roam around the room; meanwhile, the teacher suggested it would be a good time to draw a picture of him before he had to leave. The children talked among themselves as they drew, then spontaneously wrote descriptions and comments about the visitor.

Unexpectedly, the kitten jumped up on the top of a low bookshelf and immediately curled up beside a book. "He wants to read," commented one child. "I'll read to him while you draw," responded another, who was soon reading a story to the kitten while he sat in her lap. The other children persisted with their drawings and stories; the teacher walked around offering encouraging comments and help with spelling whenever it was requested. Later, after the kitten was taken to the office, some of the children held up their pictures and then read their stories.

While group experiences provide a suitable starting point for children's writing, motivation and content also derive from the unique experiences of individuals:

I have two nostrils but only one nose. I put an eraser in my left nostril. The doctor tried to get it out. I blew it out. I also got a lemon and lime sucker. I'm fine now. I will never do that again. It hurts.

Writing done by other children appears in Figures 9.10, 9.11, and 9.12.

WRITING AND READING

When comprehension is viewed as a process in which readers construct or generate meaning (15), it is only natural to think of the similarity between comprehending written text and composing it. And when attention is called to the contributions that experiences, relevant knowledge, and purpose make to reading, the similarity of the two processes seems even greater (13, 14). It is not unexpected, therefore, that the "reading-writing connection" has been a popular topic in recent years. Evidence that children do an extensive amount of reading when they reread and revise their writing (5, 8) has hardly contained the interest, nor have observations such as the following, which were made by a child who had had much encouragement and many opportunities in classrooms to be an author:

> Before I ever wrote a book, I used to think there was a big machine, and they typed a title and then the machine went until the book was done. Now I look at a book and I know a guy wrote it and it's been his project for a long time. After the guy writes it, he probably thinks of questions people will ask him and revise it like I do. (2, p. 157)

As might be expected, the widespread interest in writing as something that may help with reading has resulted in many writing activities in basal reader manuals. Some of the suggestions, in fact, are in the readers themselves. The latter inevitably include requests for written answers to assessment questions listed at the end of every selection. In the manuals, such unimaginative suggestions as having children write sentences using certain words are also highly visible. Even though other suggestions are better, glancing through any current basal program prompts thoughts permeated by the theme "too much of a good thing." Equally inevitable is regret that authors of the programs emphasize the products of writing (e.g., answers to questions) even though it is attention to the *process* of composing (e.g., be audience-minded) that has been proposed as a possible way to enhance reading ability. Clearly, a selective use of manual recommendations continues to be necessary. Otherwise, increased amounts of written busywork that foster negative attitudes toward writing (and reading) will be inevitable.

WRITING ACTIVITIES FOR READING

Obviously, whatever children write results in material they and others can read. Minimally, therefore, it provides practice. At times, however, a teacher may choose to give a writing assignment designed to help with a specific reading ability. Using details provided by an author in order to form a mental image exemplifies one such ability. Distinguishing between necessary and unnecessary details is another. A writing assignment that may contribute to both abilities is described below. (More children than are referred to – plus a teacher – could be involved.)

Child 1:   Draws a picture of a house in color.
           Writes a description of the house.

Child 2:   Reads description and draws a picture based on it.

Both: Compare pictures to note any differences. Why differences are found may be accounted for by necessary but omitted details (color of roof), or by descriptions that are vague (front door mentioned but not its location).

Child 1:   Rewrites description of the house to add essential details and, perhaps, to omit unnecessary content.

Child 3:   Draws picture based on revised description.

Child 1 and   Discuss their two pictures to see whether differences exist
Child 3:   and, if so, why.

In one second grade, a teacher chose to introduce similes in a writing activity. In this instance, the attention similes received originated in distracting behavior that occurred all too often between eleven o'clock and noon when boys from a nearby school peered in the windows. Their unwelcome appearance put *annoy* and *annoying* into everyone's vocabulary; the boys also made it natural to introduce similes with the example "as annoying as the boys who look in our windows." Examples the children provided included:

as annoying as a dog barking at night

as annoying as having to go home before a game is over

as annoying as my little sister when she cries

Whenever it was appropriate to do so, the children in this class were encouraged to use similes in their writing. Meanwhile, if books the teacher read to the children contained one or more similes, they were identified and discussed after a book was read.

Another teacher used writing to prepare one instructional group for their first encounter with the technique known as flashback. (A basal story soon to be assigned started with an account of events taking place in the present, went on to have one character's thoughts return to the past, after which the plot unfolded in chronological order.) In this case, preparations that involved the whole class centered on a hurricane whose predicted arrival – which, fortunately, never took place – caused much concern in the community. With the help of newspaper pictures of the storm that came in place of the hurricane, the children discussed their experiences while the storm was occurring. What the children's families had done before the storm was recalled next. Finally, the discussion shifted to consider how everyone felt and what they did after the storm. All this became three topics for a writing activity executed according to the following headings:

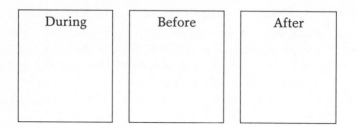

During	Before	After

Later, the sequence followed for the writing was reviewed with one instructional group when the basal story referred to earlier was about to be assigned.

In another classroom, a writing assignment came after a group read a basal selection. The basal story was about a girl named Rachel who was unhappy because nobody paid any attention to her. Told from a first-person perspective–this had been discussed before the children began their reading–it describes Rachel's efforts to get attention. In the end, she learns that showing interest in others is an effective way to get others interested in you.

After the story was discussed, the teacher said to the instructional group:

> Remember, this story was written as if Rachel were the author. I wonder if anything would be different had it been told by somebody else–by Rachel's brother, Billy, for instance. (Billy was one of the people who ignored Rachel.) Let's see if you can write the story about Rachel, but tell it as if you were her brother. In fact, let's call your stories–I'll write the title on the board so that you don't forget–"My Sister, Rachel." Have your stories finished by tomorrow. They don't have to be as long as the one in your reader.

When the children read their stories the next day, it very quickly became clear that there are at least two sides to every story and that a story may vary considerably depending on who is doing the telling.

Having discussed a few contributions that writing can make to enhancing comprehension, it might be necessary to state explicitly that writing activities should not be overdone. With that in mind, other ways to supplement basal selections are described next.

MATERIAL RELATED TO
BASAL SELECTIONS

Published books that children can read on their own and that have underlying themes similar to basal selections are not hard to find. The independent reading will add something to the basal selection and will achieve other goals as well. For instance:

BENEFITS OF EASY MATERIAL

Allows children to experience success and thus builds their self-confidence.

Promotes interest in reading.

Allows children to attend to meaning, as words are identified and understood at the level of automaticity.

Helps to develop fluency, which contributes to comprehension.

Allows for what may be the most productive kind of reading practice: reading.

To show how easy books can be read in conjunction with basal selections, let's start by reconsidering the basal story about Peter, the pioneer boy who wanted to be bigger than he was. Recall the reference to this story in the previous chapter during the discussion of story structure, in particular, of how structure can suggest comprehension assessment questions. One teacher might use the questions listed earlier as purpose-setting questions; another might decide to establish a purpose with the following assignment, which is distributed to members of the instructional group after attention has gone to the new vocabulary in the story about Peter and to the background information required for understanding it.

> Read the story about Peter. Then read the story called *Herbie, the Hippo.* (Copies are on the top of the book shelf.) When you finish both stories, write one title below that would be a good title for the two stories. Under the title tell why you chose it.

The purpose of the assignment is to learn whether the children see that the underlying theme of both stories is the same: Be satisfied with who you are. (The second, easier story is about a hippopotamus who wants to be a bird. Like Peter, he learns to be satisfied being what he is by the time the story ends.)

In another classroom, an expository selection entitled *How Big Is Big?* is in a basal reader (see Figure 14.4). The purpose is to provide information about the size of a variety of animals. Now, the book called *Let's Find Out What's Big and What's Small* (see Figures 15.2 and 15.3) would serve well as supplementary material. Although of a lower readability level than the basal selection, it deals with a more difficult concept, namely, the relativity of size.

Two further ways in which teachers have extended the content of basal selections with supplementary reading are described below.

- A series of stories in a third-grade reader dealt with jungle animals. To introduce the unit, the teacher prepared a display of colorful *National Geographic* photographs of the same animals. Each photograph was accompanied by a one-paragraph description followed by questions whose answers were not in the paragraph. Books that had the answers were also displayed.
- Since the next basal story was about a cat, one second-grade teacher started by showing the children photographs of her own two cats. This led to an animated discussion; to plans to bring in pictures of the children's cats the next day; and to an eagerness to read the basal story. By the next morning, the teacher had prepared a bulletin-board display of pictures of cats along with a table display of easy books about them.

For additional suggestions about materials children enjoy reading, see Figure 15.4 and the commentary that accompanies it.

USING OLD BASAL SERIES

The strong likelihood that basal programs will continue to be the dominant influence on what is done to teach reading accounts for the amount of space allotted in this chapter to suggestions for supplementing basal selections. Not to be overlooked in this context is the possibility of using old basal programs that have been replaced either by an updated edition or a different series. How replaced materials functioned in the hands of some inventive teachers is described next.

- One teacher tore out stories from readers that covered a range of readability levels. Stories were distributed so each child had one he or she could read without help. The children's responsibilities, to be carried out whenever they had time, were to (a) read the story in order to draw a cover that reflected its content; (b) reread the story in order to prepare questions about it; and (c) write the questions and tuck them into the story. When this was done, stories were exchanged with partners having comparable reading ability. Now they read the second story in order to answer the questions. Later, the pairs of children met so writers of questions could check on a partner's answers.

- Another teacher used illustrations in basal selections to encourage writing. The job for interested children was to write a story suggested by the pictures. (The wordless picture books referred to in an earlier chapter are likely to be more effective in developing "a sense of story." In addition, the pictures in some will appeal to older children. A reference at the end of this chapter [7] includes a lengthy list of wordless picture books suitable for use at a variety of grade levels.)

- Aware that a number of children had difficulty following written directions, one teacher cut out directions found in workbooks and attached them to sheets of paper. Copies were made in order to allow for teacher-supervised discussions of requirements for understanding directions. In some instances, the decision was to rewrite unclear directions. (E.g., "Write the letter for each definition next to the vocabulary word it defines.")

- Using two copies of brief basal reader selections, a teacher mounted individual paragraphs on cards. Paragraphs for each selection were kept in an envelope on which the title was written. Children who needed practice in following a sequence read the paragraphs in order to arrange them in an order that made sense.

- Another teacher cut out poems from readers and mounted them on cards, minus titles. Multiple copies allowed for small-group discussions of their content, for decisions about titles that reflected the central message or theme, and for a comparison of the children's titles with those of the authors.

When an entire faculty is committed to doing the best job possible, even more can be done to allow replaced materials to increase individualized instruction. For example:

- Aware of the need for more special-needs instruction, one faculty turned a summer workshop into a productive two weeks by tearing apart literally hundreds of old workbooks in order to sort out pages according to the type of practice they provided. Pages worth assigning were filed in a materials center (unused classroom) on the basis of what they dealt with and at which level. When the school year began, teachers were free to make selections from the files whenever regular classroom materials were inadequate. The following summer, time was spent not only on an evaluation of the file materials but also on presentations from the teachers on how they had supplemented them with their own ideas. Later, the best ideas were described on cards, which were also filed under appropriate headings.

Next to an elephant, a rabbit looks small.

Figure 15.2
From LET'S FIND OUT WHAT'S BIG AND WHAT'S SMALL by Martha and Charles Shapp, copyright 1959 by Franklin Watts, Inc. Reprinted with permission of Franklin Watts, Inc., p. 11.

Next to a mouse, a rabbit looks big.

Figure 15.3

From LET'S FIND OUT WHAT'S BIG AND WHAT'S SMALL by Martha and Charles Shapp, copyright 1959 by Franklin Watts, Inc. Reprinted with permission of Franklin Watts, Inc., p. 12.

Figure 15.4

Comic books, popular with children because of their action and low readability
levels, should not be automatically dismissed from consideration when material
other than basal selections is being sought. The page shown here is from a
series based on the classics. Anyone who might wonder about using comic
books in school will find it helpful to read two articles listed in the References
at the end of this chapter (1, 9). Written by women who are both mothers and
teachers, the two authors tell of the success of comic books in getting their
own children to read when everything else turned them off.

Not to be overlooked, either, are newspapers and magazines written especially for children. Among the latter is *National Geographic World*, which, like its
adult counterpart, *National Geographic Magazine*, is colorfully illustrated.* Other
magazines that attract young readers in large numbers include *Highlights for
Children*,** which offers short articles, riddles, and many opportunities to make
things with the assistance of written directions.

*National Geographic Society, Washington, D.C.

**Highlights for Children, Inc., Columbus, Ohio.

Moby Dick by Hermann Melville. Copyright © 1973 by Pendulum Press, Inc. Used with permission of Pendulum Press, Inc. All rights reserved.

CONCLUDING COMMENTS

If nothing else, the combined content of Chapters 14 and 15 should reinforce the conclusion that classroom practices like those described below are inexcusable. The account was written by a graduate student following an observation of a primary-grade classroom:

> No attempt was made to ease the children into the basal lesson that I observed. Instead, once they were seated in the reading area, the teacher began immediately to review words printed on cards. Following that, she listed new words on the board, identifying each as she printed it. She then read the entire list. There was no discussion of meanings, nor was any attempt made to put the two function words into phrases or short sentences. While all this was being done, several children in the group were looking around the room.
>
> Next came round robin reading. Since so little time had gone to pre-reading preparations, the reading was not good. But nobody really paid much attention to the oral readers—not even the teacher, as she was kept busy reminding the other children to follow in their books what was being read aloud.
>
> Each time a page was read, questions listed in the basal manual were asked. (I was surprised at how many could be answered by looking at the illustrations.) The page-by-page approach made for disjointed content; it is possible, therefore, that the large number of questions made it more, not less, difficult to comprehend the story.
>
> After the reading was done, the teacher asked members of the group to open their workbooks so that three pages could be assigned, none of which had any connection with the story. When the children got up to return to their desks, each received two ditto sheets. Apparently, they were accustomed to this, since none looked surprised nor asked questions.

Admittedly, what was just described is a basal lesson at its worse. Nonetheless, the description serves to explain why this textbook has as its central goal increased amounts of individualized instruction in every classroom, coupled with variety in materials chosen for the contributions they make to the attainment of that end.

SUMMARY

One way to highlight some of the most important points made in Chapter 15 is to refer to Teacher A; she is the one who (a) is aware of the large number of materials that have the potential to contribute to reading instruction, (b) realizes that materials are a means to an end, and (c) remembers that means can hardly be considered, much less chosen, until what it is they are supposed to be instrumental in achieving has been selected. Because many teachers rely much more extensively on basal reader programs than does Teacher A, Chapter 15 showed how other materials can both supplement and extend a basal series.

Chapter 15 also recognized the widespread interest in writing. Attention thus focused not only on some possible ways in which reading and writing can contribute to each other but also on the need for teachers to be highly selective as they examine the extensive number of suggestions for writing now found in basal manuals. As pointed out, it is unfortunate that so many recommendations concentrate on the products rather than on the process of writing.

Although discussed in an earlier chapter, language experience materials received further attention in Chapter 15. Here, the focus was on a more advanced use. Because other kinds of materials were also discussed in previous chapters (e.g., environmental text and bulletin board displays), they were not referred to in the present one.

Like so many of the earlier chapters, Chapter 15 tried to show that anyone with responsibility for teaching reading who thinks only in relation to textbooks, workbooks, and ditto-sheet exercises is working within a much too restricted framework.

REVIEW

1. It was stated many times in Chapters 14 and 15 that instructional objectives should be chosen before a teacher's thoughts turn to materials. How can those who use a basal program, either by choice or decree, follow this guideline?

2. Ideally, the work children do on their own should be as helpful in advancing their reading ability as is the work they do with a teacher. Name the suggestions in Chapter 15 for independent work and, as each is described, explain its value.

3. The idea that "If it's easy it couldn't possibly be good" may discourage teachers from having children read easy books as often as should be the case. Given that possibility, name the benefits that can derive from reading a book that requires no outside help.

4. Teachers who confine their selection of materials to one or more basal reader series will be bypassing many opportunities to demonstrate to children how useful it is to be able to read. Name other kinds of materials and the contribution(s) each can make when a teacher wants

to highlight the usefulness of reading ability. (Remember that instructional materials include anything that displays written words.)

REFERENCES

1. Alongi, Constance V. "Response to Kay Haugaard." *Reading Teacher* 27 (May, 1974), 801–803.
2. Calkins, Lucy M. *Lessons from a Child: On the Teaching and Learning of Writing.* Exeter, N.H.: Heinemann Educational Books, 1983.
3. Dionisio, Marie. "Write? Isn't This a Reading Class?" *Reading Teacher* 36 (April, 1983), 746–750.
4. Durkin, Dolores. "Is There a Match between What Elementary Teachers Do and What Basal Reader Manuals Recommend?" *Reading Teacher* 37 (April, 1984), 734–744.
5. Dyson, Anne H. "Reading, Writing, and Language." *Language Arts* 59 (November/December, 1982), 829–839.
6. Eckhoff, Barbara. "How Reading Affects Children's Writing." *Language Arts* 60 (May, 1983), 607–616.
7. Ellis, DiAnn W., and Preston, Fannie W. "Enhancing Beginning Reading Using Wordless Picture Books in a Cross-Age Tutoring Program." *Reading Teacher* 37 (April, 1984), 692–698.
8. Graves, Donald H., and Murray, Donald H. "Revision in the Writer's Workshop and in the Classroom." *Journal of Education* 162 (Spring, 1980), 38–56.
9. Haugaard, Kay. "Comic Books: Conduits to Culture?" *Reading Teacher* 27 (October, 1973), 54–55.
10. Kinney, Martha A. "A Language Experience Approach to Teaching Expository Text Structure." *Reading Teacher* 38 (May, 1985), 854–856.
11. Morris, Darrell. "Concept of Word: A Developmental Phenomenon in the Beginning Reading and Writing Process." *Language Arts* 58 (September, 1981), 659–667.
12. Policastro, Margaret M. "What's Happening: Predicting before, during, and after the Picture." *Reading Teacher* 38 (May, 1985), 929.
13. Squire, James R. "Composing and Comprehending: Two Sides of the Same Basic Process." *Language Arts* 60 (May, 1983), 581–589.
14. Tierney, Robert J., and Pearson, P. David. "Toward a Composing Model of Reading." *Language Arts* 60 (May, 1983), 568–580.
15. Wittrock, M. C. "Writing and the Teaching of Reading." *Language Arts* 60 (May, 1983), 600–606.

PART V

Making Decisions

As repeatedly stressed, the most important decisions teachers ought to be making have to do, first, with maximizing individualized instruction and, second, with making school as interesting and relevant for children as is possible. That other purposes guide the decisions of some teachers was suggested in a kindergarten in which 310 minutes were spent observing the morning and afternoon sessions. A few reasons for reaching such a conclusion will be mentioned.

To begin, the morning and afternoon sessions were identical even though the two classes were different. Each session started by having the children tear leaves from brown, yellow, and orange paper. This was done every year, the teacher said, on the first day of autumn. (As it happened, on this first day of the new season, all the trees that were visible from the kindergarten were still very green.) Each year, too, the teacher explained, she found it impossible to work with anything less than the whole class because an aide was not available. (Even though "Work Time," consisting of four activities that included building with blocks and playing in the "kitchen corner," provided an opportunity to give time to individuals or small groups, the teacher used the 23 minutes to fill out a form at her desk.)

Evidence suggesting disregard for the importance of matching programs with children was found in other comments the same teacher made. For instance:

"We make three books a year. The first is on health."

"I start teaching words in January."

Since decisions for achieving appropriate instruction in kindergarten (and nursery school) are discussed in Chapter 5, the last part of this book concentrates for the most part on the various kinds of decisions required for individualized instruction beyond kindergarten.

CHAPTER 16

Decisions: Materials, Classroom Organization, and Instruction

PREVIEW

The kindergarten program referred to in the opening to Part V might be portrayed as follows:

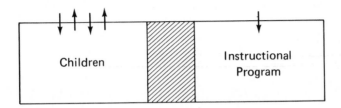

The sketch is meant to show a curriculum that remains unchanged in spite of the fact that each year, one group of children departs and is replaced by a different group the next year. It is as if an opaque wall kept the children out of the sight of the teacher, thus allowing the boys and girls to have little or no effect on instruction. As should now be clear, at levels beyond the kindergarten, instructional programs in reading are almost always defined by basal series.

How to alter this highly questionable conception of schooling underlies the content of this chapter, which deals with some topics that relate to the achievement of individualized instruction: classroom organization and management; selection of materials; and diagnosis.

The first part of Chapter 16 focuses on (a) the selection of materials for instruction and (b) classroom organization since the two topics are connected. Because classrooms have to be managed as well as organized, classroom management receives attention, too. The second part of the chapter considers ways for teachers to uncover who needs to learn what.

One trait that separates superior teachers from all others in their profession is the ability to make wise, informed decisions. This is verified whenever such teachers are observed; the products of their decision-making ability are clearly visible. With teaching, critical decisions have to do with what should be taught, to whom it needs to be taught, and how it will be taught.

The importance of knowing what should be taught accounts for the inclusion of Chapter 5 and Chapters 7 through 13 in this book. The need to know how to teach it is the reason so many illustrative lessons are in those and other chapters and why, in addition, instructional materials receive a generous amount of coverage. The importance of knowing to whom the various abilities, understandings, and skills need to be taught is one reason for this chapter. Another reason is to allow for a discussion of decisions related to (a) materials children will be asked to read, and (b) classroom organization and management. The difficulty of materials is discussed first.

RELATIVE DIFFICULTY OF TEXT

The concept *readability* is explained in Chapter 14. The need now is to consider the difficulty of text, not in isolation—as does the discussion of readability—but in relation to particular children's abilities. When such relations are in the picture, three descriptions of materials are natural outcomes: independent level, instructional level, and frustration level.

Independent-Level Material

As Chapter 15 explains, reading easy material has a number of important benefits, which suggests that encouraging children to read what they can manage on their own ought to be more common in classrooms than is often the case. As the same chapter illustrates, easy material—usually said to be at a child's *independent level*—can also be used to complement selections in basal readers.

Instructional-Level Material

Material that is too difficult for a child to manage alone, but that can be read if the right kind of help is available, is said to be at the student's *instructional level*. With help, instructional-level material should advance children's abilities.

Frustration-Level Material

Material is at the *frustration level* if it is so difficult that even with expert assistance, a child's efforts to read it would be marked by failure and thus

477

frustration. An essential difference exists, therefore, between materials offering challenge that can be met and, on the other hand, materials that put success out of reach.

Common sense suggests that frustration-level material should always be avoided. Yet, if something like a basal reader is selected not in relation to children's abilities but in relation to the grade-level sign on the classroom door, the use of frustration-level material with some children is almost inevitable.

In addition to fostering negative attitudes toward reading, frustration-level material—if its use is prolonged—also fosters the habit of reading everything slowly, regardless of its difficulty. Such material, then, like the routine use of round robin reading, helps account for needlessly slow rates of reading.

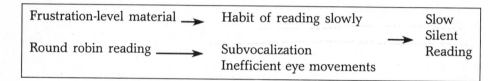

The implication of the connections displayed here is too obvious to mention and too important for teachers to ignore, especially when it is remembered that excessively slow rates of reading put a burden on a child's memory, making comprehension needlessly difficult.

CHOOSING INSTRUCTIONAL MATERIALS: SOURCES OF HELP

As stated innumerable times, selections in basal readers are what children typically read in school. This practice assumes—right or wrong—that the reading itself, plus a teacher's assistance and instruction, will result in increased abilities. With that goal in mind, the difficulty of the basal readers should be at the children's instructional level.

Various sources of information are available to help teachers decide at the start of a school year which basal readers to use with the children who are now their responsibility. One source, which is what teachers commonly rely on, are school records. Two other sources are teacher-prepared oral tests and cloze tests. Another source of information is the commercially prepared *Informal Reading Inventory*. All four sources of help for selecting instructional-level materials and, in turn, for organizing instructional subgroups, are discussed in the following sections.

School Records

From the time children enter school, a cumulative record card is kept on each student. By the end of first grade, records begin to show the materials a child has read. Since practically all schools use basal readers for the core of their instructional program, the information typically pertains to them. (If the easiest materials in a basal series – beginning workbooks, for instance – are used in kindergartens, what each child completed in those materials will also be recorded.)

Information that is approximately correct about what was read in earlier years allows for knowing – at least tentatively – the materials to use at the start of a new school year. It also paves the way for the formation of instructional subgroups. Each such group is composed of children who presumably are at about the same general-achievement level in reading. When a basal series is used, each subgroup might be using a different reader or, as sometimes happens, more than one subgroup could be using the same reader but be on different pages.

None of the procedures just described for selecting pupil texts and forming general-achievement subgroups is questionable if a teacher views the decisions as tentative, thus subject to change as more information about the children's abilities accumulates. This point is stressed because of the frequency of "once a bluebird, always a bluebird."

Oral Basal Reader Test

In theory, the best way to learn which textbook in a basal series is at a child's instructional level is to hear the student read samples from various readers in that series. (The criteria listed in Table 16.1 can serve as approximately correct guidelines for reaching a conclusion.) In reality, however, two problems exist.

Table 16.1. *General Criteria for Rating Reading Level*

Level of Difficulty	Unidentified or Misidentified Words	Comprehension
Independent	No more than one per 100 words	90%
Instructional	Five or fewer per 100 words	75%
Frustration	Ten or more per 100 words	50%

From the teacher's perspective, the first problem is finding time to give an individually administered test. The other problem is referred to in Chapter 14: the readability levels of the selections that compose each basal reader are not identical (5, 8). It is thus impossible to know to what extent samples of text are representative of an entire book.

In spite of these problems, teachers sometimes find themselves in a position where it is almost necessary to give a basal test. Children without records who transfer from other schools constitute one reason for administering such a test. Children whose observed reading abilities do not correspond to the information recorded in their cumulative records comprise another reason. That is why an oral basal reader test will be described. Keep in mind, therefore, the two functions of oral reading, both discussed in Chapter 6. Of relevance now are the requirements when oral reading is used for diagnostic purposes:

Oral Reading

Function	*Requirements*
Communication	1. Material is preread.
	2. Audience is available
Diagnosis	1. Material is unfamiliar.
	2. Maximum privacy exists.

Preparing an Oral Basal Reader Test.   If decisions about materials (and, as a consequence, about instructional groups) are to result from an oral reading test, the materials a teacher expects to use provide the best content. More specifically, if a teacher is either obligated or decides to use one or more basal series, readers from those programs should figure in the testing. Preparations require randomly selected passages of approximately 100 words from all the books chosen and a list of several comprehension questions for each passage. Ideally, a passage will make sense by itself; otherwise, what preceded it should be quickly summarized before the test starts.

Administering an Oral Basal Reader Test.   Testing begins by having a passage read aloud. While this is being done, the administrator notes errors on another copy. (A better procedure is to tape the oral reading so errors can be marked later.) Beginning with material not likely to cause serious problems is best, as this helps a child feel comfortable and secure.

Once a passage is read—with or without a teacher's help—the child is next asked to reread it silently so comprehension can be assessed. (Before the second reading, the preselected questions are read with the reminder that they will be asked afterward.) Information about the number of misnamed (or unnamed) words and the percentage of questions correctly answered allow for approximately accurate estimations of what constitutes instructional-level material (see Table 16.1).

Cloze Test

A cloze test, you recall from Chapter 8, requires readers to fill in blanks in written passages with words that make sense syntactically and semantically. Some authors suggest (20) that cloze tests "are reasonably accurate placement tools" when the goal is to select basal readers that are at children's instructional levels:

> To construct a cloze test, you simply take a selection of about 300 words from the materials you might be using. Make a copy of it, leaving the first and last sentences intact, but omitting every fifth word in other sentences. A child who can replace 40 percent of the omitted words is probably at an instructional level with respect to that material. (20, p. 447)

Informal Reading Inventory

The oral basal reader test referred to is more informative than the cloze test just described, but, like all individually administered tests, is time consuming. Even more time is required for its preparation. All this accounts for commercially prepared products that attempt to duplicate the oral basal test. They are called *Informal Reading Inventories* (IRIs) and are available from a number of publishers. A page from one such inventory constitutes Figure 16.1. Examine that page now, in particular, the directions for using this IRI.

When a teacher's intentions are to select instructional-level materials and to form subgroups composed of children reading at approximately the same general level, the oral basal reader test described earlier is superior to any IRI for two important reasons. First, IRIs are more detailed than is necessary for the two stipulated purposes (selecting instructional-level material and organizing instructional groups). Second, knowing how a child reads IRI material does not necessarily result in knowing which textbook to use for instruction. More specifically, if the readability of an IRI passage is said to be second grade, level two, and certain children's efforts to read that passage indicate it is at their instructional level, a second grade, level two basal reader will not necessarily be at that instructional level (6, 18). This limitation in particular points up the wisdom of using materials that figure in an instructional program rather than passages from an IRI.

Although the majority of basal reader programs now include placement tests, some of which resemble IRIs, their effectiveness in identifying the particular reader in the series that is at a child's instructional level is unknown (23).

Whether a teacher-prepared oral basal reader test or an IRI or a commercially prepared basal placement test is used, an observation made by John Pikulski (19) about IRIs is effective in emphasizing that the total number of word errors has no direct significance for instructional decisions. What do

Common Error	Symbol	Notes
Repetition	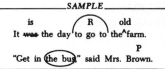 R	Mark word(s) repeated
Insertion	∧	Add additional word(s)
Substitution	—	Add substituted word
Omission	⬯	Circle word(s) omitted
Needs Assistance	P	Pronounce word when it's apparent that child does not know the word(s)

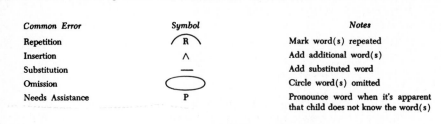

—————— SAMPLE ——————

is   R   old
It ~~was~~ the day to go to the∧farm.
                    P
"Get in ⟨the bus⟩" said Mrs. Brown.

Observe the child's general reaction while reading. If frustrated, he is likely to manifest excessive head movement and pointing, tension, a slow-labored rate of reading, or a soft whispered voice. It is recommended that the oral reading be stopped at or before the child reaches this point.

COMPREHENSION

After each oral selection the child is asked to answer five questions about what he has just read. The questions deal with the facts, inferences and vocabulary contained in each selection. The questions for each selection are in the separate Inventory Record and labeled; F (fact), I (inference) and V (vocabulary). Answers provided for each question are merely guides or probable answers to the question. Therefore, the teacher must judge the adequacy of each response made by the child.

Partial credit (½, ¼, etc.) is allowed for responses to questions. In some cases it is helpful to record the child's responses.

SCORING

WR (Word Recognition) COMP (Comprehension)

A scoring guide accompanies each oral selection. Each guide indicates the number of WR and COMP errors permitted within the limits of IND (independent), INST (instructional) and FRUST (frustration) levels of reading performance. Note (sample): each guide lists the number of errors permitted at each reading level. Therefore, the teacher must select the appropriate reading levels i.e., IND, INST, FRUST, based on the child's *actual errors* and the *suggested error limits* for each reading level.

—————— SAMPLE ——————

Scoring Guide: Second			
WR Errors		**COMP Errors**	
IND	0	IND	0-1
INST	2-3	INST	1½-2
FRUST	5+	FRUST	2½+

xiii

Figure 16.1. *An Informal Reading Inventory*

Nicholas J. Silvaroli. *Classroom Reading Inventory*, 2d ed., 1973, p. xiii. Reprinted with permission of Wm. C. Brown Company, Publishers, Dubuque, Iowa.

provide specific guidelines are the kinds of misidentifications that occur. Discussing how two children read the sentence *The boy sits on the chair and waits for his mother*, Pikulski notes:

> In the first [case], . . . substitutions and insertions did very little to change the meaning of the sentence. He made four scoreable errors. The second child read in a word-by-word fashion, needed examiner help with one word and substituted *champ* for *chair* and *water* for *waits*. A very substantial amount of difficulty with word recognition is suggested and the child received very little meaning from the sentence. Yet, the first child made four scoreable errors and the second made only three. Quantitatively, the second child did better according to conventional IRI scoring systems. (p. 146)

FORMING INSTRUCTIONAL GROUPS

As the previous sections indicate, decisions about instructional-level materials for members of a class allow for the formation of subgroups, each made up of children approximately the same in their general ability to read. Although these divisions have always had their critics, knowledgeable, experienced teachers know they would be kidding themselves were they to attempt to offer meaningful, effective instruction to an entire class. Equally clear to such teachers are both the impossibility and the inefficiency of nothing but one child–one teacher instruction. They thus accept general-achievement subgroups as a meaningful compromise, while aware that the membership of one or more subgroups may have to be altered from time to time as the reading ability of the children comes to be known with greater clarity and preciseness. When it does, the need for temporary special-needs subgroups may also become apparent to allow for instruction designed to remedy a shared problem or misunderstanding.

Aware of the importance of motivation for success, these same teachers make sure that as often as possible, children who share an interest (e.g., monsters, sailing, astronomy, basketball, horses) have opportunities to gather together to discuss what they learned about it from books and articles that may be written at different readability levels.

To sum up, then, one way to organize a class is to form general-achievement subgroups (whose membership may change during the course of a school year) and to supplement them with temporary subgroups of children who either have need for help with a particular problem or who share an interest in a topic about which they have been reading on their own. In the end, the best organized classrooms are the ones in which the organization fosters not only a maximum of individualized instruction but also an interest in reading.

DIFFERENTIAL TREATMENT
OF INSTRUCTIONAL GROUPS

Everyone naturally wants children to be winners in acquiring reading ability, but that is not the way it works. No matter what is done to help, there are always some losers.

In relatively recent years, the treatment of losers in classrooms has been the focus of a number of studies and reviews (1, 2, 3, 7, 12, 16, 17, 22). Consistent findings now suggest that what is done to help may actually contribute to the less-than-adequate achievement of such children. Specifically, when researchers compare how classroom teachers work with the poorest and the best readers, the following differences have been identified, all worthy of serious consideration by teachers and prospective teachers. For purposes of summarizing, the differential treatment reported is described from the perspective of low-achieving groups.

When working with poor readers, teachers tend to:
- Select material that is above their instructional level.
- Spend less time (than is the case for better readers) preparing lessons.
- Have almost nothing but round robin reading.
- Allow less time (than is the case with better readers) for the children to correct their mistakes.
- Stress the use of graphophonic cues, while almost ignoring contextual cues.   [phonics]
- Spend more time on individual words than on the meaning of connected text.
- Ask almost nothing but literal comprehension assessment questions.
- Spend more time (than is the case with better readers) on off-task, disciplinary actions.

Richard Allington, who has done a number of studies of teachers' treatment of poor and good readers (1, 2, 3), reached such specific (and interrelated) conclusions as the following (2):

1. Seventy percent of the reading in high-level subgroups is done silently, whereas only 30 percent of the reading in low-achieving groups is silent.
2. Students in the higher groups read about three times as many words per day in reading groups as do poorer readers.

In an article synthesizing findings from a number of studies of teachers' work with groups, author Patrick Shannon concludes:

Students in high groups are often asked to read texts which are easy for them; however, students in low groups are often placed in difficult materials in which they misread at least one in every ten words. This difficulty inhibits low group students' use of context, forces them to read word by word, and makes them rely on phonic characteristics of unknown words. Their frequent mistakes trigger student and teacher interruptions, and the unfortunate cycle begins anew. (22, p. 608)

The one positive feature of these findings is that they describe problems that are surmountable. Choosing more suitable materials, for instance, should not be out of the reach of any teacher. Independent silent reading is possible for all children—if teachers take seriously the responsibilities defined earlier as "facilitating comprehension" (see Figures 13.1 and 14.3). As for behavior problems, what else can be expected when children are in water over their heads?

How behavior problems can be minimized other than with appropriate materials and helpful instruction is discussed next, as the most perfectly organized classroom still needs to be managed well if children's learning and feelings of success are to be maximized.

MANAGING A CLASSROOM

Findings from classroom studies and the conclusions I reached after visiting schools over a long period of time match in a number of ways. Of relevance now is that the two bodies of information support the following contentions:

1. One of the greatest concerns to teachers is the possibility of losing control and, as a result, of having serious discipline problems.
2. More often than might be expected, a teacher's own behavior causes (or at least encourages) discipline problems.
3. What makes instruction effective also advances the achievement of successful classroom management.

Although one writer claims that "the nature of the teacher/student relationship is based upon a form of institutionalized dominance and subordination that emphasizes conformity and silence" (21, p. 5), the classroom management of concern here has neither conformity nor silence as its goal. It is viewed, instead, as a means for allowing maximum time for teaching and learning in a setting that is not mechanistic or impersonal. To put it differently, a well-managed classroom is orderly but not rigid, quiet but not oppressive. Most of all, it is a place where children have every opportunity to become the best readers they are capable of being.

Since the seeds are sown either for effective or ineffective management at the start of a new school year, some initial do's and don't's are reviewed first.

Getting Off to a Well-Managed Start

Just about everything I have observed, or read about, that has to do with ways for getting a new school off to a good start is in a report of a study by Carolyn Evertson and Linda Anderson entitled "Beginning School" (10). The report begins:

> Although there is agreement about what the well-managed classroom looks like, there has been very little classroom research that provides . . . specific advice . . . for achieving the smooth, well-run classroom. (p. 164)

Attempting to fill the void, the two researchers explain the purpose of their study:

> . . . we wanted to see what happens at the beginning of the year and how it affects management through the year. (p. 164)

Defining successful managers as teachers whose students consistently display large amounts of sanctioned behavior (academic and nonacademic), teachers observed to have "the lowest and highest on-task averages" were compared in order to identify "those principles that distinguished the two groups" at the beginning of the year. The comparison showed that:

At the beginning of the year, effective managers:
- Greet students at the door, see to it that they enter the room in an orderly manner, and direct them where to sit.
- Systematically introduce the new environment, pointing out what will be done where and explaining where belongings (coats, lunch boxes, and so on) are kept.
- Break down routines (lining up, sharpening pencils, and so on) into components that students understand and can practice.
- Provide instruction in a way in which "the important routines of the classroom become part of the curriculum" (p. 166).
- Work with the entire class at first in order to facilitate monitoring what is being done and to make immediate feedback possible for both academic performance and behavior.
- Are clear and specific about requirements for assignments. "Each step in seatwork is carefully explained, and the teacher watches each student as he or she performs each task" (p. 166).
- Reinforce expectations with positive comments about desirable behavior, both academic and nonacademic.
- Are consistent in enforcing rules.

When summarizing their data, Evertson and Anderson stress that effective managers have "a sound knowledge of the kinds of behavior they expect from students" (p. 165). In addition, "more effective managers begin at the first moment of the first day of school to establish themselves as the instructional leaders of their classrooms" (p. 165).

Further Reminders for Successful Management

It is said earlier that teachers may inadvertently promote what is unwanted: behavior problems. An apparent example of this is seen in a classroom depicted in Figure 16.2. In this room, who faced whom during the time scheduled for reading went completely contrary to the seating that successful managers arrange. The teacher in question faced a chalkboard as she sat at a table, while members of the subgroup with whom she was working looked in the direction of the rest of the class. Predictably, the teacher spent as much time turning around to identify who was talking or idle as she did instructing. The same seating arangements also meant that whenever she wanted to write something on the board, a child in the reading group had to do it because she was too far away.* The time all this took led to mischief among the children at the reading table. As a result of the combination of problems, only an infinitesimal amount of time was left for teaching.

Arrangements in a Classroom

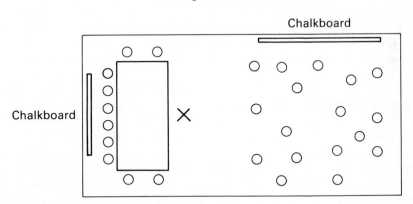

Figure 16.2.

---

*For reasons that are not obvious, basal manuals often recommend sending individual members of a group to the board to do something—cross out certain letters, underline prefixes, and so on. If those who make such suggestions took the time to visit classrooms, they would learn that adherence to their suggestions often results in inattentive and even misbehaving children.

Figure 16.2 also brings to mind another common cause of discipline problems: distractions. You may recall from Chapter 3 the references to two classrooms that had, in one case, a table display of clay figures next to the reading area and, in the other, a set of new pulleys. As said in that chapter: Do not tempt children for they will succumb!

Four other reminders underscored in previous chapters also merit being repeated:

Good managers:
- Think through what will be needed for an upcoming activity or a lesson and have everything readily available.
- Do not start an activity or a lesson until it appears that the children who need to attend *are* attending. Don't start till have attention
- Maintain attention at the start by explaining not only what will be done but what its purpose is.
- Do not distribute materials prematurely; otherwise, they will be a distraction.

Effective Instruction and Successful Management

Two more classrooms also mentioned earlier illustrate the connection between the quality of instruction and the quality of classroom management.

The first classroom is described in Chapter 14, when basal series were the primary focus. The point made is the importance of teachers' responsibilities for facilitating comprehension. In the classroom referred to, a teacher was working with the poorest readers, who were taking turns reading a story aloud. The feature of the reading emphasized in Chapter 14 was the large number of words each oral reader missed—something hardly conducive to comprehension. The point most relevant now was revealed in the teacher's explanation for having round robin reading:

> These children are too immature to read by themselves. The only way I can get them to read is to stay right with them. Yesterday I asked them to read this same story at their desks, but in less than a few minutes some were doing nothing while others were causing enough problems that they had to stay in at recess time.

Because of the large number of words the children either could not name or misnamed, what the teacher had done the previous day to prepare for reading the selection had to be questioned. Or, to state this differently, is it fair to blame the failure to read a selection silently and independently on immaturity when, in fact, the real problem might be insufficient preparation for doing the reading successfully? One can at least conjecture that had the preparation been adequate for these particular children – we will assume the text was not above their instructional level – both silent reading and the absence of discipline problems might have resulted.

To refresh your memory of the other classroom episode that demonstrates the link between good instruction and good management (and between the arrangement of furniture and good management), only those sections of the classroom that are pertinent are sketched in Figure 16.3.

Partial Diagram of a Classroom

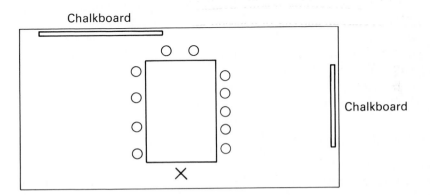

Figure 16.3.

At the time this particular class was observed, the teacher sat at the head of a long table with eleven children. Using the words suggested in a basal manual for reviewing the significance of punctuation (quotation marks) and capitalization, the teacher inquired of the group, "Does it make sense to say 'A boy was listening to the ancient tree'?" Whereas the manual said the children's response would be "No," one girl immediately responded, "Yes." She then explained, "Something might be inside the trunk that's making noise." Apparently responding to the manual's predicted response, not to the girl's explanation, the teacher proceeded to print *A boy was listening to "The Ancient Tree"* on an 8" by 11" piece of paper. (The manual recommended writing the sentence on a board, which in this room was some distance from where the teacher and children sat.) The few members of the group who were close enough to read the sentence on the paper immediately responded with comments like, "Oh, it's a story" and "He's reading a poem or something." Meanwhile, all the others talked among themselves and were soon chastised for not paying attention. Immediately afterward, the teacher shifted the focus – as did the manual – to a review of referents for pronouns.

Perhaps this can be summed up best by saying it is no accident that well-behaved children tend to be individuals whose potential for learning is being realized, mostly with instruction matched to both their needs and interests.

DIAGNOSIS AND INDIVIDUALIZED INSTRUCTION

The importance of instruction matched to children's needs accounts for the importance of diagnosis. This is so because in whatever form it takes, diagnosis – diagnosis worth doing, that is – is an attempt to learn what one or more children either know, understand, and can do, or, on the other hand, do not know, do not understand, or cannot do. (Both sides of the coin are equally relevant, since awareness of existing abilities is just as necessary as knowing what is lacking when an instructional objective is selected and instruction is planned.)

To be emphasized is that attempts to learn about abilities or the lack of them should not be conceived as special events that occur before parent conferences or for the purpose of marking report cards. Rather, the diagnosis that makes a difference and that is the concern here might be thought of as a mental set that makes it natural for teachers to be alert to evidence that suggests what is known or, to the contrary, what needs to be taught or practiced or, perhaps, retaught. Teachers with such mental sets would have no trouble completing a questionnaire like the one in Figure 16.4.

Underlying the questions listed in Figure 16.4 is what is often referred to as *diagnostic teaching* – descriptions of which have permeated this book. What follows in this chapter, therefore, is an extension of what is said in previous chapters. Or, to put it differently, this final chapter continues to aim toward enlarging the number of Teacher A's now found in classrooms.

DAILY OPPORTUNITIES FOR DIAGNOSIS

Assuming that one or more basal series are at the core of a school's instructional program, preplanned lessons in the classroom of a Teacher A are of two kinds. The first, often referred to as "a basal lesson," is fairly encompassing and typically extends over two or more days. (See Figure 14.3 to review the components of a basal lesson.) Basal lessons, as illustrated in Chapter 14, are one source for diagnostic information.

The second type of lesson concentrates on the attainment of a specific objective. Recall that the components of this more restricted type of lesson are instruction, practice (teacher-supervised and independent), and application. The second type of lesson is especially highlighted in the chapter that concentrated on comprehension because of the meager amount of comprehension instruction found in classrooms. To review the ways in which this

A Teacher's Self-Questionnaire

DID TODAY MATTER?

1. What did I try to teach today, and to whom?

    Instructional Objectives   Children

2. Why did I choose these objectives for these children?

3. How will the attainment of the objectives contribute to the

    children's reading abilities?

4. Did I take the time to clarify the connection between what I

    attempted to teach and how to be a better reader?

5. Did the children learn what I planned for them to learn?

    _____yes   _____no

6. (If yes) How do I know they did?

    (If no) Why do I think they did not?

    (If no) What do I intend doing next?

Figure 16.4.

second type of lesson provides for diagnosis, see Figure 13.2 as well as the illustrative lessons described in the section of Chapter 13 called "Reading Comprehension: Examples of Instruction."

   In order to add to the descriptions of opportunities for diagnosis, further examples are listed next in a way that calls attention to the opportunities these episodes offer for diagnostic teaching.

Episode One

A kindergarten teacher wrote *me* on the board, then asked, "How many words did I just write?" "Five!" shouted the children to whom the question had been posed.

Comment: This episode, referred to earlier, is repeated now because of the failure of commercially prepared manuals to recognize the fact that the meaning of *word* is unknown to many young children. Chapter 5 illustrates how its meaning can be clarified.

Episode Two

A page in a phonics workbook was reviewing the connection between *j* and /j/. It showed small pictures, each with a caption. Under one were the words *The juggler is in the jeep.* Asked to read that caption, a child responded, "The man is in the car."

Comment: The child's response prompts two thoughts that have significance for both material selection and instruction. The first has to do with phonics workbooks that include ludicrous material in order to present appropriate words. (After all, how often does one find a juggler in a jeep – or a yak in a yard?)

The second thought pertains to the child's use of a picture rather than relevant cues to name words. Such a procedure shows why children should *not* be encouraged to rely on picture content for help with words, even though basal manuals often recommend that. Instead, as suggested many times, a balanced use of contextual, graphophonic, and structural cues should be the goal of instruction.

Episode Three

After a general-achievement subgroup read a story about a very aggressive child, the teacher wrote *bold* on the board, said it was a word that described the boy in the story, and asked if anybody knew what it said. One child quickly identified it. In response to the teacher's next question, which asked for the meaning of *bold*, another child explained, "It means he doesn't have much hair on his head."

Comment: Clearly, this is a time for a chalkboard teacher. More specifically, the student's response points to the need to print *bald* under *bold* and to discuss the meaning and pronunciation of each word. The response further illustrates the common practice among children of ignoring contexts when meanings are considered. In this instance, the context is the story itself and, even though it may not directly define *bold*, it at least makes the meaning suggested by the student an unlikely one. The importance of contexts ("What makes sense?") should be reviewed whenever meanings are offered that are incompatible with contexts that may be as brief as a phrase or as long as a story.

Episode Four

In another classroom, *The water in the lagoon is deep* was read as "The water in the lake is deep."

Comment: Unlike the previous episode, the response in this case reflects acceptable use of a context but incomplete use of graphophonic cues. Although it is not too likely that calling a lagoon a lake will result in serious misunderstandings, a child's habitual use of one type of cue over others that are available suggests the need at least for reminders, and perhaps for some practice, in which a balanced use of cues is stressed.

Episode Five

A list of words was on the chalkboard. The children for whom it had been written were asked, "Do any of these words have a prefix or a suffix?" Immediately, one child said that *under* had a prefix.

Comment: When attention first goes to prefixes (and to suffixes), it is common to get responses like the one referred to here. They indicate the need to clarify with examples that prefixes are only attached to real words (to roots, if that term is understood). Not to be forgotten, either, is that responding in any way is more important for some children than responding correctly. Teachers need to be careful, therefore, to avoid the habit of calling on the first child who raises a hand. To do so encourages quick but not necessarily correct or thoughtful answers.

Episode Six

A teacher wrote *happen* on the board, separating its syllables with a space. Quite spontaneously, a child observed, "Oh, that's a compound word!"

Comment: This child's response parallels the previously mentioned response to *under* in the sense that the two comments illustrate the tendency of children to overgeneralize. In the episode referred to here, a review of compound words, coupled with a suitable number of examples as well as nonexamples (e.g., *carpet, notice, target*), should be helpful.

What is *not* helpful are commercial materials (see Figure 11.1) and teachers who encourage children to look for short known words in longer unknown words in order to decode the latter. As explained in Chapter 11, using the pronunciation of the shorter words is likely to be helpful only when certain precautions are taken. The precautions are described and illustrated in Chapter 11.

Episode Seven

To review letter-sound relationships and to provide practice in using them for decoding, a teacher wrote a list of unfamiliar words on the board that included *cap, pan, dip, cup, top,* and *pen.* The review began by having members of the instructional group recall the sounds associated with *c* (hard sound only), *p, t, d,* and *n.* The five short vowel sounds were recalled next. Then the teacher pointed to each letter in *cap* and, as she did, asked the children for its sound. Her next request was, "Who can tell me what this word says?" Nobody could. Once more the teacher pointed to *cap,* and asked the children to say the sound for each of its letters, this time more quickly. Still, nobody could read *cap.*

Comment: Since these children had had no previous help with blending sounds into syllables, their inability to pronounce *cap* was not unexpected. (Knowing letter-sound relationships does not automatically result in blending ability, which authors of most commercial materials do not seem to realize.) What should have preceded the activity just described was a series of lessons that would have begun with two letters, the first a vowel. Those lessons should have included modeling by the teacher of what it means to blend sounds, followed by opportunities for the children to blend some, too. At the start, the two letters need not be words; their connection with words, however, should be illustrated whenever possible (e.g., *ug-ugly, en-enter, um-umpire*). Eventually, the children will be ready to do the kind of blending that had been requested prematurely with the help of visual displays like the following:

ă	ă	ĭ
că	pă	dĭ
căp	păn	dĭp

Episode Eight

Following the silent reading of a basal story, which had been preceded by three teacher-raised questions to guide the reading, the same questions were posed again. For the most part, responses suggested very poor comprehension. Sometimes, in fact, the children's expressed conception of the story only barely resembled the one they were supposed to have read.

Comment: These first-graders, it needs to be pointed out, came from homes in which it is highly unlikely that preschoolers would be read to; thus, they lacked one of the experiences that prepare children to comprehend stories. Since basal reader programs start with stories, they can also start with problems for children like those described. (The incessant, brief, and some-what meaningless dialogues that characterize easy basal stories are often the cause of comprehension problems.) Instead of beginning with a basal reader, this teacher should have started with text as brief as single sentences. Eventually, paragraphs could be used—perhaps simple descriptions of familiar things. Later, stories can be introduced. Meanwhile, frequent contacts with stories should occur when the teacher reads to the children.

PREPLANNED DIAGNOSIS

As stressed earlier, the diagnosis of concern here is not conceived of as being "a special event," but, rather, a daily, taken-for-granted occurrence. Nonetheless, there are times when the need arises for preplanned diagnosis—that is, for deliberate attempts to learn about certain abilities or deficiencies. In such cases, one child or a group may be involved.

As seen in the following discussion of characteristics of preplanned diagnosis that is productive, similarities exist in what is required for helpful diagnosis and for individualized instruction.

Deals with What Contributes to Reading Ability

To begin, diagnosis ought to be concerned only with what contributes to reading ability. Taking time, for instance, to learn whether children can divide into syllables words they can read is highly questionable—unless the interest is in learning whether the concept *syllable* is understood.

At prior levels, finding out whether children can name letters in correct sequence is also a use of a teacher's time that has to be questioned—unless, in this case, interest lies in seeing whether the children are ready to be introduced to easy reference materials (e.g., a picture dictionary) that require knowing alphabetical order if certain information is to be located efficiently.

Seeing whether children can put roots together to form compound words is likely to be still another waste of time, since the task of the reader is to identify compounds, not to construct them. Again, the only reason that justifies such use of a teacher's time is an interest in learning whether the concept *compound word* is understood.

Has a Circumscribed Focus

A second characteristic of diagnosis worth doing is confinement to a specific focus. Although, at first, it may seem desirable to try to learn as much as possible as soon as possible about children's abilities (or lack of them), such ambition disregards the fact that everything cannot be taught right away. Since bulging folders of unused information is not the purpose of diagnosis, a more practical and valuable order to follow is: diagnose, teach, diagnose, teach . . . .

Affects Instructional Decisions

As just implied, a third characteristic of diagnosis that can make a difference is that the information it uncovers enters into decisions about what will be taught to whom. It is no exaggeration to say, in fact, that diagnosis is an exercise in futility if what is learned does not foster an increase in individualized instruction.

Even though some of you may think that "affects instructional decisions" is such an obvious requirement for diagnosis as to warrant no explicit attention, the classroom depicted in the following account of an observation may change your mind.

> When I observed this week in a second grade, I was reminded of the discussion we had in class about the critical importance of large sight vocabularies that include high-frequency words.
>
> Almost as soon as I entered the room, the teacher asked if I would listen to several children read so that I could check their ability to identify the new words in the basal story they had read earlier. Without waiting for an answer, she gave me a mimeographed list of the words she wanted checked.
>
> Here, I'll only comment on the first child I listened to, a boy named Dwayne. He brought his chair close to mine in a corner of the room and after we spent a few minutes getting acquainted, he opened his basal. Since he had read the story at least once before, he seemed bored to have to go through it again, but he did.
>
> The most apparent feature of Dwayne's reading reinforced the fact that a high-frequency vocabulary is a very useful thing to have and, in addition, that it is very important for comprehending. Dwayne was able to read all but one of the ten new words in the story including *helicopter*; however, he stumbled over, or misread, an average of about five high-frequency words per page. For example, he read the sentence *They found the helicopter on the building* as "They found the helicopter in the building."
>
> Later, when the children left the room to go to music, I discussed my findings with the teacher. To my great surprise, her response was that the children "should know those kinds of words when they get to second grade" and that about all she had time to do was "let them practice the words in the stories they read." Naturally, I left this room feeling disappointed, to say the least.

Now that the three most important characteristics of diagnosis have been identified, let's move on to examples of preplanned efforts to find out who knows what so that appropriate instruction can be provided.

EXAMPLES OF PREPLANNED DIAGNOSIS

The number of children in the typical classroom makes group diagnosis much more feasible than individual diagnosis. For that reason, the initial examples, each of which is introduced with a goal stated from the teacher's perspective, are of procedures used with groups.

Group Diagnosis

> *Goal:*   to learn whether six children remember letter-sound associations for *b, m, s, f,* and *h* and are able to perceive the five sounds in initial position in spoken words.

Wanting to know whether members of a subgroup are ready to learn additional letter-sound associations, a kindergarten teacher distributed five letter cards to six children who sat at one side of a table as she faced them from the other side. After the children placed their cards in front of them, the teacher explained that she would say a word; that they were to think of the letter that spelled its beginning sound; and that when she said "okay," they were to hold up that letter so she could see it. (Signaling when to respond was meant to encourage thoughtful responses.)

> *Goal:*   To learn whether a subgroup knows the most frequently used words introduced in a basal selection.

Constantly trying to cope with the excessive number of new words in basal selections, a first-grade teacher settled on the following plan for her work with a group of slow children: All words will be introduced and practiced prior to the reading of a selection. Afterward, additional time will go only to words likely to appear in other material. To learn whether such words have been learned, she uses the following procedure.

First, selected words on individual cards are reviewed, with all members of the group responding together. Next, sentence cards are used, each of which includes one or more of the selected words. For the diagnosis, children are directed to read a sentence silently so they will be ready to respond if called on. Now the job for individuals is to say the word that answers the teacher's question. Showing the sentence *The girl looked at the picture*, the teacher might ask, "What were the girls looking at?" since *picture* is among the selected words.

> *Goal:*   To learn whether a subgroup knows what a syllable is.

In one second grade, a teacher wondered about the large number of workbook pages that had children mark syllables in known words, presumably—she could think of no other reason—to help them understand the meaning of *syllable*. (Otherwise, why the use of known words?) Believing that the eleven best readers had no need for such practice, she gave them a list of familiar words of varying length along with three number cards. After a word was read aloud by the group, each reader was directed to hold up the card that told the number of its syllables. Consistently correct responses were accepted as evidence of what had been assumed about the children. The teacher's decision, therefore, was to skip the workbook pages and to use the time that was saved on dividing unknown words into syllables with the help of visual cues.

> *Goal:* To learn whether a subgroup can use generalizations to divide unknown words into syllables.

A third-grade teacher had been helping a group of nine children use generalizations to divide unknown words into syllables. (The instruction was not given to the other children because they had already demonstrated ability to use the generalizations.) To learn whether the extra instruction achieved its objective, this teacher distributed a list of twenty-five unfamiliar words to the nine, and asked them to divide each one (using slash marks) with the help of visual cues described in the generalizations. Results would indicate whether any of the nine required further help.

> *Goal:* To learn whether two children use contextual cues for help with unknown words.

In another second grade, the second month of a new school year was just under way. Earlier, while listening to some of the children read selected passages so that general-achievement levels could be identified, the teacher noticed that two boys, both spending a second year in second grade, seemed content to say anything whenever they came to an unfamiliar word. It was as if they didn't realize that reading is supposed to make sense. To learn more about their reading, the teacher met with the two to see what they knew about using contexts. She began by having the boys take turns reading sentences in which a word was deleted. (One sentence read: "When you come in, _____ the door.") Any word was accepted for the blank as long as it made sense. Results showed a need for attention to the semantic aspects of reading as well as to the use of contextual cues for word recognition.

Probably enough examples have now been given both to illustrate teacher-devised group diagnosis and to show its close ties to instruction. Samples of procedures used with individuals, therefore, follow.

Individual Diagnosis

Because of the difficulty of finding time to evaluate one child's abilities, let me preface the examples with a brief discussion of children who ought to be considered for such evaluation.

Candidates for Individual Diagnosis.   A child with atypically high ability will be named first because advanced readers do not figure in preplanned diagnosis as frequently as they should. Much too often, in fact, the solution for superior readers is extra and longer assignments, sometimes of a kind that add more to boredom and negative attitudes than to abilities. The question, "Just how able is this advanced reader?" should be asked (and answered) more often than is the case.

Naturally, children with deficiencies are other candidates for individual diagnosis. Whenever they are involved, an important guideline to follow is one mentioned earlier; namely, avoid trying to find out everything at once, since instruction cannot deal with everything at once.

The abilities and problems of children who transfer from other schools are often puzzling; hence, they also are candidates for individual diagnosis, as are students who have been in a classroom from the beginning, yet remain enigmas insofar as their reading is concerned.

Examples of Individual Diagnosis.   Since successful comprehension is the overriding goal to which all reading programs should be directed, the first two examples of individual diagnosis deal with that.

> *Goal:*   To learn about the ability to comprehend a main idea and related details.

The class was a second grade, and the time was early October. The instructional program in reading revolved around three general-achievement subgroups, each using a different basal reader. (In this school, basals must be used along with anything else a teacher chooses to use.) By now, the teacher felt not only ready but even eager to add other materials and other groups.

One decision already made was to use newly purchased booklets designed to provide practice in comprehending main ideas and details in expository text. The attraction of the booklets was their interesting content, written at various levels of difficulty. This allowed for a matching based on general achievement as well as on comprehension needs.

To identify who needed which practice (or who needed instruction), the teacher held individual conferences, at which time the children silently read passages written at what would be a level somewhere between the instructional and the independent. The children were encouraged to ask for assistance with words they didn't know and couldn't decode. (The level of the material selected and the opportunity to get help with words reflected the teacher's desire to separate vocabulary problems from comprehension deficiencies.)

Before the first reading, the children were asked to read three questions that dealt with main ideas and were told they would be asked to answer them when they finished the reading. The same procedure was used for a second reading of the same passage, but this time the questions focused on details.

To keep a record of what was learned about each child, the teacher used a sheet that started in the way shown in Figure 16.5. A check on the sheet indicated problems, thus helped when it came time to assign the comprehension booklets and to organize two special-needs instructional groups that would meet twice weekly for as long as necessary. Children whose comprehension was acceptable would be allowed more time for reading self-selected trade books. (Ways to initiate and foster free reading are discussed in Chapter 7.)

Record Keeping for Diagnosis

	Details	*Main Ideas*
Art		√
Barbara		√
Billy		
Don	√	√
Frances		

Figure 16.5

Goal: To assess oral language ability.

This first-grade classroom is in an inner-city school in which reading problems are rampant. Part of an effort to minimize them is a reduced class size for all first grades. The reduction to seventeen children, combined with a very conscientious teacher and a full-time aide, has allowed for more success than was typical in previous years.

Shortly after the winter vacation, at a time when the teacher was just beginning to feel satisfied with the way plans were progressing, an additional child was assigned to the room. A transfer from another school, he was living in a foster home. Knowing little else about him (no records accompanied the transfer), the teacher decided to place him temporarily with the three most meager achievers for instruction. It soon became clear, however, that the boy knew less than they did. This led to the initial effort to pinpoint deficiencies. (Meanwhile, he was kept with the group of three.)

Because of the dependence of reading on oral language, this teacher decided to start the diagnosis by focusing on the comprehension of brief, spoken sentences. Ten sentences were prepared with a question for each. (E.g., The little dog ran away. Was the dog little or big? . . . It was snowing outside. Was it summer or winter?) The large number of unanswered and incorrectly answered questions suggested the need for fundamental help with oral language. In fact, just getting this child to talk was established as the objective having highest priority. Later, with the help of the aide, the teacher expects to be able to get the beginning of reading started by using simple, brief material. Meanwhile, efforts will be made to show him the connection between spoken and written language with the help of language experience material that focuses on the boy himself.

Goal: To uncover the reason for slow rates of reading

A first-grade teacher in another school used individual diagnosis for a different reason. Among the best readers in the class were two children (a girl and a boy) who always required more time to finish assigned reading than did the other children who read well. To learn why, this teacher prepared a list of all the service words that had been taught. Meeting separately with the boy and girl, the teacher asked each child to read the list as quickly as possible. (A list was used rather than sentences because rapid reading requires automatic identifications of frequently used words.) Results indicated quick as well as correct responses.

The teacher next considered the possibility of habit being the source of the problem. Consequently, she prepared sentence cards for the second individual conference. She displayed each sentence to the children for a limited amount of time, then posed a question about the content. Now, results were different. One child did so poorly that the procedure was terminated after four sentences had been shown. The other did better but still missed five out of ten questions. Since neither the vocabulary nor the content of the sentences was difficult enough to impede comprehension, the teacher concluded at least tentatively that the problem lay with habit. That is why she plans to provide the two children (plus any others who might profit) with practice similar to the diagnostic procedure. Sentences will be displayed briefly, then questions will be asked. Once the children are successful with the limited text, the teacher plans to have them read simply written paragraphs in a given amount of time. The hope is that enough easy, timed reading will give the two children the ability to read quickly whenever the purpose for reading makes rapid rates desirable.

What this and all the other examples of diagnostic procedures demonstrate is the special value of teacher-devised diagnosis and, in addition, the close connection between diagnosis and individualized instruction.

SUMMARY

It is highly appropriate to conclude Chapter 16 with a reference to individualized instruction, since how to realize it was the decisive factor in choosing the content for this final chapter.

The content dealt, first of all, with ways for learning at the beginning of a new school year what constitutes instructional-level material for the members of a class. (Instructional-level material was defined as text that is sufficiently difficult as to allow for the advancement of abilities when suitable kinds and amounts of instruction are provided.) Because basal materials are customarily used, the recommendation was to select basal readers that are at children's instructional levels. This was followed by a discussion of four sources of information that can guide selections: (a) school records, (b) teacher-devised oral basal tests, (c) teacher-devised (basal) cloze tests, and (d) commercially produced Informal Reading Inventories. Why the latter provide the least useful help was explained.

Chapter 16 continued by pointing out that one by-product of identifying instructional-level materials is subgroups of students, each made up of individuals approximately the same in their general ability to read. Because such groups are the easiest to organize at first, reading instruction can be planned for them soon after a school year gets under way. Eventually, as abilities and deficiencies come to be known with greater precision, the need for temporary special-needs groups becomes apparent. As children's interests surface, subgroups based on shared interests are highly desirable, too. In this case, librarians can be very helpful in locating independent-level materials that deal with those same interests.

Since classrooms that allow teachers to teach and children to learn are not only thoughtfully organized but also well managed, classroom management was the next topic discussed. Specific guidelines for achieving well-run classrooms were offered.

Do's and don't's for diagnosis, the last topic considered, were outlined also. This advice was followed by support for the contention that considerable amounts of helpful information can be gleaned from children's daily responses. Subsequently, planned diagnosis was dealt with in a way that divided it into procedures that can be used with groups of children and procedures suitable for individual diagnosis.

Throughout the discussion of diagnosis, a point made repeatedly was the uselessness of collecting information if it is not of a kind that can and will be considered when decisions are made for both instruction and practice. This means-end connection explains why the commercially produced achievement tests that schools administer annually were omitted from the discussion of diagnosis.

REVIEW

1. Define the terms listed below; explain when each type of material should be used.

   independent-level material
   instructional-level material
   frustration-level material

In what way are the three listed terms different from the term *readability*?

2. Three kinds of subgroups were referred to in Chapter 16. What are the basis and purpose of each?

3. Why was it said in the chapter that procedures typically used in classrooms with poor readers—presumably to help them—may in fact contribute to student failure to reach higher levels of ability?

4. Reread the pages in Chapter 16 that deal with how to achieve a well-managed classroom. Summarize the advice given.

5. (a) Answers for an assignment that has children divide unknown words into syllables include the following:

    dress/ed   mun/ch   mis/coun/ted   e/xam/ple

What does each incorrectly divided word suggest needs to be reviewed?

(b) When children are asked to show with diacritical marks the likely vowel sounds in unknown words, one response is as follows:

sēnsé

Again, based on the response, what needs to be reviewed?

6. (a) Let's say that five children read the following sentence aloud:

    The canary flew out of the cage.

For purposes of discussion, let's also say that each child responds differently to *canary*. The five responses are: bird, canary, candy, cardinal, carry. Where would you place each response on the following continuum and what is your reason for each placement?

Best   ├─────────────────────────────┤   Worst
response   response

(b) Specify how the first part of this question shows that analyzing misidentifications, not counting them, is what is helpful for instructional decisions.

7. Starting with a definition of *individualized instruction*, explain the following:

    Classroom organization
    Classroom management
    Suitable materials for
      children   } ⟶ Individualized
    Diagnosis   instruction

8. In what ways are the characteristics of individualized instruction and useful diagnosis similar?

REFERENCES

1. Allington, Richard L. "Poor Readers Don't Get to Read Much in Reading Groups." *Language Arts* 57 (November/December, 1980), 872–876.
2. Allington, Richard L. "The Reading Instruction Provided Readers of Differing Reading Abilities." *Elementary School Journal* 83 (May, 1983), 548–559.
3. Allington, Richard L. "Teacher Interruption Behaviors during Primary-Grade Oral Reading." *Journal of Educational Psychology* 72 (June, 1980), 371–377.
4. Borko, Hilda; Shavelson, Richard J.; and Stern, Paula. "Teachers' Decisions in the Planning of Reading Instruction." *Reading Research Quarterly* 16 (1981, No. 3), 449–466.
5. Bradley, John M., and Ames, Wilbur S. "The Influence of Intrabook Readability Variation on Oral Reading Performance." *Journal of Educational Research* 70 (November/December, 1976), 101–105.
6. Bristow, Page S.; Pikulski, John J.; and Pelosi, Peter L. "A Comparison of Five Estimates of Reading Instructional Level." *Reading Teacher* 37 (December, 1983), 273–279.
7. Butkowsky, Irwin S., and Willows, Dale M. "Cognitive-Motivational Characteristics of Children Varying in Reading Ability: Evidence for Learned Helplessness in Poor Readers." *Journal of Educational Psychology* 72 (June, 1980), 408–422.
8. Duffelmeyer, Frederick A. "A Comparison of Two Noncomputational Readability Techniques." *Reading Teacher* 36 (October, 1982), 4–7.
9. Durkin, Dolores. "Is There a Match between What Elementary Teachers Do and What Basal Reader Manuals Recommend?" *Reading Teacher* 37 (April, 1984), 734–744.
10. Evertson, Carolyn M., and Anderson, Linda M. "Beginning School." *Educational Horizons* 57 (Summer, 1979), 164–168.
11. Felmlee, Diane, and Eder, Donna. "Contextual Effects in the Classroom: The Impact of Ability Groups on Student Attention." *Sociology of Education* 56 (April, 1983), 77–87.
12. Forell, Elizabeth R. "The Case for Conservative Reader Placement." *Reading Teacher* 38 (May, 1985), 857–862.
13. Goodman, Kenneth S. "Analysis of Oral Reading Miscues: Applied Psycholinguistics." *Reading Research Quarterly* 5 (Fall, 1969), 9–30.
14. Guzzetti, Barbara J., and Marzano, Robert J. "Correlates of Effective Reading Instruction." *Reading Teacher* 37 (April 1984), 754–758.
15. Haller, Emil J., and Waterman, Margaret. "The Criteria of Reading Group Assignments." *Reading Teacher* 38 (April, 1985), 772–781.
16. Hiebert, Elfrieda H. "An Examination of Ability Grouping for Reading Instruction." *Reading Research Quarterly* 18 (Winter, 1983), 231–255.
17. Jongsma, Eugene. "Research Views: Grouping for Instruction." *Reading Teacher* 38 (May, 1985), 918–920.

18. McKenna, Michael C. "Informal Reading Inventories: A Review of the Issues." *Reading Teacher* 36 (March, 1983), 670–679.
19. Pikulski, John J. "A Critical Review: Informal Reading Inventories." *Reading Teacher* 28 (November, 1974), 141–151.
20. Pikulski, John J. "Questions and Answers." *Reading Teacher* 37 (January, 1984), 447–448.
21. Popkewitz, Thomas S. "Educational Reform and the Problem of Institutional Life." *Educational Researcher* 8 (March, 1979), 3–8.
22. Shannon, Patrick. "Reading Instruction and Social Class." *Language Arts* 62 (October, 1985), 604–613.
23. Turner, Susan D. "How to Look at the Testing Components of Basal Reading Series." *Reading Teacher* 37 (May, 1984), 860–866.
24. Unsworth, Len. "Meeting Individual Needs through Flexible within Class Grouping of Pupils." *Reading Teacher* 38 (December, 1984), 298–304.

Index